With thanks & love
for your Support

NO ORDINARY PSYCHOANALYST

from Pearl.
/9/05

Carlile

NO ORDINARY PSYCHOANALYST
The Exceptional Contributions of John Rickman

Compiled and Edited by
Pearl King

Foreword by
Riccardo Steiner

LONDON   NEW YORK

First published in 2003 by
H. Karnac (Books) Ltd.
6 Pembroke Buildings, London NW10 6RE

Copyright © 2003 by Pearl King

Foreword © 2003 by Riccardo Steiner

The rights of Pearl King and Riccardo Steiner to be identified as the author(s) of this work have been asserted in accordance with §§ 77 and 78 of the Copyright Design and Patents Act 1988.

All rights reserved. No part of this publication may be reproduced, stored in a retrieval system, or transmitted, in any form or by any means, electronic, mechanical, photocopying, recording, or otherwise, without the prior written permission of the publisher.

British Library Cataloguing in Publication Data

A C.I.P. for this book is available from the British Library

ISBN: 1-85575-920-9

10 9 8 7 6 5 4 3 2 1

Edited, designed, and produced by Communication Crafts

Printed in Great Britain

www.karnacbooks.com

CONTENTS

ACKNOWLEDGEMENTS   vii

FOREWORD by Riccardo Steiner   xi

Introduction
The rediscovery of John Rickman and his work   1

PART I   **Observations on psychoanalytic theory and technique**

1   Developments in psychoanalysis, 1896–1947   71

2   Experimental psychology and psychoanalysis: a comparison of the techniques   85

3   Scientific method and psychoanalysis   98

4   Number and the human sciences   109

PART II   **The interpersonal and intra-psychic dynamics of the interview situation**

5   First aid in psychotherapy   119

6   The psychiatric interview in the social setting of a War Office Selection Board   132

7   The influence of the "social field" on behaviour in the interview situation   140

vi   CONTENTS

	8	The technique of interviewing in anthropology and psychoanalysis	148
PART III		**Disruptive forces in group relations**	
	9	Does it take all kinds to make a world? Uniformity and diversity in communities	159
	10	Panic and anxiety reactions in groups during air raids	184
	11	On the development of professional and unprofessional attitudes	197
	12	Intra-group tensions in therapy: their study as the task of the group	220
	13	Disruptive forces in group relations: war as a makeshift therapy	235
	14	Some psychodynamic factors behind tensions that cause wars	241
PART IV		**On the nature of religious and moral beliefs**	
	15	A study of Quaker beliefs	269
	16	The need for a belief in God	294
	17	Man without God?	309
	18	The development of the moral function	314

APPENDIX 1
Memorandum on training criteria   337

APPENDIX 2
A note on the concept of "dynamic structure" and "field theory"   343

APPENDIX 3
Quotations researched by Lucy Rickman Baruch   349

REFERENCES   351

INDEX   355

ACKNOWLEDGEMENTS

I would like to thank Lucy Rickman Baruch, John Rickman's daughter, for permission to make extensive use of her father's writings, and particularly for her information about the background of his early years. I would like to thank her for researching through her parents' letters to her when she was at college in America during the Second World War, and for extracting some of their comments about John Rickman's "brilliantly good work" that so impressed Brigadier J. R. Rees and his colleagues (reproduced here in Appendix 3). I would also like to thank her and her husband, Bernard Baruch, for the work they have done, checking the early and final drafts of the Introduction and giving me much helpful advice and encouragement.

I would like to thank the late Mrs Lydia Rickman, Lucy's mother, who asked M. Masud R. Khan and myself, after the first volume of John Rickman's papers was published in 1957, to go through their Rickman archival material and select any unpublished papers to prepare for publication. Lydia Rickman was most helpful to me in the task of sorting them out.

I am grateful to the late M. Masud R. Khan for working with me during this early period, selecting material that could be published as papers, and helping to devise a meaningful structure within which to present the interesting topics about which John Rickman had become concerned. It is sad that he died before we could find a satisfactory publisher for these papers.

I would like to thank Riccardo Steiner for his support and for agreeing to write the Foreword to this book and also to thank him as Hon. Archivist for his permission to use the Archives of the British Psychoanalytical Society, from which I have drawn extensively.

I would like to thank Mrs Francesca Bion for her support and encouragement and for permission to use the *Lancet* paper that her husband, Wilfred R. Bion, wrote jointly with John Rickman on the work that they did together, which is published as chapter 12 in this book; and I thank her for also permission to quote from a number of Bion's letters to John, which I discovered in the Archives of the British Psychoanalytical Society.

I would like to thank Mrs Beulah Trist for permission to use the chart published at the end of chapter 4, which her husband, Eric Trist, and John Rickman drew up together to illustrate and extend ideas in that chapter.

I would like to thank Kenneth Robinson, Hon. Secretary of the Archive Committee, for typing important letters and Memos, for making copies for me of all of Rickman's known contributions to *The Lancet*, for searching out information and checking dates that were difficult to find and for reading and commenting on the drafts of my Introduction.

I owe a debt to those who helped to transfer hundreds of letters from John Rickman and others onto the data-base retrieval systems. Among others I thank Allan Barns and Linda Carter-Jackson, who worked under the careful eye of Jill Duncan, who was then Archivist and Librarian for the Society. I would also like to thank David Leevers for giving me technical help by printing out the earlier version of Rickman's papers.

I am grateful to various colleagues who had known John Rickman or who knew of his work during the Second World War and who shared their knowledge of him with me. These were Malcolm Pines, Isabel Menzies-Lyth, Harold Bridger, Hugh Murray and Thomas Harrison.

I would like to thank my colleague, Brett Kahr, who told Oliver Rathbone of Karnac that I had already done work on John Rickman's papers and suggested that they approach me to write about John Rickman and to finish editing his papers. As well as being an active link with Oliver Rathbone, Brett Kahr suggested the title of the book and met with me from time to time to discuss any problems and to encourage me in what I was doing.

I would also like to thank Oliver Rathbone, Managing Director of Karnac, for his realization of the importance of John Rickman's work, which so many of Rickman's own colleagues either had never realized or had forgotten.

I would particularly like to thank Jill Duncan, who worked as my secretary, and who not only scanned all Rickman's papers onto her computer, but checked and typed all the references, both to Rickman's papers and to my commentary on his life and work. We regularly discussed together the different phases of my Introduction, which I had written on my computer, and she finally converted the text to the layout required by the publishers. She was my major help in the task of proofreading, and, above all, she was both knowledgeable and a pleasure to work with.

Finally, I would like to thank Elizabeth (Tina) Carlile, my friend for over fifty years, who never gave up encouraging me to finish the work I had started doing with John Rickman's papers and to whom I dedicate this work.

Note

The Archive numbers are given at the end of documents that have been quoted from material in the Archives of the British Psychoanalytical Society, to help scholars to do further work based on the book.

FOREWORD

Riccardo Steiner

Psychoanalysts usually are not very much interested in the history of their discipline, particularly today. Due to the way they often think about themselves as clinicians, what matters most for them is how to make sense in clinical and theoretical terms of what happens in the "here-and-now" of the session. This attitude has its own justifications and, in one way or another, has many analogies with the attitude towards their disciplines of the practitioners or the researchers in the field of the so-called hard natural sciences.

Indeed, very few chemists, physicists, biologists, medical doctors etc., whether involved in research or as practitioners in their field, are interested in the past of their disciplines. The past usually is considered as a series of errors or rough approximations to what they are dealing with in the present, and it therefore needs to be forgotten or discarded.

In her work in the field of the history of psychoanalysis, Pearl King, together with a few others in Europe and America, has for years tried to make us aware of the multifaceted complexity of psychoanalysis which cannot be reduced to the methodologies of research and the epistemological status of the hard natural sciences. She has over a long period reorganised, fostered and transformed, in an exemplary instrument of research in the field of the history of psychoanalysis, the Archives of the British Psychoanalytical Society. More recently she has generously helped them to survive, in the interest of future generations of researchers, with the creation of the Pearl King Trust for the Archives, supported by the British Psychoanalytical Society itself.

Using again, as in previous work, the treasures of the documents deposited in the Archives of the British Psychoanalytical Society, in writing her biographical portrait of John Rickman and in collecting and editing his major papers on which she has worked for decades, and some of which were never published or were completely forgotten, Pearl King has shown to all of us, in her inimitable way, that history and the history of its own developments are a *sine qua non*, a vital ineliminable constituent of psychoanalysis.

The work of John Rickman, one of the great pioneers of the first generation of British psychoanalysts characterised by an open and always independent mind, has been brought back to life with enormous scrupulous attention and love for detail as far as Rickman's complex and extremely personal life, his clinical interests in psychoanalysis and also the important pioneering role he played in trying to link psychoanalysis to other disciplines are concerned. Indeed, Pearl King has studied more than 700 letters as well as innumerable other documents to write her biographical portrait of John Rickman.

Having been a witness and sometimes a participant in the events that she is describing, besides having been a pupil of Rickman in her training as a psychoanalyst, gives a particular character to her biographical portrait of Rickman. Indeed, her own personal memories and observations are woven together in a lively manner with the historical narrative of Rickman's life and achievements.

The reader therefore has the chance to know about the complex and at times traumatic childhood of Rickman, his medical studies at Cambridge University, the importance of some of his teachers such as Rivers, the extremely interesting work the young Rickman, who incidentally was a Quaker, did in Russia at the time of the Russian Revolution. And then, of course, his discovery of psychoanalysis during those magic first three decades of the twentieth century with Ernest Jones, Edward Glover, the Stracheys and those belonging to the first generation of British psychoanalysis. Rickman met and was a patient of Sigmund Freud and later of Sandor Ferenczi and later even of Melanie Klein. He became a training analyst who analysed W. R. Bion among others in the late 1930s.

Besides his clinical work, Rickman's institutional activities are well illustrated too. Of particular importance, as Pearl King is able to show, and as she underlines, were Rickman's interests as an editor and translator of Freud's work and editor of psychoanalytic books, besides his long-standing editorship of the *British Journal of Medical Psychology* where he managed to relate psychoanalysis to social and clinical psychology. One should also not forget Rickman's activity as a free-lance journalist and columnist of *The Lancet*. Indeed during the 1930s and

1940s he published extremely short articles on the political and dramatic social issues of that period interpreting the events from a psychoanalytic point of view.

But there is no doubt that some of the most interesting and moving aspects of Pearl King's biography are those dedicated to the years of the Second World War when Rickman by himself and then later with Bion created among other things the Northfield experiment, at a military hospital where he could try to study the interaction between institutional and personal unconscious dynamics, focusing on traumatised soldiers who needed to be treated and sent back to fight the Nazis. All this would, besides arousing the admiration and interest even of Jacques Lacan, allow Bion later on to write his famous contributions to group psychology from a psychoanalytic point of view and was at the core of the thinking that created the psychotherapeutic communities like those of Tom Main and others, besides deeply influencing all the thinking in this field of the Tavistock group of researchers who started working with institutions and created the periodical *Human Relations* immediately after the war.

Through the personal and scientific vicissitudes of Rickman's life and his papers, we are also able better to understand the institutional life and transformations of the British Psychoanalytical Society and of psychoanalysis in general, I would say, during those years. Just think of Rickman's role in sorting out what was left of German psychoanalysis immediately after the Second World War. He also took part in a very important interdisciplinary conference on "How to Understand and Prevent Wars" in 1948 in Paris, where his skilled experience and so typically British interventions inspired by common sense were appreciated and praised by people such as Horkheimer, Reisman and many others. Rickman died a few years later, too soon, in his early sixties. The outstanding enthusiasm, loyalty and affectionate scholarship of Pearl King has managed to rescue his work now from an undeserved oblivion. I am sure his work will from now on be better understood and appreciated as it deserves, as will the influence it has had on so many aspects of our thinking and its stimulus for further research to clarify the many links that bind our present to our past in psychoanalysis.

I have just mentioned the amazing enthusiasm, loyalty and affectionate scholarship of Pearl King. This is even more astonishing if we think that she will soon be celebrating her 85th birthday! What a way to celebrate this event and what an example, for all of us, of the vitality of those who believe in the historical approach to psychoanalysis!

NO ORDINARY PSYCHOANALYST

Introduction

The rediscovery of John Rickman and his work

Pearl King

Who was John Rickman?

The Dr John Rickman whom I knew, and have since got to know better, was a psychoanalyst who combined an extraordinarily thorough knowledge of psychoanalysis with an intense interest in social processes, and he was able to throw light on some of the problems of social psychology by extending psychoanalytic concepts to cover and understand group and community problems. The setting in which his heuristic capacities flourished best was during an informal discussion group or an impromptu conversation between colleagues coming from different disciplines in the social sciences.

The creative enjoyment that John Rickman brought to such discussions was not only because of what he contributed, but also because he enabled the participants to re-experience what they had said or thought, often opening up their understanding in a way that they had not previously experienced. They were then enabled to re-evaluate themselves. Many of the letters to John that I read while editing his papers bore evidence of the impact that his way of working with colleagues had on them. I then realised how important it was for these people to have been "listened to" by John.

He was essentially an artist in understanding human relationships, and this was perhaps why a discussion with him on any problem was such a creative experience. He quickly perceived how one pattern of relationships matched another, so that he could see discrepancies that most theories would have overlooked. He often called psychoanalysis one of the "pattern-matching sciences".

Rickman believed that a knowledge of psychoanalysis for those who were not afraid to be interested in it could be of real help to people. Hence, during the 1930s he chose, as the most useful office that he could take on for the Society, "Convenor" of the Society's Public Lectures Committee. He "looked after" this committee for five or six years. Alongside this work, he started writing articles or anonymous editorials on issues of key importance to individuals and the country, for his friend, T. F. Fox, a fellow Quaker and Assistant Editor of *The Lancet*. His second anonymous editorial was entitled "On Feeling Secure", written in 1936, in the year after Mussolini invaded Abyssinia. He could discuss the real dangers, but he also used his knowledge of psychoanalysis to explain that these "real" dangers may seem worse because of the inner conflicts that individuals and groups might be facing. Referring to his clinical experience, he also indicated a way of understanding these inner conflicts, or at least another way of seeing them, which could put their conflicts in a wider, less frightening context.

John Rickman was intensely concerned with the "oral tradition", as he called it, and was aware of the subliminal meanings that were often imperceptible when translated into the printed word. His experience of broadcasting helped him to consider other factors that could impact the awareness of his audience, such as silence, the tone of voice he used, and the timing of phrases.

This did not mean that he belittled the written word. He was very concerned to discover a way of communicating in writing that would retain, as far as possible, the "music behind the words", which was so much more readily available from the spoken word, in a face-to-face situation. Hence, he was interested in the resonance in the meanings of words, and he took great care to paint a picture in words so that he and his readers could be in "a situation together".

Most of the papers included in this book seem to have been written as if to be read to an audience, although in several cases there is no evidence that they were in fact ever read at a meeting. In these cases, it seems that Rickman is writing to share his ideas with the reader, so that in reading his papers the reader may feel that he is in direct contact with Rickman and his thinking, not seeing it as an "*ex cathedra* statement of fact", but as something that he or she could think about or consider. I have attempted to preserve this atmosphere of the meeting of ideas, which was so integral to John Rickman's mode of communication.

The wide variety of topics included in this book indicate Rickman's extensive range of interests and his interdisciplinary contacts. The reader may, as it were, "listen in" to Rickman's attempts to understand and throw light on problems met with by many different professional groups including psychoanalysts, psychologists, anthropologists, general practitioners, the War Office Selection Boards (WOSBs), teachers and followers of various religions including the Shamans and the Quakers, whose teachings were part of John Rickman's background.

When Rickman left the British Army in 1945, Sylvia Payne was in her first years as the President of the British Psychoanalytical Society. John was gradually drawn back onto the various Committees of the Society and of the Institute of Psychoanalysis. In 1947 he was elected as the third President of the British Society for the next three years. As a President certain Offices had to be occupied by him, and he had no choice. He continued editing the *British Journal of Medical Psychology*, and, in addition, in 1948 when Adrian Stephen died, he took on the editorship of the *International Journal of Psycho-Analysis*, for a year.

In 1950 William Gillespie was elected the next President of the Society. He had been active in the Society during the war and had taken a responsible role in the setting up of the "Medical Committee in 1943" and in the reorganisation of the Society and Institute after the war.

At the end of May 1951, William asked John if he would agree to be nominated for the Board and the Training Committee for the next year, and Rickman turned both down. On 31 May 1951, William received a moving letter from John Rickman:

> My dear Gillespie, Yesterday you were kind enough to ask me if I really intended to refuse nomination both to the Board and the Training Committee. My reply in affirmation needs, I think, after so long a service and while I am still in reasonable health an explanation if not an apology.
>
> The plain truth is that these duties have become a burden which I have found harder and harder to bear. While I was endowed with energy which made me almost exempt from the sensation of fatigue I could take on task after task without those encroachments on reserves which first manifest themselves by irritability. Now I am finding it harder and harder to keep sweet tempered (a state of mind I prize in others and they should have the same from me) and what stock of force remains I want to employ in the gruelling task of writing—little will come of it I know, because little goes into it. But I want the Institute (I still feel myself to be its servant) to let me fiddle

with pen and paper for what remains of my youth as a good parent would without demur let a child have its bit of cloth or other of Winnicott's Transitional Objects. You would expect nothing from a child's play with a rag, expect nothing, then, of my scribbling: I do not ask leave of absence for a time (seconded to writing duties), I ask not to be asked to do work—regular routine work.

Rickman tried to support his case by insisting that he was too old at 60 and that younger members should be serving on these committees. He thought that "the management of the Institute should be (as it was in the beginning) in the hands of those in young middle age". He said that he was even in the course of retiring from his editorial responsibilities. He hoped that he would still be called on to help in "non-routine" duties, which did not stop him going off if he wished to. He said: "My mother used to say that she felt herself to be a hen with a duckling, both would be walking on the pond side and then her offspring would go off happily in a medium in which she found it difficult to follow." He ends by reminding William that 25 years ago the Institute bought their Gloucester Place building (which he chose for them) but that Mansfield House (which he also chose) had a longer lease, and "should start free from the encumbrance of old men" (CRR/F22/07).

It was clear from this letter that Rickman felt that he had done his fair share of work for the Institute and the Society. But did William, as a doctor, consider that John's tiredness might have other causes? When I first read this letter I was reminded of John's exhaustion prior to his heart attack when he worked on No. 6 WOSB during the war.

On the first Sunday in July, John Rickman went to Queen Mary's Garden in Regent's Park, one of London's royal parks, and settled himself under a mulberry tree, on one of the deckchairs, which could then be hired for a morning or afternoon for a small cost. This was where, his daughter Lucy said, he often came when he wanted both to write and to enjoy the flowers in the rose garden. When the park attendant came to collect the fee for the deckchair, he could not rouse him and he called an ambulance, which took John to University College Hospital. He had suffered a severe coronary thrombosis, from which he did not recover.

I will quote the words that William Gillespie used in his next report as President: "The beginning of the year on which I am reporting was over-shadowed by the loss of Dr John Rickman, so recently our President. His sudden and unexpected death occurred on July the first 1951. We have suffered no severer blow since the foundation of our Society and Institute" (Gillespie, 1952). He went on to report that a special memorial meeting had been held before the Annual General Meeting the previous July, and it had been decided that one of the principal rooms in Mansfield House should be named the John Rickman Room in his memory.

When I re-read Gillespie's statement recently, I realised what a deep shock it had been to William, who had to follow so closely after John—John's death occurring when it did, just before the summer break when the Institute and Society were about to move to a large and beautiful building, with plenty of space for meetings, even if the clinic area was then a bit problematic. Furthermore, halfway through Rickman's presidency it "leaked out" that he did not want to be considered a Kleinian. This had come out when he explained his position to Robert Knight of the Menninger Clinic, in the United States. As his patient, I found out about it when Michael Balint, the Training Secretary, told me that Rickman did not consider himself a Kleinian, so that I could therefore choose my second supervisor from any group I liked. (I chose Michael Balint.)

In the months and years that followed I gathered the impression that some of the Kleinians were displeased with him. Most of those who had worked with him in the army seemed to have moved to other non-psychoanalytic work and were not active in the Society; otherwise, they could have supported his memory. It was left to Independents such as Sylvia Payne and Clifford Scott (who was hoping to return to Canada to start a Society) to collect his published papers together, and to reissue them through the International Psychoanalytical Library with the Hogarth Press and the Institute of Psychoanalysis.

In her Foreword to John Rickman's *Selected Contributions to Psychoanalysis* published in 1957, Sylvia Payne described Rickman as follows: "Dr. Rickman, a tall powerfully built man with the traditional quiet courtesy of the Englishman, by his presence might appear formidable to those who had not the chance to approach him. Experience showed that he was invariably interested in other people's problems, and would take infinite pains to help colleagues as well as patients in difficult situations" (Payne, 1957). Sylvia Payne was eleven years older than John, but they both joined the British Psychoanalytical Society in the early 1920s, and in their different ways they cared for the Institute of Psychoanalysis, both being Secretaries to its Board at different crucial periods.

Finally, in the early 1960s, Lydia Rickman, John's widow, asked if Masud Khan and I would go through Rickman's Archives to see what unpublished papers we could find that were worth publication. I received ten or more large box files which were looked after carefully in my house. Masud Khan and I spent some time going through them, selecting unpublished papers that might still be of interest and which we thought were important contributions to John's thinking and scholarship.

Eventually I edited enough papers to form a book, but various publishers I took them to were not interested in them or in the way I had arranged them. Masud Khan became busy writing his own books and was then appointed Editor of Books for the Institute and Society, while I was busy working with Adam Limentani, reorganising the training arrangements of the Institute and Society. I kept copies of my edited versions of the papers, and returned the Archive boxes to Lucy Rickman Baruch (Rickman's daughter) and her husband.

As time went on I realised how few were those who knew who Rickman was or what he had accomplished or what an influence he had on people with whom he worked.

In the year 2000, Thomas Harrison published a well-researched book on the work that had been done at Northfield Military Hospital entitled *Bion, Rickman and Foulkes and the Northfield Experiment: Advancing on a Different Front*, with a Foreword by Bob Hinshelwood, who particularly responded to John Rickman's contributions, as did Tom Harrison. I was asked to review this book for the journal *Psychoanalytic Psychotherapy* (King, 2002).

Doing this review fired my enthusiasm to complete the task of editing Rickman's papers. I realised that I would have to "rediscover" John Rickman for myself. Furthermore, it had to be a serious research task. I knew that I had access to over 700 letters between John Rickman and his friends and colleagues, and also to the computerised contents of many of the Archives of the British Psychoanalytical Society, which was first set up while I was Hon. Archivist of the Society. From this material, I have been continually learning and seeing what happened to John Rickman from many different points of view.

Researching this material, together with my memories of him, have enabled me to put together and to discover many details about his life, his achievements and his relationships that have helped me in my rediscovery of John Rickman.

John Rickman's life events
and their influence on his writing and thinking

I realised that if I had learnt anything from John Rickman, I would be expected to describe not only what he did during his life, but also to give equal value to the various contexts within which he lived and worked. This I have also tried to do in this introduction to his papers.

Family background

John Rickman was born on 10 April 1891. His parents lived in Dorking in the County of Surrey, not far from London. Dorking at that time was a small, quiet town with a well-kept main street of late-eighteenth-century houses and shops. It is situated near the hills and valleys of the North Downs in the south of England, with the well-known beauty spots of Box Hill and Leith Hill in the area. As he grew up one of his pleasures was walking and later climbing, both in Austria and then in the Lake District. He had an athletic figure and was tall for his age, measuring six feet when he was only 16 years old, but remaining that height for most of his life.

Both his parents were Quakers, and he grew up in the context of the Quaker religion, with its approach to the sacredness of life and the duty of care for others. The families of his parents were engaged in "trade". His mother's father was a draper and had a business in Dorking, where John's father had run an ironmonger's shop; John's paternal grandfather lived in the County of Sussex, some forty-five miles to the southeast of Dorking. John's father became ill with tuberculosis. He went to France to seek a warmer climate for his illness, but he died there before his son was 2 years old. Thus John grew up in what we now refer to as a "one-parent family", and he missed the possible advantage of siblings and a stabilising father for most of his childhood, and his mother remained a widow for the 55 years before she died in 1948. As the little boy was left fatherless so young, the two main male influences were his two grandfathers, both of whom he had much contact with.

His Rickman grandfather lived in Wellingham near Lewes in Sussex, on a family farm dating back many years. This grandfather figured very large in John's early life. He spent much time with that family, and it was his Rickman grandfather as well as his own father who left him money that he could inherit when he reached the age of 21. This money enabled him later to visit Freud, after the end of the First World War, and to start on and continue with his career as a psychoanalyst.

His mother's parents, Grandpa and Grandma Marsh, lived near the home of John and his mother in Dorking. They were an important influence on him, and, as they were near at hand, he must have spent much time with them. They had a number of children who were much older than John, but one of whom, Harold (an uncle to John) was only five years older that him. He was more like an elder brother to him, but apparently, like many older brothers, he also bossed him.

Grandma Marsh was a devoted Quaker and was a support both to her daughter and to her grandson, but Grandpa Marsh is reported to have been a very difficult man and even to have repeatedly abused John when he was a child. Grandpa Marsh was said to have been a bully and to have created an unhappy domestic atmosphere.

Education

John Rickman attended a Dame School in Dorking. There was one held in Rose Hill House, not far from the Quaker's Meeting House, in Victoria Terrace, South Street, Dorking. The Quakers were and still are a significant group in that town. When John was old enough, he was sent to the well-known Quaker boarding school called Leighton Park, in Reading. Being an "only child", it must have been important for him to have the chance to pick his own friends as substitute brothers. One friend who also went to this school, but after John had left, was Lionel Penrose. John met him later when he lived in Cambridge after his return from Russia, when he was working at Fulbourn Hospital, and they became life-long friends. He accompanied John when he first went to Vienna to see Freud. Later, Lionel Penrose became not only an eminent geneticist but also, in 1926, an Associate Member of the British Psychoanalytical Society.

Another friend whom he met later at the University of Cambridge was Ernest Altounyan, who became a surgeon in Aleppo, Syria. He brought John into contact with T. E. Lawrence of Arabia. Rickman was *in loco parentis* to Ernest Altounyan's children when they were at school in England during some of their holidays in the Lake District. It was during one of these holidays, while he was reading Lawrence's *The Seven Pillars of Wisdom*, that Dora Collingwood, the wife of Ernest Altounyan, painted his portrait.

John was a thoughtful and observant adolescent, and, when he was retiring after fourteen years as Editor of the *British Journal of Medical Psychology*, he described his early arguments with himself:

About forty years ago a schoolboy was puzzled why on apparently the same evidence and experience there were such wide differences of outlook and opinion among his contemporaries, and between people of different age-groups, when all parties professed to base their judgement on reason. At the same time the problem seemed insoluble. It was also realised that this was the most important feature in the field of human relations and at the same time the thing which distinguished man from the rest of animal creation: he resolved to become a psychiatrist in order to approach the matter as a life work. ... In his reading he came across a book in the school library which immediately produced a profound effect on his thought. *Flatland* [1884] by "A Square" (a pseudonym for Edwin Abbott) is about a world limited to two dimensions but otherwise like our own in that its population was endowed with perception, feeling and reason. [Rickman, 1949]

From this quotation, it became clear to me that John was very aware of the boundaries and unchallenged assumptions that were restricting both himself and others in reaching a more truthful perception of the world and of relationships with people in the world, his fellow human beings.

John was very keen to go to the University of Cambridge, but he had great difficulty in passing the Latin examinations essential to gain entrance to it. He was pleased when he did get a place at King's College, Cambridge, where he entered into the sports and cultural facilities that this college and university offered. It was at Cambridge that he met Adrian Stephen and his friends, who later became part of the Bloomsbury Group. Rickman was well built and athletic in appearance, and he was particularly pleased when he won a Cambridge rowing "Blue".

Rickman read medicine but had an interest in law. He thought that law would help him to put his ideas more clearly on the one hand, but that medicine would give him the capacity to help his fellow human beings. He took a Natural Science Tripos and his pre-clinical examinations at the University of Cambridge, before he moved to St. Thomas's Hospital in London and qualified in medicine in 1916. Two years before he qualified as a doctor, the Great War had broken out, in 1914. He was under great pressure to join the Royal Army Medical Corps (RAMC), but refused as a conscientious objector, having been brought up in the Quaker religion, which forbids its adherents to take the life of other human beings.

As soon as he was qualified as a doctor, he enrolled with "The Friends War Victims Relief Committee" and went to Russia rather than be conscripted into the RAMC.

John Rickman in Russia

In 1916 Dr John Rickman joined "The Friends War Victims Relief Service". Their Unit was set up in Buzuluk, in Mogatova, in the Samara

Province in South Russia. It was staffed by Quakers from England and America, and Dr Tyler Fox was the Chief Medical Officer for the Quaker Relief mission in Russia between 1916 and 1917 and co-ordinated their activities. His aim was to establish a high-class hospital on the remote Steppe.

Some years later Rickman wrote a "Note to Obituary" of Dr Tyler Fox, and I quote from it because these comments could have been made about John Rickman's work in this Unit: "He endured with fortitude and his own quiet humour the many modifications of his ideal which conditions demanded. He would not have been successful with the peasants if he had not won their affection as a man and their respect as a clinician. It was not easy to convince them of the value of modern sanitary requirements, while persuading them that illness was not a visitation of God's displeasure proved even more difficult . . ." (CRR/F13/14). John Rickman, as a country doctor in Russia, was soon involved in trying to meet the demands of his patients, scattered over a 60-miles radius from the local, rather primitive, hospital where he and the nurses had tried to train the local girls in many things, particularly those relevant to the requirements of modern sanitation, so important to the healthy healing of their patients.

Rickman described his experiences as a country doctor in this area in a number of publications, which were collected in "Russian Camera Obscura" in *The People of Great Russia* (Gorer & Rickman, 1949). It was in this form that most people have had access to them, though some were familiar with those published earlier in *The Lancet*. It was during Rickman's work as a doctor in this region that he learned to understand the importance of group relations and group pressures, the power of belief systems, and the role of mullahs, priests and Communist activators; in other words, he was immersed in what we can now see as a "training ground" for potential anthropologists, sociologists or social workers, without the theoretical constructs to make academic sense of them. But he was aided by his instinctive knowledge that to help human beings you have to gain their confidence, and this implies your seeing and them knowing that you see and understand things from their point of view, even if you disagree with each other. This was the way of relating that he felt resulted in mutual respect between the "helper" and those "needing help". The knowledge that Rickman gained from starting with this "raw data" has informed much of his work and several of the papers included in this collection.

In 1917, Lydia Cooper Lewis, an American social worker from the Hull House settlement in Chicago, arrived with five colleagues via the

Pacific and joined the Unit. The Russian Communist revolution took place in October/November 1917. In March 1918, John and Lydia decided to get married. They had a Quaker ceremony in the Unit, but to make it official they had to have their marriage registered in the local town hall. Their marriage was the first civil marriage in the town, and the marriage certificate was No. 1.

It was becoming clear to the Rickmans that in Russia, the Great War was turning into the Russian Civil War, being fought between the Whites (anti-Communists) and the Reds (pro-Communists), and they felt that the time had come to try to leave Russia, or the Soviet Union as it was rapidly becoming. As the war was still being fought in Europe, they had to return via the Trans-Siberian Railway and leave from Vladivostock. When I started to help sort out John Rickman's papers, I remember Lydia assisting me in this task, while she described to me her memories of the long train journey from South Russia and across Siberia to the Pacific. Whenever the train was stopped and a group of men demanded to inspect the passengers, they had to decide quickly whether to show them the passes and papers that they had received from the Communists (the Reds) or those from the other side (the Whites). She said that it was very worrying. They left the Samara Province in late July 1918 and did not arrive in Vladivostock until November, shortly before the signing of the Armistice. They went to the British Consulate and reported what had happened to them, but their report was not at first believed, the consular staff thinking that no one could have survived that journey in those conditions during the Russian Civil War. They were the first people from the West to report on the situation there. Eventually they were believed, and the Rickmans sailed to the United States, so that John could be introduced to Lydia's family in America, before they came to England.

John Rickman's return to Cambridge after his work in Russia

After the war, Rickman had difficulty finding employment, for he had not "fought for King and Country", being a conscientious objector. Eventually Rickman was appointed as Medical Officer at Fulbourn Hospital, south of Cambridge. It was considered the lowest level of medical employment, but as part of his work there, one of his first tasks was to set up formal Nursing Training in the Hospital, and this linked up with the work he had done in Russia with the peasant women there and his attempts to train them. The Rickmans stayed in the Old Vicarage, Grantchester, made famous by Rupert Brooke's poem (1912).

A book about this hospital, entitled *The Story of a Mental Hospital: Fulbourn 1858–1983*, by David H. Clark was published in 1996, and it includes comments about Dr Rickman. I quote:

> In 1919 Dr Archdale attracted to the hospital Dr John Rickman, a young Quaker doctor recently returned from Relief Work in Russia who later became one of the leaders of British Psychoanalysis. Dr Archdale says in his report . . . "Dr John Rickman of King's College . . . a keen student of the mental methods of healing, has thrown the greatest energy into his medical work, and has been most assiduous in lecturing to the nurses." The report later refers to pioneering work being done by Rivers and Myers at the Psychological Laboratory in Cambridge. [Clark, 1996]

Later, Rickman wrote about this period of his life. "By good fortune I had as mentors a few men of quite outstanding 'mobility'. . . . Dr W. H. R. Rivers, a physiologist of the special senses, anthropologist and psychologist, was a person to whom it was possible to speak in terms of the viewpoint of the observer as well as the content of the events viewed . . ." (Rickman, 1949).

Through his friendship with Rivers he was also introduced to the beginnings of the Medical Section of the British Psychological Society. The people who got together to form this section were three young doctors—William H. R. Rivers, Charles S. Myers and William McDougall—all of whom had been invited by Alfred Cort Haddon in 1898 to join him in an anthropological expedition to the Torres Straits in the Pacific. The importance of this expedition lay in its influence on these psychologists in widening their horizons.

In October 1901, a small society, the British Psychological Society, was formed to study psychology in all of its branches. It had not been until 1900, when Freud published *The Interpretation of Dreams*, that an adequate theory had appeared for guiding an investigation of unconscious mental functioning. As Rickman said in pamphlet in 1938:

> If dreams were shown to be not haphazard manifestations but to be constructed according to laws, then the whole world of delusions and hallucinations, neurotic symptoms, crimes, myths, religious beliefs and social customs might perhaps be seen in relation to one another, and there was hope that they could be dealt with by a science of the mind. Here was the beginning of a psychopathology, meaning by that a systematic study of the sufferings of the mind.

The inaugural meeting of the Medical Section took place on 14 May 1919, with Rivers as its first Chairman. The title of his inaugural address was "Psychology and Medicine", and he hoped that other sections of the Psychological Society would be formed to bring in other professions, so that it would be possible "to speak in terms of the viewpoint of the observer as well as the context of the events viewed".

From early on, the Medical Section was the common meeting ground for those who were interested in medical psychology and its relationship to other disciplines. It was in 1920 that the first issue of the *British Journal of Medical Psychology* was produced; this journal was to play an important part in Rickman's life.

Rickman wrote later: "It was from Rivers that I first heard the advice 'If you are going to do anything in the field of psychiatry or psychology you must get analysed'" (Rickman, 1949).

Rivers suggested that John Rickman should go to Vienna to be analysed by Freud. Rickman contacted Freud with his request for psychoanalysis, and Freud replied on a postcard that he would undertake to analyse him and that his fee was two guineas per session. Rickman started work with Freud in 1920.

Life in Vienna

John Rickman moved to Vienna, with his wife Lydia. Lydia linked up with the Quaker Relief Unit in Vienna, and when John was not working with Freud and studying psychoanalysis, he also worked with this Unit. There was great poverty in Vienna in the area where the Quakers were then working.

Correspondence was an important channel of communication between London and Vienna at that time. On 13 May 1920, Sigmund Freud wrote to Ernest Jones saying, "My health is good, I cannot take another patient until vacancies, Rickman is excellent" (CFG/F02/26). Following this letter from Freud, Dr Douglas Bryan and the Council of the British Psychoanalytical Society agreed that John Rickman's name be put forward to the Annual General Meeting for election as an Associate Member, and he was elected on 11 October 1920.

In 1921 John Rickman came back to London to sit his MRCP examination. While he was in London, his daughter Lucy was born. In a letter to his friend Geza Roheim in Budapest, he wrote: "First we now have a daughter, aged one month and 6 days, a sturdy satisfying little mortal, full of vitality and developing quickly enough to be continually interesting" (31 August 1921, CRR/F08/26). Following the birth of his daughter, Rickman returned to Vienna to continue with his analysis, while his wife went to America to show their baby daughter to Lydia's family.

In November 1921, Rickman wrote from his Vienna address to "Dear Dr. Jones", his first formal letter to Jones, giving him a report on what the Viennese had arranged for visiting foreign analysts in his situation. He wrote:

> The course of lectures arranged by Rank for the psychoanalytic pupils who are foreigners here proceeds (with a few ups and downs) on a fairly level keel. Hitschmann who is lecturing during the current two weeks, is giving us the substance of a new book, or at least a new publication. The total number of lectures will be between 35 and 45. This seems to me an interesting experiment which may later be applied in other places e.g. in London when the psychoanalytic clinic is started for teaching as well as for treatment. [CRA/F14/01]

Another source of information comes from memoirs written by Freud's American patients. Abraham Kardiner, in his *My Analysis with Freud: Reminiscences*, comments on the jealousy of Freud's English patients—Rickman and Strachey—who complained that Freud was more "friendly" with Kardiner than with them (Kardiner, 1977).

Meanwhile Rickman was becoming interested in psychoanalytic publications, and while he was in Vienna he offered to do some translations for Freud and Jones. In a letter from Jones to Freud, dated 24 June 1924, Jones complained to Freud about business decisions, to do with publications, being discussed between Freud and Rickman during his analysis. This had created difficulties between himself and Otto Rank, who had already been asked to deal with those publication matters.

When I was working with Lydia sorting John's papers, she told me that Freud had asked John Rickman to work at applying Freud's theories to the understanding and treatment of psychoses. Rickman had worked with psychotic patients while working as a Medical Officer at Fulbourn Hospital, near Cambridge, but he had yet to start his own practice as a psychoanalyst in London. In 1922, Rickman returned to London, to start his practice and to take up an Honorary position in St Thomas's Hospital alongside Dr W. Stoddart. And on 4 October 1922, John Rickman along with James and Edward Glover, were elected to membership of the British Society.

The establishment of the Institute of Psychoanalysis in London

Before John Rickman had been elected as a member of the British Psychoanalytical Society, Jones, with the help of the "Glossary Committee", had been busy launching the *International Journal of Psycho-Analysis*, the first volume of which appeared in 1920. It was an important channel for the translation of Freud's work into English. Rickman's interest in law and legal matters while he was an undergraduate at Cambridge helped him to understand the importance of setting up a legal institution within which to contain the activities and structures of the new British Psychoanalytical Society, which had come into being on 20 February 1919.

In the first place, in 1924 Rickman assisted Ernest Jones to found the Institute of Psychoanalysis, and his concern with legal documents led him to play a prominent part in formulating the legal constitution of the Institute and to draw up the Articles of Association that determined the organisation of the membership of the Institute. It was the establishment of the Institute of Psychoanalysis which enabled the British Psychoanalytical Society to own property and to purchase the International Psychoanalytical Press, which held the rights of publication in the English language of many of Freud's earlier works. This was soon followed by the setting up of the International Psychoanalytical Library with the Hogarth Press, which body was responsible for the publication of the principal psychoanalytic books in England for many years.

The first meeting of the Board of the Institute was held on 16 January 1925, with Jones as Chairman and Rickman as Secretary, and with Douglas Bryan and James Glover as members of the Board. The minutes listed others who were allowed to attend Board meetings.

The establishment of the London Clinic of Psychoanalysis

The Institute had to be set up before the members could own the other facilities that they required to function adequately as a psychoanalytic organisation. Now they were able to purchase and own a building, which they needed in order to start a clinic in which they could see patients, house a library, and provide meeting-rooms for discussions and teaching events and, if possible, facilities for Scientific Meetings. Up to this time, the members had been meeting in houses belonging to different members, which was not satisfactory for a growing organisation. After much discussion at several Board Meetings, Rickman was asked to purchase the lease of 36 Gloucester Place, London W1. (This street was later renumbered, and No. 36 became No. 96.)

For several years, members—especially those who had been to Berlin for analysis, such as Barbara Low—had been putting forward resolutions that the British Society should set up a Clinic for those who could not afford private analysis, along the lines developed in Berlin under Max Eitingon of the Berlin Society. The Board had not only to furnish the appropriate rooms in the property, which was not difficult, but also, what was more interesting, to decide how it should be organised, who could treat patients in it, what they should be called and who should be in charge of it.

On 30 June 1926, the following decisions were agreed and placed in the Board Minutes (No. 38, Minute 2) under the heading "The Clinic" and which, for its clarity and understanding of the situation in which the new Clinic had to work, revealed the "hand" of the Secretary of the Board, Dr John Rickman. It gave the management structure and the roles that members would occupy in it. Finally, in Minute 3, the names of those who would see patients in the Clinic were given, all of whom were medically qualified. What was clear from Minute 3 was that only medically qualified members could be "appointed to work in the Clinic" and that, following the "Voluntary Hospitals Culture", they should see one patient a day free. This arrangement disappeared when the National Health Service was introduced, but the custom continued in the Institute for many years, applying to both medical and non-medical members, until it became the "Thousand Hours" requirement. It is now looked on as the contribution that everyone who trains at the Institute makes to the "Clinic".

However, these difficulties were not in John Rickman's mind when he described to us, when we were students, how he analysed the first patient to be seen in the Clinic on 6 May 1926, which date was also Freud's seventieth birthday!

Before the Clinic was officially opened by Jones on 28 September 1926, one of the Physicians to the Clinic, Dr James Glover, died, on 25 August 1926, and Dr Edward Glover was appointed Physician to the Clinic in his place. At the end of a letter to Freud, Jones writes, "The practice here is very busy and we are nearly all occupied" (CFH/F04/58). In other words, most of his colleagues had patients, and psychoanalysis was flourishing in England!

At the next Annual General Meeting of the Society, John Rickman and Joan Riviere were elected to take James Glover's place on the Council. As a member of both the Board and the Council, Rickman was in a position to make important contributions to the development of psychoanalysis in London.

John Rickman's publishing activities in the British Society

Alongside Rickman's administrative activities, he was busy working on two projects that grew out of his time in Vienna working with Freud.

The first was a bibliography that he compiled of all papers published between 1893 and 1926 on psychoanalysis, which he called *The Index Psychoanalyticus: 1893–1926*. It was an authors' index of papers on psychoanalysis. (Books were included when published by recognised psychoanalytic publishers.) It must have involved a great deal of work, not only considering what material to include in it, but also contacting analysts via the International Psychoanalytical Association and acknowledging their contributions. It contains 4,739 titles. Rickman dedicated this work to Sigmund Freud, and he must have started it when he was staying in Vienna and working with Freud. The completed book must have given both Freud and other psychoanalysts a wide vision of the spread of their ideas and interests.

At a meeting of the Board of the Institute, Rickman offered to subsidise the cost of publication if the Institute would publish it. This the Board agreed to do. It was published by the Hogarth Press in 1928 as No. 14 in the International Psychoanalytical Library.

When he had had some experience working as a psychoanalyst and in taking an outpatients' clinic in St. Thomas's Hospital, he settled down to carry out Freud's request that he should try to describe how Freud's theories could apply to the understanding and treatment of psychoses.

He published his work under the title "A Survey: The Development of the Psychoanalytical Theory of the Psychoses 1894–1926" in four parts, from 1926 to 1927, in the *British Journal of Medical Psychology*, of which he had become Assistant Editor in 1925. Rickman also produced it as a "Teaching Manual", which was later published as chapter 23 in his *Selected Contributions to Psychoanalysis* (Rickman, 1957).

In 1926, his thesis, "A Psychological Factor in the Aetiology of Descensus Uteri, Laceration of the Perineum and Vaginismus", was awarded an MD degree. Material from this thesis was published as a paper and was included in his *Selected Contributions* (1957).

John Rickman as an active member of the British Society

John Rickman enjoyed writing and contacting others through the written word. He studied how best to do so, and he developed his own philosophical approach.

First, there was his extensive correspondence, and the care that he took over writing to colleagues and others who needed advice or contact with him gives evidence of the importance that John placed on written contact with people.

His correspondence with Geza Roheim, an anthropologist and later a psychoanalyst from Budapest, started in 1920 and continued throughout his professional life. His earliest contacts with Roheim were when Rickman was working with Freud in Vienna, but Roheim soon became a friend, and the letters that Rickman received were addressed to "Dear John" not "Dr. Rickman"! Hungary, like Vienna, had been impoverished during the 1914–18 war, and Rickman tried to help Geza Roheim professionally, by sending him books by other anthropologists that were not available in Hungary. He helped him when he was moving to Australia, via London, to carry out his research on the Australian Aborigines from 1929 to 1931.

Chapter 4 in this book was originally published in 1951 under the title "Number and the Human Sciences" as a contribution to Geza Roheim's *Festschrift*, and Rickman regarded that paper, which was concerned with "one-body, two-body, three-body, four-body and group-psychology", as a breakthrough in his thinking. He was pleased when an American colleague, George B. Wilbur, one of the editors of the *Festschrift*, recognised the importance of the ideas in the paper. Wilbur wrote: "I read it with interest and approve of it .... Your essay strikes a note that needs emphasis" (CRR/F07/47/49). Rickman wrote to Wilbur to obtain his permission to circulate this paper to the British Society to discuss at their meeting on 5 September 1950, before its publication.

Second, there was his work over many years editing the papers of colleagues. In 1925 he became Assistant Editor to Dr T. W. Mitchell of the *British Journal of Medical Psychology*. This post he held until 1934, when Mitchell resigned; Rickman then took over as Editor; a post he held from 1935 to 1949. Thus, of the thirty-one years during which he was a member of the Society and a psychoanalyst, twenty-four years were spent editing this journal. But the journal was the place where professionals interested in psychology and psychoanalysis met each other and also met members of other disciplines interested in a psychological approach to understanding human behaviour. It was from this position that he made important contributions to the use of psychoanalytic ideas in exploring the problems of other disciplines, as can be seen in some of the papers included in this volume.

Third, there was his work on committees. In 1925 at the Bad Homburg Congress, the International Psychoanalytical Association passed a resolution that all Branch Societies should elect Training Committees of five to seven members, in order that there might be a uniform system of psychoanalytic instruction in different countries. And these elected committees would take institutional responsibility for selection, training and qualification of candidates, personal analysis, supervised analysis of patients and theoretical courses. It was agreed that the Training Committees of the Branch Societies should combine to form an International Training Board (Eitingon, 1925).

Accordingly, in March 1926 the British Society elected its first Training Committee, consisting of E. Jones, J. Glover, J. Rickman, J. C. Flugel and D. Bryan, and they drew up draft suggestions for the selection and training of candidates for submission to the International Training Board. Rickman was thus a member of the first British Training Committee in 1926.

John Rickman also played an important role facilitating the publication of certain manuscripts by Ferenczi and Geza Roheim among others, in his role as Secretary of the Board of the Institute.

In 1926 he was elected onto the first "Public Lectures Committee". This committee played an important function for those early analysts, who often managed to collect patients following a public lecture that they had given. Work on this committee and his editorial work must have helped Rickman to become known and appreciated in the Society and to build up his own analytic practice and experience.

In 1926 Melanie Klein moved to London from Berlin, where she had been working with Karl Abraham until he died in 1925. She was welcomed by members of the British Society, particularly those who were interested in working with children. She was followed in 1932 by her daughter, Melitta Schmideberg, and Melitta's husband, Walter Schmideberg.

Rickman's decision to work with Ferenczi in Budapest

In 1928 Rickman decided to go to Hungary to have some analysis with Ferenczi, as he felt that he still needed help with certain problems, related perhaps to past traumas, which were still causing him distress. "Dr. Rickman reported that he was going abroad for several months and it was decided that Dr. Douglas Bryan function as Secretary during Dr. Rickman's absence" (17/10/28, Minute 3).

This decision was much to the disappointment of Jones, who had come to rely on Rickman's support in administrative matters. While they kept in touch through correspondence, in his letters Jones kept asking when they could expect his return.

In March the next year, Lydia and their daughter, Lucy, went to see him in Budapest. When Lucy was describing this period to me, she said that he was very ill for some of the time that he was working with

Ferenczi. She had come across some very angry letters from her father to his mother, begging her to tell him about episodes in his childhood and more about what his grandfather had done to him when he was a little boy. When she replied that she had already told him all that she could remember, his angry reply was that she did not want to help him.

John Rickman returned to London for the Oxford Congress of the International Psychoanalytical Association in July 1929. On his return to Budapest he received a letter from Miss Mary Chadwick (dated 6/9/29), who was a nurse as well as a psychoanalyst, concerning her wish to have been able to discuss with John Rickman the unhappiness among non-medical members, who were not permitted to treat their patients in the London Clinic of Psychoanalysis, as this right was restricted to medically qualified members and associate members. She wondered why there needed to be three committees, and suggested that the Council, the Board and the Clinic Committee could become one committee. She expressed her concerns about his health: "I hope very much that things have been going better with you, for I have felt great sympathy with you in the difficult time you must have been passing through. Remember me to Ferenczi" (CRA/F14/07).

Letters were exchanged between Ernest Jones and John Rickman in Budapest discussing possible changes in the committee structure of the Board, the Council and the Clinic. Jones put forward the suggestion that any "active psychoanalyst" should be able to sit on any committee. Rickman then asked how one would define "active psychoanalyst". It would mean giving lay analysts the right to sit on any committee. This and other proposals resulted in Rickman writing a very angry five-page letter to Jones dated 19 September 1929 (CRA/F14/10) from Baden-Baden, in which he summed up all the administrative things that he felt were going wrong in the British Society and spelt out what the Society meant to him and what he had done for it. Rickman first commented on the term "practising analyst". Did this involve the analyst's "willingness to do the work of charity in serving the Clinic?" This led him to express his bitter criticism of having to work gratis for the Clinic. He had said to lay analysts: "Thank your lucky stars you are not under the obligation of medical humbug to do gratis work 'by making it obligatory'.... They should allow analysts to choose—except for pupils—and 'see if it survives or not'."

Rickman then asked "Why is there financial chaos?" and he gathered that "no Annual Meeting was called after all. He had left the clearest details to Bryan and the matter could have been done in half an hour". He lists a number of administrative failures, including that he did not receive the usual information about the Society's activities. "Even such glad news as a £2000 gift from Pryns Hopkins came to me from outside sources. Have I not scraped for money, guaranteed overdrafts at the Bank myself, given money and hoped for money for the Clinic and Institute for years and deserve to be told of your good?" He ends this sad and lonely letter as follows:

> Well, I've said it now. . . . I have no intention of resigning till I see the Institute and Clinic placed in a position when they will not be endangered by carelessness or indifference; [it may be] that joining up within the Society is the thing that needs to be done. But if you love the Society see that the Institute and Clinic are healthy organisations first. Yours very sincerely, John Rickman. [CRA/F14/10]

Ernest Jones replied on 23 September 1929:

> Your letter has come as a great shock to me, but if you feel like that it is certainly better that you wrote so that we have a chance of clearing it all up. It is impossible for me in a letter to go into all the points you mention and I shall look forward to an early interview. I can only say now that it is easy for me to show that all your reproaches are quite unjustified objectively, though I am sincerely sorry that you should have the distress of believing the opposite subjectively. . . . [CRA/F14/11]

I have quoted from these three letters at length, because they do communicate the depth of feeling that John Rickman had about the Society and Institute. Did he fear that its structure was really disintegrating, or is this what Rickman feared would happen to the "Society that he loved" without him in London to look after it? It is clear that much of his intellectual and emotional energy, as well as his money, had gone into caring for it and planning its future. Could his letter to Jones also express what he feared was happening to his own psyche or inner world?

However, Rickman's concern about money was threatening the possibility of his staying much longer in Budapest for more analysis. His money ran out abruptly when he was in Budapest, where he was earning very little, with only one or two patients, paying for his own analysis and living in an expensive hotel. In 1930 he wrote to his mother to ask her to let him have £1000 worth of securities to bolster his overdraft. He had used up nearly all the family money. Rickman's difficulty in dealing with his finances was a great worry to Lydia and increased the tension within an already stressful marriage.

Towards the end of 1930, Rickman decided to return to London, and they moved back into their house in Kent Terrace. John saw patients in the house, instead of renting a consulting-room. Lydia then decided to look after their finances, and they opened a joint bank account. It has been suggested that perhaps John's unhappy relationships go some way to explaining his drive and capacity for hard work, as well as his constant need for further analysis. But Lucy said that she had little knowledge of marital tensions in her family during that period.

Rickman's return to London and his work for the Society

When John Rickman returned to London, he was faced with the changes that had taken place in the structure of the Institute and the Society while he was away. Some of the changes can now be seen as a response to his angry outburst to Jones about what was wrong with the Society, which so shocked Jones and which was linked with the domination of the Society by the medical profession, and the exclusion of lay analysts from key committees.

At the Annual General Meeting of the Board on 2 October 1929 it was agreed that the following lay analysts should be added to the membership of the Institute: "Professor Flugel, Mrs. Isaacs, Mrs. Klein, Miss Low, Mrs. Riviere, Miss Sharpe, Miss Searl, Mr. Strachey and Mrs. Strachey."

At the same meeting of the Board in Minute No. 3 it was "resolved that the Minute 2 of the first staff meeting of the London Clinic of Psychoanalysis held on 24 September 1926, be cancelled" (they were rescinding the decision that only medical analysts could hold positions in their new Clinic) "and that in future all appointments to the permanent and temporary staff of the London Clinic of Psychoanalysis shall be made by those members of the Board of the Institute who are registered medical practitioners" (and who could take medical responsibility for their lay colleagues). What is relevant to this decision is the report of the British Medical Association's investigation into psychoanalysis which was produced in 1929, in which Jones had pointed out that their medically qualified members took medical responsibility for the patients of non-medical colleagues.

But it was not until the Board meeting on 23 June 1930, that Rickman tendered his resignation from the Council and the Training Committee. "His resignation was accepted with regret but his return in the future was anticipated with pleasure." The other matter that was discussed during that Board meeting was the obligation to treat a clinic patient free, which Rickman attacked so strongly in his long letter to Jones, but no decisions were made.

The continuing importance to John Rickman
of the Medical Section of the British Psychological Society

By 1930 John had removed himself from all major Committees in the Society and Institute, but from my initial research I was not clear what he was doing for the Medical Section. I searched through the *British Journal of Medical Psychology* which he had continued to help edit from 1925 on. What I found out, which I had not known before, was that, as well as being Assistant Editor from 1925, from 1922 to 1930 he was the Hon. Secretary of the Medical Section. These two offices he had carried on while he was in analysis with Ferenczi in Budapest.

In 1933 he took over being Hon. Secretary again for one year, during which period he put together, in a form which he published in the *British Journal of Medical Psychology*, the "Proceedings of the Medical Section of the British Psychological Society from the first meeting on May 14th 1919 to the end of 1933". Over the years many psychoanalysts had read papers to the Medical Section, and in this list he gave the dates, names and titles of all the papers that had been read; if a paper had also been published in the *Journal*, the reference was given in brackets after the title, indicating the volume, part and page numbers. Was this his farewell present as secretary to the historians of the future? The last event that he arranged as secretary was a Symposium, opened by Edward Glover and Maurice Ginsburg, on "The Psychology of Peace and War". The discussion was opened by John Rickman on 13 December 1933 (Rickman, 1934).

In 1934, John Rickman was elected as the next Chairman of the Medical Section, and the title of the paper that he read was "On Quacks and Quackery". In 1936, Sylvia Payne was another psychoanalyst elected as Chairman of the Section, for she, like Rickman, was also interested in linking up psychoanalysis with other professional disciplines.

The Board takes responsibility
for the Public Lectures Programme of the Institute

In October 1932 the Board passed Minute No. 3: "It was resolved to appoint a Public Lectures Sub-Committee to be Convened by Dr. Rickman and composed of Dr. Rickman, Dr. Adrian Stephen, Dr. Karin Stephen, Dr. Yates and Miss Low. The Committee was requested to make concrete suggestions on the subject of public lectures and communicate them to the secretary." This gave John Rickman a new role in the Society that linked up with his interest in spreading and discussing the understanding that he acquired from his work as a psychoanalyst to colleagues of other professions, which was the aim of several of the papers that I have included in this collection.

The report of the Sub-Committee appointed to deal with the organisation of public lectures was considered, and as a result of the proposals put forward the following were chosen as lecturers: Dr Glover, Mrs Isaacs, Dr Adrian Stephen and Miss Low, with Dr Rickman as chairman of the first and last lectures.

In 1933, Dr Rickman reported "that the average attendance at the public lectures was between 60 and 70. Expenses were barely covered by the fees taken. It was decided to charge a higher fee per lecture in the future. The Sub-committee previously appointed was re-appointed to consider problems concerning the organisation of lectures not of a training character and to report thereon to the Secretary of the Board who is given the authority to sanction any activities arising therefrom." It was good that Sylvia Payne was the Secretary of the Board and that they were good friends, as could be seen from her Foreword to his first book of papers, published in 1957. In 1934 the Public Lectures Committee asked the Board for a ruling on the matter of the attendance of the press at public lectures. The Board agreed that the lecturer or chairman should interview the press at each lecture and inform reporters that no case material must be reported. In 1935, when the Board considered the report of the Public Lectures Committee, they decided to appoint Mrs Susan Isaacs to the Committee in the place of Dr S. Yates who had resigned.

In 1936 the Board considered the report of the Public Lectures Sub-Committee, which they passed, and the programme presented was considered. It was agreed "that in view of the public activities of the Institute, application should be made for affiliation in the Conference of Education Societies of Great Britain provided that affiliation implied the freedom to take part in the Conference and there were no commitments." At the same meeting of the Board, Dr Jones was re-elected to the Board, and Dr Rickman was elected as Director in place of the late Dr Eder.

At the first meeting of the Board after he had been elected as a Director, an important discussion took place on suggested methods of improving the discussions at scientific meetings. Various proposals were put forward. It was decided to invite members to discuss these proposals at a meeting of the Institute before the Board came to a final decision. This was a topic that Rickman was even more concerned about when he became the third President of the Society. His very thoughtful paper, "Reflections on the Function and Organisation of a Psychoanalytical Society", on this subject was published in the *International Journal of Psycho-Analysis* in 1951 and was included in his *Selected Contributions* (1957). As a director of the Board, Rickman was gradually regaining his earlier leadership position, taking on new tasks.

At the next Board meeting it was decided to reconstitute the Public Lecture Committee, which John Rickman had convened and nurtured for the last five years. It had become an important "bridge" between the Psychoanalytical Society and the public. The Board decided to reappoint Dr John Rickman as Convenor and to appoint the following members to work with him: Dr Karin Stephen, Dr Susan Isaacs, Dr Dennis Carroll, Dr Pryns Hopkins and Dr Sylvia Payne (*ex officio* as Secretary of the Board).

Rickman became the Editor of the first four volumes of a small book series called *Psycho-Analytical Epitomes*, of which there were six volumes. The first book that he edited was entitled *A General Selection from the Works of Sigmund Freud* (1937). Rickman wrote in the Preface: "The book is an attempt to show *the development of psychoanalytic theories*. Just as each page is dated so the reader is urged to remember that each concept is dated too". This was followed by the second book in the series, *Love, Hate and Reparation* (Klein & Riviere, 1937). The third book was called *Superstition and Society*, by Roger Money-Kyrle (1939), and the fourth was *Civilization, War and Death: Selections from Three Works by Sigmund Freud*, edited by John Rickman (1939).

There was another "small" book entitled *On the Bringing Up of Children* (1936) which was edited by John Rickman, containing a short preface written by him. It consist of lectures by five psychoanalysts: Melanie Klein, Ella Freeman Sharpe, Merell Middlemore, Nina Searl and Susan Isaacs. The second edition, published in 1952, after Rickman had died, includes a "postscript" by Melanie Klein, who took over the task of editing it. I have included the above details about these publications because they cover a period during which John Rickman himself was writing papers and was sharing much of the thinking and theories used by those whose work he helped to make known. It included the work of Melanie Klein, which he always maintained was an extension of Freud's contributions. It was during this period that Rickman went into intermittent analysis with Melanie Klein until 1941, and by 1938 he had been recognised as one of the training analysts of her group.

Rickman's political concerns over threats to psychoanalysts

John Rickman's experiences in Russia working with the Quaker relief services from 1916 to 1918 gave him first-hand experience of the effect that politics could have on the lives and problems of communities, both for good as well as for ill. His inside view of what went on while he was working there, as well as while Lydia and he were trying to find their way out to America via Vladivostock, must have been "a political education" that few people have experienced! He wrote a number of articles in his attempt to show his countrymen, when he returned to England, that their "stereotyped" ideas of what had happened there did not represent the whole truth.

When Hitler was elected as Chancellor of Germany in 1933, it was clear to Rickman and his colleagues that the lives of their Jewish colleagues would soon be in danger, and they would certainly not be permitted to work as psychoanalysts. Ernest Jones wrote to Eitingon, the President of the Berlin Society, offering to help any of the Jewish psychoanalysts who felt threatened, and he invited them to come to London. The two analysts who first accepted his invitation were Paula Heimann and Kate Misch (Friedlander), and when they managed to obtain visas they travelled to London together and started to work in the "east-end" of London. In the next two or three years, the British Society welcomed other analysts from Germany. The first was Eva Rosenfeld, who had been a housekeeper to the Freuds and had helped to run the Hietzing School for children (which was one of the Rosenfeld–Burlingham schools in Vienna, under the auspices of Anna Freud), but who had left Vienna for Germany in the mid-1930s; she was followed by Herbert Rosenfeld and Hans Thorner. Later Hanka Posnanska (Hanna Segal) came from Poland via France to Edinburgh where she did her medical training at the Polish University there.

By the time that these colleagues from Europe started to arrive in London, John Rickman was well established as the Convenor of the Public Lectures Committee, and he was in a position to implement, through the public lectures that he arranged, one of his beliefs, that a knowledge of psychoanalysis can provide ways of understanding human behaviour which can make sense of situations that would otherwise seem to be illogical and threatening.

Recently I came across a list I had made some thirty years ago of some of the lectures and courses that were arranged with John Rickman, as Convenor, and it is interesting to see how the Committee had selected a cross-section of their colleagues to contribute to them. It was an impressive Society effort, and the programme covered a period from 1934 to 1937, the last lecture course being given by Rickman's friend Professor Geza Roheim, the anthropologist from Budapest.

But Hitler was not the only European to threaten the peace of John Rickman and his colleagues. In Italy Mussolini invaded and took over an independent country, Abyssinia. On 17 July 1936, Franco led a rebellion against Spain's legally elected (left-wing) government, and it was not long before it turned into a civil war, with the government side being backed by the Soviet Union, while Hitler was supporting Franco, sending him arms and planes. It seemed that some very evil and destructive political forces were becoming more powerful, and in such situations, who could see the context and try to understand what was happening?

The Assistant Editor of *The Lancet*, T. F. Fox, was a friend of John Rickman and also a Quaker, and he was concerned how to help his readers to understand and to think constructively about the situation in Europe. He approached Rickman with the suggestion that he could sometimes write *The Lancet's* Editorials, as an anonymous contributor, and comment on these events. He could use his psychoanalytic and clinical understanding to help his readers to think about what they were experiencing, as Rickman could put these events in a wider context.

Rickman's first editorial was "The Cathartic Function of General Elections", in *The Lancet* of 11 November 1935; it was subtitled "A Discussion of the Democratic Technique for Dealing with Discontent". Rickman's next editorial for *The Lancet*, on 21 February 1936, was entitled "On Feeling Secure", and it is a good example of the way that he does not deny the worrying political situation, but he uses his clinical skill and his understanding of aggressive impulses to demonstrate how human beings can survive and deal with fears that arise. His final paragraph in this editorial shows Rickman "at work":

> In a world where unrest and danger abound it sounds a mockery to speak of feeling secure, but a step in that direction is taken when we can recognise our own aggressive impulses and not blindly project them on others: we then see our neighbours more clearly and do not confuse their intentions with our own, our own with theirs. Objectivity does not give security, but it enables the darkness to be faced without morbid dread.

As the German threats became more serious, the Spanish rebels under Franco started German-assisted air attacks on Spanish towns.

Rickman and others were aware of the possible repetition of these air raids on this country. He then wrote a paper entitled "Panic and Air Raid Precautions", which he published under his own name in *The Lancet* on 6 June 1938, which is included in this volume as chapter 10. The next month, on 9 July 1938, he wrote a short "Annotation" entitled "The Psychology of A.R.P." in which he quotes his friend John Langdon-Davies and his book entitled *Air Raids*. Rickman, with the help of the Quakers, also played a leading part in organising milk for the children of Barcelona, a city that was being hard pressed by Franco's army.

It was during this period that Rickman wrote some of the papers included in this collection that were directed towards helping his readers to understand the importance of the social factors and differences that impact on us all, often without our even noticing them. For example, chapter 9 which is entitled "Does It Take All Kinds to Make a World?" was first given as two public lectures, at the time when Hitler had been increasing his attacks on Jews as well as on which ever country he planned to invade.

By the beginning of 1938 it was clear that Hitler would invade Austria, which he did in March 1938. The life and liberty of Freud, his family and colleagues were now in danger. Rickman decided to visit Freud to see how he could help.

On 11 April 1938 the Board met, and Ernest Jones "reported on the crisis in the Vienna Psychoanalytical Institute which the annexation of Austria by Germany had caused. . . ." The Board considered some of the members of the Vienna Society whom they could invite to come to London. The Board Minute concluded with: "Dr. Rickman, who was going to Vienna, was asked to collect information concerning the younger members or Associates and Candidates connected with the Vienna Society and Institute".

Before Rickman left for Vienna, Ernest Jones warned him that he was not to assume any authority in his remarks. After visiting the Freuds, Rickman then quickly left Vienna to return via Budapest, leaving Jones unclear on the purpose of his visit. Following Rickman's visit, Anna Freud wrote to Jones about her very difficult and depressing talks with Rickman. He had mentioned the resistance of some members of the British Society to the immigration of the Viennese analysts, and she wondered if he was speaking on behalf of Jones (CFF/F01/05). Jones quickly replied that he was sorry that he had not warned Anna about Rickman. Jones continued: "Now you really must not regard him as speaking in anyone's name. He has been in analysis for years, first with your father, then with Ferenczi and later with Melanie Klein (where he still is) and should have achieved some measure of stability long before this", and he emphasised that Rickman had been told firmly that he was not given any authority. "The first thing I heard was that he had invited the Balints to come to England" (Jones to Anna Freud, 25/4/38), which greatly displeased Jones, who later sent the Balints to Manchester.

Of course, the exchange lectures that took place in 1935–36 (King, 1988) were well known to have revealed certain differences between the approach of analysts in Vienna and London, but in this situation most members of the British Society were happy to welcome the immigrants. Jones was responsible for the negotiations to receive them in England, and on 6 June 1938 Freud and his family and friends arrived in England. This was followed by the immigration of other psychoanalysts from Austria or other parts of Europe and included Hedwig and Willi Hoffer, Rubenstein, Dorothy Burlingham and Barbara Lantos. The Krises and the Bibrings stayed in London for a short time before moving to America, and Geza Roheim had already gone there.

By early 1939 most of the analysts and candidates who wanted to come to London were accommodated. In Anna Freud's tribute to Ernest Jones during his Centenary meeting, she wrote: "Not only did the British Society accord the newcomers immediate membership and, where appropriate, training analyst status, they also assured their financial security by arranging a scheme whereby their private patients could be treated under the auspices of the British Society and Clinic. I have never ceased to be grateful to the British Society for their attitude at this critical moment and the memory of it influenced many of my later actions" (A. Freud, 1979, p. 286).

In 1938 the British Society passed its 25th Jubilee, since the London Society was founded in 1913 and became the British Society on 20 February 1919. Because of the reception of the colleagues from Vienna, the 25th Anniversary Dinner did not take place until May 1939, at the Savoy Hotel. The newly enlarged British Society was joined by their guests, who included the Ministers of Education and Health, professors, artists, writers and friends, showing the wide support that the Society enjoyed at that time.

The Board of the Institute considers its role should hostilities develop

At the Board Meeting in November 1938, Dr Glover reported that he been asked to join a committee under Dr R. D. Gillespie to draw up plans to deal with civilian nerve shock or mental-illness cases in the event of war. Representatives of the principal hospitals and clinics dealing with functional diseases were on the Committee. It was agreed that he should represent the Institute. They agreed to have some lectures on shell-shock. At their next meeting they discussed the position of the Institute if a new war crisis arose. A sub-committee of Dr Jones, Dr Glover, Dr Payne and Dr Rickman was appointed to deal with matters arising in this connection. Dr Glover agreed to obtain the latest information on War Committees and report as soon as possible to the sub-committee. At their meeting on 15 June 1939, it was agreed to appoint Dr Rickman to the Publications Committee, along with Dr Jones, Dr Glover and Dr Payne (Secretary).

Other appointments included were Dr Winnicott as Assistant Director of the Clinic with special responsibility for work with children. Dr Scott and Dr Bowlby were available to help him. Dr Payne resigned as Secretary of the Institute, and Dr Rickman was nominated by the Board to fill that office at the AGM of the Institute. It was also agreed to recommend that the Training Secretary should be an ex-officio member of the Board. It was as if the Board was being careful to see that the Institute was properly staffed to carry it through whatever tasks the expected war might confront it with.

Contact with other professional groups

While the Officers of the Society were too preoccupied to be concerned with relations to other professional groups, it was left to individuals such as John Rickman to try to point out to medical colleagues and others what the country was up against. He had already been to Vienna to assist in the rescue of Austrian colleagues and had seen at first hand what it was like to be invaded by the Nazis, so he spoke with authority.

He worked with members of the Medical Peace Campaign and the Quaker Medical Society with regard to their medical responsibilities during a time of risk of war. He organised other meetings and discussions with professional colleagues from different disciplines who met together in the Medical Section of the British Psychological Society to discuss psychological problems of war. While other members of the Society gave occasional lectures on relevant topics, as I have described earlier, it was Rickman who was invited by the Editor of *The Lancet* to write their leading articles whenever there was an important political crisis, and his articles were often quoted in major newspapers. He therefore had considerable influence on contemporary medical and lay opinion.

Some members of the British Society had been angry in the past because of the aloof and arrogant attitude of some of their officers, mainly Jones and Glover, in relation to their handling of the Society's relationships with other professional groups, particularly with the Tavistock Clinic, a psychotherapy clinic formed in 1920, and how little or nothing they had done to involve members of the Society in the planning for the inevitable war that would take place.

John Rickman and his work during the war

During October 1938 the Sudetenland was ceded to Germany, and by March 1939 Emil Hacha had signed over the whole of Czechoslovakia to Hitler. Chamberlain, the British prime minister, warned that if the Germans invaded Poland, Britain and her Allies would declare war on Germany. On 1 September 1939, Hitler and his armies invaded Poland.

On 2 September 1939, *The Lancet* published another anonymous editorial (written by Rickman), entitled, "A Peace of Understanding":

> Nations judge themselves by their war aims; posterity judges them by their manner of offering, making, accepting and keeping the terms of the armistice and peace. A brutal and antisocial force is at work in Germany today, destroying the peace of Europe; and whether we know it or ignore it we too are at the bar of history. We in England are united as seldom seen before in a common cause—to stop power being used for private ends. ... A war of silent hate would be long and destructive of our lives and our ideals. The will to achieve a lasting peace must include an open-minded willingness to listen to complaints and meet grievances: remembering that the peoples of Europe will have to live as neighbours to the end of time.

Participation of psychiatrists in the Emergency Medical Services

When war was declared, many medical psychoanalysts joined the Emergency Medical Service (EMS), which was set up to deal with casualties arising from the war emergency, with air-raid casualties and with members of the armed forces who needed medical care in Britain. Part of the Maudsley Hospital moved up to Mill Hill and became part of the EMS dealing with psychiatric casualties in the north-west area of London. William Gillespie and Clifford Scott worked there, and so did a number of other psychoanalysts and others who became candidates after the war.

Some of those who joined the EMS were not immediately involved and could go on working at their peace-time jobs until hostilities increased. Others moved on to join the Army as the psychiatric services became more organised. Nevertheless, in spite of the number of members who joined up, many of them still managed to attend Scientific and, especially, Business Meetings all through the war.

As described earlier, prior to the outbreak of war John Rickman had been in the forefront of organising contact with other professional groups, attempting to engage their support and understanding in the task of preparing them to meet and deal with the problems that war would confront them with as professionals.

On the day that Poland was invaded, John Rickman joined the EMS as a psychiatrist at Haymeads Emergency Hospital, Bishop's Stortford. To understand this phase of John Rickman's life, I need to explain the structure within which he now had to operate. When John started working at Haymeads EMS Hospital, and was later transferred to Wharncliffe EMS Hospital, he was working as a civilian psychiatrist, even though his patients could increasingly be military personnel. But it was soon evident to him that those psychiatrists who shared his ways of thinking were mostly in the RAMC.

Organisation of the psychiatric services of the Armed Forces

At first the Armed Forces did not want to have civilian psychiatrists and apparently hoped that they could manage with their own army-trained Medical Officers (MOs), but when they were faced with the results of mass conscription, and the psychiatric misfits that they received, they realised that they needed more skilled psychological help, and they appointed Consultant Psychiatrists for the Navy, the Air Force, and the Army (Ahrenfeldt, 1958).

J. R. Rees, the Director of the Tavistock Clinic, was appointed Consultant Psychiatrist to the Army (Dicks, 1970). He appointed a number of colleagues who had worked with him at the Tavistock Clinic, and others who had a psychodynamic approach to psychiatry, as advisors to each of the army Commands in Britain, and they were referred to as "Command Psychiatrists".

In his book *The Shaping of Psychiatry by War* (1945), J. R. Rees describes the impact that drawing so many dynamically orientated psychotherapists into the Army had on the course of the war and the organisation of the Army. It was in this way that W. R. Bion, a former tank officer who had won the DSO in the First World War, who had worked at the Tavistock Clinic and was about to start his training as a psychoanalyst, was appointed a Command Psychiatrist to the Western Command. Ferguson Roger was appointed Command Psychiatrist to Scottish Command, and Ronald Hargreaves to Northern Command. What was more important for the future contributions that the psychological services were enabled to make to the war effort was the fact that the General Officer Commanding Northern Command was Sir Ronald Adam, a soldier-scholar, who quickly realised the advantages of close collaboration with psychiatrists such as Ronald Hargreaves, with whom he worked. It was not long before Sir Ronald Adam was appointed Adjutant General of the British Army in charge of all matters to do with personnel, and on the Army Council. This meant that J. R. Rees and Ronald Hargreaves had a supporter and a facilitator at the highest levels of the army.

The first difficulty that some of the psychiatrists in the Army gradually became aware of was that they had been trained to operate the medical model of a one-to-one relationship between doctor and patient, but that as time went on there was a growing recognition of the importance of social factors in the maintenance of mental health in an army unit. It was found that psychiatric cases were "carried" in good units, while they tended to be extruded in weak ones. The usual theoretical concepts employed by psychiatrists did not help with such problems (Main, 1946).

What theory could be used to understand these and other facts that they were faced with? As time went on, those who were concerned with such issues made use of concepts from social psychology, such as Kurt Lewin's concept of field theory and that of the influence of the social field on the individual, and, when used in conjunction with object relations theory, they formed a theoretical context within which to use psychoanalytic and psychodynamic theory, with its understanding of unconscious factors in social behaviour. It was a combination of these concepts from different disciplines that was necessary if the psychiatric services were going to be able to help with problems of group relations and the healthy functioning of a large social system like the Army. Since 1939, the work of Kurt Lewin had immediately registered with Rickman, when he had got to know of it through reading J. F. Brown's *Psychology and the Social Order* (1936). Lewin's ideas gave Rickman a dynamic form into which he could fit the rich content of psychoanalytic experience, and it is this synthesis that is so characteristic of his outlook.

Work while at Haymeads EMS Hospital and The Haymeads Memorandum

While he was at Haymeads, he was given the task of visiting the EMS hospitals in his area to discuss with them their plans for the care and treatment of patients with war neurosis. At this time he also heard that Melanie Klein and Susan Isaacs had gone to Cambridge, not far from Bishop's Stortford. Susan Isaacs had been officially asked to get together a group of those concerned with the evacuation of children, in order to monitor its effect on the children. In October 1939, she asked John to chair a meeting in Cambridge to which Susan had invited fourteen people, including Melanie Klein, Donald Winnicott, John Bowlby and Sybille Yates, among others. Afterwards, Rickman wrote the Minutes of this meeting (CRR/F14/18).

As soon as he arrived at Haymeads Hospital, he produced a draft of his proposals of how to deal with military patients who were referred to the hospital. This was called "The Haymeads Memorandum". In this unpublished memorandum, dated 6 September 1939 (three days after war had been declared), Rickman formulated a new policy for dealing with psychiatric patients from the Services, in terms that made sense to medical and lay personnel. In it he particularly emphasised that as a patient may well have been traumatised by his war experiences and feel rejected by his unit, in addition to receiving help with his neurotic anxieties he should be actively helped "to a life of work and productiveness" in order to restore his morale and self-respect. To this end, Rickman recommended that an "Occupational Therapy Centre" be set up to provide meaningful activities so that the patient's energy was "turned outwards to work and normal life (not inwards to neurotic brooding)". He recommended that the Centre was to be outside the hospital, serving as a transition between illness and normal life.

I do not know how far these plans were implemented for this hospital, as he was only there until August 1940. I do know that John took his plans with him to Wharncliffe EMS Hospital near Sheffield when he was posted on 23 August 1940.

The Wharncliffe Experiment

After nearly one year at Haymeads Hospital, John Rickman was transferred to Wharncliffe Emergency Hospital, Sheffield, where Ronald Hargreaves was the Command Psychiatrist. From the correspondence it is clear that Rickman got enthusiastic backing and encouragement from Hargreaves. Soon after his arrival at Wharncliffe Hospital, with this backing, he was able to develop the plans that he had begun working on for Haymeads Hospital, but not without some obstruction from the hospital authorities. But eventually, with the assistance of Q.M. Sgt. G. R. Bryant, a regular soldier, Rickman devised a paramilitary Rehabilitation and Training Centre. This co-operation between a psychiatrist and a regular soldier was, I think, an important factor in the gradual appreciation of this scheme. Rickman obviously felt that in addition to suffering a psychiatric breakdown, the patients from the Services would have lost their role in the Forces, and if they had felt strongly about the reasons for the war, they would also feel useless and displaced. Hence his emphasis on the need to offer paramilitary training facilities, alongside the psychological care.

His activities were warmly supported by Ronald Hargreaves, and knowledge of the scheme was passed on to other Neurosis Centres under the EMS. In a letter from Hargreaves dated 3 February 1940, he wrote to Rickman, "I feel Wharncliffe may mark a new stage both in training and rehabilitation before its work is finished. Your scheme of seeing patients on the way in and on the way out is excellent. . . . I am delighted to hear that some Wharncliffe papers will be appearing soon. . . .Wilson, to our great distress is going—But since he is doing a swap with Bion, we shall have a v. good new ally in the Command" (Hargreaves, 1940, CRR/F15/01).

The fame of Rickman's work at Wharncliffe spread, and many people came to see it. In the Archives of the British Society there are letters of appreciation from them, and they are especially grateful for the time that John spent explaining his ideas to them and listening to their problems.

One person who came to see what was going on in Wharncliffe was Wilfred Bion, Command Psychiatrist from Western Command. Following his visit John received this letter dated 9 January 1941:

> Dear Rickman, Just a line to thank you for making me so very comfortable at Wharncliffe last week-end. I enjoyed seeing you again very much indeed and it was most refreshing to get somewhere where at least some attempt was being made to get some work done. I dug out my Memorandum when I got back here and was pleased to find that it did seem to suggest something like the scheme you are in fact carrying out. Not the least value of a para-military training course seems to me to be that a patient is given a world to adjust to nothing like so severe as the isolated and unsupported world which is presented to him by the bed-ridden existence, aimless and dis-

united, which he has to face in the Special Institutions I have seen so far. But I am still doing a lot of thinking about this. I think that you have given me some ammunition with which to ginger up this psychiatric service. . . . I hope I shall have a chance of coming over again. In the meantime I trust you will have every success and happiness. With every good wish, Yours very sincerely, W. R. Bion.
[CRR/F04/07]

Another person who also wanted to see "what was going on at Wharncliffe" was Eric Trist, who was then working as a clinical psychologist at Mill Hill EMS Hospital. He had been critical that there were no appropriate facilities for the rehabilitation of Service patients at that hospital, and he was also interested in the potential usefulness of Kurt Lewin's field theory and the influence of the "social field" on the individual as applied to a wider hospital environment. Aubrey Lewis, who was in charge of Mill Hill EMS Hospital, then recommended that Eric Trist visit John Rickman at Wharncliffe Hospital, to see what he was doing. While there, Rickman discussed with him the work he had been doing with Bion, who had been recently appointed as a Command Psychiatrist. He learned that they had "prepared the document which became known as 'the Wharncliffe Memorandum'". This document contained a prospectus for a therapeutic community (Trist, 1985). Unfortunately, it cannot now be traced. An attempt to put into practice some of the ideas contained in it at Northfield Military Hospital is described later in this introduction.

In January 1941, Bernard Hart, who was in charge of the EMS scheme for the whole country, sent Eliot Slater and George Debenham to make an official report on the Wharncliffe experiment, following which Slater wrote to Rickman from Sutton Emergency Hospital, "As you know we were very impressed by it and are about to give it the sincerest form of flattery." He described how a new convalescent hospital was being set up for patients from Mill Hill and Sutton Hospitals, where there would be facilities to take patients who should return to the army—"and there we propose to introduce your scheme of paramilitary training, somewhat modified of course, but still your scheme" (CRR/F16/08).

Joint Services and EMS Psychiatrists' Conferences

In order to discuss the concerns and special problems that psychiatrists in the Services and the EMS were facing in his area, Ronald Hargreaves arranged a series of conferences in Northern Command. At these conferences, psychiatric problems likely to be common to Service and EMS psychiatrists were discussed. In January 1941, one was held at Wharncliffe Hospital, which Rickman organised. Following this, in August 1941, Rickman wrote to Bernard Hart describing the Joint Conferences for the Northern Command and EMS psychiatrists, and suggesting that such meetings should be held to cover the whole country. Colonel J. R. Rees was in favour of this suggestion, as was Bernard Hart (CRR/F16/26).

This countrywide Joint Meeting of Services and EMS psychiatrists took place on 27 September 1941. Among John Rickman's papers I found the Minutes of both these meetings (CRR/F16/34). The list of those present from the army reads like a roll-call of the staff of the Tavistock Clinic. Those present from the EMS included Bernard Hart, Aubrey Lewis, John Rickman and Clifford Scott.

The conference discussed a paper by Major R. F. Barbour, on "The Relationship of the Neuroses to Service Responsibility". In this paper he supported the ideas put forward by Rickman that special training wings should be attached to Neurosis Centres and Hospitals. Following this meeting, a number of similar joint Service and EMS conferences of psychiatrists took place. Topics discussed at these meetings included morale, "unescapable psychiatric problems", the retraining of psychiatric patients, and so forth. In all of these, Rickman seems to have played an important part, including presenting the discussion paper on the topic of "Unescapable Psychiatric Problems". During the four months following this conference, Rickman arranged for "The Monday Discussions" on topics related to the work of psychiatrists to take place at the hospital every Monday from 1 September to 15 December 1941 from 8 p.m. to 10.30 p.m. (CRR/F16/27). It would have been a good "refresher course" for psychiatrists as well as a chance for them to meet each other.

One of the reasons why Rickman's scheme was particularly appreciated was that it demonstrated that some patients suffering from war neurosis would recover better in a paramilitary environment, and that all Service patients should not be sent indiscriminately to EMS Neurosis Centres, and therefore out of the military orbit, as was the case until April 1942 (Ahrenfeldt, 1958), but that they could still be rehabilitated and trained to become useful in some branch of the Services.

Gradually the army recognised the important role that their psychiatrists could play in preventing psychiatric breakdown, and in January 1942 they were permitted to recommend for transfer to special employment men working in jobs for which they were temperamentally unsuitable.

Contributions of Army Command Psychiatrists to the development of officer selection procedures

Following the evacuation of the remains of the British Army from France at Dunkirk in 1940, the army had to be reorganised, expanded, re-armed and trained, and new officers had to be selected to lead the reorganised British Army. By 1941 it was realised that there was a high rate of failure during the training of those recommended for commissions by their own officers and the traditional style of Officer Selection Boards.

In the summer of 1941, John Bowlby (a psychoanalyst) had been doing research on this rate of failure of candidates during their training. He had found a high correlation between Psychiatric Interview Assessments and success of officer cadets during their training as officers.

Following this research, a high-level discussion was held in Scotland between General Sir Ronald Adam, Adjutant General of the British Army, Major General Andrew Thorne, General Officer Commanding Scottish Command and two of the Command Psychiatrists, Ronald Hargreaves and T. Ferguson Roger. J. D. (Jock) Sutherland, who was then working as a psychiatrist in Carstairs EMS Hospital, was also asked to attend, and he described to me later what happened.

A whole day was spent discussing the problem of how to select good officers for the army more effectively. The outcome of this discussion was the decision in January 1942 to set up an experimental War Office Selection Board in Edinburgh to explore what could be done.

The core of this first experimental War Officer Selection Board in Edinburgh, known as No. 1 WOSB, included Wilfred R. Bion (a Command Psychiatrist), Jock Sutherland (an EMS psychiatrist), Eric Trist (a clinical psychologist) and Eric Wittkower (a psychiatrist from the Tavistock Clinic) and who had been working on the Selection of Other Ranks. This group was asked to think out new methods of selecting officers, which could be tried out and evaluated with the co-operation of the army officers allocated to work with them, one of whom was Harold Bridger (who later became a psychoanalyst). Here new methods of selecting officers could be tried out and evaluated with the co-operation of the army officers allocated to work with them.

A revised programme for the new WOSBs was then designed by the members of No. 1 WOSB in Edinburgh. Potential officers came in groups of thirty-two and stayed in there for two and a half days, living together with the atmosphere of a therapeutic community. Their activities included taking part in leaderless groups, where the spontaneous behaviour of men with each other in a group could be observed while they were undertaking a group task, like building a bridge. They were also given a battery of psychological tests, which included an adapted form of a Word Association Test and a shortened version of Murray's Thematic Apperception Test (TAT), as well as psychiatric interviews and cognitive tests.

It was felt that the task of the psychological specialists was to provide the army officers with whom they worked with as good a picture as possible of the candidate's personality, but that the army must choose, and be seen to choose, where to fit them in. The psychological personnel were careful to emphasise that this was the job of Military Officers.

The Research and Development part of No. 1 WOSB was then moved down to London, where it became the Research and Training Centre (RTC) for WOSBs, with Col. R. S. Ratio Kerri as a very supportive officer in charge of the Unit. The group was joined by John Bowlby, who was then responsible for following-up the results of these officer-selection methods.

Soon after this core group had started work, Wilfred Bion wrote a long, four-page letter to John Rickman dated 12 March 1942, saying that he wanted to tell Rickman about the work that he had been doing during the last six months and suggesting that Rickman "should think of coming in to it". Bion then described certain issues that made this work so important. It had emerged that the psychiatrists held a key role in the selection process, by their balanced approach, and by refusing to be certain when they were *not* certain, and by recognizing that in the selection of potential officers there really *was* a problem. "Thus we paved the way for an absence of dogmatism in our approach to the solution. Our influence in this direction has I think been as invaluable as it is difficult to measure." Bion then goes on to say that "we have been responsible for instigating reforms which I am sure are of quite fundamental importance" (CRR/F04/21).

Bion found out that the AG (Adjutant General of the British Army) had been spreading the idea that officer material in the army was bound to deteriorate, and indeed he had published this as a fact in official documents to Boards and elsewhere. Bion told him that an army at war should sprout officers, if its morale was healthy. Bion produced his gardening metaphor, including the importance of how you treat plants after you have planted them!

It is a remarkable letter for the picture it gives of the work that he and his colleagues had been doing with officers at the top of the Army

Command and his final plea to beg Rickman seriously to consider "applying to come into it" and join the RAMC.

The development of special military hospitals for psychoneurotics

Alongside the work that was being done on the selection of officers, the army authorities began to realise that it was better to keep the less ill of their psychiatric casualties in special military hospitals for psychoneurotics. In April 1942 they opened one at Northfield, Birmingham, "and provided 200 beds for hospital treatment, and 600 beds in a 'Training Wing', where the rehabilitation of soldiers suffering from psychoneurosis could be carried out prior to their return to duty" (Ahrenfeldt, 1958).

In April 1942, according to Rickman's daughter, the "Triumvirate" of Ronald Hargreaves, Ferguson Roger and A. T. M. (Tommy) Wilson, who were working with the Directorate of Army Psychiatry, "told" Rickman that he should join the RAMC, for it was clear that Bion and Rickman could not co-operate adequately belonging to two different institutions. He went through the usual entrance procedures to be commissioned as a captain in the British Army, and he was subsequently posted to Northfield Military Hospital as Major Rickman and was appointed Training Officer there for the psychiatric trainees. He had the task of helping them to acquire some understanding of psychodynamic ways of thinking, so that they could understand and help their ill patients, who were also in that hospital as soldiers. Letters received later from some of them expressed their gratitude for his approach.

John Rickman and Wilfred Bion at Northfield Military Hospital

After Rickman had been at Northfield for five or six months, Bion asked for a transfer there so that he could join him and they could both start working on the ideas that they had put together in the Wharncliffe Memorandum. Towards the end of 1942, Bion was appointed in charge of the Training Wing in Northfield Hospital, with Rickman, who was already concerned with the training of psychiatrists, to work with him. This wing housed between 100 and 200 patients, which could be seen as a rather large group. Bion used his experience with leaderless groups in the WOSBs to inform the way he related to the patients in the Training Wing, which he ran as large leaderless groups, during which he confronted the patients with their responsibility for the intra-group tensions in the group. Although they were patients, they had to be helped to remember that they were soldiers as well. Their therapy was embedded in the men's real situation, and Bion treated them as soldiers. Both Bion and Rickman agreed that one of the battles they had to wage was to prevent their patients retreating into neurosis and mental illness and thus abandoning their role as soldiers. They thought that they could help more traumatised individuals by working through groups of which they were members. Because of the nature of army life into which men were in the process of being rehabilitated, the therapeutic task was clearly identified as developing "group membership skills", which would enable the men to adapt to any community afterwards. Instead of taking up the problems of individuals, Bion's therapeutic focus was on what actions or experiences the group were having or understanding, not on the individual person's reaction or emotional state.

After some weeks, Bion could report that a sea change had occurred in the spirit of the wing. There was co-operation between men and their officers following the discussions in the leaderless groups, with the men taking increasing responsibility for helping to influence the situation that they were in. They were beginning to regain their dignity and self-worth as soldiers contributing to the defeat of the Axis powers.

The experiment, however, ended suddenly. Rickman's daughter Lucy told me that after only six weeks, both Bion and Rickman were given 48 hours' notice to leave Northfield Military Hospital and to report to other postings.

The behaviour of the military authorities utterly shocked those in the Training Wing, as can be seen from this quotation from Bion's letter to Mrs Rickman (dated 1/3/43) about these events:

> It is very disappointing to think that for the time being I shall have to be working without Major Rickman, but short as our collaboration at Northfield was I felt that I learned an enormous amount and that there will yet be an opportunity of putting it into practice. I wish that you had been able to see the enormous admiration that was felt for him by the staff, students and course at Northfield. His departure came to them as a blow so severe that the mess remained awkward and embarrassed from the time they heard the news until the moment the students' course saw him off on Friday morning; for me it was pleasant to see that even in these days his worth could strike

such deep roots. Betty joins me in sending our love and very best wishes. Yours very sincerely, Wilfred Bion. [CRR/F04/15]

The sudden removal of Bion and Rickman from Northfield Hospital seems to have been greeted with mixed responses from their colleagues. Some were shocked at the high-handed action taken against two of their colleagues, others were rather relieved because Bion's way of working was difficult for them to assimilate alongside their own approach to working with mentally disturbed patients. Bion was posted to No. 7 WOSB, Winchester and John Rickman was posted to No. 6 WOSB at Brockham Park in Surrey, which was not far from Dorking where he grew up.

If the behaviour of the military authorities utterly shocked those in the Training Wing, it must also have come as a deep shock to both Bion and Rickman, for both of them had given so much of themselves to developing this "Northfield Experiment", as it came to be called. While the new "postings" to different WOSBs meant that they could not work alongside each other, there was nothing to stop them writing to each other and trying to record what had happened in the Training Wing at Northfield Hospital at the beginning of 1943. In a letter dated 7 March 1943, Bion wrote:

> Dear Rickman, I've been trying to struggle with the memo, in spare time but not very successfully. Partly I think because the Northfield affair has required a good deal of readjustment of ideas and this has not been easy. I had a note from Doyle to say the Wing had produced a good deal of discontent at the change over and some leaders, "to safe-guard democratic principles"! If so I can see they may provide further Ammunition for our unscrupulous friends in A.M.D. 11 [Directorate of Army Psychiatry at the War Office]. ... The more I look at it the more it seems to me that some very serious work needs to be done along analytical and field theory lines. ... I'll send on more notes as soon as I get a bit further with them. With all good wishes to yourself and Mrs. Rickman. Yours very sincerely, W. R. Bion. [CRR/F04/17]

During that year, Bion and Rickman put together their report of these events and it was published in *The Lancet* in November 1943 under the title: "Intra-Group Tensions in Therapy—Their Study as the Task of the Group". From a letter dated 4 October 1943, from Ronald Hargreaves at the War Office, it is clear that the paper first arrived there before its publication. Hargreaves wrote: "I would like to congratulate you on it. It seems to me to put forward some ideas of fundamental importance in group therapy which have never been emphasised previously. In some ways I wish it were being presented to an audience more psychologically sophisticated than the readers of *The Lancet*. Yours ever, G. Ronald Hargreaves" (CRR/F18/19).

I have decided to include this paper as chapter 12 in this book, together with a statement from John Rickman when he opened a discussion on it in 1945, at the first peace-time meeting of the Medical Section of the British Psychological Society. In doing this I echo Ronald Hargreaves' hope that it will then be read by a more "psychologically sophisticated" audience.

Major John Rickman, the psychiatrist at No. 6 WOSB

John Rickman had been working since 1939 with the EMS, and later with army psychiatrists, and was mainly concerned in his work with what happened to "soldier-patients" in hospitals; he was subsequently concerned with arranging cross-fertilisation between the army and the civilian psychiatrists. These contacts led to discussions of their common problems as psychiatrists. In April 1942, John Rickman became Major Rickman, an Army Psychiatrist. And it was as an Army Psychiatrist that he worked at Northfield Military Hospital, but he was still concerned with the care of the army's patients. When Major Rickman was posted to No. 6 WOSB, at Brockham Park, Surrey, in March 1943, his type of work changed, and with it his role as a psychiatrist changed. He was not so much a healer concerned with mentally ill or stressed patients, who had been taking part in the war; rather, he was now called on to use his knowledge about people and psychology to help his military colleagues to select the soldiers who wished to become officers, and who had the best "personalities" to take responsibility for people they had been asked to lead.

The work John was called on to do as a psychiatrist in a WOSB was quite a change of role from what he had been used to from 1939 to 1943. In his previous positions in the EMS and then in the army, he had been able to have ideas and obtain encouragement and even authority to carry them out. The Command Psychiatrists in Northern Command, as well as Bernard Hart who was responsible for the EMS hospitals not under the army authority, were grateful for the work that Rickman did organising and facilitating the regional conferences of psychiatrists that did so much not only to build up morale, but more importantly, to increase the skills and usefulness of their psychiatric profession.

But when he joined No. 6 WOSB, in its beautiful setting of Brockham Park, his role was more strictly defined. He was part of a core management group, each member of which had a carefully defined role, in terms of how they related to each other and how they related to the candidates' group to which they were allocated, in the course of the two-and-a-half-day programme of activities that the applicants were following. How they assessed and shared the results was also carefully defined and kept balanced by "the President" of the Board.

This was a situation that John Rickman turned to his own creative account. Two of the chapters in this book (chapters 6 and 7) describe the various ways he used and understood the benefits of interviewing potential officers in such an unconventional setting as Brockham Park, when the manner of relating to each other was structured by a strict programme and to the achievement of the WOSBs' goal.

Rickman took seriously his own task on the Board—that of the psychiatric interview of officer candidates, in order to feed back to the core management group as good a picture as possible of the candidate's personality, so that the Army could choose and be seen to choose, where to fit them in. Rickman however, would have considered that it was part of his task to get to know the other staff members of the core group, each of whom had their own specialist skills, in the same way that he got to know the people who printed his beloved *British Journal of Medical Psychology*, which he had edited for many years. One way Rickman facilitated his relationships with other members of his WOSB was to hold informal discussions in between the visits of the two groups of officer candidates, which he referred to as "Coffee Pot" discussions. Participants could put forward their points of view or questions, and Rickman would help to facilitate their discussion. In several letters of appreciation to John after they left, these coffee pot evenings were especially appreciated.

By 1943, Rickman was known to a number of the "psychiatric fraternity", and he was asked to address their conference on 23 October 1943 on "The Technique of Psychiatric Interviewing", when members of the Expert Committee would be present! The following month, on 27 November, the psychiatrists of the three Services and the EMS met in London at the Royal Society of Medicine. Psychiatrists from the American Army also joined them and gave four papers. The Consultant to the U.S. Army over here took the chair. "If you and Pearce could say something about Northfield, it would add greatly to the value of the meeting." This letter came from "The War Office" AMD11. It seemed to me that John Rickman had become someone whom the top levels of Army Psychiatry felt to be a good example to show to the Americans. On 15 December 1943, Brigadier H. A. Sandiford sent all the psychiatrists on the WOSBs the compliments of the season and best wishes for 1944. He continued "I would like to thank you all most sincerely for the high standard you have continued to display in the strenuous work throughout the past twelve months, and it is a great source of satisfaction to feel that what we are building, we are building well" (CRR/F18/24).

It was also during this period that the Shell film unit came to No. 6 WOSB to make a film of its activities. The various officers took the same roles in the film that they did when they were working as part of a regular WOSB. Thus John Rickman, the psychiatrist, had taken his usual role of "Psychiatrist" to the Board and Col. Newman was the "President" in the film as well as in real life. I have read a copy of the "Fifth Draft Commentary" (covering 27 pages) on which the film must have been based, and it covered ten reels of film. Rickman must have spent time and energy writing and thinking about how to present what he did in the film's "Psychiatric Interview". He realised that this film was a way of training new officers to work in other WOSBs, as well as one way of introducing the idea of becoming an "officer" to younger soldiers, who could imagine themselves, through the film, taking part in the process. This particular WOSB was nearly always inundated with visitors, usually of field rank, Lt. Generals rather than Lieutenants. They moved quietly around from group to group, watching both the candidate-officers and those who were now trained in the particular skills necessary to maintain the supportive atmosphere required for their work. "Into the almost cloistered calm of a WOSB came a Film Unit." Rickman wondered how he could be affected by the intrusion of a camera and what impact it could have on his interviewee. "The psychiatrist has to get them to disclose their personality. How is this done? First of all a certain part of the work is done by the mere contrast of the setting, no running about, no hurry at all in the interview, here all is quiet: we are alone." In this setting, intra-personal tensions can be disclosed, observed and talked about. (CRR/F19/65, "Memorandum on the Preparation for Spontaneous Acting in a Documentary Film" by John Rickman.)

A colleague who had recently seen the WOSB film wrote to John afterwards: "I do think the finished product is absolutely first-class and a very balanced affair altogether. If I may say so, your Psychiatric

interview pinched the picture, particularly the Psychiatric silences. . . .
I shall certainly never forget the period we spent at No. 6. Yours very
sincerely [name illegible]" (CRR/F21/08).

On 30 May 1946, the WOSB film was shown at Shell Mex House.
Colonel Newman, the Board President, invited all those whom he could
contact who had worked in No. 6 WOSB to watch it together. He
invited Rickman to join him for lunch afterwards.

Soon after the end of the war, I was able to see this film. I was very
impressed with the film as a whole but particularly with John's interview and especially with his capacity "to hold the silence" as both a
facilitating and an integrative experience during the interview. I have
been informed by his daughter that while most of the film still exists in
the Imperial War Museum, the last few reels, which included the psychiatric interview could not be found.

On 22 February 1944, John Rickman received a "personal" letter
from A. T. M. (Tommy) Wilson from the War Office about the Army's
plans for receiving back into the community those who had been prisoners of war. It seemed that the Command Psychiatrists and their allies
had already put together some ideas on how to deal with POWs, which
Tommy enclosed with this letter. He wrote:

> Bion will have had a copy by now but the Director arranged for the
> distribution and so far as I know kept it fairly high up for political
> reasons. . . . At the moment we are trying very hard to have the
> principle accepted that the type of "handling" personnel and the
> type of atmosphere at different points during POWs re-adaptation to
> life in this country, should be very carefully considered. . . .
>
> Anyway, if you have time it would be very useful indeed to have
> any comments or views you possess on these general problems. We
> found one remarkable ally in an Australian who has actually managed to put into practice there most of the points that are vaguely
> sketched in the last paragraph of the report, i.e. techniques of handling the loss of group morale on leaving the Army. [CRR/F19/20]

This was another problem that Rickman would have been interested to
think about and make comments on, but at this moment he was beginning to find that with such extra calls on his time, he needed someone to
lend a hand with the interviewing. He asked Ronald Hargreaves if
someone could be spared to help him for a few weeks. Eventually,
Rickman was confronted with an impossible work situation, so on 13
July 1944 he wrote officially to Ferguson Roger at the Research and
Training Centre (RTC), which was responsible for allocating WOSB
psychiatrists to WOSBs:

I should like to put before you the Candidate–load in the next few weeks.
   Monday 17th July, S.B.U.C.
   Sunday 23rd July 48 Royal Marines
   Wednes 26th July 48 Royal Marines
   Sunday 30th July 48 Royal Marines . . .
   Monday 21st August Non-stop S.B.E.C.
The Royal Marine Office desires that all Royal Marines should have a psychiatric interview. Of course, 96 interviews in 3 days (with the time table at our disposal) is a possible proposition but it means spot diagnosis and guess work and at the end of the week one's interview level is reduced to the social condition of "Please pass the salt".

As this sort of thing would have to go on for 1.5 weeks and be followed immediately by about 3 weeks of high pressure Cube Boards, I wonder if you could manage to send a relief for the Royal Marines. Yours, John Rickman. Major RAMC. [CRR/F19/21]

From this letter it must have been clear that Rickman was not well. On 5 August 1944, John received a detailed reply from the RTC and signed by Jock Sutherland. Jock was glad that John was "getting his troubles properly attended to" (CRR/F19/25). He hoped that John "will feel fit quite soon". Jock then described the arrangements that he had made to relieve John of much of the work that he complained about, until he felt better. A. S. Patterson would undertake the Cube Boards from the 14th to the 16th of August for Rickman and would carry on if Rickman could not manage in the minimal way he had been doing with No. 6 Board. After Saturday, 19 August, Jock said that he could arrange for Geoffrey Thompson to take over until No. 6 WOSB went on leave.

John had arranged to see a specialist about his condition on Thursday August 10th, and because following that appointment he would probably have to take "time off", he had already sought permission from the powers that be (Brig. Rees) to spend his "sick leave" at No. 6 WOSB. This was given, unofficially, by the end of the letter.

His daughter Lucy recently found an old scrappy diary, in which she had written that her father went to hospital on August 16th (1944) and also on August 20th. The first date must have been to see a specialist, while the second was to hospitalise him as he had suffered from a coronary thrombosis. The Medical Board that saw him on 7 September placed him in Medical Category "D" and proposed that he have three months' sick leave. When he was out of hospital and feeling more like his old self, he asked to have his sick leave cut down to one month. After three weeks he knew that he could not manage working for a full day, and he applied to have it left at three months.

As soon as the news of his illness spread to his friends, the most moving and appreciative letters started arriving. On 5 September, for example, he received a letter from the War Office AMD11: "My dear John, I have been so concerned about your illness, and am thirsting for the latest news of you. I do hope that things have really settled down and that you are going still to be able to give us lots more of this brilliantly good work that you have handed out so liberally to the Army. On the other hand, you must take sensible care of yourself and try not to take on things until you are fit to do so. . . . With very best wishes to you, Yours sincerely, J. R. Rees, Brigadier" (CRR/F19/32).

He was called to another Medical Board on 7 November, and on 30 November he was informed that the previous proposal had not been approved. The official letter continues: "You have now been placed in 'Category E'. Accordingly, it will be necessary for you to relinquish your commission . . ." (CRR/F10/50). This letter was sent to Captain J. Rickman, RAMC—he was no longer "Major" Rickman!

I think that this recommendation came as a shock to John, although, being a doctor, he must have known what to expect. John's departure must have been a disappointment to Col. Newman, and in his letter dated 23 December, he wrote movingly of Rickman's importance to him. "My dear Rickman, I feel it would be ungracious of me to let the festive season go by without a word of appreciation of your efforts, during the time you have been a member of my staff. . . . In the case of my Board I do value your services not only in your official capacity as a psychiatrist but more as a pillar of strength to the Board. I can honestly say without flattery, that your help in every way has been one of my happiest experiences . . ." (CRR/F19/53).

Rickman's farewell letter to Col. Newman describes the gratitude that he felt for having had the experience of working with him at No. 6 WOSB and his sadness in having to leave this work. I quote from a draft letter dated 28 December:

Dear Col. Newman, May I for just one more occasion use this paper as a member of your mess to tell you with what regret I am leaving No. 6 WOSB and Brockham Park—my place of work and relaxation. It has been a time of expansion of spirit for me, and a constant challenge to exploit the slowly gathered experience of many years to the solution of problems whose boundaries are still to a large extent unknown. The work is not finished or even brought to a point where the extension of ideas has begun to slow down and practice hardens into routine. . . . I do not curse my fate that I should be interrupted by a medical Board in the middle of a tour of such interesting duty, but rather I reckon it such a stroke of fortune to have been summoned into such work at all and to have been posted to one of the two Selection Boards which have been pre-eminently thought worthy of a visit by technical members of other Boards . . . lay visitors (i.e. non WOSB personnel) . . . the presence of numerous post-graduate students indicates that there is a centre of creative activity worth visiting. . . . And it was during my happy months at No. 6 (only 16 months) . . . that our Board was looked on as a place worth studying by those whose life was given to scientific work. They were indeed for me fruitful and happy times and I am specially grateful to you for the encouragement and opportunity you gave me. . . . With all good wishes to you and all who are at No. 6. Yours sincerely, John Rickman. [CRR/F20/01]

On 7 January 1945, Col. Newman thanked John for his letter. He wrote: "I am glad to hear you are making a round of your old haunts, and of course you will give us a little longer than most I hope. When can we expect you? And do stay a night or two. I would like you to have a Coffee pot with our new psychi, he is very young and new to the army, but most impressions are most favourable . . . we miss you far more than I can possibly describe on paper, your help, your kindness, and the many gadgets. All send their best wishes for 1945. . . . Wells Newman" (CRR/F20/44).

The first of Rickman's colleagues to write to him after he had had to leave the RAMC was Wilfred Bion. On 7 December 1944 he wrote:

My dear Rickman, I do not know whether to be sorry or glad at your news; sorry only I think if it means that at some time it may not be easy to meet if I am moved from here, but glad from every other point of view. I don't believe there is much more that can be done in the army. . . . But I do think that it is time that we took a forward looking view and the real developments are going to be in civil practice. . . ."

After discussing the state of army psychiatry and its deterioration, Bion turns his attention to his friend Rickman:

I am very glad you mean to devote time to reading and writing. I hope that you will find it as stimulating and interesting to do as we shall find it to read. I do not know why you say you owe anything to my performances; it is quite clear to me that the indebtedness is all the other way and I, in common with all others who have had the good fortune to have your criticisms and help, have felt that anything I have done springs time and again from a stimulating and productive line of thought suggested by yourself. If you tried to dispute this I could easily muster an overwhelming number of votes against you! . . . With every good wish to yourself and Mrs. Rickman, Yours ever, Wilfred Bion. [CRR/F04/18]

This letter to John Rickman gave Bion another opportunity to point out to John how he did not seem to value his own contributions to much of the work that the army group of psychiatric colleagues, at different levels of army authority, had managed to accomplish, and particularly how much, by feeding ideas and solutions to those senior to him, John had already accomplished. He also pointed out how concerned John's seniors became when he got ill. As J. R. Rees wrote to him on 5 August 1944, "I hope that you are going still to be able to give us lots more of this brilliantly good work that you have handed out so liberally to the Army" (CRR/F19/32).

On 7 February 1945, Rickman took the opportunity to thank Brigadier Sandiford for being able to have had the experience of working under him and Brigadier Rees for three years as an army psychiatrist in the British Army:

> Dear Brig. Sandiford, I leave the Army today after nearly three years. This period in Army psychiatry has been one of the most productive and happy in my life, and I leave it with great regret, not least because it has been such an enriching experience: I doubt whether the Menninger Clinic, which has a reputation as one of the leading research places in America, will provide as stimulating an atmosphere as the team working under you has done. The Menninger has not had the direct experience of war, and army psychiatry has had the advantage of both being forced and encouraged to use its opportunity, and I for one, and I believe I speak for many, feel grateful to you and to Brigadier J. R. Rees for help in using that opportunity. Yours sincerely, John Rickman. [CRR/F02/03]

Negotiations with American psychoanalysts

On 13 January 1945, Brig. J. R. Rees received the following cable from Robert P. Knight of the Menninger Clinic, Topeka:

> VERY INTERESTED HAVING RICKMAN COME TOPEKA AS TRAINING ANALYST AND RESEARCHER PROVIDED HE COULD STAY AT LEAST A YEAR COULD OFFER DLRS 8000 SALARY FIRST YEAR PLEASE CONVEY THIS TO HIM AND HAVE HIM CABLE REPLY STATING WHEN HE COULD COME IF HE THINKS FAVORABLY OF IDEA. [CRR/F02/20]

As Brig. J. R. Rees was away, Brig. Sandiford sent the cable to John Rickman with the comment, "Sounds good to me!"

On 20 January 1945, Rickman sent this cable,

HONOURED BY OFFER AM CONSIDERING IT FAVOURABLY BUT ON MEDICAL ADVICE FOLLOWING CORONARY THROMBOSIS PROBABLY SHOULD NOT ARRIVE TOPEKA BEFORE MAY OR JUNE. AIR LETTER FOLLOWING. [CRR/F02/22]

In the air letter, dated 27 January 1945, that followed, he explained about his health and other reasons for not being able to leave for the States until after June. Rickman writes: "The prospect of teaching in your clinic for a year or so is experienced as attractive because it will give an opportunity to learn of the progress made in America in the collaboration between psychoanalysis and psychiatry and sociology, which has been my main interest for the last few years and in regard to which much inspiration has come from America. Yours sincerely, John Rickman" (CRR/F02/22).

There followed a number of cables concerning Rickman's need to obtain transport priority (the war was still in progress) and his need to obtain a visa from the U.S. Embassy in London for himself and permission to take his American born wife with him, and so on.

On 4 March 1945, John received the following rather worrying cable from Robert Knight:

YOUR LETTER JANUARY 27 RECEIVED. FROM SOME AMERICAN ANALYST WE HEAR ABOUT KLEIN VERSUS FREUD CONFLICT IN BRITISH SOCIETY AND YOUR BEING LEADER KLEIN SECTION THIS CONFLICT NOT WELL UNDERSTOOD HERE BUT AROUSES CONCERN REGARDING YOUR ESPOUSAL HERE OF KLEINIAN IDEAS IN TRAINING WHICH MIGHT NOT ASSIMILATE WELL HERE WOULD APPRECIATE CABLE REPLY AND AIR MAIL LETTER GIVING DETAILED STATEMENT YOUR TRAINING IDEAS WE HAVE HEARD NOTHING FROM STATE DEPARTMENT OR DOCTOR RICHARDS REGARDING YOUR VISA WHAT IS STATUS THERE. [CRR/F02/21]

On 5 March 1945, John Rickman replied with this cable to Robert Knight:

THERE BEING IN ESSENTIALS NO CONFLICT BETWEEN FREUDS AND KLEINS THEORIES RUMOURS OF DIFFICULTIES SCIENTIFIC NATURALLY NOT WELL UNDERSTOOD BY YOU STOP INTEGRATION OF LOGICAL AND TECHNICAL DEVELOPMENT FREUDS ABRAHAMS KLEINS IDEAS DEPENDS ON BEING UNDOGMATIC WHICH I HOPE I AM STOP FOR SPIRIT OF MY SEMINARS REFERENCE MY APPRECIATION OF FREUD BRITISH JOURNAL MEDICAL PSYCHOLOGY AIR LETTER FOLLOWING NOTHING FROM RICHARDS HERE YET. [CRR/F02/30]

On 11 March 1945, Rickman sent a carefully argued air mail letter to Knight in which he tried to take up the issues that were worrying Knight. He writes: "Your cable demonstrates anew the results of the difficulties of communication during these war years. . . . On my side I have almost no idea what your curriculum is and therefore find difficulty in complying with your request for a 'detailed statement of my training ideas'. I am therefore enclosing a memorandum which I recently submitted to our Training Secretary (Lt. Col. Bowlby) in answer to his four questions on Criteria issued to all Training Analysts (including those not now training because on Active Service)" (CRR/F02/06). Rickman adds that the full training covers four years, and in contrast with the Americans, the British Society accepted some non-medical candidates.

Rickman then described the teaching and work that he had done since 1939, when he went into government service. For the first two years in Ministry of Health Service for Military Patients, he was "in charge of a 300-bed unit for psychiatric cases and then for nearly three years in the Army doing first teaching and later officer selection work". Rickman then wrote:

> As I was not posted in the London area I was spared the often distressing discussions in the British Psychoanalytical Society. I resigned my official position as Business Secretary and I very rarely attended the meetings in that time and took no part in the controversies and have been leader of no section nor wish to be. I will now enlarge on my attitude as expressed in my cable.
>
> Psychoanalysts work with an instrument of research and therapy, the Transference Situation, and employ a theoretical device for interpreting the data which that instrument affords. The laws governing the relation of unconscious to conscious material are given in Freud's *Interpretation of Dreams*, and in his collected works we find the interaction of the ideas that that book contains with the problems presented to him by the data in the Transference Situation—here are the fundamentals of psychoanalysis. Anyone working on the basis of transference and resistance and taking full cognisance of infantile sexuality I am ready to call a psychoanalytical colleague and work with him on the basis of a vast common ground of discourse. There may be points of difference (I would not have it otherwise) but we as psychoanalysts are closer to each other than any who deny transference, resistance and infantile sexuality.
>
> I do not think it reasonable to employ any narrower basis than that just mentioned (which of course comes from Freud's writings) and within those wide limits the individual should be free to draw

what deductions he pleases and express them in any idiom he pleases provided that he can explain to his colleagues the relation of his views and his idiom to those current among them.

This kind of collaboration with give and take of ideas has been the basis of my teaching in the last five years, for though I have been out of psychoanalytical practice as such (except in the last two months when on sick leave) I was for a time in charge of teaching psychiatry and psycho-pathology to young psychiatrists in the British, U.S., and Polish armies. ... As a teacher I do not care so much what conclusions are reached as that the student should try to get his own ideas clear and to co-ordinate them to those of his fellows. In making this the working basis I believe I am interpreting the spirit of Freud.

In my cable I referred to the integration of the work of Freud, Abraham and Klein; since you asked for a personal point of view I gave it. I share with Jones and a number of others in the British Society the view that there is a logical development in this direction, which is not the same thing as an "espousal of Kleinian ideas", whether in training or otherwise. To deny the possibility of such development seems to us is to narrow the basis of collaboration among colleagues and indeed to narrow psychoanalysis itself: also such denial can hardly be reckoned scientific ... much though I like teaching the attractive feature to me of your offer is the prospect of working in an Institution known for its collaboration in different mental and social sciences. Yours sincerely, John Rickman. [CRR/F02/10]

It seems to me that John has given a clear description of where he stands as an "independent" psychoanalyst, and, from that psychoanalytic grounding, how he prefers to interchange analytic understanding and experience with colleagues and students. This letter shows that he was obviously not a missionary for anyone else's point of view. He was looking forward to the experience of teaching in another context. But from various comments that he made he was hoping to meet some of the American social scientists such as Kurt Lewin, who formulated "field theory" and J. L. Moreno, who had been quoted to him during the war by colleagues like Eric Trist.

However, it was not to be, for on 21 March 1945, he received a cable from Prof. Aydelotte of the Institute for Advanced Studies, Princeton, New Jersey:

REGRET TO REPORT IMPOSSIBLE FOR OSRD UNDER ITS RULES TO ASSIST IN TRANSPORTATION FOR DR RICKMAN. [CRR/F02/36]

This was the last chance of getting transportation to the States, for John had already been told there was "deadlock" or at best a long delay. He therefore cabled Robert Knight:

> MUST THEREFORE RETURN TO PRIVATE PRACTICE AND WITH YOUR ACQUI-
> ESCENCE REGRETFULLY ABANDON PLAN. [CRR/F02/19]

Robert Knight kept his link with the British Society, and for many years after the war, he worked with Willi Hoffer and later with John D. Sutherland as one of the Assistant Editors of the *International Journal of Psycho-Analysis*.

Other contacts with American colleagues

In April 1945, a commission of five American psychiatrists—Dr Leo Bartemeier, Dr John Romano, Dr Lawrence Kubie, Dr John Whitehorn and Dr Karl Menninger—were appointed by Brig. Gen. William C. Menninger (who held the equivalent position in the American Army to that held by Brig. Gen. J. R Rees in the British Army) and sent to England to study psychiatric techniques and programmes as developed in the British War Department. They "fell in love" with England and its people, and they were most impressed with the work that had developed in the so-called Northfield Experiments, which were "initiated" by Wilfred Bion and John Rickman in 1943 (Bion and Rickman's paper on their work is included here as chapter 12).

Karl Menninger asked Lieut. Col. Ronald Hargreaves to obtain manuscripts from those who had been working in Northfield Military Hospital, where they had treated 800 soldiers with battle neuroses of various types, primarily by group therapies (Menninger, 1946).

Rickman becomes an active member of the British Society again

When John Rickman left the British Army and returned to his profession as a psychoanalyst, he found a psychoanalytical Society that had undergone a number of changes. During the years 1941 to 1945, a series of Business and Scientific discussions had taken place among the members in an attempt to deal with strong differences of opinion between those who supported the approach of Melanie Klein in certain extensions of Freud's theories and those who opposed her point of view (King & Steiner, 1991). Edward Glover and Barbara Low from the

British Society were supported by Anna Freud and her colleagues from Vienna. Behind this conflict was another important question, which could be expressed by the question: "What kind of psychoanalysis should be taught to our students?" Sylvia Payne, who was then Secretary of the Institute, had arranged for a stenographer to record the Minutes of these meetings verbatim, so that those who were doing war work out of London could be kept in touch with the debates.

However, it had not only been scientific disagreements that divided them. There was felt to be much unfairness related to the constitution of the Institute and Society, and some members thought that as Ernest Jones had been President for many years, Edward Glover, who often presided at meetings as his Deputy, would expect to take his place for an unlimited period of office. Thus some of the more angry exchanges were often around the need for constitutional change. These two issues were not unconnected, for some thought that if Glover became President, he would not look favourably on the development of Klein's research and point of view. Finally, certain constitutional amendments were agreed that led to Glover's resignation from the Society and Anna Freud's resignation from the Training Committee at the beginning of 1944. At the Annual General Meeting in October 1944, Sylvia Payne was elected as President of the British Society and Jones was elected as the Honorary President. This was the situation in the spring of 1945 when Rickman took up his work as an "active" member of the Society again. The Training Committee was drawn from the pre-war training analysts, with no representative of Anna Freud's approach.

During 1945, discussions continued between the President, Sylvia Payne, Anna Freud and the Council of the Society concerning how they could accommodate the kind of training that Anna Freud could accept. It should be noted that they had many requirements in common. In June 1946, the Society agreed in principle to the introduction of two parallel courses, to be referred to as Course A, which would continue to be organised as formerly, teachers being drawn from all groups, and Course B, which would teach technique along the lines supported by Miss Freud and her colleagues. An Ad Hoc Committee on Training was set up to work out the details. The members were Sylvia Payne (Chairman), John Bowlby (Secretary), Anna Freud, Willi Hoffer, Melanie Klein, Susan Isaacs, Adrian Stephen and John Rickman. John Rickman was again on an important committee and was involved in the British Society, but this did not mean that he was no longer involved in wider issues that flowed from his work during the war.

The end of hostilities in Europe

As the end of the war approached, the editors of *The Lancet* started to encourage John Rickman to write another of the anonymous editorials to match the one he had written at the outbreak of war. *The Lancet* published the editorial, entitled "First Fruits of Peace", on 5 May 1945, three days before the war in Europe ended. I discussed earlier a request that John Rickman had received from Tommy Wilson to consider the plans that the Command Psychiatrists had been working on to receive the returning prisoners of war. On the day that this article was published, these plans, for the setting up of Civil Resettlement Units in different parts of the country, had now been made public.

> That a man should take up arms in defence of his country, and lay them down again, quickly returning to the arts of peace, when the danger is over, is a common-place of history; that a man feels pain on leaving home and finds joy in return is a common-place of literature: that none of these processes are as simple as they seem is a common-place of psychology. . . . An army if its spirit is good, knows how to help the recruit to make the necessary changes in outlook that group living requires . . . is there a similar awareness on the civilian side of the community that the assimilation of millions of its own people—and they are those to whom it owes life itself—is a task calling for every bit as much detailed care as that other transmutation into military formations? On the answer to this question depends not only the smooth return of our prisoners-of-war, but a fruitful issue to the enormous transformation of demobilisation, and indeed to take a still wider issue, the rehabilitation of whole populations in Europe and Asia. [*The Lancet*, 5 May 1945, p. 565]

Rickman's concern in the last line of that quote had led him to send a Memo to Henry V. Dicks, a Command Psychiatrist who had links with the Control Commission and the organisations that were planning to take over the German Army and maintain order on the Continent. Rickman was concerned with the condition of the peoples of Europe, both enemies and victims. In a letter dated 12 May 1945, Dicks says that he took this Memo to "the competent person who discussed its practicability from the 'channels' and 'admin' point of view" (CRR/F20/15). Both decided that it would take months to come into being, by which time the need for John's plans would have disappeared.

The demobilisation of the psychiatrists and psychologists

During the year following the end of hostilities in Europe, the psychological fraternity gradually began to meet each other as civilians and to discuss how they could work together in peace time to use some of the skills that enabled them to help their army colleagues, to help "society" to understand peace and its problems. A number of those who had been responsible for designing and facilitating the WOSBs decided to set up, alongside the Tavistock Clinic, the Tavistock Institute of Human Relations, among whom were John Rickman, Jock Sutherland, Eric Trist, Tommy Wilson, Harold Bridger and John Bowlby. There were others who, like myself, were members of the British Psychological Society, and of its Medical Section, who decided to join the Social Psychology Section of the British Psychological Society as being an appropriate setting within which to discuss how we could work together.

Madeline Kerr (who had been my Psychology Lecturer at Bedford College) was the Hon. Secretary of the Social Psychology Section, and she organised a week-end conference on "Present Day Problems of Peace and War". It was to take place at Bedford College on 20–22 September 1946. The following were invited to address the Conference: A. W. Walters, T. H. Pear, J. Rickman, H. V. Dicks, E. Jaques, and L. F. Richardson. Papers would be given on Saturday and Sunday, but rooms would be available on Friday evening for those who might like preliminary discussions. I attended the whole conference, and so did everybody who was anybody in the psychiatric and psychological field. This was the first time I had listened to John Rickman addressing an audience. I think that I, like most of those who heard him, was very moved. I have included his paper in this collection as chapter 13, "Disruptive Forces in Group Relations—War as a Makeshift Therapy".

Rickman's visit to Berlin on 14–15 October 1946

After hostilities were ended, the Allies set up a Control Commission to be responsible for dealing with the state that Germany and her Allies were in, and to try to round up those responsible for the atrocities that had been committed during the war. They also set up a German Personnel Research Branch of the Control Commission. British psychiatrists and social scientists were asked to take part in interviewing leading members of their intellectuals in order to select those who had not been damaged by the Nazi ideals and who could be invited to take leading roles in the reclaiming of Germany and her Allies.

Rickman described the reasons for his visit as follows:

To find out whether among the leading members of the German Psychoanalytical Society there might be any who might be suitable as assistants to the personnel of G.P.R.B.

To discuss what influence, if any, twelve years of the Nazi regime had on the personnel working in a special branch of the psychological field, both in respect of the development and enrichment of theoretical concepts and in respect of the capacity of co-operating with others in the same field but using different methods.

To establish contact again with German citizens engaged in the same line of Scientific Research, in order to ascertain whether there were ideas which might be usefully imported into England. [CRR/F21/29]

John made one long copy of his report of his interviews with five members of the German Society who had been working in Berlin all through the war, which he sent to Ernest Jones, who was then the President of the International Psychoanalytical Association (IPA), which they should now be eligible to re-join; the second shorter copy he sent to Sylvia Payne, the President of the British Psychoanalytical Society to whom Rickman was responsible as a member of that Society. For many years very few other people received copies of it, the only exception being the next President of the IPA, Dr Leo Bartemeier. It was published in full at the end of my paper, "Activities of British Psychoanalysts during the Second World War" (King, 1988).

Applications from war-time colleagues to be trained as psychoanalysts

A number of those whose work in the army brought them into contact with John Rickman and who admired his insight into the events and experiences that they shared together came to the conclusion that his approach and understanding might be related to the fact that he was a psychoanalyst. Thus during the years 1945 and 1946 a number of them applied to the Institute of Psychoanalysis to be trained as psychoanalysts. I had got to know several of these colleagues and was most impressed when they described to me what had been achieved by those working in the forces in the socio-psychological and psychiatric field. I also applied to the Institute; John Rickman was asked to interview me.

This was my first "official" meeting with John Rickman, and it took place in July 1946. What he said to me on that occasion often came to my mind as I read through his papers to prepare them for publication, alongside reading several hundred letters to and from his friends and colleagues.

What I did not know at the time was that members of the British Psychoanalytical Society had spent several years from 1941 to 1945 discussing different approaches to psychoanalytic theory and practice, as between Vienna and London (King & Steiner, 1991). In particular, they were concerned with the different approaches to psychoanalysis that had developed in Vienna and had been brought to London when Anna Freud and her colleagues escaped from Austria and the Nazis in 1938, as compared with those that members of the British Society had followed, who had partially assimilated some of the approaches of Melanie Klein.

Rickman started by explaining to me that there were two training courses; one was arranged along the lines that Anna Freud and her colleagues from Vienna had agreed and which they had called "Course B", to avoid linking it up with racial ideas by calling it "Viennese", and the other they had called "Course A" rather than "British", which catered for most of the other analysts in the British Society, among whom were those who agreed with Melanie Klein, who had said that she did not want a group for herself. In my mind I placed myself in "Course A", and I was happy to be in a group that included Melanie Klein. Rickman asked me who I had thought of going to for my analysis if I were accepted. My reply was that he was the only psychoanalyst that I knew and I would like him to be my Training Analyst.

Rickman then went on to explain that they undertook to train me as a psychoanalyst, but that it was my decision if, at the end of the training, I became a psychoanalyst or decided to use what I had gained from my training to work in another profession or discipline. At that time he would have known that many of my friends, who were also interested in being trained as psychoanalysts, were planning to start the Tavistock Institute of Human Relations, which was interested in exploring how to help sick societies or institutions to become healthier. It was only recently that I came across a long memorandum that Rickman had written in 1945, for the Training Committee of the British Society, in which he put forward the importance of a training in psychoanalysis for those wanting to work as psychoanalysts and to become future teachers in the Institute of Psychoanalysis and a parallel training for those wanting the training to help them work in another profession or with other disciplines (CRR/F02/06, see Appendix 1).

As a previous chairman of the Admissions Committee of the British Psychoanalytical Society, I now know that this approach and its advantages to psychoanalysis, had not even then penetrated into that Committee's visions of their future. In fact, an applicant who stated that he or she wanted to be trained as a psychoanalyst in order to be more effective in another profession would not have been accepted for the training—it would be considered a waste of a valuable Training Analyst's time!

Looking back after over fifty years as a psychoanalyst, I can hear John saying "What a pity!" I trained with twenty other candidates, six of whom had been Lieutenant Colonels in the army and some of whom joined the Tavistock Institute of Human Relations while they were training, which I myself also joined later for a few years.

After the war, Sylvia Payne, encouraged by Rickman, met with the Professional Committee of the Tavistock Clinic to discuss their relations with each other, and particularly with the newly formed Tavistock Institute of Human Relations. They agreed that the latter would deal mainly with the application of psychoanalytic principles to social problems, while the Institute of Psychoanalysis would be regarded as the centre for training in the technique of psychoanalysis.

John Rickman was very aware of the need for appropriate institutions to be available to offer specialist services, and he himself supported the development of three Institutions that he felt carried out socio-psychological functions in the community alongside the work done by the British Psychoanalytical Society: (1) There was the Tavistock Clinic (on whose newly constituted Council Rickman had agreed to serve), which was concerned with the provision of psychotherapy for children and adults. (2) There was the Cassel Hospital under Tom Main, which was developing as an inpatient hospital that offered psychoanalytic therapy for inpatients. (3) Then there was the Tavistock Institute of Human Relations, whose members tried to apply what they had learned from psychoanalysis and from working together during the war to helping sick institutions to become healthy. The TIHR linked with Kurt Lewin's Research Centre for Group Dynamics, in Cambridge, Massachusetts, to produce a journal, *Human Relations*. John was an enthusiastic member of the Editorial Board. His "Medical Tribute" to Lewin, reprinted from *The Lancet*, may be found in *Human Relations*, Vol. 1 (1947), No. 1, p. 133.

Rickman's contribution to the Training Programme at the Institute

When John Bowlby became Secretary of the Training Committee in 1945, he asked all those who had been recognised as part of the training scheme to let him know what criteria they would use when recommending that students in analysis with them pass from one stage in the training to the next one. Rickman's response to this request was to produce a closely typed four-page Memo containing much food for thought. This was the Memo that John sent to the Menninger Clinic to give his thoughts about training students in psychoanalysis.

I searched through the Annual Reports of the Institute and Society to find out how involved Rickman was in the training events. He usually took part in two teaching events in the course of a year. I remember most clearly his Introductory Lectures on Technique in the summer of 1948. These lectures were for Course A students. Miss Freud gave the Lectures on Technique for Course B students, and they were given at the same time. Our Course A must have numbered at least fifteen students, of whom several had been Lieutenant Colonels in the war. Rickman had sent round in advance a four-page reading list. Each item was in chronological order, with the number of pages that should be read in brackets. There were forty-two references, and they were dated from 1900 to 1947. I still have my original reading list from this course, and on it I had ticked those that I had read. When it came to the seminar, we all sat down in a circle with a space in the middle. After a short introduction, John produced a small model of a couch and strips of paper to serve as potential walls. He asked one of us to put the walls down, and he discussed with us where we would have a door and a window. We then had to say where we would put the couch and why. Would we put it against a wall? What might be the difficulties? The patients could kick and damage the wall. What about putting the couch in the middle of the room? Could their patients feel too exposed and unprotected, so that they took fright and left treatment? The next problem was, where to put the analyst's chair? Should the patients be able to see their analyst? If they wanted to do so, what would be worrying them about being in a room with an invisible analyst?

It was amazing to see how many clinical issues developed in the course of these discussions. In a short time we had learnt a great deal about technical problems that may arise when working with patients. It is an approach that I often followed when I became a Training Analyst.

Rickman's participation in UNESCO's "Tensions Project"

After the war, pressure was put on a number of international bodies to facilitate the setting up of research into factors that lead to wars between states or could prevent them occurring.

At the second meeting of the UNESCO General Assembly in 1947, a study of "Tensions Affecting International Understanding" was proposed in order to encourage social scientists to focus "on an understanding of the development and perpetuation of attitudes which make for national aggression". Hadley Cantril agreed to take responsibility for organising the conference, and in July 1948 he invited eight international social scientists to meet together in Paris to discuss this theme. John Rickman was one of the participants of this Research Conference. The Proceedings were published in 1950 under the title *Tensions That Cause Wars* (Cantril, 1950). In the Introduction, Cantril writes:

> The day before the meeting, John Rickman suggested "that we spend our first morning going around the table with each man indicating briefly the story of his life, the influences he thought had determined his point of view and his interests, together with an implicit evaluation of his own qualifications for being a member of this particular group." We had a fascinating and revealing three-hour session that first morning. And it was a tremendous time saver. For we became sufficiently acquainted so that in subsequent discussions we had enough insight into the other fellow to have a fair idea of why he was saying the things he was. [Cantril, 1950]

John was very involved in the whole event, and after the success of his proposal about the first session, he became part of a small subcommittee consisting of the Chairman, Hadley Cantril, Gordon W. Allport, Alexander Szalai and John Rickman to facilitate the clarification and sorting out of various difficulties or misunderstandings in the final statement, which was signed by all eight participants.

The comments that each member made during the personal statements of other participants were printed at the appropriate place in the final report. In this book I have included John Rickman's statement as chapter 14, under the amended title "Some Psychodynamic Factors behind Tensions That Cause Wars", but without the inclusion of the comments by other members.

One of the purposes of this conference was to encourage the participants to formulate research themes that could be carried out later. John

Rickman's proposals were based on his experiences working with psychiatrists in the EMS and the army when he helped to organise country-wide conferences of all available psychiatric colleagues, whatever their rank, to discuss both problems and good ideas, which helped to reduce tensions among psychiatrists during the war.

The first Congress of the IPA, held in Zurich, since the beginning of hostilities took place

Prior to the Zurich Congress of July 1949, Ernest Jones asked Sylvia Payne, John Rickman, William Gillespie, Anna Freud and Ruth Usher to meet with a group of representatives of the American Psychoanalytic Association (APA) to try to sort out their discontents and criticisms about how the International Psychoanalytical Association was run, its undemocratic structure and antiquated regulations, which had driven the APA Council at the 1938 Congress to wish to "go it alone" and to leave the IPA. They were particularly angry at having to report the progress of their training candidates to the "International Training Commission" in Europe. It was now obvious that the "balance of power/authority" in the IPA was not appropriate to the situation and that more authority should be shifted from Europe to America. Years later, Sylvia Payne told me that John played an important role in helping to sort these "injustices" out and to agree a better division of responsibility as between Europe and the States. The results of these discussions were well reported to the Business Meeting at the Zurich Congress of the IPA by its President, Ernest Jones.

The International Training Commission was abolished and its function was split between the APA Council which had responsibility for Training in the United States, while the Central Executive of the IPA "looked after" Training in the rest of the world. Furthermore, it was agreed that American colleagues should be proposed for positions of President of the IPA and as members of the IPA Central Executive.

This was the first Congress that I had attended as a student, but over the years I managed to discuss what various issues were at stake, and why people felt about these issues as they did, with senior colleagues like Sylvia Payne, Paula Heimann, William Gillespie and Phyllis Greenacre, who also became my good friends.

John Rickman's visits to Cairo and Damascus

After John had returned from Switzerland, he realised that his flight had not adversely affected his heart, and he started a correspondence with an Egyptian colleague and student from our Institute, Ishak Ramzy, about the possibility of spending a few days there to meet some of the leading Arabic thinkers and teachers, who were becoming interested in psychoanalysis. John was interested in the possibility of eventually starting a Psychoanalytical Society in Cairo, as several Egyptians had sought training in European Societies. John had worked with a number of students from other cultures, either as their analyst or as a supervisor, during which work many ideas must have occurred to him along the lines that there were other ways of understanding psychoanalytic experience.

Rickman offered a programme of lectures and discussion groups to cover a few days. When this was possible, Rickman booked a plane to arrive in Cairo at 9.30 p.m. on 23 March 1949. Ramzy arranged three lectures on the following three days: on 24 March, Rickman gave a talk on "The Psychoanalytic Approach to Disease" to members of the Royal Medical Association. The next day he talked about "Psychoanalysis and Human Relations" to members of the Association of Mental Health. On 26 March he addressed the members of the Psychiatric Clinical Society on "The Psychoanalytical Orientation in Psychiatry".

The lectures were to be in English, but to make it easier for his Arabic-speaking audience to follow him, he obtained permission from the British Medical Association to have his article that they published on 7 January 1949 translated into Arabic. In the afternoons, seminars were arranged around the topics of John's lectures. In order that he could meet more people, he extended his stay until 30 March, prior to moving to Damascus, where he had also been asked to lecture on psychoanalysis to members of the psychiatric and medical professions.

This would probably have been their first confrontation with a psychoanalyst and psychoanalysis. Those attending his lecture would all have had their own way of treating mental disorders, and consequently they would each have their own reputations to protect. This would not be the best situation for a "meeting of minds". In Cairo, John's colleague Ishak Ramzy had acted as a "bridge" between the audiences and Rickman, with his new ideas, but there was no such link in Damascus.

Rickman realised this and had said that he would be pleased to visit Damascus, but he would prefer to speak to medical students. He added that he would be happy if any of their teachers or other colleagues would like also to attend and hear what he was saying to the students. Thus, by not being part of the "official audience", they could "listen in" to what Rickman was saying and they would have the space to make up their minds in "the privacy of their own minds", without possibly losing face by feeling that they had to take on an opinion, before they were ready to do so!

I have not discovered in John's archives a report of this visit, but I have found a number of moving "thank you" letters to the key people that John met in Cairo, which bring together some of his thinking about this encounter and about what he had learned about Arabic culture.

> I have as you know a special place in my heart for the East, not I think sentimental but an admiration for the qualities in the culture so different from our own. And I want to see Psychoanalysis growing there with the imagination of the East—and its peculiar gift for seeing patterns—with the scientific rigour of the West. [CRR/F03/22]

> The company assembled at the lectures were impressive by reason of their diversity: it is seldom in England that one finds psychiatrists, "ordinary doctors", psychologists and educationalists all in one room, and I think it is important that they should all meet. It was the more remarkable that those who did meet were so high ranking in their professions. Such inter-departmental interest is, if I may say, a most encouraging omen for the development of psychological science in Egypt, and is rare. [CRR/F03/12]

John Rickman retires as Editor of the British Journal of Medical Psychology

John Rickman had been editing the *British Journal of Medical Psychology* since 1925, first as Assistant Editor and from 1935 to 1949 as Editor. He started his last "Editorial" by talking of "a dozen years or so" instead of twenty-four years.

John announced his retirement as Editor, alongside his great satisfaction that he could hand the Editorship over to John D. Sutherland,

> whose work has led him into the fields of general psychology, educational theory, psychiatry and psychoanalysis. But more important than such wide travelling is an interest in the integration of the ideas used in these disciplines—that he has. . . . [Rickman, 1949]

Rickman continued:

> In the last twenty-five years I have read, commented on and made ready for dispatch to the printer on the average over a thousand words a day. Though this is only a small part of one's working life, this experience provides occasion for a number of reflexions upon the field of work under consideration, and I propose to submit for publication a sort of "Obituary" of myself as an editor and the reason why I found the work satisfying. [Sadly he did not complete it.]
>
> In concluding this "pre-Obituary" editorial, I would like to say that did the custom of my family allow an epitaph (over forty of them in their small acre would shudder in their graves at the thought of such advertisement), I would simply add (by way of pointing to the greatest satisfaction which the deceased enjoyed in his public activities) after my name and dates of birth and death:
>
> > "He was for a time
> > Editor of The British Journal of Medical Psychology."

The editing of John Rickman's papers

After having completed the research work that I had done in the archives and elsewhere in order to "rediscover" John Rickman for myself, I also had to face one of my discoveries: he was probably one of the most experienced editors ever to help psychologically minded writers. His insistence that writers should not only concentrate on the item or event that they were reporting, but that they should describe the context in which it functioned and its relationship to other sources of relevant knowledge, must have been of help to those whose papers he edited, as well as of help to those who read those papers.

I have selected and prepared for publication many of John's unpublished papers that could be of interest and which I thought were important contributions to John's thinking and scholarship. I have also included two or three papers that, though previously published, are now out of print or inaccessible but whose subject-matter is relevant to the themes around which I have structured this book.

I have divided the papers into four parts, and in each part John's papers are arranged in chronological order. It should then be possible to read his papers bearing in mind the events that I have described in this Introduction, which I have entitled "The Rediscovery of John Rickman and His Work".

In part I, which deals with observations on psychoanalytical theory and technique, Rickman describes his approach to psychoanalysis, which is used in most of the papers in this book. In the next two papers, he compares his technique and approach with that used in experimental psychology and in scientific method. The last paper is a tribute to his life-long friend, Geza Roheim, which he wrote for his *Festschrift*. It deals with new ways of seeing one-, two-, three- and four-person and group "Psychologies" and encourages his readers to look afresh at what they do and what they may miss in their work.

In part II, papers that deal with the interpersonal and intra-psychic dynamics of the interview situation have been collected. The first paper, "First Aid in Psychotherapy", is on a topic that is not often discussed. It contains some useful clinical illustrations. The next two papers give a detailed study of the psychological encounter in the interview situation, including the influence of the setting of the interview on behaviour. In the last paper in part II, Rickman compares the technique of interviewing that would be appropriate in psychoanalysis with that which would be right for the anthropologist's discipline.

Part III includes papers concerned with disruptive and integrative forces in group relations. The first chapter in this section is relevant to many present-day problems: Does it take all kinds to make a world? Can a knowledge of psychoanalysis help? The next chapter, on panic and anxiety reactions in air raids, translates easily into fear of terrorist attacks—for who knows from where they may strike? Rickman's paper on professional and unprofessional attitudes explores the protection of one's profession and the dangers of losing that protection. The context from which "Intra-Group Tensions in Therapy—Their Study as the Task of the Group" arose is described in this Introduction under the heading "Northfield Military Hospital". The last two chapters in part III deal with disruptive forces in group relations which may lead to war, and psychodynamic factors that lead to group tensions that can cause wars, unless mankind can discover ways of dealing with them.

The papers in part IV explore and discuss the nature of religious and moral beliefs and their development. Rickman was born into a Quaker family, and his paper "A Study of Quaker Beliefs" shows his interest in it and his search to understand the influence it had both on himself and on others. He extends his interest in the importance that a need for a belief in God could have in the healthy make-up of human beings. "Man without God" was first broadcast as a talk on the BBC Home Service, and I remember listening to this talk. It seemed that he was expressing how he would like to have been evaluated. The final paper, on the development of the moral function, spells out the important role that education could and should have in the development of the "moral code" that each must choose for him/herself; having come to terms sufficiently with one's own excesses and impulses, one should be able to develop a more compassionate and facilitating role in relation to one's fellow human beings.

PART I

OBSERVATIONS ON PSYCHOANALYTIC THEORY AND TECHNIQUE

CHAPTER 1

Developments in psychoanalysis, 1896–1947

(1947)

Introduction and definition

Psychoanalysis is the name given to a method of research and therapy discovered by Freud (1896c) based on a study of "free associations" in the "transference situation" and to the body of data and theories about the unconscious mind and its relation to behaviour which that method of research and therapy discloses. A *psychoanalyst* is a person who uses that method of research or therapy; but speaking professionally he is a person who has been trained and registered as suitable for practice in that method in one of the Psychoanalytical Institutes recognised by the International Psychoanalytical Association (Rickman, 1951b).

Psychoanalysis deals with a part only of the field of psychology, but it contributes a part—dealing with what has been called "depth-psychology"—which cannot be clearly discerned without the use of that method of research and therapy. Just as certain classes of natural phenomena cannot be scrutinised minutely without the aid of special

---

From *Leaves for the Students' Note Books* (The Tavistock Institute of Human Relations, 1947).

instruments, e.g. a microscope for small objects, a telescope for distant ones, an electroscope for electrical phenomena, so with certain mental phenomena a special "instrument" is required.

Briefly, the *transference situation* is such an "instrument". It is a social relationship (most clearly seen in the case of two persons) which permits the spontaneous appearance of repressed unconscious phantasies of the person analysed (the analysand) to crystallise in reference to the person (and his environment) who is analysing that individual's personality and social relationships (*transference neurosis*). The skill of the analyst lies in his capacity without any impatience (it is often a slow business), and without interference (it is usually tantalizing to the beginner), to let the analysand's ideas about this social and emotional relationship emerge clearly, convincingly, and undisturbed.

It is this that requires the years of training; it is this that makes the analysis of the patient himself so time consuming—400 sessions, i.e. five times a week for about two years, reckoning holidays (intercurrent illness during the analysis is unusual), is a common figure. Psychoanalysis is therefore time consuming both for research and therapy, but, as has been said, no substitute has yet been found to accomplish the same work that it does whether for the body of theory or in the interests of the particular patient.

Throughout this introductory monograph, research and therapy have been coupled. In no other branch of psychology is this inevitable; and in this, psychoanalysis is unique. Also, and importantly, it deals with mental pain, and strives to go to the sources of mental pain in the development of the personality of the individual analysed. It provides a setting for the struggle, in which deep-seated causes of guilt, anxiety, grief and libidinal conflict are reawakened and worked through. Permanent relief is usually found and the cramping effect of inhibitions, self distrust, and suspicion of others is removed. Only with the prospect of relief from pain does the sufferer disclose (or perhaps *can* the sufferer disclose), the depths of his mind and the hidden sources of his pain. Hence research and therapy into this field of mental science at least (and how far this is also true and inevitable for the social sciences time will show) are always coupled.

Though the practitioner must in his work keep in mind the general development of the personality of his patient, it is important to note that the scientific data (which alone are convincing to the patient, strange though that may sound in reference to the notoriously suggestible neurotic) are essentially *a-historical*, i.e. as in science generally the essential data are present and discernible at the time of observation.

Though no other aspect of psychology has thrown so much light on man's development from babyhood to childhood through adolescence to adult life, or shown so clearly how one phase influences another, yet psychoanalysis is all based on experiences in the present. The realization of past and incompletely worked-through experiences *in* the present is the basis of this transference situation. The particular device that the psychoanalyst uses for dealing with the data afforded by the transference situation is *free associations*; and they are pieced together by means of a set of theoretical devices, extremely simple to apply in theory but taking years to acquire in practice, which were discovered by Freud and published in his *The Interpretation of Dreams* (Freud, 1900a). This is the sole theoretical instrument as the transference situation is the sole social instrument of psychoanalytic research and therapy.

Origins of psychoanalysis

Dr Josef Breuer, a Viennese physician, had as a patient from 1880–82, a girl who suffered from numerous neurotic symptoms which came on after she had nursed her father during his last illness (Breuer & Freud, 1893–95). She had periods of dreamy confusion in which her mind was far removed from present reality and she was compulsively preoccupied with her own thoughts. It was possible to hypnotize her and get her to talk without such confusion; her mind then kept on going back to ideas and impulses which she had to suppress while nursing her father, and her numerous symptoms were related to these suppressed thoughts. When the patient recalled these thoughts and "re-lived" in imagination these scenes, she was for a time relieved of her symptoms, but soon relapsed, so that the process had to be repeated over and over again. In the repetition the scenes dwelt on shifted further and further back in her life; eventually all of the symptoms were removed. The cure seemed to result from the reliving of the emotional experiences, which for various reasons she had avoided facing in the first place: the theory of the cure was that when the accumulated emotion which maintained the symptom found an outlet, i.e. a *catharsis*, in the treatment-room of the physician, through being brought to consciousness, the patient got better. Freud developed this technique further by abandoning hypnosis and getting the patient to talk freely. He would ask the patient to say whatever came into the mind, holding nothing back because the patient might feel it to be irrelevant or distressing. This *free association* rule (Freud, 1904a) is the foundation on which psychoanalysis rests and it makes its demand on the analyst too, for if the patient must not consider anything irrelevant, neither must the analyst, and he has the added duty of making sense of it and also of communicating its meaning to the patient.

In the course of this kind of treatment two things are invariably met with. The first is resistance. The patient's mind seems incapable of taking an objective view of the procedure, forgets the free association rule, or pleads that certain ideas should be made exceptions to it, and becomes preoccupied with what the analyst must be thinking about the thoughts disclosed or about to be disclosed. In the hypnotic treatment the patient was urged to remember, and the amount of effort expended to enable the recall of painful ideas and experiences gave a measure of the resistance to their content. In the free association treatment there is no urging but attention is directed to the reason for this tardiness of the mind to master its own content. It becomes apparent (to both parties eventually) that something has begun to happen in this social relationship of two people (physician and patient): the patient cannot recollect directly— the resistances are too strong—and he is "transferring" onto the analytic situation some of the undischarged emotion which he could not deal with in the critical phases of his development. This is the second of the things invariably met with. The therapeutic co-operation between two adults has superimposed on it all kinds of emotional cross-currents from the past of which the patient was consciously quite unaware, and of a strength and intensity which he could not believe possible. This past situation transferred to time present and dominating the physician–patient co-operation is the transference situation (Freud, 1912b). The treatment consists in disclosing to the patient the operation of these early and buried impulses and seeing them in their past and present setting; the art of the treatment lies in the maintenance of a quiet, interested, objective personal relationship throughout the storms and confusions of these transference phenomena; the science of the treatment, so to speak, lies in the employment of the simplest possible technical (theoretical) aids to the understanding of what is going on.

The data provided by following the free association rule and the transference phenomena are given some sort of order if it is assumed, and this is a basic assumption, that when any two ideas come together in temporal association there must be some common link or links of meaning. The patient's resistance frequently challenges this assumption; it is usually, if not invariably, a counter-attack to cover a sore spot. Out of the clinical application of this rule and this simple hypothesis,

Freud was enabled to construct a theory which gave meaning to neurotic symptoms, to hallucinations and even to dreams.

Dreams

First it is necessary to distinguish between the manifest content of the dream and another, latent or hidden, content (Freud, 1901a). The former is what the dreamer remembers of his dream—it is in his consciousness; of the latter we will assume that it has sense if we can but find it. Free associations to elements of the remembered or manifest dream reveal a focal point in a complex train of thought, i.e. the dreamer has made a condensation of a number of thoughts all of which are represented in a single dream element. Another feature of the dream-work is the tendency to shift the accent from an important theme onto a trivial one, i.e. there is a displacement of the emotion. Another peculiar feature of the dream-work is that a thing may be represented by its *opposite*, i.e. it seems as if there is a part of the mind which can tolerate contradictions; and finally there seems at times to be a process at work which makes the jumble look sensible and coherent. The importance of this study of dreams lay in the fact that by these simple devices of interpretation, i.e. of undoing the disguises employed in the dream-work, light was thrown on the processes going on in the unconscious mind, or more strictly we were helped to make inferences about the interplay between different parts of the mind. The *manifest* dream is that part of the total dream process which is accessible directly to the conscious mind, but by employing the basic principle of free association to the dream elements and the devices of interpretation above mentioned, thoughts are disclosed, and their relation to the manifest content is recognised by the dreamer, which seem to belong to another part of the mind and personality—to the unconscious. Something like a force seems to be keeping the two apart; the urging to remember painful episodes in the hypnotic treatment and the inability to associate freely, justify the use of some such concept as resistance and censorship.

Transference

When the urgings of the hypnotist were abandoned in favour of a neutral observation by the analyst of just whatever the patient liked to say or to impute to the analyst, or of how he tried to manipulate the relationship between them, the focus of attention of the analyst is turned to the forces in the patient's mind as the immediately significant data and these data in strangely large proportion seem apparently irrelevant to the immediate situation. The analyst is pictured by the patient to be playing all manner of roles; and it soon becomes obvious that these roles have relevance to periods and episodes of frustration and stress in the patient's past life and early childhood.

When sufficient care is given to the detail of material and the phenomena of transference are not blurred through the impatient interference by the analyst—how difficult that task is, as beginners only gradually discover!—a new sort of mental functioning becomes apparent, which is primitive, infantile and unconscious. One of its important features is the part which bodily impulses of the most elementary kind play in the personal relationship which the patient's phantasy elaborates. It is not a simple falling in love, but a complicated mixture of love and hate, tenderness and aggression that is both attraction and repulsion, ambivalently mixed; it is a mode of relationship which is strange to adult ways of thought.

The free associations in the transference situation disclosed two things. The first was the way in which bodily centred impulses of instinctual origin find representation in our imagination and outlet in our action, and the way they become transformed into the bonds which tie us in love and in hate to those nearest and dearest to us, and by displacement to our kind and our environment generally. This latter throws light on our cultural life and may provide a clue to that great gap which separates us from the animals. We are not only more intelligent than the beasts, but we have also a more flexible emotional life; if we are frustrated in our love, we displace our longing to another and seek satisfaction from a new source. Animals pine for a lost companion: man uses his frustrations, for the most part, to build, under the pressure of painful loss, an inner world—a private zone of culture—where he can work through his privation, however long and devious the path, to a solution of his longing. The richness of that inner world, which animals seem to lack, is the result of overcoming mental pain; we seem to differ from the animals too in being able to share with others the benefits we gain from our private zone of culture.

The second thing that was disclosed in the transference situation was that though there are in fact only two people in the treatment situation, the analysand frequently behaves as if there were three or more, i.e. the analysand takes the analyst as the object of his impulses and also feels a constraint, as if a third person's rights and feelings had to be taken into account at the same time. It seems as if from an early age of personal, mental development, the individual cannot easily deal with two people at a time, and if the third party is not actually present, the mind unconsciously imagines him or her to be there. The character of the behaviour and indeed the mood of the individual and his confidence or diffidence in life generally, as well as his capacity to co-operate with his fellows, is greatly influenced by his relation to this third party. The obscurity of these last statements may be perhaps diminished in a later consideration of this important topic. With a perhaps aphoristic inexactitude we may say that the barrier between human psychology and sociology is broken down when account is taken of the unconscious influence of "the third party" in the relation between two people. As this touches on society it may be one of the most momentous discoveries in human history.

Four periods of psychoanalytic theory to date

First period, 1896-1914

As has been said, one of the things disclosed by the free associations in the transference situation is the strange un-adult nature of the impulses which the unconscious harbours. They are primitive and erotic and the conscious mind repudiates them; indeed much of the above-mentioned "resistance" is a manifestation of this repudiation. Man appears to be unique in having two types of sexuality, an infantile type, which persists in the unconscious, and an adult type, which "crystallizes" at puberty. It is the persisting influence of the infantile kind which leads to abnormalities of a sexual nature in the adult and largely accounts for unhappiness in married life, and it is also one of the elements in the causation of social maladjustments, including neuroses.

The sexuality of the infant, that is, the libidinal desire for another person or part of that person, is in the early days characterised by a mouth-to-nipple relationship (Freud, 1905d). The infant is predominantly a "mouth-animal"; what it does with its mouth is exciting to it and has greater emotional value than have other activities. In phantasy the mouth activities give it control over the object of its desire and thus minister to its sense of power; they also give that feeling of access of pleasure, even ecstasy, which is characteristically erotic. Later in infantile development defecation and urination (unlike the early oral- and the later genital-activities) do not necessarily involve physical contact with another person, but in the infant's phantasy they provide a means of doing something to people. A personal and bodily substance is held in control at an orifice and then is expelled, not into a void—the child's mind peoples every cranny of its world—but towards those on whom its thoughts rest. A bodily substance and a bodily action, which biologically have nothing to do with sexuality, are used by the imagination as the medium of erotic play and personal relationships. In the course of development the genitals achieve the primacy. These organs above all others have the power to discharge the sexual tensions of the body and at the same time to bring the individual psychically into relation with another person. The increasing urge to sexual mastery and possession of the desired object, in imagination as well as in the act, brings with it a new, or rather an enhanced, source of danger—that of rivalry with another person of the same sex, typically a parent figure in the unconscious. There is rivalry in the earlier ("pregenital") activities also, but the unification of erotic activity and the differentiation of sexual objects and aims, which reach a climax with the primacy of the genital organ, increases its influence in personal and interpersonal relationships. The Oedipus complex, i.e. sexual attraction to the parent of the opposite sex and hostility to the one of the same sex, is the earliest social relationship which the individual experiences. This difficult period of development is reached and usually in good part solved by the age of five. These stresses are veiled from adult recollection by an involuntary and active forgetting; they can reappear when the effort of urging under hypnosis overcomes the resistance, and, as has been said, spontaneously and with less distortion in the transference analysis.

In the course of his work Freud found that his neurotic patients often presented scenes of seduction in infancy, in a detailed and precise way; these scenes fitted into the picture of the symptoms; but on trying to get objective verification Freud found no substantiating evidence. This was at first felt to be a blow to his previous findings (Freud, 1925d), where a disturbance of the development of the sexual impulse due to active interference was considered one of the main factors in causing neurotic illness (Freud, 1896c). Then he took a courageous and momentous step in his theoretical constructions: these events had not occurred objectively but subjectively, that is, they were occurrences in the unconscious phantasies, which were important to the child at the time. These phantasies were repressed but retained their urgency, not to say clamourousness, in adult life—of course the adult is not aware of the cause, but he *is* aware of the effect, the inner unrest. A new dimension was thus given to scientific thought by this extension of theory— what happens in the world of imagination obeys the laws of that world and can influence behaviour and a person's outlook on life; medicine and science need no longer be confined to the physical realm but had a new field to explore and conquer, that of psychic reality.

An indispensable addition to psychoanalytic thought was introduced with the notion of cathexis (Freud, 1900a), that is, the concentration or accumulation of *mental energy* (the nature of which is obscure) in some particular channel. When an object is "cathected" that object has a particularly strong interest for the person. This energy is displaceable from one object to another, for example, from a father figure to representatives of the father in later life, first to those who stand *in loco parentis*, such as schoolmasters, and later to office chiefs, rulers and so forth. Combining this concept with that of the unconscious, it is clear that the object in which the mental energy is invested need not be in the focus of conscious attention nor need the person be aware of how much he is tied in bonds of interest, of love and/or of hate, to the object. Further, there is a linking of the cathexes in the unconscious, so that the characteristics of the early cathexes tend to persist in respect to later ones in the same series, that is the patterns of behaviour which characterise early object relationships tend to be repeated in later object relationships of the same type.

Second period, 1914–23

The ego itself, it was thought, could be the focus of this interest or cathexis, and the love-impulse, or at least a part of it, might take the self as its object—as happened in the myth of Narcissus. But *narcissism* (Freud, 1914c) is not only a peculiar manifestation of the love life, it also is apt as a descriptive term for a phase that the young usually pass through, when attention is focused on the body's strength or its graces. Closer analytic observation showed that it describes also an attitude towards those who are derived from the self, for example, one's children, or objects with which there is a close, but maybe quite unconscious identification: a self-love flows over to them and they are enjoyed less for what they actually are than for being an embodiment in the external world of what the self once was or would like to have been. From this last point it was but a step to see in the attitude to an idealised object of the ego some of the primitive, but by displacement loftily aspiring, relation to the self. An ego-ideal (Freud, 1921c) thus absorbs some of the available object-cathexes so that those whose ego-ideals are over-strong display a restricted capacity for malleable and kinder object love. Many of the reformers trying to shape the world to their own often rather over-simple, if not infantile ideas could be said to exemplify this tendency.

The notion of cathexis leads to the view that the distribution of mental energy in the field of psychic life may be considered quantitatively; in the instance, given the quantity of devotion or love is portioned out between the persons ostensibly served and the image upon which they are being moulded. To the reformer himself his conduct seems to be one of selfless devotion to others, to the rest of the world he may seem rigid in manner, self-centred and ungenerous; both views are in their way correct—the frames of reference are different. The first takes its reckoning from the energy put into the ego-ideal, the second from the meagre amount of personal love (object-love) displayed. This notion of the distribution of the quantities of mental energy should not be restricted to that which is ostensibly visible in overt behaviour. The artist and the scientist, the mystic and the lunatic, for that matter all of us, have inner worlds of phantasy in which are deployed and expended considerable quantities of mental energy; whether that inner labour results in anything which is socially applauded or has social use varies with each individual. But socially useful or not, it is a source of gratification to the individual. It gives, if it is in low degree, that mood of pleasure without which mental life seems not to operate; when in high degree, it gives that rare sweeping "oceanic" exultation of spirit and ecstasy which the artists can of all men best communicate to their fellows, and which it is our humble duty here merely to try to explain.

Third period, 1923–32

In the earliest findings of analysis, the patient's unconscious mind was found to contain active elements which resulted from incompletely solved emotional experiences; these to be sure were foci of illness, but the same principle is seen—depending on the circumstances—to be operative in a constructive or "ego-cohesive" direction as well as in a neurotic or "ego-disruptive" one. Perhaps because of an underlying bisexuality the individual is orientated to two people at once, typically the two parents (Freud, 1900a, 1905d; Klein, 1945). In the early stages of our development, that amount of positive or friendly cathexis which is attached to the parent of the same sex becomes incorporated in and attached to the ego which henceforth acts as an internal representative of a once external object, a parent, guiding and supporting the ego in its struggle with its own unruly impulses. Born of a longing for the parent's approval and affection, the ego seems to split into two functions, an executive part, the ego proper, and a critical, parent-derived, part the *superego* (Freud, 1923b), which watches the ego's behaviour in relation to the crude impersonal instinct-driven part of the personality called the *id*.

When discussing the transference situation, it was said that the analysand attributes to, or *projects* into, his analyst all kinds of roles, and at times behaves as if a third party were present from whom the communications about to be made must be kept secret. We are in a better position now to place these phenomena. They are manifestations of those parts of the unconscious mind with which the ego is in conflict, that is, with the id and the superego. The task of therapy is to bring about a reorganisation of these three elements of the personality so that they work together in harmony. It comes about when they are confronted with one another in the present, that is, when the analysand comes to recognise that though his "id" is primitive and a-moral, it is a creative and tolerable part of the total personality. At the same time there occurs an amelioration of the severity of the superego, which, though broadly speaking is patterned on a parent figure, is in fact, in its early stages based not on what the parent actually was, but on what he was phantasied to be under the pressure of primitive emotion—another instance of the influence of phantasy.

Fourth period, 1932–47

The fantastic severity of the superego led to a closer study of the aggressive component in the personality. It seems, going back to the early days of personality development, that the infant has to effect a working arrangement between two opposed tendencies, of love and hate, and furthermore that his love and hate are directed to the same objects, once again the parents. When our feelings towards any object are such that we wish more of it, want it closer to us and hope that its like will never perish from the earth, we may be said to love that object and to us it is a *good object*. When our feelings are the reverse, when we want less of it, want it further away, hope it and its like will cease to exist, we may be said to hate that object, to us it is a *bad object*. For love and hate, good and bad we may on this viewing substitute the simpler concepts of motion towards or away, constructiveness or destructiveness. These two opposed tendencies are at work in the infant's relation to its first love object, the mother's breast, on which it lives. Emotional conflict is from the beginning a desperately important thing. Frustration magnifies the hate, i.e. makes the object still more bad, and yet the necessity for the breast makes the infant desire it as a thing which stills physical discomfort, so that is as a "good thing". At this stage the infant is a "mouth animal", that is, the instrument by which it attains dominion over its object is that which incorporates the object within itself; mastery of an object entails *internalising* it (Freud, 1914c; Klein, 1932). The self thus becomes filled with good and bad objects, "good" if the emotion at the moment of internalisation is friendly, "bad" if it is hostile, i.e. there are therefore dire and indeed lasting consequences from the use of the expedient of "projecting" its own emotional state upon the object and then materialising it. "Good" and "bad" have at first no moral connotation—that may come later—but can be expressed in terms of movement nearer, a desire for more etc., or the opposite. We are dealing here with the pre-moral stage, the pre-social stage, of development. When the self is filled with *bad internal objects*, its need for more and more "good" ones increases, to neutralise the bad, hence a vicious circle is developed, in which need changes to greed and greed begets guilt. As development proceeds these internalisations take on more and more the character of the actual objects, so that, to jump several stages, the person feels that he embodies the attributes of his real parents. In passing we may note that savages, still in this animistic stage of object relationship, imagine that if they eat a lion's heart they will be imbued with courage; the idea is found also in some religious rituals.

Speaking descriptively, the ego is a boundary phenomenon between an internal world, an "internal society" it might be called, since the unconscious seems almost exclusively preoccupied with personal relationships, and an external world revealed through the sense organs. Behaviour can be viewed as the resultant of several processes; the ego is driven by instinct-impulses, the id, and is also curbed by the representation within itself of parental authority, the superego, while at the same time the ego has also to adapt itself to and master portions of the external world. But behaviour may also be regarded in a rather different, perhaps a better way. The ego may be viewed as a group of cathected objects which may work in a unified way or which may show oscillating, unstable, divergent tendencies according as the grouping of forces within the ego is cohesive and unified or disruptive and diversified. These internalised objects, or superegos, may be pictured as having an arrangement in depth, the most primitive the most deeply buried, but each layer representing a phase of development influencing the deposition of and the freedom for movement in the more superficial layer above it. Furthermore, what is more difficult to conceive is that in each layer the same objects, the parents, siblings and other relations or their surrogates, which are always the central figures, recur again and again. So we find, for example, parent-regarding tendencies of differing degrees of primitiveness and complexity interacting with each other, the resultant influencing behaviour. The cathected internal objects should be distinguished from mere memory traces. The unconscious is not a sort of card-index drawer of photographic images. A better analogy would be a group of objects, people or bodily parts of people, being constantly rearranged and manipulated unconsciously, in moods of love and hate, by the individual concerned; while at the same time he is similarly manipulating objects in the external world, in the external society. There is a constant interplay between these two manipulations. Achievements no matter how sublime or base are done not alone for their effect on contemporary society or posterity, but also to adjust the relationships in the internal society, that intra-psychic constellation of social and personal forces, which is an over present and inalienable heritage of our personal past experience and development.

Now to return to the early stages of this eventually elaborate object relationship (Klein, 1940). There is stability in our emotional orientation to and hold upon objects when we are able to recognise at the same time their good and bad qualities. When despite anger-arousing frustration we can keep our orientation to them and our good regard for them unchanged. One of the several ways by which this mature attitude is achieved is by turning against the self the aggressiveness which the frustrating object rouses in us; we then become severer with ourselves for our aggressive impulses towards objects that we hold to be good, the object is spared at the cost of the self, and we suffer pangs of guilt. Pain thus caused is as it were cherished by the self, or at least there is resistance to its disclosure and removal, because it is part of a device for protecting a good object. Another way by which the mind is eased of its load of guilt is by "restitutive acts", by making good the damage done in moods and moments of anger. Sometimes restitution thus based is the main motive of an adult's life. The indefatigably, almost wearisomely, benevolent people commonly react throughout their life to impulses of great strength, operating at a nodal point in their emotional development, and as the whole process is unconscious, it pursues its course usually unchanged by time and circumstance. Apart from more extreme cases, the restitutive reaction to unconscious guilt plays a large part in the drive towards creativeness which differentiates us from the animals, whose work usually perishes or becomes indifferent after the act of digestion, of copulation, gestation and lactation. Man combines with his fellows in his restitutive work, as he also sometimes combines with them in his destructiveness. From this recognition of the need in ourselves and in others to restore and create, from the unconscious feeling and sharing of the guilt for destructive impulse, rises a community of feeling for the restitutive and constructive urges. In these feelings we find some of the roots of religion, art and science.

CHAPTER 2

Experimental psychology and psychoanalysis: a comparison of the techniques

(1937–39)

The aim of this paper is to consider the relation between psychology and psychoanalysis in the past and present and their possible relation in the future.

Psychology has roots in two disciplines, in philosophy and in the experimental laboratory, psychoanalysis in one—clinical medicine. I think it would be simpler if we left the connection of psychology with philosophy out of our discussion, because for reasons that soon will be apparent the issues can be narrowed down to workable dimensions if we consider the contrasts and similarities between experimental psychology and psychoanalysis.

Let us begin with an exceedingly simple situation in the Experimental Psychological Laboratory.

The situation in an Experimental Psychological Laboratory

The first and most obvious thing is that an experiment is going to be performed by the experimenter on the subject, but it is not going to be done to find out something about the subject personally, or his particu-

---

This paper was written under the title "Psychology and Psychoanalysis", between 1937 and 1939. There is no evidence that it was ever read or published.

lar mind, but about a mental function possessed by him as by thousands of others. The experimenter knows within limits what is going to happen and so within limits does the subject; measured stimuli will be given and the responses will be measured. Experimenter and subject participate in the experiment with awakened attention, and both are aware that the experiment can be repeated over and over again. Both can, and usually do, play the part of observers. The subject is asked after the experiment to make notes on his introspections and sensory or motor experiences at the time of the experiment. The experimenter observes the subject's behaviour in general or towards the apparatus at the time of the experiment. I want to stress that this temporal aspect, the stimulus and the response and the introspective experiences are all concerned with the present. The typical experiment deals with stimulus and response rather in the manner of eliciting a reflex. Indeed, the mind may be pictured as a reflex apparatus with a perceptual end, which receives a measured stimulus, and with a motor end that has to press a button. The experimental psychologist wants to study the motor or perceptual functions of the organism in its response to the external world. Psychologist and subject are dealing with external relations, usually of a rather impersonal kind; if they do deal with personal relationships, it is a matter of *objective* observation.

The conditions of the experiment are so arranged that the subject's attention should not be distracted by irrelevant stimuli. The greater part of the apparatus—or those parts that are interesting apart from the stimulus—are behind a screen or in another room, and even the experimenter may be at a distance and in contact with the situation only through the medium of electric wires.

It may be argued that this description of experimental psychology is over-simplified.

A study of a complete set of the *British Journal of Psychology* from 1904 onwards, however, revealed what I think is a good sample of topics of interest to experimental psychologists. Here are the first ten titles taken at random that had a connection with the laboratory or with tests:

Motor Capacity

Mental ability of "Backward" Children

Feeling-tone in Industry

Observations in Contrast Effects in Graded Discs

On Listening to sounds of Weak Intensity

Mental Examination of School Children
Musical and Unmusical Observers
Factors in Mental and Scholastic Ability
Intensity of Sensation and Duration of Stimulus
The Fall-Hammer, Chronoscope and Chronograph.

The emphasis is on the cognitive and, to a less extent, the affective aspects of mental life. All these details about the laboratory have been mentioned for a special purpose, that is, to give a starting point for some sharp contrasts. Let us now turn our attention from the Psychological Laboratory to the consulting-room.

The situation in a psychoanalyst's consulting-room

Psychoanalysis, as is well known, has its roots in medical practice. The physician has a duty to his patient. He must find out what is causing the suffering of his patient, and must subordinate his own curiosity to the needs of the patient, and whether he is interested in the problem or not he must go on searching till the pain is relieved.

The bond between the experimenter in the laboratory and his subject is either an interest in psychological problems or else that of employer and employee; the bond between the physician and patient is that of suffering; the moment that that ceases, the tie between them as physician and patient is changed.

Pain hardly enters into experimental psychology and, if it does, it is physical pain of slight intensity, whereas in clinical practice it is found in amounts so great that the patient may commit suicide. There is, of course, a great difference between physical pain and mental pain, and the two, it may be argued, should not be compared in this way. There is no doubt a difference, but it is not I who am responsible for the comparison, my patients make it and it is my business to find out why they think in that way. In the laboratory, pain (when it is given) is localised, its source is known and it can easily be stopped. In the consulting-room, the situation is the reverse.

As Antonio says in the opening lines of *The Merchant of Venice*, so might—and do—our patients:

> "In sooth, I know not why I am so sad:
> It wearies me; you say it wearies you;
> But how I caught it, found it, or came by it,
> What stuff 'tis made of, whereof it is born,

I am to learn;
And such a want-wit sadness makes of me,
That I have much ado to know myself."

Antonio's friends ask if he has business worries, and he tells them:

"My merchandise makes me not sad."
"Why, then, you are in love."
"Fie, fie!"
"Not in love neither? Then let's say you are sad,
Because you are not merry; and 'twere as easy
For you to laugh, and leap, and say you are merry.
Because you are not sad. . . ."

Salarino seems not to have reckoned with the possibility of unconscious sources of pain.

I will now attempt to describe a special piece of clinical apparatus which has been slowly devised and improved for detecting the unconscious sources of pain and in an approximate way of assessing the quantity of pain—I do not say *measuring* it. And I suggest that the clinical elucidation of the pain question has step by step thrown more and more light on psychological processes in general.

The psychoanalytic apparatus

The experimenter in the laboratory puts his subject into a room with as few extraneous stimuli as possible (within reason) in order to obtain the maximum effect from the stimuli that he is going to employ in the experiment. The psychoanalyst in essentials does the same thing. The patient enters an environment in which he is asked no questions, has no obligation to speak on any particular topic, but he is asked not to refrain from saying what is passing in his mind. The point of the procedure is to obtain the clearest impression of the "inner stimuli", the impulses to action and thought of which the patient may or may not be aware.

The patient is usually lying on a couch, the analyst in a chair to one side or behind the patient. The position is always the same, the room is within reasonable limits always the same, and the initiative as to what shall be talked about always lies with the patient.

The aim of the procedure is to facilitate a forward movement of phantasies, memories and affects into the conscious layers of the mind. So far as possible the initiation of every thought must come from within and not without. The experimental psychologist measures the response to a measurable external stimulus, the psychoanalyst observes the response to a situation where the "internal stimuli" (the instincts or conative processes) may be seen with least confusion and interference from external demands.

The analogy that I shall now use to explain the difference between the work of the experimental psychologist and the psychoanalyst is an old one and far from perfect. Reverting to the analogy of the reflex arc, a stimulus received at the perceptual end passes through the central apparatus, where it becomes connected with memory traces of past experiences and where it excites instinctual urges; the next step in the excitation of the motor end, which results in action. Freud elaborated the analogy. If the perceptual and motor ends are blocked by sleep, the excitement existing in the central part may, if strong enough, initiate a movement of energy in the psychical apparatus so that the memory systems are stimulated from within and the excitement in these may take a *regressive* path to the perceptual end of the arc, in which case the subject will experience a dream. Should this process of inner excitement be strong, the perceptual end may be stimulated from within even though there is no blockage due to sleep and the subject will experience an *hallucination*. Should the pressure of external demands be relatively small, the internal excitement may produce in the waking state not an hallucination but a day-dream. Thus dream, day-dream (both normal phenomena) and hallucination may be connected with one another by this analogy.

Speaking generally the experimental psychologist is not interested in his subject's phantasies, but concentrates on his performance of specific tests and certain mental functions, or misfunctioning. The psychoanalyst, on the other hand, concentrates on his patient's phantasies because these throw so much light on instinctive behaviour. Furthermore, the experimental psychologist deals with the *present* responses, whereas the psychoanalyst is interested in the *development* of the impulse in question. To the experimental psychologist, it is a matter of indifference whether the effect he is measuring results from conscious or unconscious mental processes; to the psychoanalyst, this is a vital difference. The psychoanalytic technique aims at *uncovering* unconscious mental processes, while the experimental psychologist's apparatus is designed for *measuring* responses.

Let us look at the unconscious mental processes more closely. The best studied example is the dream. In sleep, the subject is no longer obliged to perform the tasks which characterise his waking life. In the dream, the elements of past experience are broken up and used to express unconscious wishes and thoughts by the processes which

Freud called *dream-work* (Freud, 1901a). In order to discover what the unconscious wishes and thoughts are, the patient's attention is directed to the images or events which he remembers, i.e. to the elements of *the manifest* dream, and he is asked to associate freely to these without regard to the *rational* connection of his associations with the parts of the dream. The dream-work is undone, so to speak, by the free association, and the latent dream-thoughts are disclosed. The knowledge thus gained is conveyed to the patient in what are called *interpretations,* the aim being to relieve the patient's conflict and pain.

Now if the analyst tells his patient to say anything that comes to his mind, without giving him anything to associate to, which I have described as the basic practice of analysis, he is putting his patient in a position that comes near to that state which favours dream or daydream formation. We might go so far as to say that analysis is a process which permits of an examination of dreams in the nascent state. Should the analyst give advice, ask questions, or take part in instructing or helping his patient in his external life, he would only blur his own and his patient's vision of the emergence into consciousness of his unconscious mental processes. Let me give you an example.

Case History—B

A patient was sent for treatment because she was disturbed over her pregnancy; her doctor feared she would commit suicide or have puerperal insanity.

The patient, who had a nagging husband, feared to disappoint him by giving birth to a girl, but was also intensely anxious that she would be neglected if she gave birth to a boy. To this conflict suicide appeared to her the only solution. All arrangements for the treatment had been fixed by the doctor who had referred her, so within a few minutes of seeing me she was reclining on the couch, and was asked to say what came into her mind. No instructions of a theoretical kind were proffered. This is how things began—she was silent but I noted that she was looking at a bowl of tulips and that in looking she moved her head a little. I said that it could not really be that her mind was a complete blank, but that she refrained from talking because she did not think her thoughts were relevant. She said she was looking at the bowl of tulips, at the tulip that had its head bowed down, then at one that was looking at her; she saw its dark centre, like an eye, then at one that was looking away from her, and the base of its petals (which were almost black) made a figure like the Cross of St. John of Jerusalem. I told her to let her thoughts flow on, and she began to talk about Crusades, and then came back to the bowed tulip, which she said was herself. Then there was a silence and in it she heard through the window the sound of the chipping of ice. This brought back memories of her father (who died some years ago I learnt later) who liked iced drinks, then another silence and she went to the Crusaders driving the Saracens from the Holy Sepulchre and from the birthplace of Our Lord. Then she thought of the door-knocker on my front door (which is of a woman-figure standing on a fish of some sort). This reminded her of the Perseus legend, and so back to the Saracens and the Holy Land. Then the tulips started her off on the gardens at her father's country place, the gamekeeper and the poacher, and so to that dark eye looking at her.

All this took but little longer than it has taken me to narrate, but what wealth of meaning! Viktor Adler once said that a patient in the first few minutes of treatment if let alone will give you material the full significance of which you will only understand months later.

In this material there were three references to objects on my premises, tulips, ice, door-knocker, and each was the *starting* point of several trains of thought. So I inferred that I had come into *her nascent dream*. But I did not consider that it was *myself as* me that she was considering, but a composite picture made up of (a) phantasies of early figures in her life's experience, (b) impressions of myself coloured by these phantasies, and (c) myself as I actually was.

She had been previously informed that her treatment would be daily sessions for many months, and that I was competent to deal with the case. She did not know whether I was a Freudian, Jungian, Adlerian, or on my very own, and if I had been dubbed with a name it would have meant almost nothing to her as she had never read a book or paper on psychology. She was not concerned what sort of treatment I was going to give from the psychological point of view, but how I was going to treat her as a human being. She felt bowed down, and the question before her was whether I was going to treat her to that baleful dark look or turn away from her like the tulip with the Cross of St. John, or was I going to be a poacher or a gamekeeper. It seemed to be best to interpret this "nascent dream" on general grounds by saying that she was preoccupied not only with her own present problems but also with the question of what sort of treatment she was going to get, whether black looks or help, and whether help was going to come only if she put up with trouble from the helper (she had mentioned in further associations that the Crusaders did a good deal of violence as well as driving out the pagans). To these and similar interpretations she replied in a way which seemed to me to corroborate their correctness. She did not hail them as truths nor reject them with scorn, but continued to give associations—memories—of situations offering similar dilemmas in her past experience.

I can confirm Adler's wise and clinical remark from this case; in the months of work that followed, the themes represented in the tulips, the ice and the door knocker came in over and over again.

Interpretation as the instrument of therapy

Now the aim of the analyst is to get the patient to see his own unconscious phantasies and impulses, and one of the inevitable tendencies of the patient is to try to get the analyst to play a role in his external life, to seek his advice, encouragement or reproach for his wrongdoing. I said inevitable because the tendency of the mind to stimulate action and interaction with objects in the environment is one of the main means of obtaining satisfaction. I do not believe that the analyst can play both roles. The analyst has projected onto him figures in the patient's phantasies; in this case, at one time poacher, at the next moment gamekeeper. It is of the greatest importance that the patient should be free to project both kinds of phantasy with equal facility, for if he is to get a just impression of his own mind he must have equal opportunity to see the aggressive, destructive impulses as well as the libidinal and constructive ones. Should the analyst identify, consciously or unconsciously, with any *one* of the roles that the patient projects on to him, and express it in relation to his patient, either by action, e.g. by giving advice, or through interpretations that always run in one direction, then the patient will have succeeded in repeating in the analytic situation what he has been hitherto doing, though without realising it, in his ordinary life; that is, finding an outlet for his conflicts and impulses, in getting others to endorse his technique by colluding with him. Whether this collusion is in terms of action, i.e. behaviour or advice as in social life, or a bias of interpretation, it always leads to the same end: discharge of instinct tension without the gaining of insight. For example, there are patients who go through life trying to win the approval of others for their actions, they do this year in, year out, without perceiving that they are harbouring, let us say, a bad conscience. If the analyst is caught napping he will be swept into the patient's system of behaviour and will be giving his approval to some line of conduct, and thereby throwing away the chance to observe the deeper-lying motives for the patient's behaviour. This does not mean the analyst has to be stand-offish; on the contrary he must show benevolent neutrality to *every* kind of impulse the patient shows him. This readiness to accept all the roles which the patient projects onto him, makes him, to use another analogy, like a blank screen on which the patient can see the full range of pattern and colour of his phantasies. To go back to the tulip case mentioned, she was quite ready to accept the interpretation of myself as a helpful figure, but most loath to see me as a poacher, a scandalous Knight Templar, or that evil black eye glowering at her. But it was from an examination of the phantasies of myself as a bad object, albeit mixed up with good intentions, that she was enabled to come to terms with the aggressive and destructive components of her own personality.

That is the first point I want to make about the analyst not being able to play the role of guide and helper in external circumstances and at the same time to keep up the analytic situation. The second point is that it weakens his power of interpretation. He should be in a position to say, "This is your phantasy about me, I have not taken sides in your conflicts and controversies, it is your wish that I should be like this and now we must try to find out why you wish me to be thus". The third reason is personal to the analyst. He has a life of his own, ideals, aspirations and dislikes just as we all have; if he is going to become involved in working out in actual life—particularly the tempting *vicarious* re-living of his unconscious tendencies—he will lose insight into himself, just as his patient loses the chance to gain insight into his neurotic make-up, when he involves people in his personal problems.

Now this brings me to the question: By what means do the psychoanalysts gain an insight into another person's unconscious mental processes? What *apparatus* do they employ and of what is it composed? In a most sketchy outline I have shown that the analyst tries to reduce the stimuli coming from without, so that his patients may be free to dream freely, so to speak, in his presence, but how does he discern what his patients cannot discern—what goes on in their unconscious minds? The answer is rather complicated: the situation in which analyst and patient find themselves is a *social* relationship; there is no attempt to restrict the emotional interplay of these two people in any direction, it does not have to be friendly or severe, one of teacher and taught, superior or inferior, it has to be whatever the patient wants it to be—but there is one proviso: the reason for the relationship must be realised consciously. If the patient wants me to be a gamekeeper, we must know why she needs me to play that role in her phantasies (the answer lay in her dread of the poacher-figure), if I am cast in the poacher role we must know what she wants to steal and why. So the first requirement is for the analyst to learn to accept any role which the patient puts upon him with equal readiness; it might be expressed also by saying that he must learn not to avoid any role which is put upon him. There is a close analogy here with ordinary social tact; we must realise the part we are expected to play in any social relationship in which we find ourselves—whether we accept the role or not is another matter. And the second requirement is that the analyst must rely on *interpretation* as the sole means of dealing with the situations created in his patient's phantasies, that is to say, he must *find out* how the situation has arisen in the patient's mind and go on looking till he discovers that this is the inevitable result of the patient's life experiences that he should think in this way. The only basis for a good contact with a person showing neurotic and irrational behaviour is to assume that if all were known it would appear rational. To get to this conclusion you have of course to discover facts that were not known by the patient before, i.e. were literally unconscious. The patient's life must be disclosed to him so that he may be fully conscious of the reasons that make him act as he does. Psychoanalysis is not a way of life, and does not point out a way of life; it is a method of treatment and a method of research at the same time. The research element is not only of theoretical importance; it is, I believe, an essential part of the analyst's attitude to the work: he must not act—i.e. guide his patient—but must discover something hidden and help his patient to do the same.

The contributions of psychoanalysis to psychological research

On this matter of research I think the contributions of Freud to psychology fall under two heads, first his great piece of work, the application of the free association method to his own dreams, and secondly the evolution of the *analytic situation*. So far as I know, never before in the history of psychology had the observer let the subject go on building up phantasies about himself, and taken them quite seriously as material for scientific investigation. True, every psychologist who happened to be a father, experienced this in his nursery, but children did not count, their minds were not fully formed. The analytic situation, however, is a kind of research apparatus, into which you can put all sorts of people and observe their behaviour under comparable conditions, the normal, the insane, the adult and the child.

What has emerged in the last forty years during which this method of psychoanalytic research has been used has become familiar, but I want to single out a few of the features of interest because I do not believe these would have been discovered (at least in our day) without the research instrument of the analytic situation.

Of first importance is the *character of the early object relationships*, and their expression in the primitive phantasies of the child. For instance, the vividness and actuality of the child's belief that he is biting up the objects—the people—he is interested in, and swallowing them up, and that they go on having an existence inside him, might have been guessed, but the mechanism of it would not have been worked out without a special technique. Nor I believe would the relation of these internal objects to external people have been discovered unless the process had been observed in a special setting. Looking back over the history of psychoanalysis one can observe that there is a fairly close connection between the advances in technique and the expansion of the field of investigation.

The art of the analyst is to let the phantasies emerge without distortion, and to recognise their origin. They do not all appear as thoughts. Sometimes the phantasy formation is expressed partly in verbal association, and partly by action; e.g. by coming late or by coming at the wrong time the patient may hope to force the analyst to step out of the role of an interpreter of phantasies and take a counter-action against him. In the confusion of associations and minor intrigue one has to pick one's way very carefully and the guiding line always is the patient's phantasy about the analyst, that is, what he is at the moment phantasising the analyst to be, and how he is wanting the analyst to act towards himself. When the nature of the phantasy is more or less clear, it has to he fitted into place in the patient's past experience.

The analytic situation is a technique for examining dreams and phantasies in their nascent states. The interpretation has to match the images so obtained, with the patient's memories of his past experiences, in order that they may be convincing to the patient, and to show him the reason for his being what he is. Reduced to its simplest terms, it is a process of matching two things, and the clearer you can get the details, the more satisfactory is your matching.

Psychoanalysis is a method of research and therapy which operates in an *a-historical present*, that is to say, the data by which it verifies its hypothesis and brings conviction that it is on the right track are events observable "here-and-now" in the analytic situation. The analyst by *self-effacement* and skilful *interpretation* enables the patient to *produce spontaneously*, and so disclose, the structure and functional relations of the personal and social events he has experienced or avoided experiencing, most importantly the latter, in the past. *By re-living them in the new setting an increased understanding and mastery of the old and troublesome situations is achieved*, so that they do not worry the patient and more energy *is freed for constructive uses.*

Experimental psychologist and psychoanalyst employ different methods and cover different fields. The experimental psychologist often asks the psychoanalyst to be more scientific and the psychoanalyst sometimes asks the experimental psychologist to be more imaginative: such comments are valuable only if they point the way to an improved technique.

It is uncommonly hard to be scientific even under the easiest circumstances, and I know of no field where the difficulties are so great as in psychoanalysis. By keeping himself in the background and not being carried away in the patient's phantasies, the psychoanalyst tries to keep the field of observation clear. By having to bring the phantasies into relation with the patient's past experiences a certain amount of check is put on the analyst being carried away on his *own* hobby horses. The verification ideally required by science cannot be fulfilled, that is, two independent observers doing the analysis of the same individual. The main check is the verification of the same mechanisms in a number of people of the same type.

I now want to say one word about the present and future relations of psychology and psychoanalysis. It seems to me that the important thing is for each to develop its own research technique to the fullest extent possible. It would have been disastrous for psychoanalysis if it had all along been thought essential for a second observer to be present, because phantasy is always more inhibited *vis-à-vis* two people.

And it would be fantastic for psychoanalysts to recommend their technique for the investigations of the problems of experimental psychology. But on how many subjects could there be profitable discussions if only all parties were familiar with both fields of research? For example, let me refer to an item on our chance list already given, *On Listening to Sounds of Weak Intensity*. How varied our patients are in respect to the emotions roused when listening! Some cannot listen intently to sounds of weak intensity without getting excited, others are quite unmoved, some become "compulsive" and have to calculate the distance of the source of the sound, its probable origin, others fly into picturesque analogies, and so forth.

With regard to the present the situation seems to me satisfactory in that both lines of research seem to be forging ahead. As to the future, our view of it will be in accordance with our temperament. It may be pleasant for us to think of the day dawning when experimental psychology and psychoanalysis will employ a common technique, but I can see no special virtue in such a phantasy. So long as water continues to be drawn from the well of knowledge, it does not seem to me to matter if it is drawn in one bucket or two.

CHAPTER 3

Scientific method and psychoanalysis

(1945)

It is worth while to recapitulate principles of scientific method in their application to the theory of psychoanalysis, even though in doing so one may seem to be returning to the intellectual nursery. I do feel strongly, however, that we can never be too clear about the conditions which must be fulfilled if our theory is to continue to deserve the name of science, nor too acutely aware of the difficulties of fulfilling them that are inherent in analysis.

The ground-plan of scientific method in the so-called natural sciences since the days of Bacon has been observation of data, leading to the perception of likenesses and differences, sequences and relationships among them, i.e. classification or grouping. Minimal hypotheses are formulated in the attempt to co-ordinate and explain these observations. In the last century it would have been said that these explanations were the result of pure reason, i.e. conscious logical inference from the particular to the general, but we know now that the process is seldom as simple as this. Unconscious factors are involved, issuing in what we

---

This paper was written to be read to the British Psychoanalytical Society in 1945; there is no evidence in the proceedings of the Society that it was in fact ever presented to them.

call acts of creative imagination, unconsciously inspired logic. This is the region in which science and art appear to meet. The hypothesis itself remains an attempt to provide a logical, consistent and adequate explanation of the data observed, and once formulated it has to be verified, to be tested in relation to as wide a range of old and new data as can be achieved. All the paraphernalia of experiment in science is directed to increasing the range and accuracy of observation and to the trying-out of hypotheses.

The deductive method, reasoning from the general to the particular, from an established law to its consequences, the essential method of mathematics, is used in the natural sciences chiefly in connection with the evaluation of hypotheses. Thus, one may deduce from a given hypothesis, that certain things ought to happen and one therefore arranges practical conditions under which it can be seen whether they do happen or not. If they do the validity of the hypothesis is increased, and *vice versa*. A large number of experiments are performed in the interest of this verification. Since mathematical proof offers the highest degree of certitude, mathematical methods and processes are employed whenever possible.

While the principles of scientific methodology remain the same in all sciences, their mode of application necessarily varies with the subject-matter under investigation, and it is essential that every branch of science should develop sound techniques for dealing with its own special problems. It is the adaptation of these basic scientific principles in psychoanalysis, not as a therapy, but as a metapsychology, that I want briefly to consider.

Observation and grouping of data

First, as regards observation and its attendant grouping of data. Since all the words and works of man bear the stamp of his mental processes, our data are really coextensive with human life, but so far as practice is concerned, the consulting-room remains our principal laboratory. All Freud's major discoveries, with the single exception of the Death Instinct, issued from his clinical data, though he has applied and tried out his findings in various directions outside the consulting-room. In the consulting-room our data are still the same as in the beginning, namely, the appearance, affectivity, attitude, behaviour and verbal reports of the patient's past and present experience. Strictly speaking our data also include our own reactions during the session (Rickman, 1950, 1951a).

I will not consider in detail all the ways in which these data differ from the data of physics or chemistry, or even of physiology. I will stress only the essential point, namely, that in the consulting-room we depend solely upon our own observation since, for various reasons, it is not open to us to employ any of the mechanical or quantitative devices invented in other sciences as aids to, and checks on, accuracy and observation. Further, when we know that these data are of a type which is bound to be in the highest degree provocative of subjective reactions in ourselves, we must, I think, candidly admit that our observations are methodologically open to the highest possible degree of potential error.

The method we have developed to counteract these errors is a subjective one, namely the analysis of the analyst. Few will be disposed to doubt the utility of this precaution, but there are two things to be said about it. Firstly, its efficacy is only relative, since it is presumably impossible to eliminate all selective bias from any human being; but, certainly it can greatly increase our awareness of the direction and determinants of our individual slants, and enable us to allow to some extent for their effects. Also, it is a method which one may hope will grow in efficacy from generation to generation. The second thing is the objection raised by non-analysts that the method is one which creates and perpetuates its own errors. We shall have to refer to this when we come to verification. This criticism is rather unfair in the sense that it ignores the fact that observation in every branch of exact science involves a special training which has comparable effects. The student looking down a microscope for the first time literally does not see what the trained bacteriologist sees, and it is customary in scientific circles to attach greater weight to the observations and conclusions of trained workers rather than to those of untrained workers.

Granted that observation in the consulting-room is open to a wide margin of error, counteracted chiefly by the analyst's own temperament and training, what is to be said about the conditions under which observations are made, and the technique as a method of research? The couch and chair behind it may, I think, be considered standard routine for adult patients but, apart from this, there is no uniformity in detail. The questionnaire circulated some years ago brought to light considerable variations in technique in this country alone, not only in detail but in matters of principle (Glover, 1940). Even supposing that consulting-room conditions and the technique of the individual analyst remain constant, which they do not and cannot, repeated observations by an individual are still liable to a constant subjective error. Further, there can be no possibility of one analyst exactly repeating the observations of another, in the way in which objective or external experiments can be repeated. However much these circumstances may make other scientists shudder, their very haphazardness has one advantage, i.e. when out of all this variety there emerges a consensus of opinion on any given matter, there is perhaps as great a likelihood of its objectivity as when uniformity of results is obtained by repetition of experiments.

We are not, however, even yet at the end of the difficulties attending our observations. We have, further, to note that we are not pure observers; we constantly interfere with the processes we are watching and we can seldom limit ourselves to watching. We must, almost always, bear in mind our conjoined therapeutic task, and our freedom to experiment is very greatly limited by this double function. We know something about the effects of the analytic situation as such upon the analysand and upon ourselves, but there is a great deal about it that we do not yet thoroughly understand. The phenomena of countertransference are by no means fully investigated, and we take too much for granted such factors as "rapport".

Analysis is essentially a process of interplay between unconscious and conscious, and only secondarily a matter of intelligence. Even the people who consider that, in time and with increase in knowledge, intelligence should more and more replace intuition cannot maintain that this has been the case up to the present.

Grouping of data began with Freud's recognition of the twofold nature of mind, the existence of unconscious and conscious processes, and the dynamic relation between them. From this basic classification all subsequent groupings have issued, and have led to the stage of differentiation at which we find ourselves at the present day. We now have a well-established threefold system of the mind and a genetic theory of its development, accepted in general form by all psychoanalysts, but surrounded in detail by a host of obscurities and ambiguities, and a variety of opinions, some mutually supporting, others conflicting.

The same considerations which apply to the observation of data apply to their classification, but there are some special features. The quality of mind which enables a person to appreciate the existence of hitherto unperceived groupings or the existence of unsuspected relationships, is not universal. Only a few people possess it and, where it exists, it does not necessarily follow that the individual appreciates all the implications of what he sees. The advances made by the few are utilised by the rest of us, and our experience in so doing should provide useful evidence for or against the objectivity of the grouping. Whether it does or does not, depends largely upon our individual capacity to approach the matter in the tentative spirit of testing whether it is so or not, or whether for any reason we are animated by desires to prove it or to disprove it, i.e. how far our objectivity overrides our initial suggestibility or contra-suggestibility.

The establishment of hypotheses from grouped data

The establishment of constant groupings and relationships among data leads to the attempt to explain them in general terms. What constitutes a scientifically acceptable hypothesis?

Firstly, it must explain as logically and clearly as possible the data to which it is relevant; it must not contradict known facts.

Secondly, the hypothesis must be probable, i.e. it must derive from an adequate number and range of data. The larger the range of data of inference, the greater the chances of its accuracy. The mathematical probable error of a conclusion drawn from a small number of observations is measurably greater than is the case in one drawn from a larger number. Premature generalisation, and generalisation from too narrow a range of facts, from what statisticians call "partial samples", are fertile sources of inadequacy in hypothesis.

Thirdly, since a hypothesis is a generalisation, it must be expressed in abstract terms. Its formulation involves the by no means easy transition from perceptual to conceptual thinking.

Fourthly, a hypothesis is an explanation of facts so far as is known at the time of formulation, i.e. its probability is a matter of relative degree of approximation to truth. The healthy growth of theory, as exemplified in the history of Freud's own work, consists in the perpetual modification, retraction and expansion of working-hypotheses in accordance with the increase in data available. Too great rigidity in theory, the crystallisation of hypothesis into dogma, is invariably accompanied by an arrest of development. This tentative character of theory, which is all too readily forgotten, is in accordance incidentally with the dictionary definition. Thus, according to Webster, to make a hypothesis is to make an assumption; a hypothesis is "A tentative theory or supposition provisionally adopted to explain certain facts and to guide in the investigation of others".

This last statement indicates a fifth important quality, namely, the predictive value of the hypothesis. Present scientific developments tend to raise the predictive quality (statistical probability rather than strict predictability) of a hypothesis, especially if the hypothesis be consistent with the rest of knowledge, to a rank equalling in methodological value that of experimental confirmation, a point of primary importance in the consideration of non-metrical phenomena.

Lastly, hypotheses which are sound usually provide valuable inspiration to further research, and their fertility in this respect is proportionate to their plastic character.

The special risks of analytic theory are perhaps the following. The data available to any one individual are relatively limited, they consist of inadequate or partial samples, and the attention of any one individual is liable to be caught by a special range of data, to the temporary devaluation of other varieties. That is, our risks of premature and narrow generalisation are bound to be high. Moreover, the data are very complicated and diverse, and require to be apprehended from many different angles.

Since we are a relatively small band of workers, we have a proportionally small number of creative minds, and this is possibly one reason why we tend to absolutism. We have to make the most of all we have. Another reason is, perhaps, that the fundamental hypotheses have proved so illuminating, and have so enormously increased our understanding, that we acquire a strong conviction of their soundness. Whatever the reasons, the fact is that dogmatism is one of our patent and serious failings.

Problems of verification in analysis

Since it can hardly be denied that the conditions under which we work admit of a high probability of error all along the line from data to theory, it follows that we must pay extra-strict attention to the testing of our hypotheses. The formulation of fruitful and far-reaching hypotheses is the privilege and work of the few, but the onus of verification is a common task laid upon us all. What ways are open to us of establishing the greater or lesser probability of our theories? These ways at once fall into two groups, namely, extra-analytic and strictly analytic. Extra-analytic methods may themselves be subdivided according to whether the evidence is supplied by trained analysts or not. We cannot deny that our work is largely influenced by subjective factors, however thorough the safeguarding analysis of the analyst and, therefore, any evidence which can be obtained from completely external sources is correspondingly valuable. We should not adopt an attitude of superiority towards differently trained observers and other branches of science. On the contrary, we should aim in the course of time at closer collaboration. Correlation of our theories with other theories should, ultimately, become exceedingly useful, though at present it is only in a larval stage. The fact that so little of our theory is susceptible of experimental proof is rather a reason for encouraging such possibilities as may exist.

One of the most important fields open to the trained analyst outside the consulting-room is behaviour observation, systematised or unsystematised. The wider a range of facts any given hypothesis explains satisfactorily in the outer world, the greater its probability. The more widely we can range the more likely we are to rule out fallacies arising from the numerical smallness of consulting-room data and selective sampling. It is not my intention to discuss extra-analytic methods at length, but only to emphasise that verification from such sources is to be desired and valued, and that possibilities in that direction should be sought and encouraged.

As in the case of data, so in the case of verification, it seems to me more useful to concentrate here on consulting-room methods. The situation appears admirably simple at the first glance. We listen to a given hypothesis and to the evidence on which it is based, we return to our consulting-rooms and each see if similar evidence is provided by one or more of our patients and if the explanation appears to fit more accurately and better than any previous explanation. If the result is positive, we have some grounds in experience for judging the hypothesis to be sound and can testify to this effect. Again, at first glance, it seems a direct adaptation in analysis of the ordinary scientific procedure of proving results by repeating experiments. But this first impression is rather misleading. However fully the evidence is given in support of any hypothesis (and it is impossible to give all the evidence, since it must reach us selected and summarised) it is radically impossible for us to recreate approximately the same conditions in the way in which one can recreate the conditions of a controlled experiment. The only way the isolation of a problem can be effected is by concentrating our attention on it, and this may of itself defeat our ends, since if we are looking intently for certain things, other things escape us. Even our concentration can be only relative, since it is impracticable to conduct an ordinary therapeutic analysis with the single aim of testing a given point.

The position is a thoroughly contradictory one. On the one hand, testing in our own practice is our only way of estimating the working value of a hypothesis, and our final acceptance or rejection of it should be based on personal experience of it, not to mention that it may take a long time to reach any final decision on grounds of experience. On the other hand, however careful we are, the probability of our personal conclusions being sound is reduced by a variety of objective and subjective factors. The only way out of this impasse appears to lie in the pooling of results. It is this pooling alone which offers a possibility of cancelling out extraneous interferences, though it is not a complete safeguard especially against subjective trends. Nevertheless, a consensus of opinion which proves stable undoubtedly has a claim to a real degree of probability. Indeed, it is upon a few such generally accepted principles that the structure of analytic theory is based.

While agreement raises the degree of probability, disagreement is equally important. No minority opinion which makes any claim to be based on facts ought to be disregarded. On the contrary, every serious disagreement ought to be carefully and thoroughly investigated. We should follow the example of Darwin, who paid less attention to his supporters than he did to the objections raised by his opponents. Opposing views may have all kinds of different motivations, but a strong minority opinion is suggestive of inadequacy of some kind in the majority view. Indeed, one reason why pooling, comparison and correlation of results, together with investigation of apparent and real disagreement, are so imperative lies in the immense complexity of our material and the necessity of approaching it from such a variety of different aspects. Individuals are drawn to some aspects rather than to others, and only if their results are co-ordinated with the results of other workers approaching the problem from a different angle is there a chance of getting a whole picture with each aspect in due perspective. From this point of view again, the more various the lines of approach, the richer and more complete the picture and, in this sense, it is an advantage to have analysts with different professional backgrounds. We should, I think, lose something if all analysts were medically trained. From the point of view of theory, however, it is to be desired that analysts should have had a previous training in some educative discipline involving scientific methodology. Our greatest difficulty in problems of verification is the difficulty of approaching them in a scientific way and of sustaining our objectivity in regard to them.

The scientific attitude

What then is this necessary scientific attitude of mind? It is primarily an attitude of wanting to find out what the facts are, how they are related, and what is their most probable explanation, irrespective of whether we like them or not. It is a tentative attitude, which does not regard explanations as having more than a greater or a lesser degree of probability. It allows for the necessary growth of knowledge and expects the hypotheses of today, not necessarily to be discarded, but to be subsumed in wider hypotheses made possible by the continuance of investigation. In short, the scientific attitude is objective, and tentative. Complete objectivity is an unattainable ideal for human beings, but a greater or lesser degree *is* attainable, and we do make every effort to practise it in relation to our patients and to encourage its growth in them. Indeed, it is our boast that we approach the human mind to see what is there, and not what it had been taken for granted is or ought to be there: and indeed this boast is legitimate. Nevertheless, when it comes to matters of theory, we seem all too easily to discard this attitude, in spite of the fact that theory demands at least as high a degree of objectivity as practice. It may be that we use up all our tolerance in our practices, but the thing we should aim at is to create the same atmosphere of disinterested enquiry in our scientific discussions as obtains in consulting-rooms. We cannot leave our own subjective trends and feelings outside the door and we certainly should not hoodwink ourselves about them, but just as during an analytic hour we subordinate our personal ends to the ends of the patient, so we should try for a similar subordination in scientific discussions in the interests of theory as a whole.

The receptive tolerance that we extend to our patients is precisely the attitude which, alone, is genuinely favourable to free and constructive discussion. In fact, we seem to leave behind in the consulting-room the attitude which is so urgently required in theoretical research and, instead, carry over something which is entirely out of place, namely, the habit of interpretation in terms of subjective motive and clinical diagnosis. We cannot avoid receiving impressions of other people's subjective problems, and there is no reason why we should try to avoid this. But there is every reason to avoid using such impressions as weapons in discussion. The subjective history, the genetic development of an opinion in its owner is one thing, the assessment of the objective validity of the opinion as a contribution to theory is quite another, and it is with this latter process alone that we have any concern in scientific discussion. In any case, the pot can always legitimately retort that the kettle is black because if there is one thing that is fairly certain, it is that every one of us has a specific subjective bias, from which we cannot escape and which does determine our approach to theoretical as to all other problems. This is the reason why pooling and collective research is so imperative. The genetic development of a theory is a legitimate branch of research in itself, but theory as a whole will be aided by discussion only insofar as this is concerned with the truth of what is said. Our concern is with ideas expressed, not with their sponsors. Everyone and anyone should ideally feel free to say exactly what they think about any idea, no matter whose idea it is.

A great stumbling block to freedom of discussion is a tendency to regard criticism as personal attack. We all have frustrated aggression problems, and heated argument does offer a channel for hostility discharge; and what is felt to be hostility is naturally resented. We must tolerate occasional quarrels but it is improbable that they will contribute much to the advance and consolidation of theory. They may be a refreshing outlet for individuals, but the positive and constructive uses of argument are not the annihilation of the opponent but the exchange of information and explanation. I believe it is a mistake in method to defend oneself instantly against criticism. Not only does it prevent one from pausing to consider whether there is any reasonable foundation for the criticism, but it is a mistake to take it for granted that the purpose of the critic is destructive. The most fruitful type of argument is not a battle but a concerted attempt to elucidate a problem and to understand the reasons underlying differences of opinion. It is not conflict itself but the solution of conflict which is progress.

At the same time, because the appreciation of differences and the understanding of their causes is so essential to sound progress, even heated arguments are, perhaps, to be preferred to glossing over genuine divergences. We must remind ourselves over and over again that our business in discussion is with theories, not with persons. I often think that in dealing with theory we tend to regress to infantile modes of reaction, to swallow it whole or to spit it out, and the adult habit of mastication is easily inhibited. It is not an easy matter to grow up to intellectual maturity and many of the impediments to scientific thinking may be traced to faulty maturation. Our intelligence is easily seduced from this, so exacting an objectivity by the lure of infantile goals. It is immensely hard, for instance, to forego belief in the reality of perfection somewhere, and we do sometimes display symptoms of the fairly widespread tendency to find in science a substitute for religion. If we do not try to find in theory the consolations of religion, it is still far more peaceful to rest upon the bosom of authority than to make strenuous efforts to think for oneself. But progress is effected only when people find the courage to think for themselves. Since we are all differently endowed, a certain division of labour is inevitable and desirable, but we can none of us escape our share of responsibility for the future of analysis.

Summary

We call ourselves scientists because our purpose is to build up an objective psychology; and we act upon the general principles of scientific method inasmuch as we employ the basic processes of observation and grouping of data, formulation of working hypothesis, and verification. We cannot, however, employ these processes under conditions which diminish the possibility of error to anything like the extent that is possible in so-called exact sciences. Within the sphere of analysis itself we have two principal ways of counteracting this greater probability of error, namely, the subjective way of analysis of the analyst, and the objective way of pooling, interchange and comparison of results. One of the most vitally important points in collective verification is the thorough examination of divergences of view. Discussion will be constructive insofar as it is true, and no method of furthering useful discussion will succeed unless we can manage to create an atmosphere of tolerance and objectivity in which intellectual honesty is encouraged.

CHAPTER 4

Number and the human sciences

(1951)

Suppose one of those oft-spoken-of but seldom-met travellers from Mars had visited us to satisfy his native curiosity about psychology: he would find a state of affairs that might at first seem somewhat puzzling. In the write-up of his field work he would report on one-person psychology, two-person psychology, three-person psychology, possibly a four-person psychology, and a multi-person psychology; what would strike him most would of course be the interrelation of those aspects of the subject.

"The break-up of the whole field of psychology into categories according to the minimum number of persons essential to the study of each branch of the subject is the first thing that strikes the visitor", he might write in his thesis, adding that distressing confusions sometimes occurred because these simple categories were thought to be irrelevant to the study of detail by the practitioners of each category and the implications so disconcerting that they were generally ignored.

Reprinted from G. Wilbur & W. Munsterberger (Eds.), *Psycho-Analysis and Culture* (New York: International Universities Press, 1951, pp. 150–155), a collection of papers written as tributes to the work of Geza Roheim. Also in J. Rickman, *Selected Contributions to Psychoanalysis* (London: Hogarth Press and the Institute of Psycho-Analysis, 1957).

One-person psychology

"One-person psychology" concerns itself with what goes on inside one person taken in isolation. It studies the neurological aspect of the mind, sensation, reaction time, learning and forgetting, memory, imagery, hallucinations, introspection etc., a very varied field. It is true that in the study of some of these phenomena an experimenter or observer is usually present, but with the present richness of imagination and ingenuity now given to the construction of apparatus of all kinds it would be possible for most of the experiments in this branch of psychology to be carried out, not to be sure designed, by a robot. Where for reasons of economy or of scientific curiosity an observer is used in place of a robot to carry out the routine of testing, in the case of one-person psychology the relation between the observer and the person observed is reduced to a minimum. In situations where the responses of the subject of the experiment annoy the observer, in one-person psychology the experimental situation is usually considered to be vitiated in some degree because only one person's responses are relevant to the problem being investigated. In the language of two-and three-person psychology the ego ideal of the observer in one-person psychology is a robot. The basis of the research in observations is the a-historical present, the "here-and-now" of the laboratory. People with a gift for investigating harsh names would include much of what they call rat psychology and brass instrument psychology under the heading of what is here called one-person psychology.

Two-person psychology

In "two-person psychology" we enter the psychological region of reciprocal relationships; in this it differs from one-person psychology but is linked with some if not all of the other psychologies. It studies the relation existing when two persons are in a more or less closed region and are tied to one another by simultaneously acting aims, tasks or needs. The example of two-body psychology which has proved of outstanding utility in both theory and practice is the psychoanalyst and his patient in the analytic transference situation, which is in one sense a closed region devoted largely but not exclusively to the study of a-historical events observed in the "here-and-now". The two psychologists who laid the foundations of this research are of course Freud and Ferenczi. (The transference phenomena seen in *statu nascendi*, though originating in the past, are noted by both analyst and patient in the present, and the countertransference phenomena are reckoned with by the observing analyst and frequently noted by the observant patient.) The analytic situation also gives insight into another occurrence of two-person psychology in the mother–child relationship, particularly in the stages of the nursing couple and the sphincter interests which they share and dispute.

Three-person psychology

Investigations in this seemingly closed two-person relationship, however, disclose that it is not in fact closed; though there are only two persons shut up in one room there is forced on the attention of both of them that some of the patient's behaviour can only be explained by the fact that he cannot consider himself alone with his analyst, but is acting as if the analyst's wife (or husband), were in the closed region too. Thus a "three-person psychology", which goes by the name of the Oedipus complex, is forced on the observer under the conditions of the transference situation in analysis. A more direct observation of this kind of psychology, based, however, on the findings of analysis, is recorded by Dr D. W. Winnicott, when he makes his clinical examination of babies seated on the mother's lap. Doctors from time immemorial have interviewed two persons at once in clinical consultation, whether they be husband and wife or parent and child.

What is striking about this fact is that in all this time these good observers have contributed almost nothing to the psychodynamics of the three-person relationship; perhaps we may return to this later.

Four-person psychology

Another derivation of the analysis of the transference situation is a study of sibling rivalry as a side issue in the examination of the Oedipus complex. This branch is not very clearly developed as yet but there is just enough to warrant the establishment of the "four-person psychology".

Multi-person psychology

With "multi-person psychology" we enter a quite different phase of research. Though in the analytic situation only the images of the other parent and/or sibling were present (i.e. they were not present in the flesh) they were really present in the sense that the effect on behaviour was comparable to that of their being present in the flesh, and on the definition of reality by Kurt Lewin (what is real is that which has effects) we can speak of a three- or a four-person psychology in a two-person situation. With more than four we have group psychology, and where this is multi-structured we have as yet almost no clues. Freud has given us an outline of group psychology in relation to the analysis of the ego based on a three- and four-person psychology. He chose for study the groups with the simplest structure, the army and the church, where the individuals were all of one sex and related to one another through a father-ego ideal; neither of these are typical of groups generally. We are, in fact, without an adequate theoretical frame of reference for a group dynamics where there are more than four persons related to one another in more than one way. Our poverty of a well-ordered frame of reference in this field, though embarrassing for progress, should not surprise or shame us, for mathematicians tell us that the growth of complexity of the dynamics of ordinary particulars (they despair to touch such complex things as human beings) increases enormously as the number increases. Indeed, only under certain limited conditions can they speak with certainty about the dynamics of three bodies considered simultaneously; with four, five or more the complexity is beyond their unravelling. There may be a further reason for our lack of theory, i.e. that the subject is distasteful.

When Freud described psychoanalysis as the third blow to man's narcissism (the other two being delivered by Galileo and Darwin) in that it showed him he was not master within his own house, there was left the hope—fostered perhaps by a remaining shred of that same self-concern—that if he knew himself better he would attain that mastery of the forces within. But suppose a study of group dynamics shows us how we are more than the children of our time and generation, are indeed its slaves, that we are in fact ruled from without by group forces of which we are unaware, then our narcissism would get another nasty knock and flinching before the scattering of another illusion, we would pull round us the consoling blanket of incomprehension and keep our minds engaged within the cosy circle of the family and its simple social derivatives. A hint of this possibility is seen in some of the objections to field theory, which are reminiscent of the more polite but vigorous repudiations of psychoanalysis after it delivered the third blow mentioned above, for though field theory does not halt at considerations of number, it is prepared to give full reckoning to the influence of the next higher phase of complexity, being at least as important as the lower one on which there is general agreement.

The limitations of predictions in the psychological field

Those who use this classification of the psychologies, assuming that it has any use at all, will choose one or other aspect of it for employment. One of the first things which has struck the present writer is the hint that it gives as to the limitations of prediction in the psychological field generally. Thus the strict student of one-person psychology is unable to predict much about what goes on in a two-person situation; for instance, the unclinical psychology that is taught in the classrooms and laboratories, though useful in the highest degree (and for obtaining higher degrees, incidentally) in the academic psychology of introspection, sensation, perception, learning, memory, and the like, is nevertheless almost useless in a clinical situation, particularly the analytic situation. Of course, if the student has heard of the theories and findings of the psychoanalysts and uses them in his thinking and in action, he is not strictly speaking a one-person psychologist any more. Similarly a two-person psychologist who shut his mind to those transference manifestations which brought in the third party would not be able to make many useful predictions concerning three-person psychological situations. The range of accurate predictions is limited, it would seem, to social or psychological situations based on a comparable number of persons, or a comparable degree of complexity in the structure of the psychodynamic unit under consideration to that on which the basic research was done.

Assuming for the moment that the conclusion last mentioned is correct, an inference can be drawn on the relation between psychoanalysis and anthropology, i.e. that psychoanalysis as we understand it today, however valuable its aid to anthropology may be, can *never* provide a framework of theory that will cover adequately the multi-person, multi-structured psychodynamic units with which anthropology is mainly and usually concerned. To say this is not in any way to belittle the amazing power and suggestiveness (indeed also the provocativeness) of the ideas that derive from, and could only be derived from, the work of psychoanalysts in their thorough studies of two-, three- and four-person psychologies in their encloistered consulting-rooms.

Two features of psychoanalytic work are outstanding in importance for the human sciences. The first is its a-historical character: this gives it its power to resolve the complicated phenomena displayed into its component elements; the second is the fact that the problems of the subject under investigation have priority over the intellectual curiosity of the observer—the patient's associations settle the direction of the investigation, not the ingenious contrivance of the scientist's questionnaires. In the researches in multi-person psychology the same two features are found in the work of Dr W. R. Bion (Bion, 1948, etc.) and researches stemming from his study of groups. It is as yet too soon to appraise this work, and it may be many years before it will be applicable to anthropology, but it must be mentioned because the psychodynamic unit that is investigated consists of about eight persons.[1]

The matter of prediction is an important ore for any science, even for the "pattern sciences" (such as psychoanalysis, anthropology, aesthetics and the like) where it is less used than in the "measuring sciences" such as physics. Geza Roheim predicted once that a tribe in Australia would be found (if not extinguished already) having such and such myths; and he was proved correct. This kind of prediction was not, I think, based directly on psychoanalytic researches but rather on a study of culture contact, e.g. on the pattern of totem animal relationships. But the verification of a hypothesis often comes at a later stage in the development of a science than is either psychoanalysis or anthropology at the present time. In the matter of following clues and co-ordinating them we have received much aid and stimulation from Geza Roheim's work.

If I knew a shred of the grammar and syntax of anthropology I could write in praise of his work, perhaps with sense and understanding; not being so endowed I can only record my relief over twenty years ago to hear that an anthropologist was going into the field who had in the course of his dual training to face and uncover his own infantile amnesia, i.e. who had been analysed. To see a strange culture clearly when the major defence against a perception of one's own mental processes had not been breached was, as Rivers pointed out to me just after the First World War, a thing anthropologists would not for long expect to do, His recommendation that every young psychiatrist and anthropologist should first be analysed was not quickly followed. Geza Roheim was a pioneer, and, as such, however ignorant of his speciality we may be, we salute him.

---

[1] It is incidentally interesting that the "span" of the observer varies considerably. Thus one observer can stretch his observations over only five persons in group discussion—beyond that number individual and group "outlines" get confused—while another observer can encompass seven or eight. One observer, whose work is known to the present writer, could easily span a dozen and with a little effort fifteen, but before he took up this occupation he was a sports journalist and had for years kept a lively eye for the personal characteristics of a scrimmaging mass of athletes in the usual ball games of his culture; number here relates to the range of the observer's power, not to the category of psychology considered.

A Table of Psycho-Social Relationships
(based on a discussion with Trist)

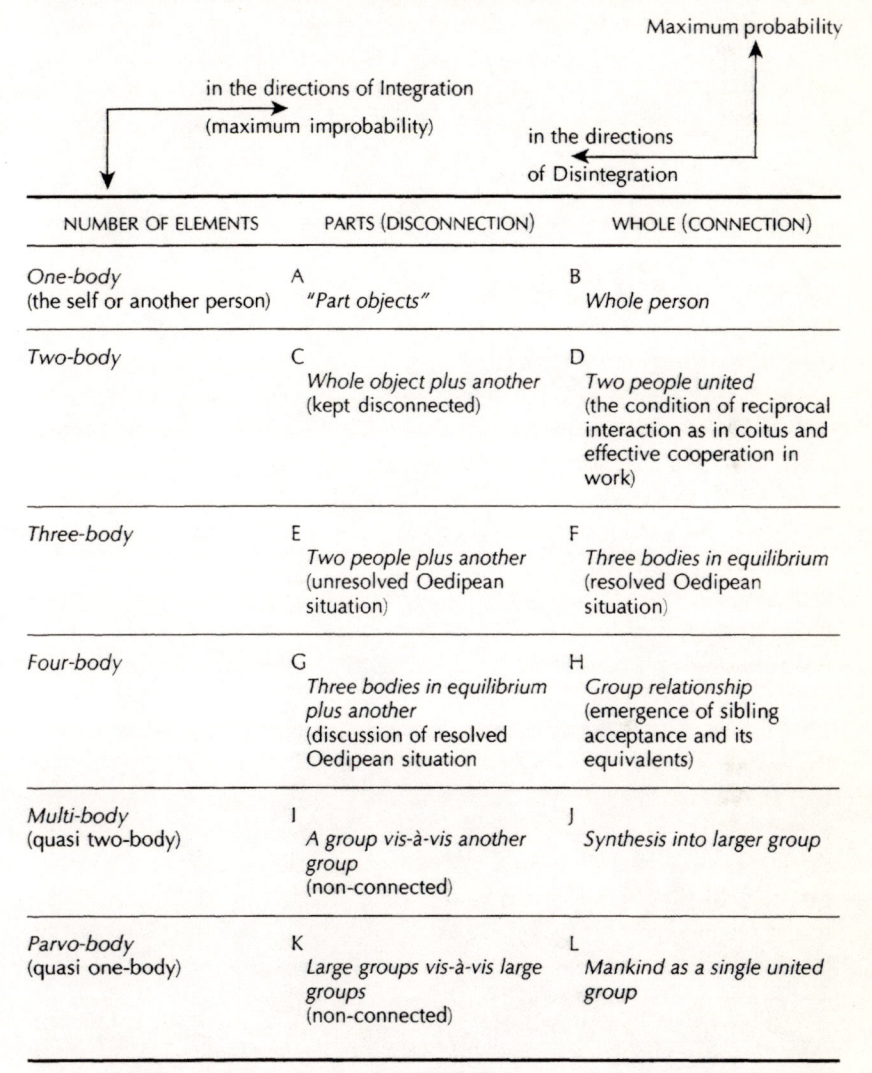

in the directions of Integration
(maximum improbability)

Maximum probability

in the directions of Disintegration

NUMBER OF ELEMENTS	PARTS (DISCONNECTION)	WHOLE (CONNECTION)
One-body (the self or another person)	A "Part objects"	B Whole person
Two-body	C Whole object plus another (kept disconnected)	D Two people united (the condition of reciprocal interaction as in coitus and effective cooperation in work)
Three-body	E Two people plus another (unresolved Oedipean situation)	F Three bodies in equilibrium (resolved Oedipean situation)
Four-body	G Three bodies in equilibrium plus another (discussion of resolved Oedipean situation	H Group relationship (emergence of sibling acceptance and its equivalents)
Multi-body (quasi two-body)	I A group vis-à-vis another group (non-connected)	J Synthesis into larger group
Parvo-body (quasi one-body)	K Large groups vis-à-vis large groups (non-connected)	L Mankind as a single united group

Editor's note: This chart was discovered in the Archives of the British Psychoanalytical Society among John Rickman's papers. It was the result of a discussion between Professor Eric Trist and Rickman and, in the opinion of the Editor, showed an extension of some of the ideas put forward in this paper, which linked up with his work on Lewin (see Appendix 2).

PART II

THE INTERPERSONAL AND INTRA-PSYCHIC DYNAMICS OF THE INTERVIEW SITUATION

CHAPTER 5

First aid in psychotherapy

(1936–38)

On first reflection it may seem odd that there is no literature on first aid in psychotherapy comparable with that in general medicine. This omission cannot be explained on the ground that emergencies in mental life are very rare and that when they occur they are trivial. We know that they are occasions of the greatest discomfort to the general practitioner and that he dreads nothing in his patient's illnesses more than a nervous breakdown. The dread is all the greater because he has no technique for dealing with the emergency except either to call in a specialist, or to certify the patient, or to recommend a sea voyage for the patient. The general practitioner may look forward with some misgiving if called to a bad roadside smash; his aid may be called in too late and the injuries may be severe or his skill hindered by darkness or cold weather, but at least he knows how to set about his work, he can do something. In psychological crises he often feels helpless from the very start.

The many reasons for this feeling of helplessness have often been considered; first there is the lack of preparation in the curriculum;

This paper was written between 1936 and 1938, but there is no record that it was read to any group.

second, the fact that what training is provided consists of the exhibition of incurable cases in a distant and forbidding institution, instead of the demonstration of everyday mental disorders in the wards and outpatient department; and thirdly, the lectures centre on the symptoms of the medico-legal disorders called insanity and the medico-legal restrictions which may be imposed on the sufferers. The atmosphere is thus so charged with crisis and hopelessness that it is little wonder the student and practitioner look on acute mental illness as the bugbear of professional life.

There is another feature in physical medicine which distinguishes it from psychological medicine, and perhaps more than has been commonly recognised this feature has led to an over-emphasis on the physical to the neglect of the mental side of medicine—I refer to the uniformity of the human body and the diversity of human behaviour. Organs are to be found in the expected places, this applies to young and old; even in the cases of the two sexes, with notable exceptions, the same holds. The body is a piece of mass-production goods, standardised to such an extent that every doctor's surgery, every clinic in the world is a service station of competence, since all the mechanics have had their training in the assembling and dismantling of the same machine. It seems to be quite a different matter in the case of the human mind. Here we find diversity the rule not the exception "What's one man's meat is another man's poison" is not true in the world of physiology and pharmacology; in the matter of preference, of wishes, desires and taste there is no uniformity:

> Jack Sprat would eat no fat,
> His wife would eat no lean,
> And so betwixt them both
> They licked the platter clean.

The medical practitioner has to feel his way with each case of mental illness relying on intuition, because he has nothing comparable with a *fixed* anatomy and physiology, and therefore a norm, to guide him.

The contrast between the orderliness of physical medicine and the empiricism of psychopathology may cause a bewildered doctor to turn away from mental disease in despair. But I think there is another and stronger reason than this. His curriculum shows him how the horrors of physical injury can be put right, gaping wounds are sewn up and heal as we say "by first intention", we know how to aid nature because we understand her ways. The wounds of the mind gape and cannot be closed because we do not understand the processes of injury and repair, and they fester because we cannot keep them clean. We are no longer frightened to see diseased or injured bodies, we have remedies. Mental disorder wakens unknown or, rather, unremembered dreads and we lose our nerve.

A case for discussion

The following history will serve to illustrate several features of importance in making a preliminary examination of a nervous breakdown, and therefore of service in emphasising some of the techniques of first aid.

The first interview

A young married man of 29 [referred to J.R. in 1935] is with some difficulty persuaded by his employers to come and see me on account of an increasingly troublesome "interference". An unknown man with a wireless appliance began three to four months ago to read his thoughts and speak to him; now the fellow has begun to read his business correspondence as well. I am clearly given to understand that the trouble is purely external. He himself is sound in mind and only comes to me because as a doctor I am also an expert in all matters pertaining to the influence of electricity on the nervous system. In short, he wants to know from me how he can switch off the wireless man. And yet he is not hostile to the wireless man, whom he calls "Hawk-eye"; he even smiles when he mentions him. He said that when the interference became intolerable he went to the police telling them that if they captured the apparatus they would have a valuable instrument for detecting spies and reading the documents of foreign powers. So even the weapon that torments him is not wholly evil.

At this point in the interview I came to a provisional conclusion that Hawk-eye was not an embodiment of his own hostile phantasies which he had projected outwards onto the environment and which was now turning against himself, that is to say, did not represent his own hatred of someone else that was recoiling back on himself, but was a reflection of his own conscience. At a guess he had done something for which his conscience reproached him, but instead of feeling guilt, he suffered from the torments of what he felt to be another person. It was risky to get the evidence for this, because "Hawk-eye" might slip back into him, so to speak. In other words, his conscience might become acutely aggressive and he would be suicidal.

I asked him when the interference of Hawk-eye began and was told that it was in October, it grew worse in November, stopped in early December, began again before Christmas, and in January and now it was terrible. The cessation of the trouble in early December gave me a chance to ask if there had been any change in his mode of life about then. He said there was not. Becoming rather bolder, I asked if there had been anything of consequence in September or October which had upset him. Again he said there had not been anything unusual. On the assumption that there had been something disturbing at that time, it seemed that his defensive device of projecting his conscience was a fairly stable and efficient mechanism, and if there was no precipitating factor of guilt, there remained the possibility of a shock of some kind followed by amnesia or an internal alteration in his phantasies of which he was unaware.

So, changing the subject, which I could now do fairly easily because it seemed to go away from the painful subject, I asked about his work. He was at once friendly and communicative. From the work was but a step to his life in general, and then he told me that he was married. In fact he had married in April. There had been some tiffs and awkward times, but in general he and his wife had got on very well. At this point there was an absence of the earlier defensiveness, he was eager to talk. I asked myself whatever caused the change. There were two possibilities. Either his marriage and sexual relations were an easier subject than the persecutory ones, because the latter touched on this queer relation of intimacy, spying and bickering with a man (unconscious homosexual phantasies), *or else he had something he wanted to confess.* So I let him range pretty freely in reminiscence, the usual adolescent yearnings, a visit to Paris where a sexual adventure made him feel disgust, followed by a spell of religious interests, etc. There was nothing special here. Then he told me how he came to choose a flat for himself and his fiancée. A month before the marriage he found an upper maisonette; the landlord's wife was lonely, felt deserted, needed love, he had an outburst of erotic feelings, took her out in his car, they kissed, petted, and he wrote her passionate letters. Then his fiancée came to look at the place, was introduced to the landlady who took to her at once. He was married, was impotent the first night, but not afterwards, and the two households got on splendidly. In July he had a terrible attack of remorse and told his wife of the petting parties. She was very cut up but recovered. In September he heard the landlord say quite casually to his own wife, "Have you got the letters?" It was recognised to be an innocent remark as he was going out to the post, but it struck the young lover as having terrible possibilities. He resolved to move. Then he had a psychotic outburst. When both families were taking coffee together in the evening, he said to the landlord, "Now, out with it! What about those letters?" The man was dumbfounded, thought he must be drunk, was tactful, pacifying, and finally wrote my patient a solemn declaration that he knew nothing of any letters or about any blackmail schemes.

At this point I gently asked if he could see any connection between the things he had just been talking about and Hawk-eye's interferences, he replied that he could see none. Letting the talk run on for a bit I brought it back to Hawk-eye and now got a great deal of new information.

The interference began with a sort of mental comment, not a voice nor yet a thought, directed towards himself. For example, "It's quicker to go from Oxford Circus to Dover Street by Conduit Street than round by Oxford Street and down Bond Street." And the counter-thought rising spontaneously in his mind "Yes, so it is!"—the mental comment was friendly and advisory, and yet felt as a distinctly foreign influence in his mind; for the first time at least in the last few years, he detected something uncanny. In technical language, he was beginning to dissociate. A friendly supporting element in his personality which was till recently a part of himself was becoming separated off and projected outwards. For about a week the mental comment continued, with increasing force because more detached, the advice becoming more sharp and admonishing. One day he heard a short nasty word within his mind, "Shit!" It was foreign to his nature to use such a term. It shocked him and he knew it was directed at himself. It meant that he was a shit. The projected conscience became more personal still, but never divulged the fact of the rides in the car and the petting parties. The patient was called a fornicator and a dirty blackguard, but never a reference to the immediate occasion of the crisis was established.

Up to this point the work had been comparatively simple, I had avoided the cardinal mistake of frightening him by attacking his "delusion" about the wireless man. But had I done anything positive? What right, for instance, has this case to inclusion in a paper on first aid? We are now obviously on the threshold of a theoretical discussion which lies at the heart of our theme.

The function of first aid in psychotherapy

First aid is a remedial measure undertaken after a preliminary diagnosis has been made. Its aim is to enable the patient to survive the immediate crisis, and as far as circumstances permit, to restrict the ill effects of injury. It does not pretend to be a radical cure, but gives the doctor time to make better arrangements for the patient's well-being and relieves the patient as far as possible of his discomforts. A cardinal point in first-aid work is that nothing should be done to make either a fuller diagnosis or subsequent treatment more difficult. For example, in physical medicine it is recognised as thoroughly bad practice to load up the patient with morphine to make him comfortable unless one is absolutely sure that such artificial relief will not obscure the symptoms of, say, internal haemorrhage.

We can in physical medicine speak with assurance saying, for instance, that this is thoroughly bad practice, this must never be done, that is a *sine qua non* because we are dealing with standardised goods. But can we speak with an equal sureness in psychological medicine where there seem to be such wide individual differences? Only, I think, if we fall back on psychopathology as our sole guide in matters touching the mind.

If we ask a biologically orientated physiologist what he conceives to be the central purpose in all the elaborate biochemical devices in the body, I think he would reply that they served to keep the internal conditions as constant as possible, and to enable the animal to reproduce and repair tissue loss by eating. At least such an answer gives coherence to the many processes—for example, that of regulation of blood contents, etc. If we bring the biologically minded physiologist to look at a patient suffering from severe shock, all his theories seem upset. The temperature is falling and yet there is no shivering to generate heat, the kidneys and lungs slow their action and the blood picture changes without the usual measures of recovery. In the case of severe shock, outside aid is essential if the patient's life is to be saved. What are the analogies in psychological medicine? They are familiar to every reader of psychopathology and very similar to what has just been described in the physical field. The majority of mental processes are devoted to keeping the level of excitement in the mind as constant as possible, the balance being upset by the instinctual drives which lead to a psychical relation to objects.

The commonest error in psychiatry is to confuse the mental crises with the condition of physical shock and therefore to assure that the normal regulative processes are suspended. The mental patient has not lost his object relationships, which would be the analogue of shock. He is in the liveliest dread of losing them. The symptoms which seem to laymen so peculiar are, to our more practised eye, *defence measures against the loss* of *objects*. When the body is cooling to a fatal degree during shock we can arrest the process of cooling by applying heat from the outside; we may be unable to stop the important disturbance, but we can at least prevent the automatic physical process of cooling from making the body an untenable habitation for the spark of life. In the case of mental illness we can do no more by first-aid methods than this. We cannot replace the patient's lost object in an emergency, we cannot provide a substitute. All that we can do is to prevent the disruptive processes from occurring too rapidly.

There are three kinds of psychotherapy. The patient seeks for a love-cure—that is to say, he wants to find a substitute for a love-object that has been lost. The second kind of therapy is reassurance. It is based on the assumption that the patient is right in wanting a love-cure, but the reassurance-therapist tells him in effect that though he is a thoroughly fine fellow he should turn elsewhere. The third kind of therapy is analytic. It is based on the assumption that the patient cannot help wanting a love-cure and does not pass on the burden of being the object of the patient's interest but shows him how it came about that his object was lost and how his conflicts prevent him from accepting substitutes. I do not want to waste time in discussing the various kinds of psychotherapy. The severe disciplinary technique is of course the love-cure on a sadistic basis. The spiritual element in many kinds of therapy is obviously a technique of handing on the patient to a Divine rather than a Harley Street specialist, and belongs to the reassurance method.

The conclusion of the first interview

Let us return to our patient who it will be remembered did *not* apparently want help except to stop an outside (projected) interference and who was just beginning to tell us how Hawk-eye was reproaching him and calling him bad names. At this point he changed the subject once more and began to talk about electric waves. I took that to mean that he was asking for help on account of the next thought that was about to emerge, and if I could relieve his anxieties he would be able to talk about it. The way at this point was fairly easy. I went over the ground again concerning the Paris adventure, the amorous landlady and his intended marriage, trying to get him to reconstruct those last fateful weeks, suggesting that perhaps some disgust (which he had mentioned in connection with Paris) still lingered from his last sexual relations and he wanted to experience a more romantic affair before his wife came to live with him. It was a very superficial explanation but I thought it would fetch out something in contradiction if not in confirmation. He replied that there was nothing in that and returned to Hawk-eye. I then asked if a lady took part in Hawk-eye's talks with him, and heard that she did. She was intimate with Hawk-eye and exercised a restraining influence on him in connection with the patient. Here was my chance—if the lady could influence the relationship it was possible that I could also. He was silent for a moment with face slightly turned away as if listening to something. I ventured a shot in the dark, "Well, what is being said?"

Patient: "Hawk-eye is talking about you."

J.R.: "What is he saying?"

Patient: "He is saying that you are a decent fellow."

I asked the patient to report whatever was being said and got the immediate response that Hawk-eye was strongly opposed to psychoanalysis. I was exceedingly careful not to take sides in a controversy, so confined my remarks to the observation that Hawk-eye appeared to like me as a person but disliked me as an analyst. I then gave out a general reassurance by saying that I did not think Hawk-eye would find anything to fear in me as an analyst either. The patient replied that Hawk-eye did but he himself did not. We then discussed the possibility of his being treated (not by me but by another analyst) and he was to return in a few days to take up the point again.

The psychopathology of the case

I shall now discuss the psychopathology of the case with reference to first aid.

It is obvious that his increasing anxiety was closely related to the petting episode; it is equally obvious that he stood in no dread of the loss of his wife's affection, at least not in the present or immediate future. She had forgiven him. She had, as the phrase goes, "returned to him". No, if there is any loss of object relationship it does not concern the patient.

I took this as a cue not to refer to his relation to his wife in terms of reassurance. It would have increased his sense of guilt to regard her as an injured and forgiving woman. It would have also been equally fruitless to take the popular line that now that he and his wife were settled down such things would not be likely to happen again. The *future never consoles a person in acute anxiety or guilt.*

I assume that his trouble was due to the loss of an object because the affair was an attempt to get love satisfaction and to give it. You will remember that the lady was lonely and felt neglected. It would be easy to connect this episode with his family relationship in two ways: first, his mother was left a widow; secondly, when he was about 14 he went to spend the summer with a married sister whose husband was away. It was not therefore a case of a simple oedipal wish to possess the mother, but to give her what her husband did or could not accomplish. If this was all there was to it—giving consolation—there would seem to be no occasion for the opprobrious epithets which Hawk-eye poured on him. It is therefore highly probable that in his phantasy he had ousted the husband as well as given the lonely lady what she desired. This gave a further ground for not trying to console him with reassurances about the future—the trouble lay not in the recent act of unfaithfulness, but in his phantasies which dated almost certainly from the distant past. Hawk-eye represented the ousted landlord and also the father, with whom in memory and in delusion he was on good terms (his very first "interference" was directing him from one place to another by the shortest way). He was injuring a friendly figure, and it seemed that that same figure was reproaching him.

Of the early life and phantasies, night terrors, memories, dreams, I got not a word. There was an apparently impenetrable wall between the present and the past. Now since I was out for a preliminary diagnosis and only first-aid treatment (I could not take him on myself), I had to decide on how to reduce the tension *vis-à-vis* Hawk-eye and whether or no to try to dig up the past. I decided that the latter was dangerous. A first-aid examination must not disturb the patient overmuch. I had also to bear in mind that if he was going to get help from another analyst I must do nothing to jeopardise an effective transference to that other person. The problem was how to deal with the guilt centred in the "project" of his conscience; then I remembered that the situation became intolerable when Hawk-eye read his business letters. Now this, I thought, might have a double meaning. On the one hand it referred pretty obviously to the landlord and the indiscreet letters, on the other with his business, which was confectionery. It was a terribly long shot, but I coupled in my mind the business of forwarding orders for sweets from little shopkeepers to his firm with the earliest relation to a good and toothsome object, the breast. It occurred to me that the taking and giving of sweets might have been a matter of concern to his father (hence Hawk-eye's interest in the letters) or that his own watching of someone else at his mother's breast might have been of importance to him; he had a younger brother. So I spent a long time in talking to him about his daily work, what sort of women kept the little shops, how he felt when meeting them alone, what his relations to the firm were, and so on. It had to be carefully done because I might become a Hawk-eye myself. He seemed at first a bit bewildered by my interest in the details of the daily round but soon warmed to it.

The second interview

His first visit was on Thursday. On Monday he asked to see me again. In the meantime he motored with his wife to his home town, dropped her at her relatives and then went on to visit his mother. She was in bed with bronchitis; he sat for hours in the stuffy room just listening to Hawk-eye and his woman jabbering away, and to his mother talking to his brother and his wife. "And what was the talk about?" I felt prompted to ask, since here was another wall of silence. It was nothing of interest I was assured, the most trivial domestic details. But still I persisted with the question. Well, his younger brother was having to break up his home temporarily, and mother was going to house the furniture. She would put a table here, put a cupboard there, and so on, and so on. And while he sat in the bedroom saying nothing but half listening to these domestic trivialities Hawk-eye faded out; it felt quite different from any previous endings of the interference. Hawk-eye faded away, and he found that things around him were different: the same but different—the difference was the quietness of the relief from strain. He could not account for it, did not want to, in fact. It might, he thought, be due to the talk with me, but that he considered was unlikely since there had been no "treatment", and yet he connected the relief of strain with his visit to me. I observed a discreet silence, thanking the Fates that he should have thought of going to his mother, who was in bed, and have had renewed evidence of her kindness in housing one of her sons who had temporarily to break up his home. He had regained to some extent the position which he had lost by his peccadillo with the landlady, and his belief in his capacity to retain contact with a good person had been in some measure restored.

On the therapeutic handling of the first interview in first aid

First of all *every crisis is due to loss of satisfaction in object-relationship* and dread of never getting satisfaction again. The cause is never obvious. If it were obvious the patient would be sad on account of his loss or in pain or grief but not ill. The distinction between fear and anxiety is that fear is experienced at the possible loss of an object of satisfaction of which the person is conscious, and anxiety when the loss of an *unconscious* love object becomes imminent. The precipitating factor may be conspicuous enough, the specific factor is only to be got through search. This leads to the second point: *the patient's story is like the manifest content of a dream*—it may or may not in itself tell us something. The cause of the breakdown is, like the *latent content*, unconscious.

The technique of dream interpretation may be applied to the first exploratory interview. By technique of dream interpretation I do not mean asking the patient what comes to his mind in connection with a dream, but the analyst's technique of interpreting dreams, by regarding the next association as more relevant than the next but one, and reckoning any remark, gesture or omission as associative material.

The problem in the first interview is whether to press for a quick psychiatric diagnosis or risk losing bits of history for the sake of a deeper insight into the patient's phantasy life, his object-relationships and capacity for enduring frustration (Rickman, 1950, 1951a). The answer to this question depends on the urgency of the need for certification or special care (e.g. special supervision in a nursing home). For if there is a great risk of suicide or homicide, treatment in the immediate future must be subordinated to more radical measures in the present; but in general the accuracy of a psychiatric diagnosis is of smaller account than a psychopathological survey of the patient. By psychiatric diagnosis I mean classification according to psychiatric types. At this point I should like to take up a problem lying on the border between questions concerning the first interview and first aid, i.e. the special difficulties of the general practitioner in any psychological examination.

General practitioners have often said to me that it is far easier for a consultant to make a thorough mental exploration than for a general practitioner who sees the patient in his family relationships. The patient is more shy of revealing himself to his ordinary medical attendant than is the case when talking to a stranger. I think this difficulty is exaggerated. If the doctor knows his subject, the patient responds in a medical rather than a social way. The thing which inspires real confidence is the understanding of the underlying difficulties and the way to remedy them. The specialist is in just the same predicament if he is connected through a personal acquaintance. But nevertheless there is a difficulty. If the therapeutic talks touch on the unconscious, the chance of rousing powerful emotional drives, either erotic and aggressive, is far greater than if the contact is "purely medical". The general practitioner does not want to have to face his patient's unresolved unconscious transferences without the means of removing them. The general practitioner is in as awkward a predicament as the relations, if he starts a psychotherapy which he cannot finish. The consultant is not faced daily with his failures for the rest of his life; the "usual medical attendant" is, and it is little wonder that he treats psychological medicine as he does medical jurisprudence—a thing to be avoided.

The technique of reassurance, which is never radical in its effects, may lead to two major errors, both dependent on a few words of encouragement rousing and powerfully stimulating old beliefs in magic.

One physician was understood by a patient to say that psychoanalysis was necessary but was "a mere matter of form". He was induced to undertake it nevertheless, and over two years were spent before he could be effectively moved from the position of "magical indifference" to the analytic work. The error lay in its implication that cure could come about by magical means.

In another case of severe inhibition I had at the first interview given no hint as to the probable duration of the treatment, but later to a relative, who seemed sensible, I said I thought it would take at least two years. This was reported to the patient as "cure at the end of two years", and she took this as a "magical promise", a contract, and it delayed the work enormously, the patient holding firmly to the belief that she need do nothing but comply by regular attendance, and I would do the cure for her as a reward of her punctual attendance. In both cases the remarks were intended to reassure, but failed in the cardinal feature of first aid, to make "second aid" easier.

The technique which saves trouble in the long run is that of interpretation. A patient reproached me for putting him into a mental hospital, but his reproach lacked the spontaneity one would expect from a restriction of liberty. I pointed out that he was reproaching me for not having put him in earlier, since the moment he got inside the place he was easier in his bearing and relieved in his mind. This remark was followed by much more detailed analysis of his recent associations;

even my putting him in a "looney-bin" did not affect his good relations to me. I used to think certification absolutely broke up an analysis, yet even this first-aid measure is not irremediable if it is brought vigorously into the transference analysis. I recall another patient certified during analysis under urgency order, with his mother as petitioner. The patient had phantasies that his mother and his own lover were my mistresses, and yet the certification did not interrupt the work of analysis. The most depressed patient does not want encouragement, because he cannot use a good thing when it comes his way—that's his illness. He wants an immediate reduction in his anxiety and guilt tensions. Such reduction cannot be achieved by reference to conscious levels or contents of the mind, but only by reference to the unconscious.

Another point almost strong enough to be a rule may be put thus: never explain in terms of theory nor in reference to the past if the patient is in any distress but always in terms of his present feelings. If he has drawn the physician into his psychological system—some do this in five minutes—interpretations can be directed to current transference situations. For example: a woman patient, who came in the greatest distress because she felt she would strangle her husband and then take an excess of sleeping draught, gave indications of this early inclusion of myself in her psychological system. She tried to explain her feelings of hate by talking as if a tiger were inside her and controlling her, so that she was not safe. "I could scratch him [the husband] to pieces. I want help badly." She paused, looked at me and added, "No, I can't!" Meaning, I thought, scratch me. So I said that she wanted me to assist her but she was afraid that if a helpful person came along, he would get the full force of her destructive impulses and that her warning me off the case was a measure to protect me, since if I was experienced as "good" to her, it would pain her to destroy me, and she would suffer an exacerbation of guilt. She had denied previously, by the way, that guilt played any part in her life!

The handling of the immediate situation on the spot is what I call first aid in psychotherapy.

CHAPTER 6

The psychiatric interview in the social setting of a War Office Selection Board

(1943)

The theme of this paper is the "Psychiatric Interview in the Social Setting of a War Office Selection Board". The words "in the Social Setting" are important, because the psychiatrist was a technical member of a team of observers, who were regarded by the candidates collectively as a board. The members of the board were a group whose component units were necessary to one another for information and advice. The candidates were also necessary to one another because one of the characteristic features of the selection method employed by the War Office Selection Board was the assessment of qualities of personality as displayed in a group relationship.

It is perhaps well to bring these points forward prominently at an early stage, because when joining a WOSB team, the psychiatrist has to make some adaptations of his usual approach to his subject. For that matter, the other members of the Board have also to learn to discard the traditional picture of the psychiatrist as an alienist and to see him as a

---

Compiled from papers read to technical conferences of psychiatrists and psychologists employed by the War Office Selection Boards, 1943.

technical adviser, whose main function is to assess the positive (constructive) qualities of candidates from a medical (psychiatric) standpoint, and also to point out, where there is any doubt, the negative (obstructive or destructive) qualities in the candidates as viewed from the point of their group or social relationship.

If the psychiatrist has to protect the Army from the dangers of commissioning neurotic or psychotic or psychopathic individuals, he has no less a duty to the Army to prevent the candidate of fundamental good quality from being misjudged by a nervousness of superficial origin, by poor *self-salesmanship*, or by his being *a slow-starter*. The psychiatrist can do these services to the Army and the candidate best, in my view, if he makes the psychiatric interview the culmination, not the beginning, of his contact with the candidate.

It will clarify this proposition best if I describe the procedure and the reasons for the details of the procedure at the Board where I was stationed.

The task of the psychiatrist in the selection procedure

At the end of the President's address of welcome he introduces the psychiatrist as a member of the Board and asks him to say a few words. The aim of the psychiatrist in these few minutes is to establish a contact with the candidates as a group and to disclose the line which will be taken in the interview, namely, that the psychiatrist's special line of country is a study of jobs and of how people fit into them and what proves difficult in the job, whether it is civil or military, to the person carrying it out. In this connection, psychologist and psychiatrist can be taken as the same, except that the latter has a medical degree and is a Medical Officer as well. The candidates are told that if their notion of a psychiatrist is simply to get mental defectives out of the Army and neurotics into and out of hospital, then they have something new to learn. And then, in an aside apropos of learning, they are told that the WOSB's tests are a new experience and they are invited to participate in them as observers and not as mere victims, and to feel free to ask questions about the aim of the tests. The talk ends with the remark that an intelligent interest in the proceedings improves performance and that their best is what is wanted by the Board.

The aim of this is to present the psychiatrist to the candidate as a person who will talk about practical matters. All candidates attending a particular Board have the same objective basis to work on; their various ways of responding to it serve as a guide to their individual differences. Those who after this say that they would rather go through a battle than face a psychiatric interview, have been fortunate in their enemies or had misfortune with the psychiatrists, or are unfortunate in the burden they carry of hostile or persecuting phantasies. Directly after the psychiatrist's talk they settle down to Board Questionnaires and the Intelligence Tests.

If time permits, the psychiatrist sees the candidates while they fill up the Medical Questionnaire, to answer any questions that may arise in that connection.

That afternoon and evening the psychiatrist spends about five hours in making notes from the documents (Questionnaires I and II, the Self-Description, Word Association Test results, Thematic Apperception Test results and other attached papers), so that when the candidate is next seen something is known about him.

The candidates' next view of the psychiatrist is while they are in Group Discussion, where he silently takes notes. The Group Discussion is usually divided into two parts: a free discussion and that projective test turned into a parlour-game which we call the Train Journey. This gives the psychiatrist a chance to see the candidate handling a group situation and to observe his manner of opening a talk with the passenger of his choice. Speaking for myself, this last is the most important single clue, more important than even the Self-Description, to the way the psychiatric interview should be handled.

The best way to put the candidate at his ease is to give him just that which he has been led to expect. So I begin by asking him about his civil job and what led him to choose it, what he liked best in it, how his experience in it has helped him in the Army and in what he found disappointment.

The manner of discourse is conversational, having on the writing pad on my knee the details of his own, his father's and maybe his brother's jobs, details from his Self-Description and Word Association Test. I do not refer to documents during the interview, but from his records interpolate questions and information, so that the talk is fluid and balanced by informed statement from my side, not at all a string of questions. Indeed the only interrogations I at all regularly employ are those which psychoanalytic practice has shown me are least disturbing even in highly unbalanced and nervous people—for example, "How old were you at that time?"

So the first point is that the candidate gets what he has been led to expect—that is, a talk about his relation to his job.

On conducting an interview with an ambitious candidate

The second point is that from his manner of handling this interview situation of friendly enquiry I judge how next to proceed. Suppose we take as an example a pushing, ambitious type of fellow. If he speaks of the prospects and hopes he had built up I may recall similar details from his documents, and then I need to find out if in his career there was a regard for people as people or whether the world was only his oyster. Then, and particularly if he chose an ambitious egoist for the Train Journey, we get to talking about the people he modelled himself on. His father maybe is introduced here (for usually by this time he will be ready to describe his father to me), men his seniors in business, his relatives and friends, then he is led to speak of school.

It seems to me that at a WOSB, the ambition of many candidates is specially aflame and in these in particular it is important to know to what extent and how readily they may be got to speak of persons as *persons* directly after they have been dilating on their projects and successes. This young fellow will, if he can, try to use me; by his push and vigour he will persuade me that he is the very man for the job. But the Army needs in an officer one who will befriend his men as well as one who will bedevil the enemy. The battery of outside tests, obstacles and the like may give a measure of his dash; we need also a test for his capacity for "compassion".

Well, I know of none that as easily and patently demonstrates *compassion* as some of the obstacles show up *dash;* I know of no questions whose answers stenographically recorded will prove this gift of compassion. But what the psychiatrist can do is to arrange a social setting so that if a person, though caught up in the narration of his ambitious dreams, is brought up against a situation where his sense of obligation to others, his capacity for considerateness is present in himself and a potent factor in his personal relationships, then it will have a chance to express itself.

I ask myself at this point of the interview: how far am I being used as an instrument in his designs, how far is he allowing me to guide his imagination—now this way to his career, now that way to his home life—and how far is he ready to let me see, or in any way to share, as an equal, in the good and pleasant things he has experienced.

After I have got a provisional glimpse of this candidate's social relationships and seen how he has managed the interview, I endeavour to discuss other aspects of his life which would corroborate this first impression or lead me to examine other directions of his personality development.

Finally, I watch him after the interview is ostensibly ended, particularly as he is going out of the door, for at this point he may betray a cynical or contemptuous attitude which he could control when sitting during what he regarded as the interview proper.

On conducting an interview with a shy candidate

Let us now discuss, as an example, another type of candidate, a shy man aged between 25 and 30 years old. Starting again with the civilian job, it is usually easy within a couple of minutes to get him talking of his daily work; the conversation is then led to his difficulty in meeting people. Next as a rule my *time question* is brought in: "Now looking back over your life," I say to him, "tell me when you really began to get over your shyness." The normal answer is that he hasn't overcome his shyness yet; my answer to this is, "be that as it may, the situation is no doubt better now, and if we can find what brought an improvement in the past, we can see in what way you can help yourself still further in this matter in the future".

The point of this approach is just to give the candidate a reassuring feeling that the psychiatrist views impediments as something that can be overcome; the usual result is that he talks fairly freely and in detail of his shyness, of when he is shy and when not. This gives material for studying his social relationships.

It is a kind of *quid pro quo*: he gives the psychiatrist rather embarrassing details of his shyness, in return he gets a method of dealing with his difficulty. Almost invariably such candidates leave the interview relieved and appreciative and often thank the psychiatrist, it is sincere, for the privilege of the interview.

It must be remembered that on a Selection Board a psychiatrist's duty is not psychotherapeutic, but it is useful to employ a therapeutic technique for the purpose of getting a fuller picture of the candidate's past experiences and present personality. Those not trained in psychotherapeutic procedure are at a disadvantage when such devices are called for.

The psychiatric silence

While speaking of psychotherapeutic procedures I may mention a powerful diagnostic technique, whose method is inconspicuous, namely, what I call the *psychiatric silence*. It is particularly useful in cases where the candidate is one who blusters or bluffs his way through difficulties, or tries to. When he has brought this aspect of his personality forward the psychiatrist becomes a relaxed, attentive listener, lacking impatience, lacking special interests, blandly curious about whatsoever the candidate says. Those who try "to work up an effect" find this bland silence particularly trying. The psychiatrist has at this point to *watch himself* to see whether he is getting an irrelevant satisfaction from the effect he also works up to. His aim should be to keep his mind alert to the drift of the candidate's talk, to watch him to see if he talks to "blind with science" the officer before him, to flatter him or to see if be collapses under the strain and starts an appeasement policy. The non-responding but attentive psychiatrist may turn into a persecuting figure in his mind, or into a friendly one, or into a fool to be kicked out of the way. Whichever role he unconsciously chooses to put me in, I accept and let the situation develop. If the candidate's behaviour is a surprise to himself, then we have at once a measure of his insight; if he seems to be heading for a familiar tirade, then we know something of his underlying personal relationships. In either case, as soon as the psychiatrist has got the diagnostic information he wants, he breaks the silence and steers the talk to easier and more reassuring channels.

The duration of these *psychiatric silences* seldom exceeds two or three minutes and at their conclusion they can be sealed off with an ordinary amount of psychiatric skill and experience.

The prognostic significance of the psychiatric interview

We may now touch on a matter of some importance, both in psychiatric practice and in the work of WOSBs, namely, the significance of the interview for disclosing the spontaneous behaviour of the candidate when under strain.

To many candidates the psychiatric interview is more of a strain than, say, the interview with the President even, or than the outside tests. The reason for this is that the boundaries of the psychiatric investigation are not clearly defined in the candidate's mind. If he is uncertain of himself he is liable to imagine the widest and wildest variety of probes and investigations into his personality, and to fear that his weaknesses will surely be found out! If such is his dread he will take defensive or evasive measures against such onslaughts. Now in the field of action, till action begins, there are some elements in common with this situation; weaknesses will be tested, the most frightful onslaughts will be made upon him, and he will have no supporters. I am aware that the difficulties in the interview are internal, whereas in the field of action there is a source of strain that is external, but it is now well known that where the internal difficulties are great, the external stresses are more likely to prove overwhelming.

Considerations of this kind lead me to view the prognostic significance of the psychiatric interview as important.

We can approach the problem from another angle. There are people whose mental make-up is such that they wear a friendly and reassuring mask, but at the same time have a tendency to hurt the feelings of those dependent on them or who show friendliness to them. They are usually quite unaware of this tendency which may be called an *unwitting negative attitude*. Such people lack the quality that was called earlier in this paper *compassion*.

In the field of battle the soldier is called upon to exert the utmost ruthlessness to the enemy and the utmost consideration to those on his own side. The boundary between the disposition of love and hate impulses is clearly drawn. Clinical investigations show that of those who are much given to the unwitting *negative attitude* to their friends, a proportion adopt an appeasing attitude to the enemy. They may be witty and amusing in company but they are not reliable in action. It seems to me that the duty specially falls upon the psychiatrist to spot these sources of danger.

The sealing-off process

There is another device in an interview related to the *sealing-off* technique; it is designed to leave the candidate with the feeling that he has had a square deal; he is asked if he has any questions he would like to put to the psychiatrist. The tables are turned in favour of the candidate. This fulfils the promise made on the first day, that the Board would be ready to answer questions, though the candidate is not directed to ask any particular ones. Of course, the questions he puts are turned back for him to answer, the amount of help he needs being a measure of his grasp of the situation.

As a rule in longer interviews this matter comes up halfway through, because after it the candidate feels more ready to talk. If the candidate is seen towards the end of the three days he is asked to comment on the tests if he wishes.

These two questions throw light on his relation to the officers on the Board, and on his capacity to think freely in their presence and to criticise their work in a constructive (or destructive) way without loss of social contact.

The reason WOSBs were so effective is that the candidates' responses were seen and evaluated in a *social setting*. What we needed to know about these men was their capacity to endure and manipulate intra-group tensions so that hostile impulses will be turned out towards the enemy and their friendly impulses will strengthen morale in their own unit. The psychiatrist was in a favourable position to make estimates of this potentiality, because he was first seen as an officiating member of the Board, then in his interview he moved from the detachment of an assessing officer to a talk about the candidate's own adjustments to social and personal relationships and finally, with the sealing off process, returned to the impersonal position again. The candidate's capacity to follow these moves was a measure of his social flexibility.

To conclude, I will return to the interview again and ask, what should have been the feeling in the mind of both candidate and psychiatrist? I think they should have felt that both have learnt something interesting and valuable about the candidate and the candidate in his turn should have been able to realise that he has discovered something new and interesting and valuable in Army methods.

CHAPTER 7

The influence of the "social field" on behaviour in the interview situation

(1943)

It is sometimes permitted in scientific work to use the broadest or, if you prefer, the crudest generalisations if by so doing a new point of view be thus obtained and a new basis established for making more exact observations. Two such crude generalisations will now be considered; both employ the concept of "psychological or social movement".

We can simplify the relation of the organism to its objects, to one of simple positive or negative "tropisms" or movements. If the object is "good" the organism desires to approach it, to hold it within its grasp, to have more of it, to wish that its like may never perish from the earth. We might say that in certain cases the organism "loves" that object, or simplifying still further we can say that the relation is a "positive" one. If the object is "bad" the organism desires to put a distance between the object and itself, to shun it, to have less of it, to wish that its like may perish from the earth. We might say that in certain cases the organism "hates" the object, or simplifying still further we can say the relation is a "negative" one.

The terms *good object* and *bad object* have no moral connotations whatsoever. They refer to the kind of relationship, positive or negative,

---

This paper was compiled by the Editor from a series of appendices originally attached to chapter 6, which were written by John Rickman while he was working as a Major on a War Office Selection Board, during 1942–44.

subsisting between this particular individual and that particular object or class of objects. Indeed, the only criterion as to whether an object, for this individual, is to be classed as good or bad is his behaviour towards it. His statements about it may, of course, be at variance with his deeds.

The interplay of forces between the "social field" and the "personal field"

The quality *good* or *bad* is, of course, not always a constant one in respect to an individual's relation to a particular object. It depends on the resultant of forces within the personality and, in particular, on the inter-play between the forces in the external or social *field* and the internal or *personal field*, many of the latter forces being unconscious (Rickman, 1950.)

An object can be a person or a thing. It can also be a group of people, and, further, it can be an *atmosphere*, a mood or *feeling* in a group of people of which the individual is a member. Thus a person may not have any particular ties to the members of a group, but he may enjoy the social atmosphere which that group creates. If we express this in terms of movement, in such a case he would do what he could to keep the group together and not to disrupt it by unpleasantness. His endeavour would be to keep every member of the group in such a frame of mind that they regarded the existence of the group as a pleasant experience, so that their *movement* in respect to it would then be *positive*.

If we apply the same simplified concepts to the behaviour of groups, we can think of a group, usually unwittingly and quite spontaneously, creating an atmosphere which is group-cohesive or group-destructive. The forces which produce these effects are probably, though not certainly, of much the same character as are operative in the positive and negative movements between an individual and his object. People vary in the degree to which they contribute to a positive or negative *group-movement*. Their influence could be called *group-centripetal* or *group-centrifugal* respectively, meaning that their presence and activities tend to increase a positive and cohesive group feeling or a negative and disruptive group feeling.

Ego-development viewed as the growth of an "internal society"

If we employ the concepts of Kurt Lewin (Lewin, 1941), we can distinguish two kinds of approach to the problems of clinical psychology and to the problems of the War Office Selection Boards. In the one approach the question is "What *type* of man is this", while in the other, it is "What *forces* are at work here?" The former tends to a static, the latter to a dynamic, view of clinical medicine. If we follow the latter view, in the light of recent developments in psychopathology, we may come to the notion that an individual can be regarded as a *field of forces* in which the component elements, though operating of course in the present time, had in some cases their origin in past events. In a word, personality is a composite structure growing round a central, ever developing, ego-nucleus. There are two ways of looking at this process of growth. One is in terms of a moulding of the ego which is pictured as a plastic recipient of impressions, and the other is in terms of an agglutinative process, so that personalities, or aspects of them, experienced particularly in the formative and impressionable years, are incorporated into the ego-system and continue to be active within that system. (This is another way of describing superego formation in terms of field theory.) If we do not think of the effect of social experiences and the influence of up-bringing in terms of the "conditioning" of a reflex system (a notion not without its usefulness in a restricted field of research), but think of them as adding to the number and character of *"personality inclusions"* which are retained within the ego-system, then we can go a step further and think of a group of forces within the personality which are, and often even by the subject actually can be, related to persons of importance in the past. The personality in action, to use an analogy from the WOSB, is like a candidate-group doing a group task; but, of course, with this difference: whereas the candidates are all separate people, assembled for tests and all present to the consciousness of the others all the time, in this analogy there is only one body visible. The other members of the group are invisible, present only as incorporations within the personality, in many cases not appearing in consciousness, but all of them nevertheless exerting an influence hardly less than if they had been at a family conference. In a word, the complexity of human personality and our knowledge of its growth justifies us in constructing a working hypothesis of it as if it were a Group Structure, and highly structured. There is an internal *society* which, through the mediation of what we commonly call "the ego", is in constant and ever changing inter-play with the *external society.*

A description of the social structure and the social dynamics of a WOSB

To illustrate some of the points I have made, I would like to describe the sequence of events in a particular WOSB and to show the place of the psychiatric interview in the social dynamics of the Board's activities.

The candidates come individually to the railway station on Sunday or Wednesday. They are first brought together as a group by the Sergeant Major, who meets them and bundles them into a lorry. On arrival they are divided into squads, and each subgroup of eight or ten is shown its own Nissen hut. They are told they will sleep, eat and work together as a group. They have lunch at their own tables, their first common or shared activity. After lunch they go to the gymnasium and "Theatre" where they may sit where they like for the President's Opening Address and for the Written Tests. At this point, the relationships in candidates' groups are unstructured. The President and other officers now file in, and the two talks mentioned previously [see chapter 6] are given, so that the President and the psychiatrist emerge from their officer-subgroup for a few moments to address the candidate-group as a whole. They then recede into their officer-subgroup, which files out of the hall, leaving the psychologist, who speaks about the Tests as a member of the officer-subgroup to the whole candidate-group. Any candidate can ask questions, of course. After tea the psychiatrist, time permitting, goes down to answer queries about the Medical Questionnaire as a Medical Officer member of the officer-subgroup. At the first supper the Military Testing Officers have their meal with the officer-subgroup. not with the candidates. After supper the Military Testing Officer gives a talk to his own candidate-subgroup. From this moment to the end of the board, the Military Testing Officer leaves the officer-subgroup (except for sleeping, tea and breakfast) and has meals with and spends about eight hours a day with his subgroup. His opening words to his candidates, "We are a Group (A, B, C, etc.) and I am your Military Testing Officer, and my name is ____", indicate that he joins their subgroup. The Military Testing Officer assists his subgroup with advice about the concert, given on the last evening (Tuesday or Friday), that is he shares with his candidates some of the responsibility for amusing the other candidate-subgroups, the Staff, the Auxiliary Territorial Service and visitors. On the morning of the Board (Wednesday or Saturday) the President alone gives a farewell address to the whole candidate-group. After this address the candidates file in one by one to the Board Meeting, and meet the officer-subgroup for the second and last time. Immediately after the Board interview the Sergeant Major recovers the candidate's arm bands, and they reacquire individual status.

In passing it should be pointed out that Psychiatric Interviews for follow-up purposes after the Board is over are unsatisfactory, because not only is the lorry waiting at the door to take the candidates away, but the social structure of the WOSB has been broken up, by then, for that particular group of candidates.

Returning to the outline of the social structure and the movement of individuals past a subgroup barrier to meet for interview a member of the officer-subgroup, it will be noted that a candidate has to make this passage normally on two occasions: when he interviews the President or his deputy and when he sees the psychiatrist. A candidate coming to the psychiatrist for a minor medical or surgical treatment traverses the barrier, and the reason for this should be sought. It may be due to accident-proneness, or to a wish to relate himself to a member of the officer-subgroup as an individual, to get sympathy, special attention or masochistically to show his sores, or a wish to get away from his own subgroup. The reason is usually more psycho-social than organic-medico-surgical.

The candidates may also have Psychological Re-tests. This is often done on the whole intake (the opportunity is usually appreciated). Perhaps because tests are usually done by a Sergeant, the barrier-crossing is not conspicuous, chiefly, I think, because the result of the test is thought to be for the officer-subgroup as a whole.

On the two occasions when a member of the candidate-group and of the officer-subgroup must leave their subgroups, during their several interviews, both must cross barriers to meet as individuals. When the interview is over each returns to his subgroup and the contact is a group-to-group one again.

On the social structure and the dynamics of the interview relationship

Within this highly structured setting the psychiatrist has to construct a social framework in which to operate and to be aware of its boundaries and its relation to the social structure of which it is a part. The view that the Psychiatric Interview is a simple personal relationship, particularly when the two participating units are in the Army, is one which, in my opinion, ignores important though admittedly complicated psychological factors.

At this particular Board the psychiatric interview was usually held in a sumptuously furnished, fantastic "Chinese Room" with a fine view; the pictures on the walls, unlike so many others in the house, were restful to the eye and did not inflame the imagination. Visitors to the Board often asked whether the room did not put the candidates off. Some asked "Where is the soothsayer's crystal?" As a Thematic Apperception Test it was, at times, useful. With some candidates, on or soon after entering the room, their attention got fixed on the red lacquer, pagoda-like hangings and other "Sino-Tottenham-Court-Road" oddities; this I learned to interpret as part of the candidate's flight from a personal relationship.

I would now like to mention an experiment. On my arrival at this Board I found installed in the Chinese Room a psychiatrist, my junior in years, rank and psychiatric experience. I was introduced to the candidates in a humble apartment—my domestically furnished bedroom on the top floor—which was once the night-nursery of the tycoon's palace which housed the Selection Board. I did not expect the simple furnishings to attract the candidates' attention. To my surprise many looked puzzled, then let their eyes wander round the roost and their gaze return to the crown on my shoulder. My room had no door-plate. The Chinese Room, on the other hand, had PSYCHIATRIST written in large capitals over the door and the name of the captain-occupant at eye level. Though I often asked, from no single candidate did I get an explanation of their puzzled look, which incidentally shows the relatively shallow level at which the talk proceeded, which was far removed from the relaxed free-association level of psychoanalytic procedures. My inference, from their looking now at my crowns, now at the plain, rickety painted furniture, was that the mild bewilderment was due to their rumination about the social relationship existing between the Senior Psychiatrist and the rest of the Board and particularly the Junior Psychiatrist. "Why this banishment to an attic?" was my guess at the reason for their behaviour. Whether it was a topic of conversation among the candidates, or whether it influenced their social approach at a lower, less-conscious, level only, I did not discover. I do know this, that after the Junior Psychiatrist had left the Board, my crowns were hardly ever glanced at in an interview and that when candidates looked about the room, I could usually tell from the context that their mind is turning *away* from something, not, as in the attic, ruminating *about* something.

This experience stimulated further experiments. For a time I turned over the Chinese Room almost exclusively to Psychological Re-Tests and interviewed the candidates in a French-windowed, lavishly equipped bedroom with a balcony, or, weather permitting, on the balcony itself. There was no crown gazing here, practically no looking about. But balcony-interviews, even though screened from gaze when seated, were not satisfactory.

That "walls have ears" is true of only a small proportion of cases, mostly those struggling against persecutory ideas; but can one say "Outdoors is all eyes" of a greater proportion of people? I think this self-consciousness is more strong *vis-à-vis* a psychiatrist than in most other interviews. I observed that the relationship of candidates to a Military Testing Officer *protected* the candidates from self-consciousness before outsiders. This *protection* was a function of the special social *role* of the Military Testing Officer, which enables him to be in the subgroup of candidates and also attached to the subgroup of the Staff, who are all members of the main WOSB group. To test my theory, I moved the candidate and myself back through the French window during a number of interviews and got a more direct contact in every case after the move and sometimes immediately after the move. Later, I returned to my attic and sometimes interviewed there while Sergeants gave the Koh's Blocks test in the Chinese Room. This time there was no crown gazing nor bewildered scrutiny of the job-lot furniture, because, I surmised, there was no thought of intra-group tensions in the candidates' minds.

All this may be interpreted thus: The physical attributes of an interview-room probably play far less part in influencing the atmosphere or rapport of the Psychiatric Interview than does the social relation of the psychiatrist to his own subgroup, the Staff of the Board, or to be more precise, what the candidates imagine that relationship to be. If they think the psychiatrist is banished to an attic they are disturbed. If he moves freely, they will approach as freely to meet him, or tend to do so. What hesitations occur will result from their own mental make-up; their hesitations and temporary detachment will not be precipitated in the psychiatric situation by tension already existing (or thought to exist) in a social field they are entering.

This last point is perhaps important. What I have called the officer-subgroup to the candidate represents both the high authority of adviser to the Army Council and also a social-group (the class of officer) which he is about to enter. He is in a state of great sensitiveness to the mood and interpersonal relationship existing between the officers on the Board. It may be that as psychiatry develops, more attention will have to be paid to studying the effect on the candidate or patient of the social tensions within the observing group of which the psychiatrist is a member. Our technique for studying the effect of intra-group tensions, of a positive or friendly, as well as of a negative or hostile kind, upon the individual, particularly as they affect his capacity for social mobility, for example, when entering another group, is in its infancy. When that time comes it should be more possible to describe the manifestations of the candidate's personality relative to the field of social forces in which they appear. Perhaps the WOSBs have afforded a favourable occasion for such observations, for candidates were seen in the social setting of their subgroup, those with whom they did their tests, with whom they slept and had their meals; no less did the candidates observe us, the officers, in the subgroup with whom we ourselves slept, ate and worked. The aquarium in which we all swam had at most glass partitions; one lot of fish were residents, the other lot were visitors-on-probation. It was natural for the behaviour of the visitors to be affected by the social atmosphere of the residents. The forces that affected the candidates thus did not need, of course, to be apparent to the residents themselves, unless they were ready to observe it.

The three-day scheme to select officers has been described as "Exercise Goldfish", but this bowl has no sides: all are observers, all are observed.

CHAPTER 8

The technique of interviewing in anthropology and psychoanalysis

(1949)

The study of the technique of interviewing is a difficult, and I think a very important undertaking, for it is one of the main methods by which we collect the data used in the human sciences. Anthropologists in the main, from the data they choose and collect, *describe the structure and function* of social communities; I, as a psychiatrist specialising in psychoanalysis, am employed by people who are aware of their lack of adjustment, or by relatives of these people, to effect a better harmony with themselves and between themselves and the community in which they live; that is, my job is to produce a *change of function*.

Anthropology may be called pure research. In my kind of work, the answers to questions I want to put must come second to the need to find a solution to the patient's problems. I would hesitate to apply such a lordly title as "research" to the method I use, were it not for the fact that something essential to the research worker is a necessary ingredient in the attitude of those who follow it.

The work of anthropologists and psychoanalysts is alike in this, in that both depend on skill in establishing and maintaining a particular kind of human relation called an interview.

Read before the Royal Anthropological Society, 1949.

In both cases we are in need of information which can only be got from the person or the group of persons we talk with. But the list of similarities soon ends, for in his self-appointed tasks the anthropologist does not have to make the information of use to his interlocutor; in my task that is essential. In his task the data are for the most part readily within the span of memory and conscious realisation of his informants; in mine the process is more in the nature of a joint enterprise to discover something that neither party knows, or at least has not fully realised before. And there is a further difference. In his work, the anthropologist is troubled to find an incentive that will keep his informant continually informing *him*. In my work the incentive—pain—is plentifully present. The patient wants to get rid of his incentive. The trouble is to keep him continually willing to collect information about himself (the parting with the information is less difficult), for he resists self-knowledge.

The diagnostic interview

The handling of a psychiatric case that proves suitable for psychoanalytic therapy may, as regards interview technique, be reckoned to have two stages: the first is diagnostic, the second therapeutic. In the first stage, the psychoanalyst endeavours to get as exact a description as possible of the patient's complaints, and then to obtain a personal and family history with particular reference to similar occurrences of mental pain or worry which the patient suffered earlier in his life. This process is called a *"history taking"*. All events are threaded together along the development in time of this single and particular individual. The object of the investigation is to discover how this person comes to behave today, this very day, in the way he does now. The underlying idea being that only by making a study of the origins of the present-day personality, with its multitude of troubles and joys, will the present be fully understood. This genetic study is essentially *historical*. But if psychoanalytic treatment is begun the method is essentially *a-historical*. The focus of attention is on what is occurring at the very moment of speaking in the interview; nothing exists for a certainty that is not being experienced at the moment—the rest is more like hearsay. This situation is so important and in some aspects so peculiar that I must expand it, but before doing so we should consider the diagnostic interview in more detail. The patient seemingly is in primary need of having his complaint understood, he is in some sort of pain of mind (and maybe of body too), and he will submit to an examination of his private and family life from a professional man whom he believes competent and willing to relieve him of his suffering. One kind of barrier is down, that which inhibits the normal person from speaking of his weakness, failures and shameful thoughts and impulses, or more correctly, it is partially down. The interview is a two-way process: the patient gives information to the physician in exchange for an understanding of his condition that will lead to the relief of suffering. A great deal of painful information can be given provided that there is a corresponding relief of mental strain.

Lest you should think that the value of the two-way process is peculiar to interviews with neurotic patients, I would like to report on 2,000 interviews I had during the war with candidates for Army Commissions. Here the starting point of the interview was certainly not that of a history of mental suffering. They knew I was a psychiatrist, or "trick-cyclist" in army slang. Many of them had heard frightful rumours about these interviews, but in the great majority of cases to my simple remark, "Well, tell me about yourself", they answered frankly, and surprisingly often in a short time, with matters concerning their personality that puzzled them. Those people had to be helped on the way to the solution of those puzzles. Though employed by the War Office to advise the Selection Boards on the suitability of the candidates for a commission, my terms of employment and specialist pay included my role as a psychiatrist, and as such I had to help solve problems of personality when asked by the person concerned. From the War Office point of view the time thus spent was well spent. I was able to use the data obtained through this matching process, in which thousands of people were interviewed under the same conditions, to draw what are called "personality profiles" for each member of the series.

A *matching process* best describes the psychiatrist's work in the diagnostic phase. The conditions of interview are kept as constant as possible. Personally I do not employ any small talk about the weather or similar social introductions, but go straight to the point, "What may I do for you?" I never mention anything of interest to myself, keep the conversation as flat as possible in choice of language and range of inflection. The room is furnished with reasonable comfort and unobtrusively; I smoke and offer cigarettes or tobacco, the only action of an ordinary human being—the rest is strictly professional. This dull shade of sociableness enables me to see more clearly what the person interviewed does with the situation he is offered. Studies often have dull-coloured walls. My psychiatric presence is socially dull in order that I may more easily perceive the social and personal colouring of those I interview.

You will have noticed that I have shifted the frame of reference somewhat when speaking of the psychiatric-diagnostic interview. I began by referring to data concerning the patient's complaints and his past history, and I have just ended by reference to such intangible things as the "social colouring" or mood of the interview. The kind of mood or colouring which the patient introduces into the interview, nay, *forces* upon the interview is, provided that the psychiatrist remains in his role, part of the essential data for the diagnosis. The psychiatrist's aim, to use a familiar simile, is to be a blank screen on to which the patient unwittingly will project his own phantasies. The patient will try to get the psychiatrist to play a role, the nature of which is determined in some part by the patient's conscious wishes, but in larger part by his unconscious desires and fears.

The psychiatrist's art in this two-body relationship is to be sensitive to the smaller indications, which the patient unwittingly gives, of the role that he is thrusting upon his physician. The psychiatrist must listen on two levels at once: one is a conscious level, and the other is an unconscious one. For example, a rather boisterous patient who begins an interview with the remark that he believes in frankness, and says, "if you don't trust your doctor or your lawyer or banker, where are you", may respond to a gentle non-committal silence at this point with the remark, "yes, I know what you are thinking, you are wondering how you can catch the fellow out". Such a one must be listened to on two levels. On one level he is trying to be polite and reassuring to his doctor, he is trying to reassure himself; but, on the other level, he is suspicious, he wants to test his interlocutor and trap him into some action which will justify his own secretiveness, But if this should happen, he would then be without the helper he needs. This dilemma is painful; what happens is that if the suspiciousness is ascribed to the psychiatrist, the patient then can regard himself as straightforward in his personal relationships. If the psychiatrist had answered to the first remarks by saying that he himself was to be trusted, that he kept confidences, the Hippocratic Oath, and so on, my experience shows that he would not have got the second statement, at least in the naive form in which it was presented. The psychiatrist can seldom respond to a single statement; he must first sense the patterns of attitude which the patient presents both wittingly and unwittingly.

How does the psychiatrist sense these rather subtle intentions of the patient? The answer is by a gentle but inward compliance with what the patient pushes upon him. To react overtly to the patient's behaviour is foolish. To put up a barrier of resistance to what the patient desires of him is equally foolish. The useful course is to be willing to let the patient, in limited degree, work on one's feelings, but remain sensitive to the movement thus created at an early phase of the action.

You will have guessed by now what is one of the principal instruments of this kind of research. It is, of course, the receptiveness to small changes of direction in human relationships *within the physician himself.* It sounds dreadfully unscientific, but there are measures for reducing somewhat the waywardness of human feelings in this sort of social contact. For example, the psychoanalysts in the course of their training give about 1,000 hours to this task spread over a period of four years, first with a personal analysis and then with 300 hours of supervised analysis of selected cases. The aim of this training is to get the practitioner's own mind supple in sensing the patient's moods and intentions and in not reading his own ideas into the mind and expressions of his interlocutor. This is one part of what I call the "social instrument" of psychoanalytic research. I think this point has some relevance to certain kinds of anthropological research too, but less to the pure than to the operational research. To understand the other part of the "social instrument" it is necessary to explain the postulate on which the whole of psychoanalysis (and all its derivatives) is based—namely, that when a person allows his mind to wander freely any two ideas that emerge to consciousness in temporal contiguity are linked in meaning. The person may not see the meaning which underlies both ideas—that is quite another matter—but there is a link all the same; the mind cannot jump out of its own context so to speak. This useful postulate alone is not sufficient to carry the research worker far, but with the aid of the four laws governing the processes of dream work which Freud set out in his *Interpretation of Dreams,* further light is thrown on the link in the meaning of associated ideas.

The influence of past emotional experiences on the psychiatric interview

I want to go back to the other part of the "social instrument" of psychoanalytic research. The patient is told to say whatever comes into his mind, and to let anything come in. With the aids to understanding I have just mentioned, the analyst listens to the flow of ideas. To begin with they related to recently experienced worries and mental pains. It soon becomes clear that the character of the associations is being influenced by factors at first not at all prominent, i.e. characteristics ascribed to the analyst by the patient. These characteristics are not conjured up anew; they relate to persons relevant to the patient's past history. In a word, the patient is trying though unwittingly to find in the present a solution for present unsolved problems and also—though he does not realise this—unsolved emotional problems of the past. Regarding those two levels on which I said the psychiatrist had to listen, the unconscious one is that which is expressing past unsolved problems. The situations that thus press for re-attention but in a disguised form are early experiences screened from memory by the barrier of an infantile amnesia. The task of the psychotherapy of individuals is to overcome the resistance to the memory of those old and painful experiences and to liberate the energy which was being wasted by holding them repressed.

The reason why I introduce all of this about repressed infantile experience in a paper about interview technique is that it illustrates a point I wish to make, namely, that this class of important data can only be got by a process of interview in which a prodigious deal of effort is required to overcome an active resistance to change; even though the patient is suffering acutely he cannot easily relinquish the defences set up in his mind against any alteration to those defences. He is afraid to change them. Only by the experience of a relief from his suffering can he gather sufficient energy and courage to make another attempt to effect a change—a consciously desired change—within himself. So clear is this within the field of which I am speaking that some of us have coined the phrase "No Research without Therapy, and No Therapy without Research". I emphasise "within the field of which I am speaking"; but what is that field? It is any field in which anxiety and guilt operate to the extent of altering behaviour. Only when the research worker has shown himself ready to face along with the subject of his research the painful influence of anxiety and guilt, when the research worker's bona fide has been tested by the subject and the latter is convinced that the next step in the investigation will be profitable, because the last one was, only then will the next step be taken to disclose and investigate a further series of experiences which involve a study of the misery of insecurity and fear and guilt.

The psychiatric interview and other research techniques

Now a great deal of valuable research has been done in psychology in which the research worker has thought out the questions to which he wants answers, has gone to his subjects, interrogated them and made experiments upon them, and has never come upon a trace of what I have been talking about: he has met with no resistances, nor seen a sign of anxiety or guilt—indeed, for him and his researches such things might not exist. Further, throughout the investigation, and after, he has seen no sign that his subjects have had problems of their own to solve, or if they have such problems these certainly have not interfered with the research. How is the discrepancy to be explained?

I must remind you that there are two kinds of research—pure research and operational research. It is in the latter kind, where the research worker and his subject are both involved in an undertaking the failure of which would mean a great sacrifice to both—it is in operational research that these awkward, but I must add *revealing*, resistances are met with. If they do not occur in pure research I can only conclude that it must be the intention of the planners of it that these awkward things should not appear.

The greater part of my remarks have been concerned with the two-way traffic between psychiatrist and his patient, the latter employing the doctor to perform a job of work, usually for a fee. But there is also another kind of research where the investigator is called in by a group of people to bring about a better adjustment in the social relationships existing in that group.

It we construct a frame of reference in respect to the relation of the research worker to his employer we have at the one end the pure research worker, who is self-employed and who seeks for answers to his own questions, and at the other end the operational research worker, who is employed by the persons he investigates and who has to settle their problems before answering his own. In between and nearer to the "pure" end are the group expeditions, organised by Haddon, for example, in 1898, who took with him to the Torres Straits Doctors Rivers, Myers and McDougall (I mention this in affection, for they were my teachers). But there is now another class of work, i.e. where the investigator is an employee of a paramount power. Clearly such investigators are not free agents. They are subject to pressure from their employer to find means to carry out the policy of the paramount power, and this hinders an intimacy of contact with the people they investigate. Such intimacy, such fusion of interests, is essential for operational research.

Let us return to operational research where the investigator is called in to effect an adjustment in communal relationships. His technique is not the same as in an individual interview but rather it is that of a clarifier at a conference. He has to bear in mind that there are two agendas for the conference: a written one and an unwritten one. The former is in the consciousness of all those present; the latter, the unwritten agenda, is a general name for all of the items—the aspirations which have not yet been verbalised by the individuals or collectively by the group, i.e. things they need to have done in order to lesson their mental stresses.

This kind of operational research is in its infancy. The work is exceedingly difficult. The casualty rate is enormous, i.e. the investigation is often stopped by the very community who called in the aid of the investigator. This is very reminiscent of the early days of psychotherapy, when the *number* of failures to achieve an adjustment within the individual was considerable. But the important feature of this kind of research activity is that it is concerned with the social forces operating in the community concerned. This study of group-tension deals with the moment-to-moment oscillations between group-cohesive and group-disruptive forces, forces which often prevent group decision where hasty action is undesirable. The pioneer in this field of research, in my view, is Dr W. R. Bion, whose first exposition on group tensions was published in *The Lancet* in 1943 [see chapter 12], and whose later contributions were published in *Human Relations* (1948). No one should even begin to undertake this kind of work who desires above all things to live a peaceful life. In the group interview of the kind I have in mind, it is often found that one of the first things the group does is roundly to attack the person they have called in to help them, because he does not provide them with an agenda they can work to—this, be it noted, before even the outlines of their problem are clear. It sounds stupid, but—hard though it is for humanity to realise—an unstructured group in distress at its incompetence to cope with its own group-disruptiveness does often what seem to be foolish things. Indeed, we find with groups, as we find with individuals, that they will go to great lengths to conceal from themselves the nature of their dilemmas, at least such of them as arise in the main from their own instability of purpose and from the conflicting nature of their own aspirations. And, as is the case with the treatment of individuals, the therapy of groups can only go step by step in assisting the process of self-understanding as step by step they are relieved of some of their intra-group tensions.

I have given a warning that this kind of research is not for those who pine for a quiet life. I gave the same warning to medical students nearly thirty years ago in regard to taking up psychotherapy. The latter situation has changed—changed because the training in interview technique has improved. In another few decades the study of group dynamics may be a quieter job. Anyone who has lived through two world wars and is still brave enough to read the daily papers will not doubt that to be a member of a changing community is a strenuous activity.

I would like to end with reference to a topic that has been on my mind for many years. When reading anthropological work and hearing accounts by anthropologists of their field work, I have been struck by the static nature of the social organisations described. This is in part due to the fact that so few anthropologists live long enough in the communities they study to be able to observe changes, and partly because they want to get the structure of these organisations clearly defined, for purposes of comparison. Just as the psychiatrist observes many persons pass through his more or less constant psychiatric interview situation in order to draw profiles of the different types of patient, i.e. he is an investigator of the structure of the personality, so anthropologists pass a great number of groups under review with the same end in view. The psychoanalyst, on the other hand, passes the same patient through the same analytic interview situation very many times and thus the analyst gets a view of changing structure, i.e. functions. "A structure", as Lundberg (1939) says, "is merely a persistent function, while a function is merely a series of changing structures."

PART III

DISRUPTIVE FORCES IN GROUP RELATIONS

CHAPTER 9

Does it take all kinds to make a world? Uniformity and diversity in communities

(1938)

I would like to explore the question implicit in the title of this paper, "Does it take all kinds to make a world?" If we are philosophers, we shall say that there are only two answers, either it does or it does not; but perhaps this answer is rather too simple. This question is a problem which is not only of importance in the immediate present, but is, I think, one of the major problems that humanity will always have to deal with.

We see at the present time two tendencies in political life: on the one hand, there is a movement to induce all of the members of a group to hold identical opinions on political and social questions; on the other hand, there is a tendency to preserve diversity in political and social

---

This paper is based on two lectures that were delivered in March 1938 in a series of public lectures sponsored by the Institute of Psychoanalysis, and which included the following topics: "Types of Groups", "The Future of Penology", "Why There Are Sects", "Primitive Social Relations", Incapacity for Work", "Emotional Life of Civilized Men and Women", "Some Guiding Principles in Upbringing", "Social Revolution", "Can Wars Be Averted?", "The Crime-Free Pacifist State: Is It an Illusion?", and "Is the Criminal Amoral?"

life. In the one case, the ideal is a single-party system; in the other, the conception of a multi-party system as essential to the political life of the community. I am not concerned here with the question, which of the two is the better system, I am only concerned to enquire what kind of satisfaction each brings to the members of the group, and what factors may play a part in causing the acceptance or rejection of either position. But before I go on to discuss the matter in more detail, it should be remembered that we find the same two tendencies in other fields than politics. In some schools, for instance, it is considered healthy for every boy to show enthusiasm for games, even if he has no inclination to do so, otherwise he will let down his school; in another institution, a boy will let down his school only if he does nothing at all, and provided that he is productive in his own way the group-spirit is satisfied. In religion we find just the same. For example, there are strong forces towards the formation of sects and at the same time towards having a Universal Catholic Church.

My problem is this: what advantage, what sense of security, is derived from uniformity in the one case or diversity in the other. The matter can be put in another form: that for the purpose of obtaining a sense of security, there is in the one case a focusing of attention on an aspect of social life which presents uniformity (or diversity), but that really the total amount of diversity and uniformity remains the same. There is merit in considering this last point, because it directs our attention to the fact that what we have to pay most attention to is the *composition* of groups, not merely to outstanding opinions; for, without necessarily defining the term in the way of types, there are all sorts of people—the question is whether we want a variety in our world or not.

The homogeneous group demanding uniformity as its group-ideal

We will take first the point of view that it is desirable to have the highest possible degree of uniformity of behaviour and opinion, that is, that the group will feel most secure from internal disruption and the individuals will feel that they are living the fullest life, if the members act and think alike, or in more psychological terms, if their impulses find expression and their fears are mastered in the same way.

This is not necessarily synonymous with fanaticism, as people usually understand the term, that is, as a wish for uniformity through the use of violence, if need be, to attain the end in view. To illustrate the concept of uniformity carried to a high pitch without physical violence, I will take an experience from my medical practice in a remote country village in Tsarist Russia. It was a village sixty miles from the railway, fifty from a metalled road, it had no telegraph, there was no big landlord within fifty miles and there were no Kulaks (landed peasants). The Staroster, or selected head village elder, came to me rather apologetically to know if I would turn "vet". Someone had gashed the hamstring muscles of his favourite white mare with an axe. While sewing up the wound we talked about the affair. A notoriously bad-tempered and evilly disposed man in the village had got the notion that the Staroster was retaining some pension-money due to a member of his family. He had been told by others that this was not the case, but still holding to his view had taken the path of private vengeance in the manner described. I asked the Staroster if the miscreant was going to be handed over to the police, and he asked in return what good that would do? It would do nothing to alter the man's views about the alleged theft of money nor to alter his disposition, and in addition his wife and family would be most undeservedly hard hit by his prison detention. No! He was a neighbour and whatever his conduct, he must be treated as such. By kindly remonstrances, but no condoning of the offence, the villagers would give him every opportunity to change his relation to their elected chief and to themselves. This forbearing treatment was adopted. The wound of the horse healed more quickly than the rage of the man cooled, but, at least for the time, the patience and forgiveness of the peasants won a victory. This illustrates the extraordinary tolerance of the monjiks towards a refractory member of their community; but it was not always the same to an outsider. In that same village after the Revolution I was asked to treat a young man who had come to them from Moscow. He was trying to instil some new ideas into them, and they endured it for as long as possible. Because he wouldn't stop, they whacked him on the head with a beer bottle and made him a case for the surgeon. Thus silenced, he became an object of pity and I was asked to go and stitch him up. If they had hit a bit harder he would have been given a respectful burial, that is, with a coffin paid for from the village chest, as they did to another man they murdered soon after. But the propagandist, on coming-to, did not wait for my ministrations, nor more of theirs, and made off. Other men from Moscow coming later showed more tact.

Here we have the same group acting first with great forbearance, later with intolerance, to what we may speak of as dangers to the cohesion of the group, dangers coming from within and without. In the case of the horse-slasher, a member of the group had erred in his ways and no effort was too great to restore harmony. The village formed a *leaderless* group, and the bond which held the members together was that they shared a *common ideal*. The assailant's conduct had not in their view put him outside the group because of the ties of affection and of kinship, and because he had once been "one of us", as they put it. His offence, furthermore, was not directed against the group as a whole, but seemed to them a personal though deluded grievance; but the propagandist had bored and insulted them as village peasants and so they had no great compunction in silencing him, for he was not "one of us". He was a menace because he might have split the monjiks into small groups, and therein lay danger. Returning to the first case and using the tools that Freud has provided, I think that we can explain the way in which the aggressive impulse was dealt with by each of the three parties. Everyone was deeply moved by the atrocity. The villagers I assume identified themselves with the criminal's destructive impulse, that is, they felt as if it was a part of themselves that had done the evil deed. This accords with our general experience that we cannot feel deeply about anything that we keep remote from our imagination. To win over a horse-slasher requires a good deal of this empathy. The villagers' relation to the Staroster was also temporarily changed; he was thought of as an injured person needing their help, and as an idealised parent-figure who does not return evil for evil. There does not seem to me to be anything strange in supposing so many different identifications going on at once, because they relate to different institutions within the mind. The identification with the criminal is a link with the instinctual part of the self (the id); they identified with the Staroster the parental figure (the ego-ideal or superego), and the bond with each other, which was strengthened by this work in common, was effected by an identification of their egos. If we consider the Staroster himself we find the same three mental institutions at work; the curbing of his revenge impulses is strengthened by his sharing an ego-ideal with the villagers. He cannot attack the criminal personally, nor redeem him personally; the identification with him is too strong. But with the support of his friends and in order that there may be no break in the spirit of love uniting them, he can hold his aggression in check.

What of the criminal? First, their quiet reproach increased his sense of guilt. It was an agony to see his remorse, I was told. For a time he kept away from everyone, and was persuaded back to join in the fellowship of the village. It was a purely moral punishment, and the period of expiation was not short. Once the conscience of every member of the community was cleared, and not before, was his own free.

On hearing this story you may think that it properly belongs to the psychology of crime, but it belongs just as much to the psychology of groups, because an important part of group-formation is doing things in common, and the curbing of aggression is itself a mental action of the greatest importance in group-formation.

I have described how those monjiks dealt with a criminal and with a propagandist. I want now to describe how they came to a decision in the Village Council or "Mir". When a topic came up for discussion someone would begin speaking in a guarded, vague and rather long-winded way; after a bit the conversation became general but in a loud voice, so that everyone could hear the tentative proposals made without either the speaker or the listeners being committed to a yea or nay. By constant repetition of argument and many contradictory assertions made by nearly everyone present, the members of the group, after several evenings' talk, arrived at a fair guess at which way the wind was blowing. Personally, I never saw a vote taken. Everyone's "face" was saved by this method. There was no minority, no one in particular had carried the meeting, no one was defeated.

The procedure is understandable if one remembers the isolated life of the group, shut off from an open labour market, tied to the soil, almost without home industries to develop personal talent and initiative. Aided by these factors, perhaps in large measure produced by them, there is a very strong drive to uniformity of thought. No man dared hold an opinion unless everyone held it, except on a philosophical problem without significance to practical or religious life. My exploration of this is that a distinction was not drawn in the unconscious between thought and action. To hold an idea in the mind which other people might disapprove of was the same thing as doing the action which follows from the thought. Thus to consider the merits of a republican regime is as dangerous as murder of the Tsar. The peasants told me that they could not hold an idea firmly in their minds if it involved politics unless everyone held it too. The conscience behaved as if the holding of an individual opinion was an unsocial act.

At this point I want to throw out some questions: When you read the account of the Staroster's horse, did you think the villagers tolerant? And did the behaviour to the propagandist show tolerance? And did the Mir, or Village Council, show tolerance? Of course, a moment's reflection shows that the same word cannot be used appropriately for the three situations. The first revealed a *forbearance* with the outbreak of hate in a member of the group, that is, a forbearance with the direct expression of instinctual gratifications. The second showed fear that outside influences would upset the equilibrium of forces within the minds of the individuals, so that they could no longer lean for support on the conscience of the community in their struggle to keep the aggressive impulses in check. The third showed, among other things, a dread of anyone achieving leadership in the group and fear of breaking up the unity in the village.

I have dealt at great length with this village group because it differs in certain important ways from the groups usually taken for consideration, for example, the Army, the Church, a school, or a nation. People did not "join" the village as they can join a church or a political party, they were born into it. There was very little coming and going from the towns. The village was made of a homogeneous group of all ages belonging to one race and religion and engaged in only one occupation, agriculture.

I have described one of the ways in which the village dealt with the *disruptive* forces in the group. But now I want to mention a point of importance in group *solidarity* in a small community, i.e. that though there was no freedom to express individual opinions on any matter affecting the group as a whole, there was great liberty of expression in the "ornaments of life", if one can use such a term without in any way belittling them. I believe it true to say that the arts form a far stronger group-bond in homogeneous than in mixed communities. In my village, through singing, dancing, needlework, colouring, washing of walls, in fact through any of the arts, each man and woman could show his or her pride and skill for the glory of himself and the pleasure of his neighbours. But not in a skilled trade! An endeavour to separate oneself as a joiner or smith was not encouraged. The standard of skill was accordingly simply appalling, and I have seen horses grazing on nearly ploughed over pasture—so careless were the peasants in the alignment of the furrows.

I now wish to recapitulate some of the points I have discussed. These groups have a dread lest a member of their group should rise to leadership or even rise to be conspicuously skilled. A dread lest the group should be split into factions led to a heightening of sensitiveness to the opinion of the group and self-abnegation before it, so that personal initiative is paralysed. Independence is thought to be an aggressive act against the group, and is condemned, and the elimination of competition, except in late adolescence at the time of mating, leads to the perpetuation of a low standard of life. And in a district subject to crop failures a low standard of life spells a high rate of death.

The idealised group and the idealised family

This group that we have been considering was an island of humanity on a sea of steppe, but its *psychical* isolation was the creation of its members. What went on in the group was felt to be "good"—that is, it gave a sense of security—but outside the group everything was dangerous. The only things the members could depend on were those blessed by the group. This is a familiar situation with us all. In our early days we build just such a picture of an idealised good family, in whose bosom is all goodness, security and peace, and in the environment is all uncertainty and danger. Of course no family actually matches this ideal, because by the projection of our own hate, we are specially prone to attribute our hate to those nearest to us; but nevertheless, there continues to exist an image of a perfect family, a perfect group, which will meet our every need. This picture has however its counterpart, that the perfect family is surrounded by enemies. They are of our making, but as projections are rarely perceived as such, we do not realise this. There is another phantasy that is also active in our early years, i.e. that if we harbour hostile thoughts or impulses against the good parents then all the bogies in the environment will rush in and finish off the destruction. The concept is made terrifying because in the unconscious, a distinction is not drawn between thought and deed, that is, a magical omnipotence is attributed to thought, which must accordingly be kept on a friendly tone or else all that is valued runs the risk of destruction. Because of the danger to our good objects from our aggression, we are unconsciously on our guard to protect them from our hostile thoughts and intentions, and because in the early days our ego was weak and our impulses were strong, we tended not to believe that the things which we prized could get on without our constant vigilance and support. In other words, we carry with us from childhood a picture of parent figures who must not be attacked and who are helpless without our support. In the course of development this concept becomes modified. We discover that the parents are not destroyed by critical thoughts, and indeed, that they can get along very well without us. But the transition to this rational and by no means unfriendly attitude to our parents is beset with difficulties. We do not renounce either the phantasy of our malevolent power or the sense of responsibility—also in phantasy— without a struggle, nor can we relinquish the concept of the perfect parents lightly. Some of the god-like qualities that we attributed to the parents is displaced towards the heavens to form a Divinity. Some is displaced by hero-worship onto powerful figures in the environment—kings and more intermediate rulers—and some is attached to the concept of the group in which we live. The more dependent we are on the group, the more likely are we to endow it with the characteristics that we imagined our parents to have, while we ourselves were in the dependent stage. It becomes once more the protecting parent which must be cared for in return, and when the group is given this position it becomes a blasphemy to challenge it in any way.

Feelings of respect and affection for the community spring from very deep sources in our experience. Even those whose demeanour would seem to imply great contempt for it show, if we look closely enough, that the outward scorn masks an inner feeling of an opposite kind. But it would not be true to say that affection was the only deep-lying emotion here, any more than in the infantile attitude to the parents. The group is a force which restricts our gratifications and enforces the laws which keep others from the enjoyment of hurting us, and us from hurting them. It is not only the group that imposes restrictions on our sexual pleasures; this is also done for the most part by our own sense of guilt. But the group is *thought* to be the source of this frustration, and for that reason it comes in for a great deal of our hostility. The evidence for this may be found in the behaviour of adolescents who have a double or ambivalent attitude to the group, regarding it as a tyrant and also as an object which calls for their most altruistic endeavours, an attitude determined in the main by an unconscious attitude to the father and mother respectively. The way of dealing with the love and hate feelings towards this idealised object (once a parent figure, and now by substitution, the group) shows every degree of gradation from a primitive impulsive, all-or-none reaction, on the one hand, to a more discriminating but not less loving response on the other.

The simplest response is that adopted towards all idealised objects—that is, to regard them as all good or all bad. The group-regarding sentiments are split into two; the community in which the individual lives is considered as wholly good and all other groups are bad. It is not a once-and-for-all decision, but a process that is going on all the time as our love and hate feelings are generated or roused. This division into good and bad groups has a great psychological merit. It facilitates the discharge of emotion through action. Aggression can *quickly* find a relatively guilt-free outlet by attacking bad groups in the environment, and the conscience can applaud the ego in this task because it is *defending* a good and valued object—the home.

Aggression and co-operation

Man may be described as an animal that is continually seeking guilt-free ways of being aggressive.

The concept of a group that is wholly good inevitably leads to a search for outlets for the impulse of obstruction, that is to say, too gross an idealisation of one's own group tends towards war. The enemy becomes the scapegoat, which must be driven from the earth. But there are two other ways of dealing with aggression. One is to turn it against the self, the other is to turn it outwards, not against men but against inanimate nature. When turned against the self (a process that is not part of a conscious plan, but is unconscious) the individuals suffer excessively from conscience and the group becomes puritanical. This is not a stable solution of the problem, because there seems to be a limit to the amount which normal people can become strict with themselves. Furthermore, when hate is turned inwards it leads to depression. The second way is by an attack on nature. Now it is obvious that all work, handwork and brainwork, is a blending of destructive and constructive impulses. The peasant must cut down trees before he can build his house; the farmer must rip up the ground before he can plant the seed in it effectively; the thinker must pull his own and other people's systems to pieces before he can find out how they are connected and before he can construct one of his own. We do not even swallow our food whole. Work provides a satisfaction to aggression and usually it gives satisfaction in proportion as we see "results". Work as such and by itself does not contribute to group bonds any more than does sexual love. But communal work, which we experienced first, by the way, in the nursery (the prototype for all subsequent co-operative plans), brings the members together in a specially intimate way. It contributes, for instance, to the comradeship of the war.

There is a limitation in this direction too, and one that comes specially near to our topic. The work has really to be done in common; it must in other words be the same for all. If the work done by each is different it tends to have the character of work done for the self; jealousy soon comes in. For example, it may be felt that this man's work is easier, is cleaner, is more praised; and what at first seemed like a solution of the problem of dealing with the aggressive impulse in a harmless way, leads to a renewal of the tendency to disruption.

Let us consider another obstacle to the application of the gospel of work—it is after all impersonal! An individual has to be gifted with a special faculty to "work over" inanimate material and "bring it to life", that is, he must be an artist before he can find the deepest satisfaction for his soul in working with dead stuff. The aggressive impulse was first roused in us by our passionate and excited contact with living flesh. Throughout our lives the connection remains. There is a limit to sublimation and it seems that man cannot find it in him to renounce this early impulse entirely. The zest for attacking a fellow human being lies dormant, and when the channel of sublimated aggression finds even a temporary check, the impulse takes a turn against fellow man and the community sharing of work in common begins to look for scapegoats. If scapegoats could be really established it would no doubt be pleasant for the group, but the process of projection is not a once-and-for-all operation, like the removal of the appendix; it is a makeshift way of dealing with anxiety. The members of the group believe themselves to be persecuted by aliens in their midst, the attack on the alien being regarded by those who make it as a *counter-attack*, and therefore guilt-free.

It is time for us to look at the main question once more: does it take all kinds to make a world? I have taken a homogeneous group intent on maintaining uniformity in thought and behaviour among its members. It is no part of my business to pass judgement and say whether it is a good or a bad arrangement, but to show the advantages and the disadvantages deriving from the process. I would like to stress one of the advantages that I have not indicated fully enough. I spoke of the group being, in the unconscious of its member, a direct derivative of an infantile conception of the parents. The forces which come into play in the formation of a group sentiment are the tender (or aim-inhibited libidinal) impulses which once were directed to those we loved more than anyone else in the world. If the hostile impulses can be mastered or deflected from the loved objects and the members can feel towards each other, as a group, the passionate tenderness of which children are capable, the result is an emotional tie that is extraordinarily satisfying. As Freud has pointed out in his scientific writings, and as countless poets have shown in theirs, love gives to our phantasy a sense of independence of fate. If we can, in full trust, enjoy the love of a kind and strong person and feel that we can love in return, then let come what may, we have our heart's desire. In this state of mind we feel that no enemy can vanquish us, and we are glad in the assurance that life will go on!

We are accustomed to associate this confidence in love with the relation between the sexes, but it applies to the child's attitude to his parents, and in certain conditions to the member's feeling towards the group. I believe it is because of a wish to *re-create* this feeling of being supported by a force as strong as fate and of being fortified against a terrifying isolation, that people unwittingly evolve the homogeneous kind of group where all think alike.

Such a group makes very great demands on its members, for example, a degree of submission that few, who have grown up in a heterogeneous world, could contemplate with equanimity. It calls for sacrifices akin to those asked by religion, a surrender of the self to a superior power without reservation, and for a reward which is primarily spiritual.

Factors leading to the need for uniformity in group-ideal

The group I have described evolved this attitude towards uniformity (and away from diversity) over a long period of time. It is uniformity "in pure culture" so to speak. But this type of *Weltanschauung* has been adopted by about 250 million people in the last two decades, many of them being, if not exactly *new* to it, at least unfamiliar with its extreme form. When great states make a drive towards homogeneity, they do so under a leader. In this they are unlike the village group described. It may be asked what factors Soviet Russia and Nazi Germany had in common to lead them to the same kind of attitude to political diversity within the group? They had both lost their rulers, and the culture that went with them. Both had been subject to disruptive forces from without at a time of internal strain; and the means of subsistence or trade of practically every member of the group had been threatened. The state, which is endowed with parental authority, must show a parent's power and must govern within its own frontiers. If it can do this the members of the group not only endow it with some of the attributes of the superego, but feel an identification with it; the aggrandisement of their state sheds glory on themselves. It requires unusual tenacity for an individual or a people to maintain an affectionate identification with *any* object that is undergoing dissolution. After an exhausting war and a perfidious peace, the people of Central Europe had nowhere to turn, no one in whom they could trust. The impulse to accept a regime demanding uniformity not only proved irresistible but was inevitable. It offered unity. Complete trust in a leader would bring cohesion, and affection for him would give them peace of mind. Some of the mystical attitudes to life, which religion has now largely relinquished, appear to be returning in the field of politics.

There is no place to assess the success of any regime or political theory but only to indicate advantages and difficulties of a psychological nature.

Yet, after what I have said about a homogeneous society that had uniformity in thought and behaviour as one of its ideals, you may still feel like asking the question "But surely there was a butcher and a baker?" If you do this, as well you may, it goes to show how very difficult it is to picture a kind of society differing from our own, for we in England are accustomed to a community in which the widest development of skill in trade and the arts is applauded and diversity is part of our political system. For example, "the Leader of His Majesty's Opposition" is paid a salary on about the scale of a Cabinet Minister— a state of affairs that is unthinkable in certain totalitarian countries. Furthermore, one of the arguments in favour of our adopting tariffs was that though humanity as a *whole* might derive most benefit by a policy of free trade, yet in any given area, say England, the specialisation of activities, which would result from each country regulating its production *solely* according to the world market, would restrict the full exploitation of the potential skill of the members of the community. Variety of occupation, according to this view, is essential to the healthy growth of the community.

To make the contrast between the homogeneous and the heterogeneous groups clear, I am going to recapitulate the points already raised. In the homogeneous group, the ideal was towards uniformity in thought and behaviour, competition among the adults was deprecated and even in boys' games there was no scoring of any kind. The group was leaderless or rather the place of the leader was taken by an ideal of non-aggressive behaviour towards fellow members of the group.

One point I omitted to discuss earlier was the activity of the women. Although women were admitted on equal terms to men on the Mir, speaking generally they did not have the same submissive attitude to the Village Spirit. Their technical skill seemed to me to be on a far higher level to that of the men and they seemed more intelligent.

To summarise: the solidarity which came from substituting the emotional dependence on the parents by dependence on the group in this specially thorough way, that is, by letting the group function as the egoideal, gave a sense of great security to the members both against the hardships of fate and against the individual's own impulsive tendencies. So long as submission to the group was complete each member felt magnificently strong and secure. In the main this feeling of security is derived from two sources, or to be more exact, from the way in which both the love and the hate impulses are dealt with. The *group* is put in the place of the idealised good parent, and is loved as was its personal prototype; the hostile parent-directed impulses are turned outwards towards some other group or authority, in this case the Central Government. More typically it is directed against foreigners and scapegoats, where expulsion is thought to purify the group. Some of the aggression is turned inwards and takes the form of a highly sensitive conscience and a readiness to submit to the rulings of authority. Some of the aggression is also directed to other members of the group in the form of vigilance over their behaviour.

One of the main sources of attraction to the group in a homogeneous society lies in the fact that it is pictured to the unconscious as good, all idea of badness in regard to it is suppressed; though this gives scope, in phantasy, for the feeling of boundless satisfaction, it requires far more effort to maintain this condition than the members of the group commonly realise. And where a constant output of energy is required for this purpose the condition is unstable.

It is comparable with repression which is not a once-and-for-all act of abolishing an idea or impulse from the mind, but a constant application of mental effort though the person concerned is not aware of the fact. It is the same in holding any idealised image before the mind: an effort is required to keep it clear of hostile thoughts, to keep it enshrined so to speak.

But we have to remember that the idealised image is attached to a real figure and for the combination to be effective it is important that the real figure should not seem to fail in its purpose. The protecting parent image must protect. When in fact conditions become hard or faith in the idealised object weakens, then there is a risk that the aggressive impulses will turn with vehemence against what was previously considered holy.

Those villagers that I mentioned earlier were on the brink of a famine; the situation was met by the device of the in-turning of aggression. The priest prayed for rain and God's blessing on the crops, and told the people that if they did not have a good harvest it would be a divine punishment for their sins. I have described their low standard of technical efficiency and how personal initiative was hampered by the dread of rising superior to one's neighbour. Yet no word could be raised against inefficiency because it was tolerated in the service of the ideal of non-competitiveness. I think some of the bitterness in the ruthless and stupid Anti-God campaign in Russia came from a reaction to this technique for dealing with aggression, a technique which sacrificed Man entirely to the maintenance of an unworkable concept of God in heaven and the Tsar on earth.

The search for scapegoats is a magical, phantasy-ridden procedure; it maintains the illusion that the self can be made perfect by embodying some of its own hostile impulses in the person of the scapegoat and expelling that from the self or the community. We find this process in every country in greater or less degree. In Russia the results of their inefficiency lead to alarm, and to allay the apprehension, a score or more technicians are shot in order to purge the country of evil. I do not dispute the element of discontent and that the wish to sabotage may—indeed *must* be—widespread with so much terror exercised as an everyday expedient by the executive, but the method of seeking for scapegoats is irrational, leads to more terror and underground activity.

The peasant villagers lived in the greatest trust of each other because they knew each other well, but they lived in great distrust of all strangers. In a community where everyone cannot be known, latent suspicion is easily roused. When it lies in any man's power to be an informer, his own ill-will towards his neighbours has more scope, and some of the hostility which he unconsciously projects onto others returns upon him (in his phantasy) from the environment he has endowed with evil, and he fears his neighbours, begins even to fear his own thoughts. Hundreds of millions of our fellow Europeans are now faced with the choice of dealing with the mental dilemmas I have just outlined or else shut out free criticism of political or social problems from their minds altogether. There are many people—and those not the least valuable socially—to whom this is impossible.

Another great disadvantage accompanying a rigidly maintained homogeneous society is that the group loses too many of its vigorous men not only on the gallows but by emigration. America has gained for a century and a half a valuable import of human energy which Europe was too rigid to use and so has lost. Nor is it at all certain that if migration is forcibly prevented those energies will be freely available for use at home. The social problem of migration probably has a fairly close connection with the psychological problem of casting loose home ties, and with that point in mind I think we can make a beginning with an investigation of heterogeneous groups whose general ideal is a multiformity in society.

The heterogeneous group

If we watch the development of children in our own community here in England, we are struck by the great range of adult activities with which they identify themselves. At one moment a boy's main ambition is to be a postman delivering letters to everybody's door, and the arrival of this uniformed functionary is one of the big events in his day. Later he may wish to be an engine-driver and if his holidays are spent on the coast he may for weeks after his return inland still show a hankering after the life of a lighthouse keeper. The arrival of a circus to his town may change his habits for a time to clowning, and if the summer manoeuvres are in his neighbourhood he will give his mind to the serious business of fighting.

We do not regard such changing roles as abnormal in a young child, but rather as a sign of healthy interest in the world around him. If we look into the causes of this versatility, we find that each of these activities gives expression to a different kind of phantasy.

In phantasy the mind finds outlet for instinctual desires in the relation between the self and its objects, and phantasy is the medium in which the child's mental life finds its liveliest expression. Phantasy is exteriorised and made visible and tangible to the child itself and to others in play. If we watch a child at play with sufficiently discerning eyes we may note how the simplest object is endowed with different personalities and plays many different roles. Its toy horse is at one moment a docile friendly helpful animal, like a strong father (to the child's phantasy it *is* the father) doing benevolent works; later this same creature will be stamping, smashing and biting everything to bits. The child's ego, its executive self, remains the same, but the toy is being transformed now into one kind of creature, now into another, according as the instinctual desires of the child change in the course of the story it constructs in its imagination.

The exploration of diversity through imagination

Now what are the stories that go on all the time in the minds of children? How are they related to real life, what purpose do they serve it at the time of play, and how do they relate to our theme?

The story is derived from two sources: the impulses of the child himself supply the motives, and the actual events in the environment supply sub-plots, so to speak, that have to be woven into the pattern of the drama. The toys (human, animal and inanimate) play roles of father, mother, brothers and sisters; they have sexual relations, they fight, eat each other and make it up again, in endless varieties of ways. Even though the child himself becomes more and more of a social being, he will still have some phantasy objects that are refractory to every attempt at education. The life of phantasy allows scope for the expression of some aspects of instinctual life that have not yet been fully integrated into the personality.

When thinking of early mental life we should avoid such narrowing concepts as the conditioned reflex in which our responses are confined to a single or very limited number of actions and the stimuli, even though intense, are few. The child does not have a "single-track mind". If we are looking for an analogy, the ballet with a full cast is to be preferred. The number of principal performers may be limited, but their relation to one another is reflected in the diverse minor characters who play in the background, each one catching up some part of the main theme and colouring it with their own personality and characteristics, and reflecting back upon the chief actors of the drama, features of the love and hate, the jealousies, doubts and cares which the great ones are feeling and showing, perhaps with greater intensity but with no greater truth.

So it is in our mental lives. From a very early age we experience within ourselves, and with great intensity, the emotions which formerly were thought to begin with adolescence: the longing for love, the hate of rivals and the loneliness when, as it seems, all goodness has gone out of our life.

An important feature of early mental life is that it is essentially *unfinished*. It is a period of beginnings, new starts and innumerable abandoned undertakings. It is not simply a preparation for life. It is a life of its own exploring the potentialities of pleasure to be found in the environment and trying out the resources of the self in every imaginable way, or rather, it could be this way. All too often the individual is inhibited, loses pleasure in his initiative and becomes a docile follower of other people's plans, having none of his own. One cannot stress enough the fact that the mental life of the child is *"unfinished"*. There are many impulses or tendencies to action which do not get fulfilled, and though they are apparently abandoned, the wish to take them up again lingers on in the unconscious. This may in part explain the power that a novel like *War and Peace* or *Anna Karenina* has over us. In them Tolstoy seems to have picked up every loose thread and woven it into the pattern of his story.

My references to phantasy so far have been descriptive. They have not touched on the forces at work in them, nor the way in which the ego adapts itself to meet its inner requirements *vis-à-vis* the environment.

The part played by processes of identification in early development

We must remember that the executive part of the mind, the ego, is weak in infancy in relation to the strength of its impulses. It needs support against its impulses, if it is not to succumb to the anxiety and depression which would result if they had unrestricted sway. One means of steadying the ego is through the process of identification, as a result of which the ego moulds itself upon the pattern of another person, who is conspicuous in his success in overcoming the difficulty in question.

This brings us to a special type of identification for a specific purpose. The conscience is a device of the mind for preventing the execution of destructive actions; it warns the ego against its own tendencies. The conscience is a part of the ego, but it is also a part of the outer world; the injunctions of the parents are identified with and incorporated within the self and made to function as if they were a part of the ego itself. Freud called this modified part of the ego the superego (Freud, 1923b) but he pointed out that the superego has another and vitally important function besides that of prohibiting evil action. It also encourages the ego and supports it as does a loving parent.

The concept of the superego has been widened in recent years, and investigations by Melanie Klein and others have disclosed the fact that in the unconscious there is not merely the registration of parental prohibitions and encouragements, but also the subjective feeling that there are objects incorporated from the environment, installed within the ego, and that these may be felt to be good or bad (Klein, 1932). *The contents of the self*, therefore, are far more complicated than we once thought.

I want to give an example of this process from an everyday experience. We observe in the growing boy—the same applies with appropriate changes to girls—that early in his life he takes his father as an ideal, and says that no one is his equal, no one knows more, is stronger, and so forth. But when he gets to school, the place of this ideal, in his conscious thoughts at any rate, may be taken by a schoolmaster, and his father as an idealised object is regarded now from a different standpoint. The father is still a splendid person but the schoolmaster *knows* more. So it goes on through life, one ego-ideal after another is added to the personality, to the inner treasury of experience on which the individual relies.

I say "*added* to the personality", for the point is important. The change from one ego-ideal to another does not mean that the former one is discarded, but only that it is not in active use at the moment.

Now this succession of idealised persons—parent, school teacher, and the other heroes—represent but one aspect of mental life. Under the guidance of our impulses we evolve in our phantasy masterful and destructive idealisations as well. The docile horse of our infancy readily turned into a brute that stamped and bit people to pieces, and the precipitates of these phantasies also lie in the store-house of our minds, and act in the unconscious as a superego, or an ideal for the ego to copy. The ego does not copy *all* the dictates of these superegos, whether good or bad, but it uses them in phantasy, in acts of pure destruction or as a foil for the impulses of an opposite, constructive, kind. Unless we recognise the bad superegos (the antisocial tendencies in ourselves) our inner life is meaningless.

The part played by the process of projection in early development

Now I have dealt at length with the process of incorporating objects into ourselves to form those semi-foreign accretions to the personality, the superegos. It is necessary to pay an equal attention to the effects of projection on the patterning of our mental life. We thrust onto persons or situations in the environment what we do not wish to recognise in ourselves. The bogies which haunt children in our culture (and both children and adults in primitive cultures) are the embodiments in the environment of aggressive impulses having origin in the self.

Our picture of the world, in our early days at least, is far from objective. It is made up of people who are fantastically good and fantastically bad. The extreme tendencies in *both* directions are the products of our imagination. And the more bogey-fied the environment, the more do we need the help of magically good objects to counteract the evil that the bogeys may do to us and to the persons we value.

After all, the splitting into these two sharply contrasting groups, the excessively good and excessively bad, is a device for preserving what we value from the contamination of what we fear and hate, whether it be within ourselves or in the environment. Our inner and our outer world is thus highly complex, both are full of good and bad objects, and there is a continual interplay between the inner and outer world and between the objects (good and bad) composing them.

Now when the ego is dominated by anxiety there is an immediate tendency to stop this interplay. In extreme cases there is an unconscious tendency to do nothing lest the bogies get at the self from without and lest those inside do damage to loved objects in the environment. In other words, there is a paralysis of action in order to paralyse the forces of evil. The unconscious may also go to the length of paralysing thought, for thought and deed are in the unconscious often regarded as identical. The anxiety arises when the destructive impulses are felt to be getting out of hand and when valued objects are within their reach. The separation of good from bad is one device for preserving the good, the paralysis is another. Both are in the long run ineffective, for if an ordinary and carefree life is to be had at all, there must be a minimum of paralysis and a maximum of freedom of contact for the objects inside the self and in the environment. The quandary in which this state of affairs places the infant is overcome by a device as simple as it is universal. Interest is diverted to new objects which have not the same emotional value as those most precious people—and most hated also—in the family. The field of interest spreads. When this happens the newly chosen objects do not afford the same potential satisfactions but usually give more *actual* satisfactions. The hating of them is the occasion of less fear and the loving of them is accompanied by less guilt, for the possessive element in the love does not come up against the self-reproach that we are taking from anyone whom we love. But the relation to these new objects of interest is not completely free from the disturbances that have complicated the first love and hate relationships. Some of the idealisation of the early attachments flows over to the new object of our regard and some of the projections colour it with our unconscious attitudes.

When the real characteristics of the new object more or less coincide with those that we imagine him or her to have, then the relation is a stable one: if not, the individual turns attention to someone else or starts a sequence of misunderstandings and bickerings which usually end in an emotional deadlock.

Heterogeneous groups that demand uniformity of group-ideal, but permit diversity of occupation

We speak of a difficulty in transferring libidinal interest from the early objects of attachment to other people as a *fixation*, and *fixation* accounts for a great deal of the world's troubles, for it means that persons thus restricted in their choice of love-object and hate-object cannot readily adapt themselves to a new, and particularly to a changing, environment. It means furthermore that there is restriction also in the capacity to fuse love and hate impulses, so that affection cannot neutralise the devastating effects of hostility. A further consequence of fixation is a carry over of the dependence on the idealised parent figures onto that of a substitute figure, either a personal hero or the group as a whole. Hero-worship is a fixation of interest to one aspect of the idealised parent figure. It is a concentration of all goodness and power into one object and removing it above criticism. There are certain factors in connection with hero-worship that should be considered. First, it is an idealisation of the father's potency and creativeness, at the expense even of the individual's own power, but the identification with the glorified image gives back to the individual some of the glory bestowed on the idealised object. Hero-worship has a second value. Acts done in the service of the ideal are themselves idealised, even though they are of a kind which under ordinary circumstances would be reckoned mean or even criminal. Religious wars provide the most striking instances of this peculiar twisting of conscience, and since mankind is less and less inclined to glorify war for its own sake, the number of *Holy Wars* is increasing. Under the mask of service to an ideal, the greatest barbarities are deemed permissible, even against helpless and unarmed persons. The sanctity of a Holy Crusade can even be stretched to cover private vengeance, if the object of attack has been placed by the hero beyond the bounds of pity. Hero-worship, furthermore, undoubtedly strengthens certain types of group bonds for a time. All the members, who take the same hero as their ideal, feel a bond of brotherliness to one another. In the strength of this mutual tie they can tolerate a certain amount of diversity among each other provided that one thing is not touched—the nature and the extent of the submissiveness to the hero. His reign must be regarded as perfect, eternal and unchanging, or else it is subject to disrupting suspicion. Even to point out that these very features partake somewhat of the nature of phantasy rather than reality is dangerous to the cohesion of the group.

The sense of group solidarity is specially important to people who have a group-ideal, such as I described earlier, and to the people who worship a hero, because the narrowing down of emotional choice leads to intensification of the opposite tendency, hostility. The conflict thus aroused over a single sacred object is dangerous to equilibrium. The method of hero-worship has a further disadvantage. Since it is dangerous to criticise or feel any hostile impulses towards the hero or the group he leads, the aggression has to be turned outwards and the individuals have to find a free—that is, guilt-free—outlet beyond the group frontier. The extreme bellicosity that may thus be produced is sometimes said to be an expression of a "will to peace". We must not reject such a notion as absurd because it contains a partial truth. The projection of the aggressiveness beyond the frontier is an act of protection to the good objects within the frontier. The home is *not* being attacked by this act of aggression but some despised foreign country, which has become the dumping ground for phantasies of badness.

The state of satisfaction which comes from an idealisation of a homogeneous group, or a single person as a hero, is not an easy one to maintain. It seems to contain inherent instabilities though they are never apparent to those taking part until the structure begins to break up. The reason for this I have tried to trace to an unconscious wish to reinstate a phantasied situation of childhood where all good things, security and love, were centred on one person. The danger lies in the inadequate provision for the discharge of aggression.

I want to turn now to the main theme of this discussion.

I have tried to point out that we are not simple reflex machines, or ones that are influenced by a series of conditioned reflexes from the environment, but rather that the composition of the inner recesses of our minds is exceedingly complex, containing more or less organised tendencies to the most diverse actions. However good we are, however much our lives may be filled with creative and constructive works, we cannot live adequately on one plane alone. Those more destructive than ourselves afford us, through identification, a gratification of the destructive component in our emotional lives. We need in the environment some of what we regard as evil, in order to help us to keep our own tendencies in that direction from breaking out. We also need it to attack. If we were all alike and all grew up in the image of our idealised good parents, to vent some of our energies in hostility to our neighbours would be the same as to attack what we regarded as most good. The diversity of our types affords us an outlet for aggression without evoking the paralysing effect of too much guilt.

I wish to emphasise that I am now referring to outlets of aggression within the group, that is, towards members of the same group. Now if this is to occur without disruption of the group, for example, as by civil war, several factors must be present in the right proportion. Firstly, the destructive element, obviously, must not be too strong.

Secondly, the constructive element in the aggression must be strong. For example, in the old Liberal versus Conservative days in English politics, one party could go to great lengths to push the other out of office, but it must not attack its opponents except as political opponents. Shooting or concentration camps were not even thought of, and at all costs the two parties must, within pretty wide limits, respect the Constitution and/or the Crown. The third factor is contained in the last point. The separation of good and bad elements, even in political opponents, must not be regarded as absolute, and transfer from one party to another must be possible if reasons can be given that are in conformity with the group ideals. The elements in the group must recognise differences compatible with group unity. I regard the tolerance towards a serious change of political view and intolerance of too rapid or frequent change of party as an important criterion, when trying to assess a nation's political health, and all such barriers as those of race, colour, baptismal affiliations, and the caste system as dangerous, because they introduce a rigidity into politics. This rigidity makes the approximation of what is thought to be bad to that which is thought to be good, more difficult.

Heterogeneous groups that permit diversity of group-ideal and occupation

I have described two kinds of groups. In the first, which was leaderless, uniformity was thought to be desirable in occupation, mode of thought and every ideal. There was a uniformity of ego and ego-ideal. In the hero-worshipping group there was a common ideal, but there could also be diversity of occupation, that is, a uniformity of ego-ideal but not of ego. There is, however, a third or completely heterogeneous group, in which there is no insistence on uniformity of political ideal. There can be diversity of ego, and to a large extent even of ego-ideal, among its members.

Two questions arise in connection with this third group. Firstly, what are the group bonds, and secondly, what are the difficulties inherent in the association? A good example of this third class is the United States of America. The ego-ideal or leader is found in two sections: there is the Constitution to which all high officials swear loyalty, and there is the President. Both are alterable by the will of the people. In England there is the Crown and the Constitution as permanent but alterable ego-ideals, and a removable portion of authority, the Cabinet.

The Government can thus be attacked without overthrowing authority. The ego-bonds are provided by our everyday social and commercial contact with one another.

The vastly increased means of communication, which science has provided, while it does nothing to alter the psychical mechanisms underlying our social life, has greatly changed the emphasis on the ego, as distinct from the ego-ideal factor. Another product of civilisation, the mechanisation of the means of production, has also strengthened the egoistic, as distinct from the ego-ideal, bonds which hold the group together. Indeed, we could, without total inaccuracy, describe the differences between economics and politics as sciences affecting the group bonds of the ego and of the superego, respectively.

Now for the difficulties inherent in a heterogeneous group. First: its lack of coherence makes it weak in face of its enemies in time of war, but not paralysed. The British, with their great capacity for maintaining internal quarrels for long periods of time, frequently disappoint their enemies in this respect. The most charming example of this trait being the resolution, carried into effect, of the Sailors Committee during the Mutiny at the Nore in 1797 to dress the ship when some foreign admirals came to inspect the Fleet. The Admiralty showed confidence in the mutineers as Englishmen in allowing distinguished foreigners near the place at such a time, and the sailors suspended their business of hanging officers from the yard-arm to show their preference even for the Admiralty yoke to that of a foreigner. The moral of this is that disruptiveness is relative and if the sailors at the Nore, the workers on the one hand and the Admirals and employers on the other, can regard each other as *people* with a different point of view and different interests—in a word as *people* and not *bogies*—disruption cannot go very far. There are few real grounds for disruption and they are not strong in proportion to the power of cohesion. There are, however, many *phantasy* grounds, and when there is a strong *belief* that other people are dangerous and disruptive, that is, when a phantasy is carried over from the nursery to the group, then group cohesion is in grave danger.

The main disadvantage of a heterogeneous group is that the trajectory of projections, so to speak, lies within the borders. We may draw a distinction between the first two types of group and the third by saying that in the first two the conflicts of jealousy and hate, carried over from the nursery in the unconscious, are solved by a device of suppressing jealousy in the first case, and idealising the father in the second; whereas the assumption has been made that in the fully heterogeneous or third type of group the infantile conflicts have *not* been solved and must be worked out laboriously throughout life.

This is the central part of my thesis. The conflicts of our early years are not in any of us solved by the time we grow up; we have seldom come to terms with our early jealousies and fears. Brothers and sisters are in part our good companions, in part the recipients of our most evil projections. They are people we hate as well as love, and to save them we divert the terrifying impulses to outsiders. The Communists, the Jews, the Capitalists, the Roman Catholics or doctors, politicians, or trade unionists—any of these people may be endowed with evil in a measure far beyond their deserts. We say consciously, if we have any insight at all, that we are prejudiced against such and such a class of people, but that does not tell us enough. The source of our prejudice is the displacement of a nursery animus, and by that split we attempt to keep the home free from quarrelling, and displace our squabbles to the political and social field.

There are ideologies which regard squabbles in politics as almost indecent, a derivative, I think, of the phantasy of an idealised peaceful home. Another view is that they are irrational in a society where the means of production belong to the community. The last point seems to beg the question since there can be two opinions on how the job should be done. The further assumption that party politics is a result of a society in which there are possessing and dispossessed classes seems to me also wide of the mark, since it assumes that there can be no other basis for an ego-identification than the *possession* of the means of production.

I would like in conclusion to make one point as clear as I can. I have been drawing parallels between the child's behaviour in the nursery and the man's behaviour in the big wide world, but I have even gone further than drawing parallels. I have implied that political squabbling is largely due to unresolved nursery conflicts, and that our view of the society in which we live is derived from our early attitude to parents, brothers and sisters. All this seems to me to be a reasonable assumption, if we keep in mind that the early experiences exert an influence unconsciously throughout life, and at times we give way to this influence and at times resist it. There is a pull in the direction of reason and actual adult gratifications, and I would not minimise this, but the explanations which rely only on reason do not, in my opinion, explain enough.

I have placed politics in the centre of this discussion, because it is so much a field of action and aggression, in the group. This has given a very one-sided picture of our emotional life. In essentials, I think the problem is the same in the field of morals, aesthetic taste and religion also, and that mankind is always facing the task of shaping its group life, so that it shall be either an embodiment of an early ideal of perfect uniformity, or else that it shall be a place of struggle, with an *ultimate* aim of peace.

CHAPTER 10

Panic and anxiety reactions in groups during air raids

(1938)

Definitions

Since air raids may produce panic in the civilian population it is well to consider the factors that facilitate or diminish panic, and what steps, if any, may be taken against it. First let me quote definitions of relevant words.

> Fright, fear, apprehension are incorrectly used as synonymous expressions: in their relations to danger they admit of quite clear distinction. . . . *Fear* requires a definite object of which one is afraid; *fright* is the name of a condition to which one is reduced if one encounters a danger without being prepared for it; it lays stress on the element of surprise. [Freud, 1920g]

> Anxiety has an unmistakable affinity with expectation: it is anxiety about something. It has a quality of indefiniteness and lack of object. In precise speech we use the word "fear" rather than "anxiety" if the feeling has found an object. [Freud, 1926d]

Anxiety can be a more or less normal phenomenon or it may be neurotic.

First published in *The Lancet* (4 June 1938), p. 1291, under the title "Panic and Air Raid Precautions".

Objective danger is a danger that is known, and objective anxiety is an anxiety about a known danger of this sort. Neurotic anxiety is anxiety about an unknown danger. Neurotic danger is thus a danger that has still to be discovered. [Freud, 1921c]

There are two reactions to objective danger. One, an affective reaction, is an outbreak of anxiety (or fear). The other is a protective action . . . the two reactions can co-operate in an expedient way, the one giving the signal for the other to appear. But they can also behave in an inexpedient way: paralysis due to anxiety may set in, and the reaction spread at the cost of the other. In some cases the characteristics of objective anxiety and neurotic anxiety are mingled. The danger is known and objective, but the anxiety in regard to it is over-great, greater than seems proper. [Freud, 1926g]

The foregoing definitions are clear and would be generally acceptable. In regard to *panic* there is less agreement. The word is popularly used in three ways:

- to denote a dread not warranted by the occasion—this is covered by "neurotic anxiety";
- where dread exceeds certain bounds—this places the accent only on quantity and does not take into account the special characteristics of panic, i.e. its relation to other people and its "nameless horror";
- for any collective dread—and this emphasises the social bond but it ignores the fact that in panic the social bond is broken.

These three between them contain several essential features of panic, but they do not go far enough; they ignore the loss of self-control.

Causation of panic

Aetiological factors have been divided into four classes (Freud, 1895f): predisposition, specific, contributory causes and exciting or releasing cause. Without the predisposition and the specific causes, the effect—i.e. panic—could not come about; contributory causes need not be present every time there is panic and cannot by themselves produce it.

This formula helps to clarify the issues, for since panic occurs (though infrequently) apart from external dangers and may occur when the external dangers are diminishing, we cannot regard external danger as "the" cause of panic; though of course external dangers contribute very much indeed to the release of panic, just as bad housing or malnutrition contribute to the onset of tuberculosis. In both disorders, resistance is very important.

The predisposition and specific cause in panic is not clear; it may have something to do with a tendency to nervous breakdown, which under normal conditions is not apparent. External danger mobilises aggressive impulses. If there is no opportunity for immediate outlet, the executive part of the mind in dealing with the increased mental tension is forced to effect a redistribution of love and hate impulses. It may be that an incapacity to effect such a redistribution rapidly enough is the predisposing cause of panic. A direct attack on the panic problem by "getting at the roots", i.e. altering predisposition and specific cause, is very probably not possible, at least as regards the community as a whole; but this should not deter anyone from attempting to grapple with the contributory factors, difficult as this may be.

Panic in an organised group

In an organised artificial group, such as an army (Freud, 1921c), the outbreak of panic, or its absence, does not depend on the amount of objective danger; of more importance is the lowering of the resistance to dread.

In an army in panic, orders are not obeyed; the mutual reliance on authority is lost and the members of the group act as individuals, i.e. the group tie holding them together (sharing the submission to the officers and the solidarity that comes from sharing an ideal) is lost. "Each for all" gives place to "each for himself".

The ties that bind a member of the gunship to other members also serve to keep in check the unrestricted expression of the individual's emotional reactions; loyalty to the group facilitates self-control. Some of the self-esteem that is lost by submission to the group leader, or by the acceptance of the group-ideal, is compensated for, while the group tie is strong, by the good regard or moral support of the group. When the group ties are broken, few individuals can in the face of danger readjust themselves quickly enough to the sudden demand for self-reliance (before, there had been reliance on the group); and, having no support either within or without, they are the victims of the "nameless horror". Panic when it comes is always a surprise, the unexpectedness arising not from a new external situation (the degree of danger may not have changed) but from a revelation of internal confusion or lack of control.

Members of an organised group turn some of their affection towards other members of the same group, but their hostility is in the main turned outwards; the cohesion of the group is thus maintained by the maintenance of bonds of affection and hate—safely distributed. When group cohesion vanishes, some of the affectionate ties have lost their object, i.e. are now available for persons outside the group, and the forces of hostility heretofore mainly directed outwards are now detached from their object and may turn inwards towards members of the same group. A part of the "nameless horror" is due to the turning back of outwardly projected (and therefore formerly "safe") hate upon persons who had stood near to the self in time of danger and were loved and trusted. Thus the breakdown of the group system has personal as well as social consequences; hate is once more dangerous, and its exercise, even in thought and intention, is felt to jeopardise persons who have not merited such hostility. In panic, to the mental distress of anxiety is added that of guilt.

But the state of panic goes a step further and the subject feels that he is without friends at all, he can trust no one; he is alone, or at least friendless. Not really alone, however, because the "shortening of the trajectory of hate" (no longer extending mainly outside the group) turns former friends into potential enemies, and his self-knowledge that panic increases his own egoism tells him that others are now less willing to bear him goodwill. Therefore another source of the "nameless horror" is not mere loneliness but the suspicion that one is surrounded by potential enemies.

Yet another source of the mental anguish of panic is the realisation that one is helpless to defend those one loves. Not only are the group ties broken, but the capacity to do any constructive action in the face of danger is lost. The loss of inner resources against disaster renders one powerless to stop destruction, and there is a tendency under these conditions to join with the enemy and start destroying what lies nearest, which is usually also dearest. This perhaps is the greatest reason for the dread of panic; the victims realise or are dimly aware that it is a condition in which values disappear and all the evil in themselves may be loosed on what is good about them.

Panic in an unorganised group

It is a mistake to think of panic as a sudden state of collapse from a previous condition of perfect self-control. It is in the extreme case a condition of uncoordinated impulses to action and unpremeditated actions, but there are intermediate stages in which some degree of response to group feeling remains and the ties of affection and duty still control behaviour.

The main difference between panic in an organised and an unorganised group lies in the greater resistance to panic in the organised and in the greater difficulty in re-forming emotional ties in the unorganised group. The organised groups, e.g. Army, Church, Boy Scouts, Women's Institutes, are usually also more or less homogeneous and with a leader; the unorganised groups, e.g. family, township, have no visible structure: they are united by various ideals and interests (sometimes in conflict) and the emotional ties that bind them are often weak. Their resistance to panic is therefore not so easy to strengthen by prearranged plan.

Since there is a tendency to the spontaneous formation of groups it is desirable that schemes (if and when devised) should not attempt to institute new and artificial groups unless it is beyond doubt that these will be effective.

In the preliminary stage of panic there is a tendency for the larger group loyalty to be abandoned in favour of smaller group formations. When this occurs, those whose position in the administration leads them to think that they govern the people may regard the situation as out of hand, or even hopeless; whereas in fact it is a redistribution of group loyalty to meet mental strain. The situation only becomes dangerous when the smaller groups develop hostility to one another or to the central authority. (As a measure to reduce the risk of this the provision of many food depots seems desirable; the fear of starvation—a dread from which no man is exempt in time of danger—is closer to consciousness than civilised man commonly realises.)

A sign that the anger of the population is finding outlet against a common foe is that of increased volunteering for national service. There is reason to think that the voluntary system, as distinct from conscription, acts as a conduit for the discharge of pent-up anger in the small groups from which the volunteer comes, i.e. the volunteer is the proxy in aggression for his group. Anti-panic schemes could utilise this mental mechanism but should weigh the risks of concentrating too much loyalty on the central authority (cf. totalitarian countries).[1]

Group bonds and self-control

Group ties are an acquisition, not an inheritance; they develop in infancy during the period of great dependence and are influenced by the

---

[1] A discussion of the democratic technique for dealing with discontent is to be found in the first leader of *The Lancet* of 16 November 1935.

child's need for help from its parents in obtaining control over its own impulses. Thus conscience is partly acquired from the environment and is developed for dealing with the instinctual part of the personality.

Group bonds and self-control are closely connected at the beginning of mental life, and in adult life in time of danger the close connection is once more apparent. The early attitude to the parental authority is in later life displaced onto the Government (nation) or the GOC (Army), Pope (Church), etc., and these must fulfil in some measure the ideals attributed, in the unconscious, to good parent figures; these must (i) govern, i.e. keep order and dispense justice fairly, and (ii) *protect*, i.e. supply needs and distribute them fairly, giving equal opportunity to each member of the group (Freud, 1921c). When these conditions are fulfilled the authority of the group is accepted as a good parent figure (in the unconscious); the members unite in respect for their authority, and their friendly relation to one another is facilitated.

A group tie based on this equal treatment facilitates self-control. Envy (the wrecker of nurseries) if not mitigated even in later life by fair play leads to increase of hatred, which induces mutual distrust (the wrecker of societies). That is to say, self-control is easiest when there is no sense of injustice.

Self-control is aided in large measure by the "ego-ideal", the power of parental injunction and that of other superiors being vested in this controlling force (Freud, 1914c, 1921c). There is both a "regulator" of conduct and a source of "inner support" in this internal mental factor, which from the first is closely related to social life.

One of the functions of the Authority is to *protect*. This concept must not be treated narrowly in a military or economic sense, but rather in the psychological sense. Physical danger and severe threat to economic security do not in themselves produce panic, provided that the individual has an "inner support" (self-confidence); but these factors may endanger the inner support by activating unconscious impulses which have to be kept in check, i.e. they increase the "internal dangers".

External and "internal" dangers

Air raids are likely to produce mental strain, arising from two sources—external danger and "internal danger".[2]

---

[2] The clearest account in non-technical language of "Internal Dangers" and the way in which they are overcome is given in *Love, Hate and Reparation* by Melanie Klein and Joan Riviere (1937).

Strain arising from external danger

The emotional response (fear) produced by an external danger is normally a signal to the mind to *do* something to remove the source of danger, and if the appropriate action is not adequate or is impossible, the emotional strain inevitably increases. It seems, therefore, since the civilian population cannot reach the source of danger and stifle it, that an increase of affect without adequate discharge is inevitable. This however is not the same as saying that there are no measures that can be taken to support the ego, or executive part of the mind, during the time of stress.

Strain arising from "internal dangers"

The part of the mind in which the internal dangers operate is *unconscious*, i.e. not accessible to conscious introspection. The important elements operating in this unconscious part of the mind are infantile impulses, phantasies and anxieties, and the emotional relation to people arising out of these impulses. Phantasies of attacking and being attacked occur in every child, and these phantasies—and the impulses which give strength to them—persist in the unconscious of the adult. They are activated by any factor which puts an increased strain on the ego or conscious executive part of the mind. Normally much energy from these infantile phantasies is exploited (sublimated) in work and in social life in useful ways, but in crisis the energy may be withdrawn in greater or less degree from socially useful employment in the external life and be diverted back to the reactivation of these early phantasies. For instance, to the risk in an air raid of physical injury to the self, there may be added in phantasy a certainty of the most painful mutilation; this is so because the unconscious takes no reckoning of probabilities but goes to extremes: "All or none." This phantasy may so far absorb mental energy as to paralyse a person from taking precautions against the risk. But the mind may react against the impending panic by another device, and, reverting to a belief in omnipotence (a characteristic of infantile modes of thought), it may deny that there is any danger (omnipotence of the self), or may assert that the government (parental authority) is omnipotent and gives full protection; thus it may put implicit trust in everything the Government says, or even read into official statements, ideas that the Administration does not hold. Such statements as the "100 per cent efficiency of the gas-mask" are stretched to cover all kinds of gas-risk; balloon barrages and anti-aircraft defences are thought of as conferring immunity from attack, and so on. This attitude leads to omission to take proper precautions.

The stability of a mind which adopts denial of danger as its mode of defence against panic is liable to suffer sudden collapse and then it is too late to set in train the "manipulative activities", i.e. doing something useful for the self and for others in an orderly way, which tend to strengthen the ego against panic.

The gravest of the internal dangers, however, arise from the mobilisation of aggressive phantasies directed against loved persons, through identification of the self with the enemy. The person thus feels himself to be in his heart an enemy to his "loved objects" and has to stifle a conflict within himself before he can face his own conscience within or the enemy without. It is not certain but it is in my view probable that this is the principal factor in loss of ego control when faced with dangers of the kind we are considering and therefore in the incidence of panic. The central point of this concept turns on the term "loved objects". This must not be taken narrowly as meaning only persons with whom one is in love, nor confined to present-day persons (here the peculiar "timelessness" of unconscious mental processes comes into prominence); it must rather be regarded as a relation of love and affection to all objects that are or have been endowed in the mind with the attribute of "goodness" (of being helpful, supporting, kind, love-worthy)—objects to which one feels drawn. The term also includes ideals, causes, and beliefs which are felt to be nearly as precious as life itself. Because these impulses and phantasies and the objects to which they relate are unconscious, it is impossible to predict the incidence of panic, and for the same reason it is impossible to take direct precautions against its outbreak. Inner dangers cannot be removed with certainty except by means which get into the inside so to speak; but once again this is not the same as saying that all measures against panic are useless. The internal dangers which we have all struggled with as children, and in lesser degree still struggle against, we have in the past for ordinary situations largely overcome: in extraordinary situations, such as air raids, it is reasonable to adopt so far as possible the same measures which earlier have proved more or less effective.

As objective experiences, air raids may be to most of the population new; but the essential elements—attack from an invisible foe, explosions, and poisonous gases and incendiarism—are so much in line with unconscious infantile phantasy that it is not expedient to regard air raids as new experiences subjectively. There is even something encouraging in this, for what once succeeded in allaying mental strain may be used to that end again. If we think of external dangers only, we can see no rational remedy; but if we consider also "internal dangers", we are not utterly without hope.

Psychological precautions

The essential causal factors of panic cannot be altered by any one measure, but attention to the contributory factors may lessen its incidence. Panic is not a new experience for any of us, but a veil of amnesia covers our most important experiences of it.

Four main factors increase mental strain: isolation from the group; absence of means of removing the source of danger or rendering it less harmful; unreliability of belief in omnipotence; and distrust of Authority. In infancy these factors made mental strain worse and led under certain conditions to panic, which was then overcome by formation of groups, by mastery of the sources of danger (external and internal), by increased reliance on objective experience and diminished reliance on magical beliefs, and by coming to terms with Authority.

Group membership and the reduction of dread

Membership of a group usually reduces dread. Opportunity for friendly interchange and for a mutual "hate" against the enemy keeps away the feeling of complete isolation, which often rapidly passes over to feelings of worthlessness, and acts as a support for the ego. So far a truism; but the psychological consequence of this is not quite so obvious. The mere huddling together of people, even when they have occasion for a mutual "hate", does not constitute the most efficient group-psychology defence against panic. A group cannot be welded effectively by hate.

Panic is probably best allayed by doing something for those one loves. This is presumably the basis of the Air Raid Precautions (ARPs) advice that people should stay in their homes and make them gas-tight, each person being given a duty. The group here is a "natural" one, that of the family; but this assumes that the family ties are good to begin with and will not be made worse by the strain of a raid. The stay-at-home policy (for which one could devise a slogan "Do not go out to seek safety. Make it-at home!") does not, however, take into account the degree of aptitude for, and satisfaction from, manipulative activity (this varies greatly): it omits consideration of the mental state of persons with a claustrophobic tendency (the number of whom is many times greater than of those with manifest claustrophobia), and above all it does not take into consideration the fact that many find their group feelings roused more deeply and more readily in the company of their own sex, or in a society based on community of work or social interests.

The chief objection to the stay-at-home policy (apart from the fact that of the three dangers—high-explosive, incendiary, and gas bomb—at best it may afford some protection only from the last) is that the Government does not appear in this policy as an active partner. A great wave of hate and distrust will come if it fails, and as air raids are likely to be repeated this is a thing no Government could or should risk. In time of danger, a Government cannot rely on working up a spirit of loyalty if in the preceding months it has not won the respect of the public by showing an energetic and realistic endeavour to protect and a fairness in the distribution of the protection.

Such measures as evacuation of a part of the population, and the organisation of groups of householders into units for ARP work, can be considered as regards the type of group formed and its effect on increasing resistance to panic. A group may be given a leader by the central authority but may nevertheless be leaderless from a psychological point of view. Though given a structure or hierarchy, in a moment of crisis the group may still behave in an unorganised way. A paper organisation which breaks down might be worse than none at all. Since the English are not particularly docile and still think of their home as their castle, the home-staying policy may be the best we can organise *en masse*, unless we are willing to spend much money and effort on very numerous, very well-protected shelters.

Mastery of the sources of danger

As we pass from infancy to childhood and to adolescence we grow less afraid; not because we grow strong in the control of external danger but because we grow less afraid of the sources of internal danger—our own aggressive impulses. In this process of mastering anxiety, doing things, particularly for others, plays a significant part. In time of crisis the more primitive mental reactions again become important, and the opportunity to be vigilant on behalf of others and to get busy oneself strengthens the mind to resist panic. Therefore ARP instructions which lay stress on active measures of preparation will tend to reduce panic. The mastery of the "Sources of Danger" should not, therefore, be considered solely in terms of dowsing incendiary bombs or shooting down bombers, but as covering all measures which give self-confidence and divert attention *outwards*. The allotting of duties within the shelter (of whatever kind it be) sets the mind going in an active and constructive direction and so lessens the risk of uncontrollable dread; even if the chance of doing anything "100 per cent effective" is small, nevertheless the doing something in the right direction tends to diminish the strain of mind which comes from a purely passive resistance to apprehension.

Diminished reliance on magical beliefs

In time of mental stress the mind often tends to rely on magical beliefs. Danger lies here in two directions: first, the magical remedy against danger may be suddenly doubted, i.e. the resistance to panic may suddenly collapse; secondly, the reliance on a talisman, if this is provided by an Authority, may lower the capacity for group activity or the full utilisation of group bonds.[3]

"I, in my mask, am secure: the devil take the hindmost!" is more likely to be adopted as a way of thought if the gas-mask is declared to be "100 per cent efficient", i.e. is claimed to be perfect.

One-hundred per cent efficiency is not in any case probable; it requires an effort of mind to contemplate it rationally, but many will jump at the idea as a consolation. Is that consolation to be denied to these nervous people? The question is not well put: it is, rather, "What measures will best meet the craving for security in a situation of great insecurity?" No one would stop a man practising his private magic—if he needs it he will make a talisman of his own—but the question is, what is best for the Government, public authorities, and scientists to do when faced with a demand for what in fact is magic? If there was likely to be only one occasion of panic, the Government intent on prosecuting the war could afford to take the risk (even in democratic England) of adopting the attitude of omnipotence and omniscience by saying, "Obey me and you will be safe!" But air raids may be repeated, and therefore from a military point of view the Government would be unwise to lend too much of its prestige to magic; for magic is an unstable ally. Just as those in need of talismans (and other objects of

---

[3] The medical man may be asked by his patients for advice about analgesic drugs in case of injury. The giving of such drugs may be attended by psychological risks in unstable persons, and the matter should be considered with an eye to mental as well as physical effects.

private protective ritual, such as a horse-hair tied round the finger) will make them for themselves, so those in need of the belief in an omnipotent governmental authority (parent figure in the unconscious mind) will in time of crisis exalt the Government to a position of a Protective Deity, and nothing can stop them from doing so. But it is wiser to encourage reliance on appropriate action rather than on consoling beliefs. In my opinion, therefore, the Government should give a lead in rationality; for example, not saying "gas masks are 100 per cent efficient", which no reasonable man will believe, but that they give protection for so many hours in the concentration of such and such likely to be met in the case of the probable gases in an air raid; and stating the probable proportionate risks of high-explosive, incendiary, and gas bomb. The public in fact should be instructed to think in terms of relative quantity, of more-or-less (reason, conscious mental action) rather than of all-or-none (blind belief, unconscious mental action). It is no valid argument that the public wants plain statements and that therefore the niceties of relative quantities are likely to lead to mere confusion of mind. The risk we are considering, and which has to be combated, is a state in which confusion of mind is completely dominant, and the aim must be to strengthen the controlling forces in the mind. These find support in action—mental action no less than physical. The publication of simple but accurate statements of the various risks, of detailed reports on the effects of aerial bombardment in Spain and other areas of modern warfare, and of the ways in which risks have been effectively dealt with, so far as these are known, therefore seems desirable as an Air Raid Precaution.

Besides giving a lead in protection from an external danger, another way of assisting in panic-prevention is open to the Government. It can contribute to the sense of security by providing a quite different kind of "internal support" from that we have been considering, but one of great psychological importance, namely, food. The confidence that, even though the physical structure of civilisation (railways etc.) may be badly smashed up, this essential support will be distributed regularly to each individual, and fairly as between the various classes in the community, will go far to create a solid group spirit and a good relation to the Government.

The relation to authority

Mention has been made of the danger of blind submission to Authority; but in time of crisis complete emotional independence from Authority is for most people neither possible nor desirable; there is need for leadership and a desire (not necessarily prominent in consciousness) for guidance in action. This favours the quick and loyal submission of the individual to the Group or Commanding Officer, and two things are required: a leader who will really lead, dealing fairly between all members of his group, and a group with which the individual can readily identify himself. These are the factors required to bring stability to an unorganised group and so to reduce the risk of panic. Training in submission to orders is an advantage to rapid group formation, and activities such as fire-drill practice, "physical jerks", boy-scout and girl-guide work, and military drill all work to this end.

Summary

There are probably no really effective specific remedies. Two that have been given much consideration as a recipe against fear may be mentioned: Totalitarianism (even if acceptable in this country) is a brittle crutch; and Religion is apparently easier to prescribe than to dispense.

In conclusion and to repeat: panic in the adult is not a new experience; it is a recrudescence of an earlier state which is screened from us. This gives some of the nameless horror to panic, but it also gives a key to reducing its incidence. Unable to attack its specific causes, we can endeavour to reduce the contributory causes and can follow the ways taken to overcome the periods of panic when our minds were immature: by formation of groups, by manipulative activities, by turning slowly from blind and magical beliefs to a more reasoned interest in the world around us, but above all by acquiring the capacity to recognise and control our own egoism and impulses of hate. On this last depends the success of group-formation and group activities which always exercise a large influence in checking the outbreak of panic.

CHAPTER 11

On the development of professional and unprofessional attitudes

(1934/1938)

Doctors are not the only professionals who find themselves faced with unprofessional rivals, and it should be possible to discover general features of this situation, whether the direction of the activity be the administration of medicine, the drawing up of a deed or an audit, the building of a house or a bridge, the planning of a campaign or the cure of souls.

The present-day professions may be arranged in a series according as they are related to the laws of nature on the one hand or to the customs of men on the other. Thus, we have at one extreme the physicians with their close connection with the disciplines of biochemistry and biology, and at the other extreme the accountants and lawyers whose minds are turned to the intricacies arising from the interplay of human interests, and who have not such a direct connection with science as have the physicians and engineers. This serial classification of the professions shows us at a glance that the criterion used in this paper to distinguish the mental qualities of the unprofessional practitioner

---

This chapter was compiled by the Editor from two overlapping papers entitled "On the Professional Attitude" and "Quacks and Quackery", the latter being the title of Rickman's Inaugural Lecture as Chairman given to the Medical Section of the British Psychological Society in 1934.

cannot be employed with an equal ease in the case of all professions, for they do not all rest on a similar mental basis or share a common history.

Attempts to define the unprofessional attitude in terms of current practice seem to me liable to a considerable disadvantage, because the professions do not regulate the practice of their members but only their education and "professional ethics". The enquiry to be fruitful should be directed to the attitude of the person in question towards the body of knowledge already existing in his subject and to the mental discipline of the student in the face of that body of knowledge. We may thus be able to link up the person who refuses to undergo that discipline, with the attitude of those who, having once oriented themselves to their profession, have later turned their back on the body of knowledge common to their colleagues for the sake of some special fancy of their own.

A word about professional education. The hasty or light-minded student is inclined to think that this is primarily designed to give him facts, that is, to help him to acquire something of the vast store of present knowledge. I regard this as a secondary point, valuable though it is. The main task of a professional education is to show the student how the body of knowledge has been acquired, that is, to put him, as far as practicable, in possession of an instrument for dealing with the unknown. True education is oriented to the unknown and helps the student to face it with the best equipment available. It must give him courage to face his own ignorance in the presence of pressing and difficult situations by showing him the methods by which similar tasks have been solved by his seniors in the past.

A brief historical summary

The first "professional man" was the Shaman, the magician medicine-man, who to this day treats sickness in the primitive Siberian tribes and in other parts of the world. He was the first "professional man", because he was the first person to separate himself from the rest of the community and offer specific services for a specified remuneration. He was thus distinguished from the rest of the community as regards a livelihood by the fact that he received a specified remuneration for a special service. He was not elected as in the case of tribal elders, nor was he usually a hereditary officer as is a king; his position was attained as the result of personal aptitudes. Though the office of Shaman was not hereditary the secrets and tradition were handed down from one to another within the profession.

PROFESSIONAL AND UNPROFESSIONAL ATTITUDES   199

If we consider the following data about the Shaman, not as a collection of amusing facts collected from a little anthropological reading, but as a clinical entity, we may then be free to speak of Shamanism as we would speak of Dementia Paranoides, and later to use just the same psychological instruments of thought when we speak of Priestcraft and Scientific Medicine. We may consider the development of medicine as an example of the evolution of the capacity for objectivity, and if we can get this subject straight in our minds we shall be ready to deal with Quacks and Quackery, which is always an important question, not only because the public looks favourably on quacks but because the tendency to quackery lies in ourselves.

I propose to divide the development of professional life into three categories. They are not three defined historical periods, like three dynasties which succeed one another, though in a measure this is true. They are three kinds of attitude to the Unknown, one might almost say three syndromes, which for convenience I shall call those of Shaman, Priest and Scientist.

The Shaman

The Shaman[1] characterises an animistic attitude to nature in which the world is ruled by forces for the most part hostile, and the illnesses from which men and beasts suffer—including death itself—especially death—are always due to somebody's malice. The way to cure an illness is to fight the evil demon by employing another demon that is stronger. These two will fight, the weaker demon will die and the patient will thus be cured. The Shaman effects the cure by using his ancestral spirits, and the struggle between the two demons takes place inside the Shaman, and he has a fit. A very powerful illness may require several fits. Illness of every kind is regarded as having the same fundamental cause, a bad demon is projected into the patient by a hostile human being or hostile element in nature, by the Gods of the Sky or Earth. In a word, illness is caused by malice, and for cure a malice-extractor or malice-neutraliser is required.

There is a corollary to the notion that every ailment is due to someone else's malice, namely, that the self is perfect and would remain so if it were not for the action of enemies. From this we can go a step further

---

[1] The Shamans referred to in this paper are those from the Altai region of Siberia, among whom the characteristics described here are most clearly observed.

and say that by regarding illness as a thing which can penetrate into the body and be pulled out again, primitive main unconsciously believes that all disease is a form of sadistic coitus displaced from the genitals into the interior of the body.

The cosmology of these people is relatively simple. The demons in the sky and earth are thought to spend their time, when not pouncing on a mortal, in perpetual copulation of the most bloodthirsty kind, so that it is not difficult to connect in one formula cosmology, aetiology and therapy. Thus, the aim of the Shaman is to restore the feeling of perfection of the self which the patient has lost owing to the anxiety caused by the violent coitus of demons inside. The technique of the Shaman is to take part in the proceedings, absorb the copulating elements into himself, let them do their worst and thus to lower the tension in the patient's mind.

These demons are not, I think, the patient's parents so much as a horrible jumble of the parents' genitals in sadistic relation to one another. The difference is significant. If they are really parents and not muddled-up organs, we should expect to find in the cosmogony and in their medical tradition some traces of cohesion of thought and some systematising of their odd beliefs. But both resemble the notions of dementia paranoides patients, and the only way in which they can be reduced to order is to use the rules of dream formation, a code that is valid in a world of one person, the self alone.

There are several points here of great importance for our theme. First of all, the underlying conception is that the self is perfectly healthy except when attacked by a malicious object; secondly, the usual site of the operation of cure lies in the Shaman himself. He becomes in his very person the embodiment of force and therefore of healing. A third point is that the mental mechanism chiefly employed by patient and Shaman alike in this conception of illness is that of projection, the attribution of evil to external agencies, a device of the mind which serves to foster the notion that the self is perfect. In the process of cure the Shaman *impersonates* the forces in the struggle and is possessed by the contending demons. His own *"little death"* and resurrection is a triumph of his power over death itself.

The external world of the Shaman and his patients is made up of what may be regarded as more or less isolated bodily functions, fertility spirits, the demons of mind, rain, thunder, hailstones and so on. These spirits are in almost continual warfare with each other or with man and the beasts. The therapeutic struggle within the Shaman may be regarded as a struggle to master bodily functions in their most dangerous concentration, a conception which tallies with the most primitive notions of the small child.

The "Shamanising" serves a useful function in that it reduces the patient's anxiety, at least for a time, as he has paid a more powerful demon to work for him.[2]

Though the Shaman may only "half-believe" in his magic, that is, he may be willing to let his patients deceive themselves about his powers, he is no reformer in the sense that he wishes them to change their outlook on the world of nature without or within themselves.

In addition to the exhibition of magic powers, the Shaman has a certain crude skill in the use of drugs and manipulative surgery, but the greater part of his professional education is devoted to the less objective but more spectacular aspects of his occupation. In the Altai region of Siberia, for instance, the training of the novitiate lasts for nine years, during which time the pupil changes his sex, fasts, is nearly frozen in winter (Siberian winter) and baked in summer; he has to learn to go off into a fit at command and to endure the tortures of his Elders in order to acclimatise himself to the even worse rigors of the demons. It is a thorough professional training, characterised by a systematic disciplining of the student to meet the problems of the unknown. It teaches him whatever is known to his elders of the lore concerning nature and the control of the body by means of drugs and above all by demons. It seems to me, from the cases on record, that to become a Shaman is a means of dealing with mental breakdown. They defend themselves from this eventuality by submitting to the crudest expression of the paranoid phantasies which we meet with in the adult psychotic or in the infant. In this connection it must be remembered that the communities in which they live retain a normal if primitive mental outlook towards each other, in time of health, while simultaneously harbouring conceptions which we only hear freely spoken of in a mental hospital.

The characteristic of the notions of the Shaman and his patient may be summarised in a phrase: their aggressive impulses are only to a slight extent blended with loving or restitutive tendencies (Klein & Riviere, 1937). Illness scares both Shaman and patient. The Shaman sets about at once to fight the demon through the process of introjective identification, but by so doing he loses touch with the patient until such time as he is less frightening. The anxiety of these people is easily roused and this makes them lose objectivity. Their technique for deal-

---

[2] The Shaman, like his professional brother in another stage of culture, does not usually get paid by results: no cure, no pay is not the rule among them.

ing with anxiety is restricted, because they have not been able to achieve a harmony either in their own personality, or in their conception of the external world. The professional education of the Shaman is sadistic because fear of the destructive forces within themselves prevents them from making any contact with their patients or each other, except in a hostile way. They resemble the psychotic in cherishing within themselves the conception of a good force or good objects which must be kept from contact with other people. Their aggression is probably a defence against phantasied danger from their patients (I am referring here to their unconscious mental processes) and, as in the case of all people who have found but little means to soften their impulses of hate by a tender component, their capacity for sublimation is reduced.

If we ask what is handed on from one generation to another of Shamans, and frame our answer in terms of infantile phantasies (usually, in our culture, unconscious ones), we arrive at a simple but terrible answer. The world is governed by fighting demons, whose hate must be met with the magic of counter-malice, and the technique for doing this is to decrease the capacity for sensibility of every kind, even at the cost of mental dissociation. No hope can have no fear. To have no love spares the mind from any loss. The result of this education is to make a profound separation between the Shamans and the rest of the tribe. The Shaman is feared because he is associated in the mind of his patients with the forces of destruction. Though evil, he is tolerated because he protects them from greater evil.

This, unless I am much mistaken, was the state of affairs when professional life began. I wish to emphasise one point, i.e. that Shamanism was (and is) a profession with a long discipline and professional standards of behaviour. We may deplore the technique, but we must recognise the fact that it is an organised attempt to deal with the unknown along lines which were proper to the culture that the profession served.

The Priest

The change from Shamanism to Religion was no doubt gradual; the two exist side by side in the purest forms—for example, along that vast boundary between China and Siberia—but, taking extreme instances which yet lie properly within each type, the differences are enormous.

First of all, the true priest does not take part in the personal affairs of the community in at all the same way as the true Shaman, He never at any time identifies himself with the spirits, but stands between the people and the Gods and Demons and acts as an interpreter as Moses did, as a messenger from God to man or man to God.

The Shaman deals with the forces of nature by taking them into himself and letting them fight within him: he *impersonates* them. The Priest, on the other hand, stands aside from the battle, he mediates between the Gods and men. The difference between these two functions is profound, for the Priest does not claim for his own person any special power but only such power as he is given by the Gods. The Shaman is a master of the demons, the Priest serves both Gods and man.

When the Other World is regarded as made up of what, for want of the proper anthropological word, I would call bodily functions (fertility, wind, rain, thunder, hailstones, etc.) and only these, each requiring its propitiation, and these spirits are engrossed in sadistic coitus, there is no opportunity for a personal go-between, because *neither* of the protagonists is a unified personality. The spirits are thought of as embodiments of organic functions, and men are thought of as perfect beings ravaged by these organs. The change from Shamanism to Religion can be ascribed to a unification of the spirit organs into Divine People, which process is but the reflection in heaven of an internal mental change due to an alteration in the ego.

The difference between Shamanism and Religion may be followed in more detail. In the former, the forces of nature resemble bodily functions; in the latter, they are more integrated and take the shape of people. In the former, they are fighting or engaged in violent copulation; in the latter, though they fight, they also engage in constructive occupations such as creating the world, or as master smiths, messengers and farmers. The behaviour of the Gods and Demons is a fair index of the organisation of infantile phantasy upon which the culture has stabilised itself, but is not an exact index for the whole community. In the Shaman culture, the predominant unconscious phantasy appears to be that of a persecutory insertion of dangerous objects into the personality, and the predominant resulting attitude to the self is that of hypochondria. In the Priestly culture, the predominant attitude is not so markedly projective, the self is in increasing degree regarded as the seat of evil; and in the later stages of the culture, the predominant attitude to the self is that of *guilt*. Speaking generally, the priests tend to turn aggression inwards and to increase the sense of duty to the Gods, later to the neighbour, as a means for overcoming the sense of isolation and misery which is liable to arise in the mind.

In its struggle to master the excitements generated by the instincts, the mind adopts a peculiar device for acquiring an equilibrium. It absorbs objects from the outside world and attaches these to the ego so that the excitement can be spread over a greater area so to speak, and thus more easily tolerated; this absorption is called superego formation. Thus when the Shaman is faced with a wilderness of demons, he calls in the aid of his ancestral spirits to help him, and this, in the form of a horse, for example, takes possession of him, or more correctly he takes the horse-strength into himself.

The character of this ego-annex depends on the character of the primitive instincts at the time of the annexation, that is, when the ego was driven by fear to take steps for its better security.

Using this as a criterion for ego-development, we can see that Shamanism is based on a more primitive kind of contact with the outside world than Religion, because in the latter the objects annexed are more developed and co-ordinated, or to put it more simply are more like real people than is the case in Shamanism. The complexity of the tasks of the ego, which the increasing moral sense brought in its train, helped to alter the attitude to the outer world as well as to the self. In religion there is, furthermore, a greater opportunity for progressive development in the character of the objects annexed. Whereas Shamanism must of its very nature stay on the level in which the essential elements are related in a sadistic coitus, religion offers vastly greater scope for sublimation and the personality of the protagonist reaches the level of organised and well-disposed human beings.

Speaking generally, the Gods in the Priestly culture were kinder than in the Shamanistic and were influenced by Man's constructive activities instead of being overpowered by greater diabolism. When God is pleased with the work of man's hands humanity is encouraged to vie with the Gods in creative activity. Progress in culture depends on man's capacity to identify himself with a father-image who produces good things: put in another way progress depends on the acquisition of a helpful superego.

Whatever the causes may have been which led to an alteration in the character of the superego, the result was a profound change in the attitude towards the external and internal world. Nature became less an object of fear and more an object of study. Though the wish to control the Gods was not extinguished it was thought necessary to study the manifestations of their will. The seat of omnipotence shifted from the self to heaven when and only when the Gods came to be regarded as benevolent.

The importance of these changes for our present topic lies in their effect on professional education. When the accent is no longer laid on the student or novice acquiring magical control over demons within himself, a less divided attention is directed to the behaviour of and control over an object lying outside the self. Put in another way, when the student's or novice's (unconscious) fear of his own destructive impulses is lessened he is in a position to recognise the interplay of forces outside himself. The rule of law cannot be grasped while the mind is struggling with chaos within itself. Insofar as the Priest puts himself under a discipline it is to curb his own bodily passions, so that he may be in a better position either to bargain with the Gods in the more primitive religions, or, in the later developments of religion, to detach himself from the forces of nature in order to be more receptive to divine manifestations. The self-discipline of the Priest shows every gradation between Shamanism and science.

We must not forget that the main duties of the Priests were not to make observations of symptoms of bodily or even mental disease but only to appease the Gods. As the belief in God's benevolence grew so the Priests became more concerned to preserve in every way the flock under their care, and thus they began to be concerned with healing. But their primary function was to regulate passions. They were most concerned with sin, and their therapy was the casting out of devils, but by a new technique. At the same time, the seat of perfection gradually shifted from the self to the person of God. Sin and disease were defilements that had to be searched for in the behaviour and subjective feelings. The Shaman dealt mainly with hypochondria, the Priest with guilt.

The differences between the Shaman and the Priest can be illustrated in two further directions, namely, as regards their capacity for objectivity and as regards the level of the mind on which they sought to bring relief. The Shaman is clearly dealing with unorganised forces and he regards the outside world as chaotic as the fighting demons inside his mind. The Priest, in establishing the rule of a personal God, is reflecting the relative calm which he has established within. In more technical language, the superego of the Priest is more co-ordinated, more of a person than that of the Shaman; consequently he is prepared to recognise a reign of law.

The Scientist

The liberation of the mind which the Priest's independent position gave, led to a restricted but useful degree of objectivity. The possibility of external law led to a curiosity about the whole of the processes of nature instead of merely her terrifying moments. Perhaps the most important factor in the development of medicine lay in that passionate love for the human body which characterised the Greeks. The feature of most psychological importance seems to me to lie in the fact that among the Greeks the ailments of the body did not arouse the same fear in the mind of the practitioner, as they did in previous ages. Injury and disorder of function aroused pity instead of stirring up beliefs in demons. In fact, a vast change had taken place in the ego of the practitioner. He was able to look at disablement and disease without losing his objectivity, or we might say that his capacity for *object-love* overcame his fear of anything which reminded him of castration.

I have described earlier the training of the Shaman, which lasted for about nine years, and the ordeals which their training entailed, at least in the Altai region of Siberia. The medical student of the Greeks also submitted himself to the influence of his ancestors, but in a different way. He had not to be terrified of them, but to learn about their observations in the book of nature. I think the reason why their minds were so free to observe, lay in the fact that they had libidinised the aggressive component in their minds and were able to guide their energies towards the outer world in a co-ordinated and constructive way, irrespective of the appearance of their patients. They did not believe that their patients were full of demons, good or evil, but that they were human beings. The operation of object-love overcame their anxiety.

The removal of inner anxiety leads, as we know in clinical experience, to a sense of the person being a single being, which is not the case in neurotics and still less in psychotics. When there is a unification within the personality, the outer world is found to be harmonious also; the latter is dependent on the former. I take it that this is the reason why Scientists assume that there is only one kind of science. It is impossible to assume two kinds of mental processes of equal validity, which contradict one another, if the intellect is the instrument of a single controlling force within the personality.

It is a curious fact that the more a person regards the outer world as an ordered place the more simple do his instruments of thought become. The Shaman seeks to overcome demons by a combination of the most terrific powers that he can assemble. He lays the accent on the personal strength of his mind and asserts that he can discern the cause of disease in every case afresh. Contrast this with the humble task of the Scientist, who patiently matches one experience against another, one patient's symptom with another, until he has built up a clear picture of two things with points of resemblance and difference, both independent of each other and both in the outside world. His work is as little as possible subjective, as little as possible exciting to his emotions. The Scientist delays the feeling of pride in his work until the case before him is fitted into the framework of laws which he can understand and use. The Shaman does not match two external objects, but insofar as his work deals with observation at all, it is the matching of an external object with a figure in his phantasy. He cannot construct an ordered picture of external forces because his own subjective feelings thrust themselves into his view of the world, that is, he has no capacity for objectivity.

The change from Shaman to Priest can be expressed in many ways; we can regard it as a change in the concept of the Gods or in the ways of overcoming anxiety or guilt. The change from Priest to Scientist can in the same way be viewed as an alteration in the attitude to the external or to the internal world, which results in an important change in the attitude to knowledge. The Shaman and the Priest have secrets, the Scientist publishes whatever he discovers. From this point of view, the Priest again stands in an intermediate position, for the earliest recording of observations was done by Priests, but for their own secret purposes. In contrast, the Scientist publishes his work for anyone to use.

The psychological and social factors which led to the development of a scientific habit of thought in different periods of history lie outside the scope of this discussion, but we may consider some of the more recent social results of the development from a religious to a scientific outlook.

When the means of controlling nature were thought to be magical and the persons employing those means were thought to be of a different kind of human being to the ordinary, the regulation of the professions by the community was out of the question because the professions regulated the community.

An example

An example may illustrate this point. So far I have not mentioned the function of Shamans and Priests as ambassadors between the tribes, nor of their regulation of the economic life of the community. No undertaking of any importance was begun until it was ascertained from Shaman or Priest that the attitude of the Spirits or Gods was favourable. Even in so high a culture as pre-revolution Russia, the peasants (at least in the Samara Government) would not begin sowing the Spring wheat before a particular Church Feast, unless the Priest gave them leave. As the Feast was movable the planting of grain was sometimes at a favourable, and sometimes at an unfavourable, season. The condition of the ground was thought by some to exercise less influence than the will of God. It was thought by others that God would be offended if the planting was done before the ritual of the death and resurrection of the God. Though the district was periodically stricken with devastating famines and they had the evidence before them of the better husbandry of their Tartar neighbours in the next villages (the Priests of Allah laid no such agricultural restrictions as did those of the Christian God), yet fear of the jealousy and wrath of God overrode rational, self-preservative tendencies. The laws of nature were thought to be different according to whether people leaned on a Christian or Mohameddan God. No other laws were known, and, outside the framework of religious belief, there was thought to be nothing but chaos.

The change from status to contract

With the development of the idea that knowledge was a more effective instrument for controlling nature than magic, public attention turned in its own interest to the regulation of the professions. In the case of England, in respect to medicine in the last century, for instance, the legislators in effect struck a bargain with the medical profession in these terms: In return for an obligation you will be accorded certain privileges, the law will not limit you in respect to the methods you employ but will insist that you have a reasonable amount of information about the methods that are and have been employed, and a reasonable amount of understanding of the reasons that have led to those methods being adopted. In return for the obligation of education, the executive will only appoint to public offices persons who are registered as having passed examinations, the general character of which will be decided by appointees of the executive and of the profession. Further, such certificates as affect public interest—for example, those of death— and such as cause a drain on the treasury—pensions and health certificates—will only be accepted if signed by a person who is on the Register. Persons on this Register will be allowed to recover reasonable fees in a Court of Law, in payment for the knowledge they obtain in the course of their education and the skill they acquire in the course of their work. It has been made very clear and definite that persons on the Medical Register *are not a* privileged group *within the community*.

This brief outline may be summarised in the well-known aphorism of Sir Henry Maine, who said that the history of the professions is but another example of the *change from Status to Contract*.

Psychological basis for the professional attitude

A community which believes in magic will also believe that illness can only be cured with the intervention of a different kind of person; a community which believes that the forces of nature are subject to laws, as distinct from the notion that the forces of nature can be controlled by the superior force of personal magic, will employ for therapeutic purposes persons who have studied those laws.

A belief in magic may, as is well known, make an individual or a community impervious to the evidence of the senses, so that it is most unlikely that the professional attitude belonging to the "contractual period" could develop in a culture of the "status period". In the "contract period" both parties must be "contractually minded", and if we seek for the causes of the development of the "contractual attitude" in the community, I think it will be found in the absence of secrecy about the phenomena of nature (more positively in the impulse towards publication of discoveries) which characterises the science-oriented cultures; secrets, which once were thought to bind the Gods, bind those who keep them for themselves. A body of men united in publishing all they know must in the end prevail over a group which relies on a special relation to the uncertain Gods.

A genetic study of the professional impulses

Psychoanalytic studies of the most important but most obscured period of our lives, infancy, show that in its early, and as yet unorganised and unintegrated state, the mind is ruled by phantasies of two kinds: destructive and constructive. These phantasies, and the response of the self to them, constitute the mental basis on which the subsequent activity is built up and determine the individual's attitude towards his fellow men and towards the outer world.

Three factors are of special importance: the strength of the impulses in question, the way in which they are blended, and the methods by which the destructive component of the instinctual life is curbed. The first is presumably entirely due to heredity, the second and third depend in part on the first, in part on the environment. We know too little about the obscure hereditary factor to justify its inclusion in this discussion. But we can give an example of the blending of impulses. The destructive impulse finds expression in chopping things to pieces, the constructive or more correctly *reparative* impulse finds expression in putting them together again. Our complicated culture finds use for both of these impulses either separately or in fusion; thus the butcher and the surgeon, the woodman and the carpenter chop or cut objects to pieces, and we would be in a sorry way without these four people, but there is a difference in the mental attitude of the surgeon and the carpenter which we may discern without prejudice to the high social value of the activities of the butcher and the woodman: the former not only cut up but they fasten together what they have cut.

Speaking generally, the putting-together activity calls for more skill than the cutting-up, and cannot be developed without help, although it is important to remember that the *impulse* to put together exists at a very early stage of mental life.

The strength of the putting-together impulse appears to be derived from two sources. In the first place, it is an expression of the loving, constructive tendencies (derived from the genital impulse to create things), in part it is a reaction to the anxiety and guilt which arise in the mind when the destructive impulse has its way, for we must remember we are dealing with animistic phantasies in which inanimate objects are thought of as people whose destruction is ultimately terrible calamity.

The defences against the influence in the mind of the destructive component of our instinctual life, play a large part in our culture. One way by which the destructive component is rendered harmless is by an identification with and imitation of a "good father figure" in our phantasies. First of all this is almost entirely an imaginary figure, a beneficent and God-like concept, but later it assumes more human proportions. As this humanising process proceeds, interest in *technique* increases; the wish to make things, or to repair things, becomes more and more strongly bound up with the *way* of doing so.

We refer to the inner and unconscious aspect of this alliance with a constructive figure in the phantasy life as the superego; its more conscious and external aspects may be referred to as the ego-ideal.[3]

As a result of superego (and later ego-ideal) formation the individual's attitude to his own impulses and to the outer world undergoes change. Two consequences of this change are of special concern in connection with our subject: first there is set up in the mind a critical

---

[3] The development of the earlier psychoanalytic concept of the superego may be followed most conveniently in *A General Selection from the Works of Sigmund Freud* (Rickman, 1937). For its later development see *The Psycho-Analysis of Children* (Klein, 1932) and Melanie Klein and Joan Riviere's *Love, Hate and Reparation* (1937). For its special relation to the destructive component, see Klein, "A Psycho-Analytic Study of the Manic-Depressive States" (1949).

faculty which judges the influence that the instinctual forces exert in the mind, and secondly, when several people adopt the same ideal, their relation to one another alters so that they readily form a group (Freud, 1921c).

The discipline of the ego-ideal (the more conscious aspect) derives its strength and ultimately its direction from the more primitive and unconscious superego, and may be described as a positive and negative injunction: "If you do as the ideal does you will receive the support of a benevolent father figure; if you go against the ideal, you will lose the support of this benevolent father figure." When combined with the second factor this becomes: "If you do as the group does you will receive its support; if you go against the group you will stand in painful isolation." At first sight it would appear from this that the superego (ego-ideal) always worked in the direction of traditionalism. This is in the main true, but it must not be forgotten that the impulse to investigate and experiment may be supported by the superego, and that the support which is valued most is that which preserves the mind from the consequences of its own inner conflicts. There may therefore be strong forces working in the mind in the direction of research and new scientific creations as well as towards the most arid traditionalism. It depends on the character of the ideal whether the outcome will be progressive or not.

We may now re-examine the three periods of professional development with the superego factor as a criterion. It is clear that in the case of the Shaman the ego-ideal was one of personal power (to a lesser extent this applies to the Priestly stage); the goal was to be a powerful magician influencing directly the lives of men. In the third or scientific stage, the omnipotence of the self is curbed by a criterion lacking or nearly lacking in the other two: the criterion is an understanding of how the forces of nature work. The wish to be omnipotent may be there, but the ego-ideal says "You shall not enjoy that feeling of power until you have discovered how these forces operate." The pleasure is not denied, it is postponed—in its full strength, it is indefinitely postponed. The Shaman says "I and my Spirits cure", the Priest, "I will call on the Gods to help you", the Scientist "the application of this method may cure".

It may be observed that this distinction between the three types does not refer to the motive which leads the individuals to acts of therapy. The wish to relieve suffering is an impulse which springs from the very early days of phantasy activity and may be combined with the greatest degrees of magic and mysticism or the purest refinements of the scientific spirit.

A genetic study of the unprofessional impulse or of the nature of "quackery"

As I have shown above, clinical observation of a wide variety of people shows that the wish to heal others is not the expression of a simple instinct, but is the end product of various tendencies which date back to the early phantasy activity of infancy. Among these are the wish to cut up and explore the insides of other people, to stop them having children, to make children themselves, to regulate the alimentary contents in peculiar and magical ways and to control the breathing, eating and sleeping of themselves and others. In some people these phantasies persist not in the conscious mind but in the unconscious as tendencies to action, and determine the choice of a profession. The phantasies are not to be thought of as embodying the principles and practice of physiology, pharmacology and medicine. On the contrary, quite "innocent" children indulge the most awful thoughts of chopping people up, stewing the bits in poison and then, after a pang of guilt, making the people whole again and ready for another "doctor game". In fact very little children behave rather like Shamans, later they behave rather like priests and try to curb their destructive impulses with piety, and later still they develop a quiet or seemingly quiet interest in the world about them.

It is important to know this fact about our own childhood because, by understanding it aright, we approach the subject of quackery from a new angle. The usual medical—registered medical—opinion is that a quack is a danger to the community because he does not know enough. Remembering how much I myself have forgotten, this view does not impress me as much as no doubt it ought to. The subject of quackery can be approached also from the side of the *emotions* and not only of the intellect. One can ask what difference exists between doctor and quack in respect to the control of these wayward phantasies which affect our choice of a career.

The way in which as children we tried to curb the forces of these crude impulses has already been described as superego formation. I can describe the later stages of this very roughly as the acquisition of an ego-ideal in which the self submits to an internal discipline of the emotional life in order to become more like an admired person—an ideal. This ego-ideal can be shared if several people adopt the same idealised leader, and when they do this a strong group feeling may develop between them. Furthermore, the leader need not be real—it can be an abstraction such as "The Profession"—but its essential features remain. The essential features of the professional ego-ideal are that it is adopted in order to keep discipline in the mind; it admonishes the self when its rules are disobeyed or praises the self if the codes of behaviour are maintained and it promoted group-formation. This is expressing in popular language and rather inaccurately some of the aspects of the superego.

Now the whole question turns on the kind of object which is regarded as an ideal, whether the behaviour of the individual is in a social or sublimated direction or in an egocentric or destructive one. Psychology calls an aim an "ideal" if it is such to the ego, irrespective of whether it is so regarded by the community. One of the worst quacks I ever came across had a very strong ideal, but it was a destructive one. But whether it is good or bad, an ideal is one of the most important factors in a man's mental life and, as much as anything else, shapes his behaviour. The matter can be summed up as follows: the ideal is acquired from a superior, though the choice of who is idealised is the result of unconscious factors in the mind; but the purpose of the ego-ideal is primarily to act as a guard against the carrying out of the infantile phantasies in an unmodified form.

Let us return to the subject of quacks: I shall define them as persons who refuse to submit to the discipline of a profession, while claiming the privileges of the professional man. From my own rather restricted experience and from the wider experience of my colleagues, I have drawn up the following reasons why quacks do not undertake professional qualifications. Firstly, the quack has an unconscious hostility to or suspicion of society, which makes it almost impossible for him to accept a mandate for practice without rousing guilt feelings, so he sets up an opposition camp which at one and the same time gives expression to his unfriendly attitude to the community and ministers to the sense of his own importance. Secondly, the quack fears that the "hackneyed routine of the curriculum" will take away a special gift that he regards as his most cherished possession; he calls it the "gift of healing". It is usually a belief in magic in one disguise or another; in some it is a genuine skill in manipulation or facility in a restricted kind of diagnosis. Thirdly, the quack believes that the medical profession has, through its own sinful pride, its worldly success and the favour of the Government, been corrupted so that it can no longer see the Truth, and God has raised him (the man in question) up to give a new Gospel for the regeneration of mankind, which the medical profession is out to suppress.

We might call these the aggressive quack, the timid quack and the deluded quack, without prejudice to another grouping that includes all three.

Now you may ask why I did not begin this section with this statement. My reason was that the significance of these objections is not apparent without a consideration of the influence of the demons or bogies of our childhood, or the device of superego and ego-ideal to curb our criminal tendencies. A man who goes to a medical school and says "I will learn the art of healing from you, I will spend my life in association with you and submit to the discipline of my colleagues in my relations to the public and my patients", is showing a certain amount of willingness to curb his impulses and to take on the guidance of an ego-ideal which will tend to unite him to the community. My experience is that doctors and surgeons had rather more than the average of the destructive phantasies in their childhood, and it has been said that their profession is a choice forced on them by the pressure of an early and unconscious sadism. I do not even refute that we doctors may be unconscious sadists. I want, rather, to point out that in choosing the discipline of the curriculum an attempt is made to bring the restraints of an ego-ideal to bear on the destructive impulse and to guide it in harmless fashion on to the outside world.

I can interpolate one of my conclusions here: the difference between the doctor and the quack is not so much that the former is learned and the latter ignorant (important, when valid, though that distinction is) as that the doctor shows willingness to continue his ego-ideal construction far beyond childhood, while the quack does not give the same evidence of this, in respect to his professional training.

To make the significance of this clear I must go back to the earliest situations again when the child thought of demons inside himself and outside as well. The acceptance of helpers in the form of a friendly ego-ideal is clinically an indication that the major part of the struggle is over, and that the violent impulses will be kept in check in the normal way. When a benevolent ego-ideal is not formed the outcome is always precarious because the subject is more liable to become suspicious of authority and to develop on lines that are not consistent with one another, i.e. to become deluded. A helpful ego-ideal strengthens the ego and increases objectivity; a destructive ego-ideal increases the feeling of self-importance *vis-à-vis* the world and decreases the power of constructive thought. Without the internal help of a benevolent ego-ideal there is a danger of regression to an earlier phase of the struggle with instinctual impulses. To put it crudely, regression may end in Shamanism. I am not such a fool as to think that the taking of a medical course is a guarantee against the regression to Shamanism or that it will do more than assist whatever power of objectivity is already there. The measures of education are powerless against a defective or destructive ego-ideal, but the wish to co-operate with those who already possess the learning and tradition of the profession is a good index that the student has taken a step towards the outside world that is characterised by the incorporation of what is good, and is not going to exploit his rescue and restitution phantasies unchecked.

It is clear that the acceptance of the present medical profession as a teacher does not imply that the student should not be free to criticise and later to lead his fellow practitioners in whatever direction he thinks is wise and good; but to reject the assistance of the professional training, because on some point it seems wrong, indicates to my mind a hypersensitivity to particular and usually symbolical problems that is certainly far from satisfactory.

Clinically, we find that when one feature in an otherwise desired individual causes great revulsion, the explanation that this is due to a heightened and delicate sensibility is only half the story; the visible symptom is like a buoy anchored over hidden rocks. The man may make declarations of passion and undying devotion to his lady, but if he shudders at the thought of some blemish, his relation to her will almost certainly be shipwrecked by unconscious anxiety.

I have found in psychoanalytic practice that when a patient rails or argues against a department of medical activity, he is masking anxiety regarding one of his own phantasies. I recall one who sneered at the doctor's pills and potions and only with the greatest difficulty discovered his unconscious delusions of being poisoned. Several have jeered at the errors in diagnosis made by medical men, who had failed to detect their hysteria, which they only themselves admitted with a terrible struggle. The list could be lengthened endlessly. The point is that these attacks conceal an underlying anxiety due not to fear that the medical man will fail in attaining truth but due to the unconscious hostility to the doctor and to other father figures, and the guilt which this arouses makes them hinder the doctor in his work.

We discover in our clinical work that the capacity for objectivity is usually weak in places, or that where it is weak the mind builds up defences. For instance, the attacks on the medical profession, which, we hear from our patients, are in some cases due to an unwillingness to acknowledge indebtedness due to guilt feelings. The same impulse leads people to attack the Church and Religion, not because these institutions stand as barriers in the way of Truth which is the conscious reason advanced, but because the Church tries to bring consolation to those who have a bad conscience, a point that touches them nearly. I believe that the charge, often made by quacks, that the medical profession refuses to co-operate with them, is a projection due to their own guilt feelings that they have neglected to equip themselves for their work in the way that one of their ego-ideals recommended. I think that the aggressive quacks all suffer from a bad conscience—or, in other terms, their superego or ego-ideal is not a benevolent one—and so they find a co-operative relationship to a professional-ideal painful. I do not wish to be misinterpreted at this point. I do not say that quacks with an unco-operative ego-ideal necessarily and always do harm to their patients. They may deserve all the gratitude they receive, but they have not adjusted themselves to society or to science, nor have they adjusted to their own internal conflicts.

I want to say a few words about the timid quack who fears the "hackneyed routine of the medical schools" will spoil his gift. I know a few such whose gift is precious to them for a very good reason: it is a delusion that stands between them and the outbreak of intolerable anxiety. The overvaluation of their "gift" as a curative agency for humanity is based on an assumption made unconsciously by nearly all quacks that other people are going to be cured by the agencies that they themselves find useful, another instance of lack of objectivity and incapacity to distinguish between the external world and internal phantasy. "Sovereign Remedies" are regarded as magical talismans, and on this point we may offer two comments. They make the quack feel that he himself is not dangerous to his patients, so their function is to allay the quack's anxiety in respect to this unconscious intentions towards his patient. The sovereign remedy ministers to the quack's sense of magical power; the implication is always that other waters possess no such patent drug. Those who have real self-confidence are not ashamed to acknowledge a limitation of their powers. I believe that the argument that patients require of their medical attendant an omniscient or omnipotent attitude, and that to deny them the pleasure of reliance on a "strength" outside themselves jeopardises the treatment, is a fallacy. When suffering, the patient requires benevolent attention and knowledge. If the medical attendant indulges in magic he raises the bogey-fears in his patient's mind without knowing that he does so. The remedy for bad bogey-fears is not more magic but the experience of an understanding fellow human being.

Of course many medical students have romantic-defensive phantasy-delusions of the kind I have been ascribing to the quack. I do not believe that the medical education does a jot to cure them of such delusions, but it helps the student to sublimate the remainder of their less destructive phantasies and so lessens the urgency of the dominant pathological one. The medical school has this effect because the students themselves take the step in the direction of reality.

I now come to another aspect of the subject which is easier to treat under the heading of quackery than quack. It is the gradual dilution of the objective scientific attitude in already qualified men—by magical beliefs, at first respecting the peculiar efficacy of certain remedies, or the special dangers of certain techniques, and proceeding, usually gradually, either to a doddering old-fashionedness or else to a belligerent modernism or trailing after new cults. I think two principles already foreshadowed in the earlier part of this paper will guide us in our judgement of these schismatic people and their followers. The first principle is that if they retain their interest in the profession they have adopted and try to convert their colleagues to their ideas, they may be in error but they are not quacks. In the terminology adopted here, they share the ego-ideal of the profession and are colleagues still, and in the long run they are a blessing because they keep us critical of ourselves. If they break away from the profession, to start another organisation that is nearly the same but with an improvement, they are fighting out in the external world an internal mental conflict and have already lost their objectivity.

Revolutions and nationalism may have a place in the social world because the persons affected must have some control over their own lives, no one can endure unlimited frustration. But science is not the place in which to initiate the factions and cliques of political life. Anyone who increases the resemblance to politics has turned away from a constructive ego-ideal. Change must come from within; slow it may be and fatiguing to those whose work is not appreciated, but in science one must be willing to endure unlimited frustration.

This brings me to the second principle. The final test of quackery is not whether it works cures but whether it adds to knowledge. The thing that convinces me that the medical profession is on the right lines and the organisations of rivals are on the wrong lines is not that the profession has the support of authority but that it adds to our understanding of the outside world. I believe that objectivity and the capacity to increase the richness of science is the only reliable test whether a profession is moving along the right lines. Other organised professions may arise, have arisen, and will arise, but they will not flourish if they are based on the deflection of aggressive impulses onto the medical or another profession. If they borrow our text-books and distort them, borrow our nomenclature and confuse it, they will have no power of doing permanent injury because the ego-ideal which holds them together is based on hostility and not on respect for what is good; hatred breeds fear, and fear reduces the power to see clearly. The aetiology, nosology and therapy will regress to Shamanism, and the public, which in the end is never foolish, will go where their complaints are best understood.

Professional education

We may now return to professional education, which is of two kinds: the "ad hoc" and the "historical".

"Ad hoc" professional education

By this I mean that the student is told how he is to deal with such and such a situation. Its extreme form is found in the courses of salesmanship which some firms hold for their travellers. Here the student is told the latest methods of obtaining a customer's attention and confidence and is given "sales talk" to "push" the particular "line" of goods to be marketed. It is "ad hoc" because the orientation of the education is to a particular problem and the best of the present known ways of dealing with that problem are given, without the background of experience which led to the selection of the method.

There would be no reason for mentioning "ad hoc" professional education (which is to be distinguished from post-graduate or "refresher courses" by the fact that these are based on a previously acquired academic background) were it not for the fact that it forms a large part of the syllabus of some of the medical cults that claim professional status. The length of training which some of these groups emphasise in their favour is not the important criterion, but the proportion of it that is educational.

Historical education

An education is "historical" when it is so arranged that the student can follow the growth of knowledge in his subject. The importance of this from a psychological point of view cannot be overemphasised. Although the presentation of information, however convincing intellectually, will not remove the unconscious tendencies to primitive or magical ways of dealing with the phenomena of nature, a presentation of the development of scientific thought will assist the student, if he has imagination, to identify himself with those who have contributed to knowledge.

The process of superego (ego-ideal) formation, though strongest in infancy, continues throughout development, and when a student begins a new phase of his career he is in a receptive state of mind to form "transferences", that is, to repeat—but without his being aware of the repetition—his infantile attitude to the figures in his phantasy who formed part of his superego. It is a period in which the "professional attitude" begins to take shape once more. I say "once more" because there is a rudiment of the professional attitude in the early phantasies of all children. When they want to be engine-drivers, doctors, soldiers and so forth, they build up a picture not only of driving engines and operating on people, but on being the person, in his relation to other engine-drivers and doctors as well as to engines and patients.

This "transference" can be guided to a limited extent only by educational methods, but within these limits the direction taken by educational influences is important. The main strength of a professional group in a "contractual"—that is, on the whole non-magical—culture lies in its members' possession of a highly developed critical faculty and of sharing the same "instruments of thought".

The aggressive component of the instinctual endowment of every individual needs outlet, and if this can be employed in a socially constructive way the community is going to benefit as well as the individual. The impulse to attack can be employed, again only to a limited but by no means negligible degree, in "attacking problems". When the "enemy" is the cause of disease, the aggression is by sublimation turned upon inanimate nature, and the common ideal in this work is an effective group-bond. There is, however, another direction in which aggression can be turned with great immediate satisfaction to the individuals in the group, and that is to a rather similar but rival group. A group which relies on this for its main group-bond is, from a psychological point of view, taking a "regressive path" and in the long run suffers through lack of the inspiration which comes from successful attacks on scientific problems.

CHAPTER 12

Intra-group tensions in therapy: their study as the task of the group

(1943)

The term "group therapy" can have two meanings. It can refer to the treatment of a number of individuals assembled for special therapeutic sessions, or it can refer to a planned endeavour to develop in a group the forces that lead to smoothly running co-operative activity.

The therapy of individuals assembled in groups is usually in the nature of explanation of neurotic trouble, with reassurance; and sometimes it turns mainly on the catharsis of public confession. The therapy of groups is likely to turn on the acquisition of knowledge and experience of the factors which make for a good group spirit.

This paper was published jointly by W. R. Bion, DSO, BA(Oxon), MRCS, LRCP, and John Rickman, MD, and is reprinted from *The Lancet* (27 November 1943), p. 678. "A Scheme for Rehabilitation" is a report of the work of Bion; "Application of Group Therapy in a Small Ward" is a report of the work of Rickman. The paper was reprinted under the same title in *Experiences in Groups* (Bion, 1961).

A scheme for rehabilitation

In the treatment of the individual, neurosis is displayed as a problem of the individual. In the treatment of a group it must be displayed as a problem of the group. This was the aim I set myself when I was put in charge of the training wing of a military psychiatric hospital. My first task therefore was to find out what the pursuit of this aim would mean in terms of time-table and organisation.

I was not able to work at this task in an atmosphere of cloistered calm. No sooner was I seated before desk and papers than I was beset with urgent problems posed by importunate patients and others. Would I see the NCOs in charge of the training wing and explain to them what their duties were? Would I see Private A who had an urgent need for 48 hours' leave to see an old friend just back from the Middle East? Private B, on the other hand, would seek advice because an unfortunate delay on the railway had laid him open to misunderstanding as one who had overstayed his leave. And so on.

An hour or so of this kind of thing convinced me that what was required was discipline. Exasperated at what I felt to be a postponement of my work I turned to consider this problem.

Discipline for the neurotic

Under one roof were gathered 300–400 men who in their units already had the benefit of such therapeutic value as lies in military discipline, good food and regular care; clearly this had not been enough to stop them from finding their way into a psychiatric hospital. In a psychiatric hospital such types provide the total population and by the time they reach the training wing they are not even subject to such slight restraint as is provided by being confined to bed.

I became convinced that what was required was the sort of discipline achieved in a theatre of war by an experienced officer in command of a rather scallywag battalion. But what sort of discipline is that? In face of the urgent need for action I sought, and found, a working hypothesis. It was, that the discipline required depends on two main factors: (1) the presence of the enemy, who provides a common danger and a common aim; and (2) the presence of an officer who, being experienced, knows some of his own failings, respects the integrity of his men, and is not afraid of either their goodwill or their hostility.

An officer who aspires to be the psychiatrist in charge of a rehabilitation wing must know what it is to be in a responsible position at a time when responsibility means having to face issues of life and death. He must know what it is to exercise authority in circumstances that make his fellows unable to accept his authority except insofar as he appears to be able to sustain it. He must know what it is to live in close emotional relationship with his fellow men. In short, he must know the sort of life that is led by a combatant officer. A psychiatrist who knows this will at least be spared the hideous blunder of thinking that patients are potential cannon-fodder, to be returned as such to their units. He will realise that it is his task to produce self-respecting men socially adjusted to the community and therefore willing to accept its responsibilities whether in peace or war. Only thus will he be free from deep feelings of guilt which effectually stultify any efforts he may otherwise make towards treatment.

What common danger is shared by the men in the rehabilitation wing? What aim could unite them?

There was no difficulty about detecting a common danger; neurotic extravagances of one sort and another perpetually endanger the work of the psychiatrist or of any institution set up to further treatment of neurotic disorders. The common danger in the training wing was the existence of neurosis as a disability of the community.

I was now back at my starting-point—the need, in the treatment of a group, for displaying neurosis as a problem of the group. But, thanks to my excursion into the problem of discipline, I had come back with two additions. Neurosis needs to be displayed as a danger to the group; and its display must somehow be made the common aim of the group.

But how was the group to be persuaded to tackle neurotic disability as a communal problem?

The neurotic patient does not always want treatment, and when at last his distress drives him to it he does not want it wholeheartedly. This reluctance has been recognised in the discussion of resistance and allied phenomena; but the existence of comparable phenomena in societies has not been recognised.

Society has not yet been driven to seek treatment of its psychological disorders by psychological means because it has not achieved sufficient insight to appreciate the nature of its distress. The organisation of the training wing had to be such that the growth of insight should at least not be hindered. Better still if it could be designed to throw into prominence the way in which neurotic behaviour adds to the difficulties of the community, destroying happiness and efficiency. If communal distress were to become demonstrable as a neurotic by-product, then neurosis itself would be seen to be worthy of communal study and attack. And a step would have been taken on the way to overcome resistance in the society.

Two minor, but severely practical, military requirements had to be satisfied by the training wing. The organisation should if possible provide a means by which the progress of the patients could be indicated, so that the psychiatrist could tell if a man were fit for discharge. It would also be useful to have an indication of the patient's direction, of his effective motivation, so that an opinion could be formed about the sort of work to which he should be discharged.

I found it helpful to visualise the projected organisation of the training wing as if it were a framework enclosed within transparent walls. Into this space the patient would be admitted at one point, and the activities within that space would be so organised that he could move freely in any direction according to the resultant of his conflicting impulses. His movements, as far as possible, were not to be distorted by outside interference, As a result his behaviour could be trusted to give a fair indication of his effective will and aims, as opposed to the aims he himself proclaimed or the psychiatrist wished him to have.

It was expected that some of the activities organised within the "space" would be clearly war-like, others equally clearly civilian, others again merely expressions of neurotic powerlessness. As the patient's progress was seen to run along one or other of these paths, so his "assets and liabilities", to use a phrase employed in the sphere of officer selection by Eric Wittkower, MD, could be assessed with reasonable objectivity. As his progress appeared to be towards one or other of the possible exits from this imaginary space, so his true aim could be judged.

At the same time the organisation could be used to further the main aim of the training wing—the education and training of the community in the problems of interpersonal relationships. If it could approximate to this theoretical construct it would enable the members of the training wing to stand (as it were) outside the framework and look with detachment and growing understanding upon the problems of its working.

The experiment

The training wing, consisting of some hundred men, was paraded and was told that in future the following regulations would apply:

1. Every man must do one hour's physical training daily unless a medical certificate excused him.
2. Every man must be a member of one or more groups—the groups designed to study handicrafts, Army correspondence courses, carpentry, map-reading, sand-tabling, etc.
3. Any man could form a fresh group if he wanted to do so either because no group existed for his particular activity or because, for some reason or other, he was not able to join an existing similar group.
4. A man feeling unable to attend his group would have to go to the rest-room.
5. The rest-room would be in the charge of a nursing orderly and must be kept quiet for reading, writing or games such as draughts. Talking in an undertone was permitted with the permission of the nursing orderly but other patients must not be disturbed; couches were provided so that any men who felt unfit for any activity whatever could lie down. The nursing orderly would take the names of all those in the rest-room as a matter of routine.

It was also announced that a parade would be held every day at 12.10 p.m. for making announcements and conducting other business of the training wing. Unknown to the patients, it was intended that this meeting, strictly limited to thirty minutes, should provide an occasion for the men to step outside their framework and look upon its working with the detachment of spectators. In short, it was intended to be the first step towards the elaboration of therapeutic seminars.

For the first few days little happened; but it was evident that among the patients a great deal of discussion, and thinking, was taking place. The first few 12.10 meetings were little more than attempts to gauge the sincerity of the proposals; then the groups began to form in earnest. Among other more obvious activities there was a programme group to chart out working hours of groups and their location, to make announcements and to allocate tickets for free concerts and such-like. In a very short time the programme-room, which showed by means of flags on a work-chart the activities of every man in the training wing, now growing rapidly in size, became almost vernal in its display of multi-coloured flags of patterns suggested by the ingenuity of the patients. By a happy thought a supply of flags bearing the skull and crossbones was prepared, ready for the use of such gentlemen as felt compelled to be absent without leave.

The existence of this brave display gave occasion for what was probably the first important attempt at therapeutic co-operation at a 12.10 meeting. It had been my habit, on going the rounds of the groups, to detach one or two men from their immediate work and take them with me, "Just to see how the rest of the world lives." I was therefore able to communicate to this meeting an interesting fact observed by myself and by others who had gone round with me. Namely, that although there were many groups and almost entire freedom to each man to follow the bent of his own inclinations, provided he could make a practical proposal, yet very little was happening. The carpenter's shop might have one or two men at most; car maintenance the same; in short, I suggested, it almost looked as if the training wing was a façade with nothing behind it. This, I said, seemed odd because I remembered how bitterly the patients in the training wing had previously complained to me that one of their objections to the Army was the "eyewash". Its presence in the training wing, therefore, really did seem to be a point worth study and discussion.

This announcement left the audience looking as if they felt they were being "got at". I turned the discussion over at that point as a matter of communal responsibility and not something that concerned myself, as an officer, alone.

With surprising rapidity the training wing became self-critical. The freedom of movement permitted by the original set-up allowed the characteristics of a neurotic community to show with painful clarity; within a few days men complained that the wards (hitherto always claimed to be spotless) were dirty and could not be kept clean under the present system of a routine hour for ward fatigues. They asked and were allowed to organise under the programme group an "orderly group", whose duties it would be to keep the wards clean throughout that day. The result of this was that on a subsequent weekly inspection the Commanding Officer of the hospital remarked on the big change in cleanliness that had taken place.

Some results

It is impossible to go into details about the working of all the therapeutic aspects of the organisation; but two examples of method and result may be given.

Shortly after the new arrangement started, men began to complain to me that patients were taking advantage of the laxity of the organisation.

"Only 20%", they said, "of the men are taking part and really working hard. The other 80% are just a lot of shirkers." They complained that not only was the rest-room often filled with people simply loafing, but that some men even cut that. I was already aware of this, but refused, at least outwardly, to have its cure made my responsibility. Instead, I pointed out that, at an ABCA [Army Bureau of Current Affairs] meeting some weeks before, this discussion had at one point centred on just that question—namely, the existence in communities (and the community then under discussion was Soviet Russia) of just such unco-operative individuals as these and the problem presented to society by their existence. Why, then, did they sound so surprised and affronted at discovering that just the same problem afflicted the training wing?

This cool reply did not satisfy the complainants; they wanted such men to be punished, or otherwise dealt with. To this I replied that no doubt the complainants, themselves, had neurotic symptoms, or they would not be in hospital—why should their disabilities be treated in one way and the disabilities of the 80% treated in another? After all, the problem of the "80%" was not new; in civil life magistrates, probation officers, social workers, the Church and Statesmen had all attempted to deal with it, some of them by discipline and punishment. The "80%", however, were still with us; was it not possible that the nature of the problem had not yet been fully elucidated and that they (the complainants) were attempting to rush in with a cure before the disease had been diagnosed? The problem, I said, appeared to be one that concerned not only the training wing, or even the Army alone, but to have the widest possible implications for society at large. I suggested that they should study it and come forward with fresh proposals when they felt they were beginning to see daylight.

It is worth remarking at this point that my determination not to attempt solution of any problem until its borders had become clearly defined helped to produce, after a vivid and healthy impatience, a real belief that the unit was meant to tackle its job with scientific seriousness. One critic expostulated that surely such a system of patient observation would be exceedingly slow in producing results, if indeed it produced results at all. He was answered by reminding him that only a few days previously the critic himself had spontaneously remarked that the military discipline and bearing of the training wing had improved out of all recognition within the short period of a month.

The second example illustrates the development of an idea from the stage of rather wild, neurotic impulse to practical common-sense activity.

By far the largest group of men proposed the formation of a dancing class. Despite the veneer of a desire to test my sincerity in promising facilities for group activity, the pathetic sense of inferiority towards women that underlay this proposal, by men taking no part in fighting, was only too obvious. They were told to produce concrete proposals. The steps by which this was done need not detain us; in the end the class was held during hours usually taken up by an evening entertainment; it was confined, by the volition of the men themselves, only to those who had no knowledge at all of dancing and the instruction was done by ATS [Auxiliary Territorial Service] staff.[1] In short, a proposal that had started as a quite impractical idea, quite contrary to any apparently serious military aim, or sense of social responsibility to the nation at war, ended by being an inoffensive and serious study carried out at the end of a day's work. Furthermore, the men concerned had had to approach the Commanding Officer, the ATS officers and the ATS, as a matter of discipline in the first place and social courtesy in the second.

In the meantime, the 12.10 parades had developed very fast into business-like, lively and constructive meetings and that in spite of the fact that the wing was now receiving heavy reinforcements of patients new to the organisation, as well as losing others who had been discharged from hospital, often when they had become very useful.

Within a month of the inception of the scheme big changes had taken place. Whereas at first it almost seemed difficult to find ways of employing the men, at the end of the month it was difficult to find time for the work they wanted to do. Groups had already begun to operate well outside what were ordinarily considered parade hours; absence without leave was for a considerable period non-existent, and over the whole period there was only one case; patients not in the training wing became anxious to come over to it; and despite the changing population, the wing had an unmistakable *esprit-de-corps*, which showed itself in details such as the smartness with which men came to attention when officers entered the room at the 12.10 meetings. The relationship of the men to the officers was friendly and co-operative; they were eager to enlist the officers' sympathy in concerts and other activities which they were arranging. There was a subtle but unmistakable sense that the officers and men alike were engaged on a worth-while and important task even though the men had not yet grasped quite fully the nature of

---

[1] [The Auxiliary Territorial Service was a branch of the British Army staffed by women. *Ed.*]

the task on which they were engaged. The atmosphere was not unlike that seen in a unit of an army under the command of a general in whom they have confidence, even though they cannot know his plans.

Comment

It is not possible to draw many conclusions from an experiment lasting, in all, six weeks. Some problems that arose could not be fully explored in the time; others may not be openly discussed while the war is still in progress.

It was evident that the 12.10 meetings were increasingly concerned with the expression, on the part of the men, of their ability to make contact with reality and to regulate their relationships with others, and with their tasks, efficiently. The need for organisation of seminars for group therapy had become clear, and the foundation of their commencement appeared to be firmly laid.

The whole concept of the "occupation" of the training wing as a study of, and a training in, the management of interpersonal relationships within a group seemed to be amply justified as a therapeutic approach. Anyone with a knowledge of good fighting regiments in a theatre of war would have been struck by certain similarities in outlook in the men of such a unit and the men of the training wing. In these respects the attempt could be regarded as helpful; but there were also lessons to be learnt.

Some of these raised serious doubts about the suitability of a hospital milieu for psychotherapy. It was possible to envisage an organisation that would be more fitly described as a psychiatric training unit; and, indeed, some work had been done in the elaboration of an establishment and a *modus operandi* of such a unit. With regard to the psychiatrist, also, there was room for some readjustment of outlook. If group therapy is to succeed it appears necessary that he should have the outlook, and the sort of intuitive sympathetic flair, of the good unit commander. Otherwise there will always be a lingering suspicion that some combatant officers are better psychiatrists, and achieve better results, than those who have devoted themselves to the narrow paths of individual interview.

Finally, attention may be drawn again to the fact that society, like the individual, may not want to deal with its distresses by psychological means until driven to do so by a realisation that some at least of these distresses are psychological in origin. The community represented by the training wing had to learn this fact before the full force of its energy could be released in self-cure. What applied to the small community of the training wing may well apply to the community at large; and further insight may be needed before wholehearted backing can be obtained for those who attempt in this way to deal with deep-seated springs of national morale.

Application of group therapy in a small ward

An experiment in the application of group therapy, in the newer sense, to patients in a ward of fourteen to sixteen beds was made in the hospital division of the same institution. Each patient had an initial interview with the psychiatrist in which a personal history was taken in the usual way; thereafter there were group discussions every morning before the hour's "route march"; and after it, as the patients returned to the ward, they could call in at the psychiatrist's room to discuss privately the topic of the group discussion, which had usually been the subject of conversation on the "route march", and their personal feelings about it.

The therapeutic talks centred on their personal difficulties in putting the welfare of the group in the first place during their membership of the group. The topics of the group discussion included the following:

(a) Since residence in this ward is temporary, some going into the training wing and others coming from the admission ward to take their place, how is this changing situation to be met? We (the distinction between physician and patient, officer and other ranks was another special topic) should have to accommodate ourselves to people entering our group to whom our attitude to our ward (it was always referred to as "our ward") meant nothing at all; either we could regard them as outsiders or as imperfectly accommodated insiders. So too with those who "went out" into the training wing: they could not expect to retain the ward-group attitudes indefinitely, nor could they expect to include the much larger training wing in their ward group; they would have to find their place in the new groupings and allow their ward experience to be but a memory, but it was to be hoped a helpful memory. Then there was the further point, whether those in the training wing should come back to the daily group discussions, the question being not what they would get out of them (there seemed little doubt they were among the most interesting experiences we had ever had) but whether, coming from another group-formation, or while losing their ward contact, they might not prove a distraction to those who were finding their feet in the ward group.

(b) How far were the differences of rank acquired "outside" to determine the behaviour of the members of the group to one another while in the ward? Would an attempt at equality work, or would it be better, while not forgetting the rank acquired outside, to consider what equivalents of rank emerge when in the ward, and if so the basis of these equivalents?

(c) What makes for discontent in the ward? Is it something peculiar to this ward, or any ward, or to any association of people?

(d) What makes for content and happiness in the ward? Is it the exercise of individual initiative having for its sole criterion the free expression of the person's own private enterprises, or does that come only after recognition of what the ward needs from the individual? Is there a fundamental incompatibility between these two points of view, and if so does it apply to all or only some members? If to only some, what causes it to appear in these, and is it a characteristic they carry through in their lives all the time or is it sometimes more strong than at others? If it varies, can the ward diminish it without being oppressive to those individuals so endowed?

The effect of this approach to the problem of neurosis was considerable. There was a readiness, and at times an eagerness, to discuss both in public and in private the social implications of personality problems. The neurotic is commonly regarded as being self-centred and averse from co-operative endeavour; but perhaps this is because he is seldom put in an environment in which *every* member is on the same footing as regards interpersonal relationships.

The experiment was interrupted by posting of personnel, so I cannot give clinical or statistical results; but it seemed to show that it is possible for a clinician to turn attention to the structure of a group and to the forces operating in that structure without losing touch with his patients, and further that anxiety may be raised either inside or outside the group if this approach is made.

Conclusions

We are now in a better position to define the "good group spirit", which has been our aim.

It is as hard to define as is the concept of good health in an individual; but some of its qualities appear to be associated with:

1. A common purpose, whether that be overcoming an enemy or the defending and fostering an ideal or a creative construction in the field of social relationships or in physical amenities.
2. Common recognition by members of the group of the "boundaries" of the group and their position and function in relation to that of larger units or groups.
3. The capacity to absorb new members, and to lose members without fear of losing group individuality, i.e. "group character", must be flexible.
4. Freedom from internal subgroups having rigid (i.e. exclusive) boundaries. If a subgroup is present it must not be centred on any of its members nor on itself—treating other members of the main group as if they did not belong within the main group barrier—and the value of the subgroup to the function of the main group must be generally recognised.
5. Each individual member is valued for his contribution to the group and has free movement within it, his freedom of locomotion being limited only by the generally accepted conditions devised and imposed by the group.
6. The group must have the capacity to face discontent within the group and must have means to cope with discontent.
7. The minimum size of a group is three. Two members have personal relationships; with three or more there is a change of quality (interpersonal relationship).

These experiments in a rehabilitation wing of a military psychiatric neurosis hospital suggest the need for further examination of the structure of groups and the interplay of forces within the groups. Psychology and psychopathology have focused attention on the individual often to the exclusion of the social field of which he is a part. There is a useful future in the study of the interplay of individual and social psychology (viewed as equally important interacting elements), and wartime makes this study an urgent issue.

Discussion of W. R. Bion and J. Rickman's "Intra-Group Tensions in Therapy"

About twenty-five years ago an even then fairly well known psychoanalyst giving advice on how the patient should be introduced into the analytic situation said among other things that he should be reassured that what he said would be treated as confidential and that as he (the analyst) did not drink there was no risk of his breaking secrecy by talking in his cups.

Such crude reassurances are surely never or but seldom given today even by those who are beginning a freelance career in self-taught analytic therapy. The reason why the instance given seems to us now so shocking is also a measure of our appreciation of what a good research and therapeutic instrument was thereby imperilled—that remark sullied the future clarity of the transference situation. (In parenthesis we may reflect that in the quarter century the most important events in the field of research into the psychology of the individual have been in the direction of clarifying our ideas on the transference situation.)

With that said by way of preface, I want to refer to a remark I heard when a (commissioned) group therapist opened a series of group therapy sessions with a new batch of soldier patients in a Military Hospital. He said among other things "You can say what you like here, for within these four walls we are not in the Army!"

One reason why this remark was so shocking lay in the fact that it jeopardised the development of a free and good relationship within the group. The characteristics of free and good relationships within the group—surely one of the most important objects of study if one culture is to survive—of course are by no means always clear, nor are the reasons why groups break up or become ineffective necessarily clear even to the participants. One of our many debts to Bion in the last few years has been the provision of a technique based on and comparable

---

A discussion of "Intra-Group Tensions in Therapy" was held at the Medical Section of the British Psychological Society on 19 December 1945 at the Royal Society of Medicine, and this is John Rickman's opening contribution to the discussion.

with the psychoanalytic technique for studying the immediately present and emerging phenomena of group relationships.

It is possible that the discussion of Bion's paper may be facilitated if I make as clear as I can the differences which I have observed between Bion's handling of groups and the handling by people who have not been influenced by his ideas. I am going to stress the differences between Bion's work and other people's because perhaps out of modesty he may not let it be sufficiently apparent that a pioneer *is* different from those who have not broken new ground.

There are in fact two kinds of group therapy, first those in which people are assembled together for discussion of their nervous complaints or to obtain relief by the catharsis of public confession, or to hear from their therapist either words of encouragement or explanations of the cause and cure of neurosis. These methods have their usefulness, as have their analogues in individual therapy, but they are not at all like Bion's, which is the alternative method. *He does not steer the discourse when handling groups.* This must be taken literally. I recall watching a group therapy session taken by a person who said that he let the group find their own subject and that in this respect he followed the analytic method. What in fact happened was that he opened with a discussion on the nature of neurosis and after that for a few minutes at any rate let the group chew his remarks to bits. I give this instance because he was under the impression that he had not steered his group in any way.

On another occasion a group of soldiers after discussing why they were in a neurosis wing of a hospital began complaining of the way in which they were treated by the civilian population outside; this was ruled to be outside the topic they agreed to discuss. Of the three or four group therapists then present only one (and he had been influenced by Bion's work) spotted that the discourse had been deflected to a material extent. It would seem that it is not easy to be objective on the question whether one is steering a group or not, and it is relevant to say that just the same applies to an individual analysis.

The second point which comes near, as I see it, to the main characteristic of a Bion group is that the attention of everyone present is led from time to time to *what is happening at the moment in the group*. This is not steering the discourse in the same sense as above, it is more near to an interpretation in the psychoanalyst's sense of the word.

For instance, a group of Bion's more or less agreed to meet at 6.30 for ninety-minute sessions; after about half past eight while the discussion rambled and dragged on Bion said "Let us see what has been happening lately. We agreed to go on for an hour and a half and yet no one has suggested that we get up and go." He paused and one person who had been trying to take the lead accused Bion of looking at the clock ever since eight, another accused the last speaker of talking too much; all agreed that the discourse had been fitful, hot and then cold, no one connected this behaviour with the time-element. Bion here made what I think may fairly be called an interpretation—that is to say, what he said added no new topic to the events covered by the interpretation but synthesised those events so that what was before subliminal (I do not want to discuss the kind of unawareness) became clear and events, which though everyone was aware of them before, seemed more connected. Bion's interpretation was that though everyone was restless no one was willing to bring the ill will of the group on himself by ending the session.

I am aware how thin and indeed even arbitrary this must sound. It was a revelation to those present, and the implications of this discovery was the subject of much further reflection, not only in the Group Sessions but in its application by individuals to their own group relationships in industry.

I have just used the word *discovery*; something seems to be *discovered* by the group (with the characteristics of surprise, relief and quickened resolution to know more) about its own tendencies to behaviour and its own potentialities to productivity and to futility. Of the discoveries the most surprising, the most relieving, the most stimulating are those which disclose the reason why the group was not functioning smoothly. To use the language of psychoanalysis, the overcoming of something analogous to a resistance increases the fluidity, the cohesiveness and creativeness of the group. We should however be on our guard against applying the psychodynamics of the individual to that of the group, just as we should be on our guard against thinking that because we know something of the treatment of individuals we are thereby qualified to treat groups.

By Bion's application of the essentials of Freud's technique of research to groups a new phase of development in group psychology is beginning and this Section of the British Psychological Society does well to open its postwar Scientific sessions with such an important topic.

CHAPTER 13

Disruptive forces in group relations: war as a makeshift therapy

(1946)

The unconscious need for war

War is an event which almost all people profess to loathe, and yet it is of frequent occurrence. In an attempt to explain this state of affairs it seems reasonable to assume that there are unconscious factors in its causation analogous, perhaps, to the neurotic compulsions which are beyond the conscious control of the individual.

If we look at the reasons why nations go to war, we find that participants on both sides are firmly convinced that they are fighting for some ideal and for the defence of some idealised object. They each feel that the right is on their side and that their opponents are wicked and ruthless. The enemy is felt to be "bad" and to be the "cause" of the troubles while "our side" becomes the embodiment of all that is good and noble.

There is present, in such situations, an excessive need on the part of the combatants to attribute to each other their own aggressive impulses

---

A contribution by John Rickman to a week-end conference organised by the Social Psychology Section of the British Psychological Society on "Present-Day Problems of Peace and War" at Bedford College, London, on 20–22 September 1946. Compiled from notes from which Rickman addressed the conference.

or desires, which for some reason had become too intolerable or disruptive to deal with through intra-group mechanisms. It is this projective mechanism which appears to facilitate the outbreak of hostilities and which deserves careful study.

Individuals differ greatly in their capacity to tolerate internal or mental tension and it is not unreasonable to assume that a capacity to tolerate intra-group tension varies also with different groups. Individuals often try to deal with their unbearable, internal tensions by irritability in social relationship, so that the site of the tensions is shifted from an intra-personal to an interpersonal one. The source of the trouble is then felt to be external to the individual and its cause can then be attacked with greater safety.

Thus, by placing the source of danger, and the threat to the group, outside the group, away from loved ones and in the "bad" enemy, the group can achieve a lessening of internal tension and once more experience some internal cohesion and safety. While this technique of relieving intra-group tension does not necessarily lead to war, there is no doubt that it will eventually do so, unless the groups or nations concerned can get insight into this pattern of behaviour. But because a considerable lessening of tension is achieved by sharing a common enemy or object of hate, and the group does experience a well-being and togetherness as a result, and because the mechanism involved is unconscious and has as one of its aim the *avoidance* of the recognition of the state of internal tension, there are strong forces at work which make it difficult for a group to obtain insight into its own behaviour. It may be assumed therefore that the cost of war in terms of mental pain is *less* than the expenditure of emotional effort that would be involved in overcoming the distress of recognising the depth and the extent of the social disharmony.

In the individual the *resistance* to the recognition of a disruptive tendency (i.e. one which interferes with a good relationship to desired and loved objects without and within the self) is a measure of the strength of that disruptive tendency, a measure of the mental pain which would follow a too sudden disclosure of that disruptiveness. Such recognition can only occur with conviction, and with a permanent alteration of the individual's toleration of and capacity to master the internal disruptiveness, when conditions are such that the pain can be alleviated.

Research into fields of activity where mental pain is involved can only be effective when the unconscious conflicts which cause the pain can be solved by therapy. In other words, in these fields of activity I think that there can be no effective research without the possibility of some alleviation of the pain through therapy.

Applying these ideas to the social psychology of war, it is probable that unless the research worker applies himself to the problem of solving intra-group tensions in the group of which he is a functioning member, his research will be less useful than it might be.

War as a "makeshift therapy"

Since war is so intimately linked up with pain, and its gratifications are so soon glossed over, a study of war which does not expose the pain for which war is probably "a makeshift therapy" is not an effective study of war.

The notion that war may be "a makeshift therapy" needs a word of explanation. It is based on the assumption, familiar to psychotherapists, that neurotic symptoms are a substitute for gratifications that are held under the constraint of repression, and that they are defended by the patient and clung to despite their manifest disadvantages, lest a disturbing outbreak of anxiety should occur. In other words, a neurotic symptom, unpleasant though it may be, is a makeshift therapy, it protects the individual from worse pain. Arguing by analogy, war is not unconsciously felt to be the worst of all calamities to befall a people, but rather something well worth the cost.

We can add a further notion by analogy with neurosis that this "makeshift therapy" satisfies a number of unconscious tendencies, that it is "over-determined" in the sense that the elements of a dream, a neurotic symptom or a work of art, are over-determined.

In individuals, a large part of the internal tension can be expressed in terms of anxiety. This, in turn, is felt *both* as a painful manifestation of the sense of powerlessness to make a good and abiding relationship to loved people or objects, *and* as a dread of dependence on those objects. This dread of dependence arises partly because of our ambivalence towards them, and partly because our capacity for restitution is unconsciously felt not to be as powerful as the degree of destructiveness which we feel in relation to those loved objects.

The work of W. R. Bion seems to indicate that the thing a group most dreads is its impotence *vis-à-vis* an enemy, and its worst enemy is its own unfaced group-disruptiveness. He found that when the study of intra-group tension was made the task of a group, that group became more at peace with itself, its capacity for constructiveness rose and, also, its ability to work with other groups in friendly rivalry increased [see chapter 12].

There are, however, two kinds of psychotherapy. There is that which seeks to diminish the contributory or aggravating factors which maintain the sick condition, which we can call "ameliorative therapy". Then there is the therapy which seeks to alter the dynamics of the unconscious, which, with perhaps too little modesty, we can call "radical".

Our understanding of the possibilities of Sociotherapy, or Sociatry as it is sometimes called, is greatly hampered by ignorance of the dynamics of the unconscious forces at work in groups. At present we tend, perhaps overmuch, to grope towards them from the basis of our still small knowledge of the psychodynamics of the individual.

War is usually a contest between *men*. If war is a "makeshift therapy", to reduce the tension in the minds of individuals, the kind of auto-therapy that results from war is probably related to the kind of frustration that precipitates it. War redistributes the social life of the community into sex-segregated groups, perhaps in an endeavour to solve an early failure in adaptation to the first love objects. In other words, war helps us in our distribution of homosexual impulses. Men in our own army can be loved without stint, those in the enemy army can be mutilated or killed without qualm. I am speaking now mainly of the unconscious aspect of these relationships.

The line of therapy for this component is not primarily to attempt to produce an alteration in adult sexual behaviour but to do more research into the upbringing of children, for the homosexual impulses concerned lie near to the basic bisexual roots of our earliest relationships with people and objects. However that may be, it seems that the camaraderie of the sexes in American co-education as compared with the Student Korps of the prewar German universities for instance, is more likely to foster a constructive attitude to personal relationships than a highly ambivalent homosexual component.

Social structure as a defence against internal disruption

The structure of the political system of a country may favour a pacific or a militant attitude to foreign affairs. If the political system provides the people with a means for expressing its discontent with the government without at the same time endangering the flow of loyalty to the central authority, the tendency in that country is likely to be more pacific than in a regime where discontent inevitably overthrows the central government entirely, as in dictatorships. In England we have a permanent Head of Government—the King or Queen—and a removable Head of Government, the Prime Minister; we can remove the latter without disturbing our orientation to the former. Discontent is constitutionally legitimate. The legitimacy of discontent and public control of the channels of its expression is fundamental to a political democracy; tension is thus kept low and there is not likely to be a need for the projective notion of encirclement in order to canalise discontent over the borders.

But political discontent is not the only kind which disturbs a community. There is also economic discontent. The greater the control the community has over the means of production the more likely people are to wage only defensive war; for under such circumstances aggression is more likely to be turned against nature than against people. But the validity of this point is greatly dependent on a basic tolerance of frustration by a community and on the freedom that exists in that community to express discontent politically.

The task of the social therapist

Though the preceding paragraphs have been concerned with war, they are not altogether without relevance to present-day problems of peace. Perhaps the therapeutic aspect should be considered in more detail.

The psychoanalysts effect changes in the distribution of forces in the unconscious by dealing, and only dealing, with those which manifest themselves in the transference situation. Their work is fundamentally a-historical; only what is present, and therefore active, has power to effect permanent changes in the mind. The analyst is a participant in the field of social forces; he is in it on a bread-and-butter basis, he has to produce results or stand impeached, and he will fail in his endeavours unless he understands and uses for his constructive purposes the hostile forces which tend to wreck the relationship. The social therapist who attempts to help groups to deal with their disruptive tendencies should, in my view, try to, dare to, attain the same position. There are three points which seem to me to be fundamental to the technique of the social therapist. The first is that the only effective force at his disposal is that which he can demonstrate as having emerged out of the real-life situation in which he is professionally engaged. Discourses on historical tendencies avail nothing; only the present operating factors convince. The second is that hostility to him and all his works (if he knows his job) is an expression of the discontent which he was called in to treat, and praise of him and all his works is an expression of diminished anxiety, and not a true index of Sociatric or therapeutic success. The third is that the reason for the difficulties he encounters in comprehension and acceptance of his therapeutic endeavours lies in the fact, so simple to state, so important to believe, that mental pain is unbearable. He is a man professionally engaged in dealing with unbearable ideas in a group setting.

Finally, shall I be original if I add that I do not think there are "Present-Day Problems of War and Peace" of any importance which have not been harassing mankind throughout history. But perhaps we have at our hand a task of discovery—that is, the ways in which our group relationships are shaped by mental pain, which we go to great lengths to avoid recognising.

CHAPTER 14

Some psychodynamic factors behind tensions that cause wars

(1950)

If asked to reduce the content of what follows to its original sources I should indicate six "events" in the history of mental dynamics. The *first* concerns Freud's work: he did not run away from his patients' problems, he listened to their neurotic complaints; by virtue of his genius he hit on a key (the best so far found) for tracing the connection between conscious and unconscious mental processes, and from the application of that discovery is derived the greater part of our understanding of the psychodynamics of the individual. The *third* event (numbered in chronological order) is Freud's excursion into anthropology in *Totem and Taboo* (1912–13) which linked behaviour in social life with processes occurring in the development of the individual. The *fourth* event was Freud's *Group Psychology and the Analysis of the Ego* (1921c), in which the ties binding the group together are discussed with reference to the impulses of love and the growth of the superego (sometimes called conscience).

The *second* event is a technical point of importance in therapy and of great interest to all research workers in the psychological and social

---

This paper was first published under the title of "Psychodynamic Notes" as part of a UNESCO Conference Study, *Tensions that Cause Wars*, edited by Hadley Cantril (1950).

241

field, i.e. the extent to which the events in the psychoanalytic treatment situation relate to the patient's transferring into the present all of the unsolved emotional problems of the past; the date for this event being about 1909. This can be restated in the more modern terms of Gestalt closure, but the gist of it is that such is the nature of our mental life (and if we did not have the insight and the technical equipment of thought we could always see it) that every detail of our behaviour is a resultant on the one hand of the working out of unsolved past problems and on the other of an endeavour to find satisfaction for present needs. (If the reader at this point is inclined to remark that everyone but an ass has thought this from time immemorial, my reply is that it is one thing to think it to be true, it may be quite another thing to shape your own behaviour as it if were true.) This event cannot be referred to a single paper or book, it is, rather, a gradually dawning and extending understanding of a phenomenon of the mind.

The *fifth* event has something of the same nature and is a result of the application of the foregoing development of psychoanalytic theory and practice. It is still a matter of controversy, which is wholesome, but, as I see it, the main feature is a concept of the ego as a boundary phenomenon between two distinguishable classes of process. That the ego is a boundary phenomenon between the core of the instinct life in the individual and the external world was a notion put forward with great force and clarity by Freud in *The Ego and the Id* (1923b), but if I grasp Melanie Klein's theories aright, the ego may also be viewed as a boundary phenomenon between our inner world of fantasied internalized objects and an outer world.

Thus the ego viewed in one way can be regarded as a psychophysical mechanism acting reflexly to external stimuli while under the pressure also of the "stimuli" or instincts from within—the organism is, so to say, a solid object with a sensitive boundary membrane, the ego, which mediates between two classes of "stimulus" impact. The ego can also and without contradiction be viewed as a container or storage arrangement. This is sensitive to its contents, which are social situations of the past, and also sensitive to its external social environment—the ego looked at this way is a boundary phenomenon which mediates between two classes of "social" impact.

I confess that this is rather obscure to myself and it is a view by no means generally regarded as worth much consideration; to me the importance of this perhaps over-simple concept is that it helps me to see more clearly the way in which the field of action can get shifted across the "ego boundary". To give but one instance, a person who feels persecuted from within gets a sense of internal relief if he "projects" the persecutor into the outer world, for, when the persecution is regarded as in the external world the patient feels that he can do something effective against it and that his inner world is more peaceful.

The events I have enumerated are of unequal importance for the immediate application of psychodynamic theory to problems of international tension; the one which is easiest to apply in this connection is that of the superego; it is almost too easy! It offers so many interesting solutions and it has already produced a vast literature.

Now to the *sixth* event.

Freud's and Ferenczi's development of the research and therapeutic method of psychoanalysis could be summarized in a few words—it is an endlessly patient examination of the events existing "here-and-now" in the social relationship occurring between analyst and his patient. W. R. Bion applied this same simple notion to a group and, of course, met with opposition within the group to making the study of the conflicting tensions occurring "here-and-now" in their very midst the major task of the group. The resistance which a group displays to the examination of its own group-disruptive tendencies is impressive once one allows oneself to take cognizance of it. It is in some ways similar to the resistance which the patient displays towards the dispassionate study of his own socially and personally disruptive tendencies.

A situation of tension cannot be treated *in absentia*, nor, I think, can it be fully understood unless the participants are prepared to make its study their major task. Theoretical disquisitions, however learned, do not suffice to solve human emotional problems; these can be solved only by those who are prepared to face them and face the consequences of facing them in the presence of those concerned. Freud faced his patient, Bion his group; hence these are events of note: I am speaking of facing a person or a group in a particular sense, i.e. endeavouring not to evade issues, being as ready to see evasion in oneself as in others and study the evasion wherever it is seen as the most important problem to solve and the one to be tackled first.

In this introduction, I have singled out six events that seem important to an understanding of a psychodynamic contribution to this Tension Project: I am well aware that this is a personal choice and that others from the same body of experience and the literature could select other points of equal importance.

Now a concluding word to this introduction: much will be said of tension and group-disruptive tendencies. It is well to recall that these are not new to human experience. Yet humanity has proceeded on its way perhaps towards a greater cultural maturation, so there are group-cohesive and -constructive forces of equal if not greater power. When reading what follows, this point should be kept in mind—when discussing tensions which lead to disruptiveness, much attention inevitably is given to disquieting features of our mental life. The fact that they are being studied by a worldwide organization is itself both novel and reassuring.

Caution regarding a physician's analogies

A physician approaches the problem of tensions between nations with considerable hesitation; he is professionally occupied according to usual custom with one person at a time, or, if he is a medical officer of health, with matters affecting the "physical" health of the community. The constructs which a physician uses (pathology, diagnosis, symptom-complexes, and so forth) are designed to apply to that biological unit that we think of when we speak of "a person", and it is by no means certain that they can be applied with an equal relevance to a community. A physician therefore can offer to sociology "analogies", some of which may be useful, some misleading—that is a matter for others to judge. A doctor should be reticent about making such assessments.

A psychiatrist can approach our problem with rather more assurance than a physician, particularly if he has a psychoanalytic training, because in his professional work he has occasion to observe the way in which a cultural pattern influences the development of the simple biological unit, the person of his patient. He also has occasion to notice the way in which the personality of the patient influences or tries to influence those around him. His work is on the borderline of sociology but is definitely not sociology. But the psychiatrist also works under the limitation of dealing professionally with individual people; the factor of number is important. In the case of psychoanalytic research, which has added so much to our understanding of human behaviour, the data actually observed occur in a "two-body relationship", in this instance the analyst and the person he is analysing. From such data inferences can be drawn regarding "three-body", "four-body", or "multi-body" relationships. But with increase of number, other factors may come in that lessen the accuracy of the inferences; though I could make an exception to the "three-body" relation, for I think the analytic theories about this are the most powerful additions to sociology yet made.

Physician and psychiatrist, however, share an experience denied to the sociologist; they can in their examination of the patient (the unit they are professionally concerned with) survey that person's life history in detail, noting his interaction with his environment, his impulses and moods, his aspirations and his fears, and can regard—indeed must regard—everything discovered as relevant to the totality of that person then and there before him. The sociologist cannot do this, if the unit is large, e.g. a nation cannot be seen all at once at the same time. But whether the unit is large or can be measured in dozens of individuals, sociology has not yet got such an integrated thing to deal with as the doctor's patient. Its life cycle is less defined, its coherence less understood. Analogies with the body and mind (if they are separate) of the individual are tempting but not trustworthy.

The work of the physician and the psychiatrist differs from that of the sociologist in another important respect: the patient goes to his doctor because of a need for help. In the course of the examination, pain is often experienced; sometimes it is physical, sometimes mental. This pain is endured, and can only be endured, by the patient for the sake of a better outcome of the treatment. The psychiatrist and the sociologist may be called in by one element in the community, as they were for instance in the British Army during the Second World War, and as they sometimes are by an industrial firm. But to be consulted in this way is only the first step; the consultant has to make his inquiry accepted, and therefore ultimately acceptable, by all "sections" of the "unit" which he is consulted about. The same is true of a psychiatrist (here the analogies begin): there are in every case parts of the personality which resent the intrusion of the doctors; his therapeutic art consists in getting the whole of the personality to co-operate in the process of diagnosis and therapy.

A medical interview is a "two-way" process. The more the patient gives himself to the process of examination, the more the doctor can give back in the form of diagnosis and advice. The doctor's part consists also in a similar wholehearted exploration of the situation then and there existing; if he brings to the interview questions of his own to which he demands an answer, however lofty and scientific his motives, by that much he is distorting the doctor–patient relationship and jeopardizing its therapeutic success, i.e. the removal of the pain. It is possible—a clinician would say probable, again using analogies—that the sociologist's interviews may fail to be fully revealing if he brings to the interview his own questions for answer and does not give priority to the "unit" he is interviewing. People cannot—by a clinician's analogy—disclose the roots of their discomforts unless they have not merely the assurance but some actual relief of their suffering. But there is as yet no clear definition of the "structure" or the nature or even the boundaries of the "organism" which suffers in the case of a group.

In his work the psychiatrist, as is now commonly but not universally recognized, has to deal with forces in the mind of which the patient is unaware; they operate in the region of the unconscious and are held away from consciousness by a force of "resistance", i.e. a force acting against their becoming conscious. In the individual these processes are beginning to be understood, but whether the sociologist can transfer this concept *in toto* to his own field is an open question at present; again it is a matter of our ignorance of the basic structure of group psychology.

Money-Kyrle's study of normality

A consideration of normality is useful because it helps the reader to place quickly the notions being discussed in a frame of reference. For whether we acknowledge it theoretically or not, the fact is that we use some notion of normality continually in our daily life and judge people and their views by it. In the present case Money-Kyrle's outline will be followed.

Money-Kyrle (1944) begins by discussing what he calls "the negative characteristics of normality" which are present in abnormal people and to a small degree, if present at all, in normal ones.

(a) The "paranoid tendencies": people with these tendencies feel themselves to be persecuted and hated by others. In fact, at the beginning at any rate, they are the haters, but they cannot tolerate the inner tension caused by their hate and so they attribute or "project" it onto others. This, however, does not solve their difficulty, because the outer world now feels hostile (the projection was a defensive device for reducing the tension due to hostile feelings within themselves) and they then have to attack their persecuting enemies.

This delusional condition is seen clearly in a relatively small number of seriously mentally ill people, but traces of it are found in nearly everyone. Most people can match up their feelings and ideas about the outer world and so control their "projection" and find reassurance in their normal contacts with their fellows.

This much from psychiatric experience. Something remarkably similar was found in Nazi Germany. Hitler and those who accepted his ideas projected their hate beyond the frontier and imagined that Germany was beset with enemies, even at a time when in fact her neighbours were friendly. Once the projection process is underway a vicious circle is established. Now what was originally hated? It was Germany itself, but there were also feelings of good regard for the motherland. As the conflict was intolerable, a solution was reached by turning the hate outwards. This will sound nonsense to anyone who cannot believe that there can be love and hate for the same person, but the observation of individuals and inferences from political events leave no doubt that such contradictions are possible.

This turning outwards of the hate has a further motivation—it is protective to the good or loved object (at least in the case of individuals, that is what examination of the paranoid person reveals). These processes occur for the most part below the threshold of consciousness and so are not under the patient's control.

In defence of a good or loved object the patient feels that any action, however violent and destructive, must be justified; nor can, or rather dare, the patient reverse the process once the vicious circle has been established. If he acknowledges that the neighbours are in fact friendly he has to face the resurgence of his own hate upon himself or on his loved object. Their appeasement is regarded as weakness or a trick; in either case his aggressiveness is still further excited.

(b) The second of Money-Kyrle's negative characteristics of normality is that of "appeasement". Here the evil motives of an aggressor and the danger from him are denied. The reasons for this are complicated. First a fight against him is pictured unconsciously as far more horrible than in fact it could really be. Bad though the enemy may be, the image of him is far worse. In place, therefore, of standing up to him, his point of view is seen and sympathised with even though it goes flatly against the subject's own interests; a passive attitude is adopted in the face of his giant strength. Some of the reactions in prewar England to the threat of the Nazis took this appeasing form.

A further step in this direction is taken by the "Quisling", who, however, in despair of protecting his motherland from an external menace, allies himself with the enemy and leads the attack from within.

The Quisling is in deeds more active than the appeaser, but in his inner attitude he is more passive and helpless before the exciting menace of the aggressor.

(c) The "Pacifist" does not, as in the case of the appeaser, deny the badness of the enemy nor is any attempt made to placate him. But he is not attacked. The aggressive impulse is so loaded with guilt feelings and anxiety that the assertive action is inhibited. There is a certain degree of passivity to the enemy but not that almost complete inversion which characterises the Quisling.

(d) "Moral Negativism": the cynic regards no object or cause as worth fighting for, or even living for—at the root of this attitude is a profound despair.

Money-Kyrle also considers the "positive characteristics of normality". These must include not only some freedom for aggressive action but must also recognise that the normal person will be discriminating in his aims (which the paranoid person cannot be). Aggression should not be blocked as it is with the pacifist, nor of course turned against its own good objects through a passive attitude to the enemy as with the Quisling. Nor will the normal person be saddled with an unrecognised despair like the cynic. He will have aims and ends of supreme importance and will attack only those who really stand in the way of his aims. Nor will he be impatient in achieving his aims, since he will not see enemies where there are none nor ascribe to them attributes they do not possess.

From this point of view the possibility of further wars is not excluded and no stand is taken for or against war. But it is important nevertheless to consider the psychological conditions which would reduce the number of unnecessary wars.

If clinical work with individuals is a guide to a general attitude on this subject, one could say that humanity is more likely to listen to the pros and cons of war and aggressive nationalism being discussed if the organizations making the investigation show an absolute impartiality. For though one of the most constant cries of mankind has been for the abolition of war, the fact is that wars have continued and therefore have fulfilled some need. That need may well have a neurotic origin or contain self-destruction. But it is a need, and perhaps it can only make itself felt explosively because there is no graduated outlet or understanding of its nature.

Confusions regarding aggression

Some people say that war is a product of aggression. And some of these, who regard war with greater abhorrence than anything else, go on to argue that aggression must therefore be bad. So they turn to psychologists to ask how aggressive instincts or impulses can be eradicated. It is probable, but not certain, that aggressive impulses of some sort are part of man's constitutional make-up, and if so they cannot be eradicated.

By aggression I mean an impulse to dominate and control the object of the impulse. Usually and basically the "object" is a person, so we will speak always of persons, though aggressions can also be applied to things. Probably the drive or urge behind the aggressive impulse is derived from a basic instinct of destructiveness. But in action it is, at least from a very early age, blended in greater or less proportion with loving or constructive impulses as well. A consideration of whether basic impulses are desirable or not seems to me to be a futile undertaking. But actions may be so considered, even though the study of them may be difficult. A man chopping down a tree is giving expression to a destructive impulse, but he may be doing it to build a house—an action, therefore, cannot with any wisdom be judged in isolation but only considered in relation to the total mental attitude of the person performing the action in the social setting in which he does it.

Aggressive impulses as such are not the point at issue, it seems to me: the "repressed aggressive impulses" are the significant thing. If an impulse is recognized, fully recognized in its actual application (I do not speak of the evasive generalisations we are all inclined to make about painful subjects; I mean plainly faced and acknowledged in actual application), then it can nearly always be controlled or modified. If an impulse is repressed, i.e. denied access to consciousness, it cannot be controlled, yet it does not cease to exist but shapes behaviour in indirect but none the less disturbing ways.

To explain the importance of repression it will be necessary to make an excursion into psychodynamics. In the course of this, several new issues will be raised (unfortunately a linear exposition of the subject is not possible; it spreads out in all directions). But there is one central point to be emphasised again—that we are not concerned with this or that impulse, aggressive or destructive, but with the controllability of impulse, and that an impulse cannot be controlled if its existence, its effects, and its implications are repressed or denied to the mind.

Some of the origins of man's insecurity

The origins of man's fundamental insecurity lie deep in his experience, perhaps also in his nature. Though in regard to some bodily needs we closely resemble what we are pleased to call the lower creation, we differ greatly in two respects. Generally speaking, the beasts do not appear to suffer from anxiety nor from guilt; it is their misfortune, since they keep on being much the same as their ancestors: it is our destiny in each generation of individuals and of society to reshape and readjust ourselves in ever new ways to the end that we may achieve a peace of mind.

We begin as helpless creatures ill-equipped with a regulating nervous system, utterly dependent on another person for sustenance and nearly every kind of satisfaction. We cannot work for our living, we can only get what we want when it is put in our mouth. Such was the foundation of our mental and social life. And according to the way that foundation was laid, so is the superstructure shaped.

The distinction in the first year of life between the Me and the Not-Me is not the same as in later life, but the mode of dealing with that "ego boundary" in those early days influences subsequent behaviour.

The child is an intensely subjective creature and its mind is active from the earliest days, but the material its mind has to work on is differently apportioned from that which occupies us in our adult years: predominantly it is a world of sensations, moods and wants. The child's fantasies (we would speak of daydreams as the nearest thing in adult life) are "real" in the sense that they are the stuff it deals with, unchecked of course by the matching process we later use in our "testing" of reality.

By the incorporation within ourselves of objects taken from the outer world there is formed an "inner world" within but yet part of the personality; henceforth there are two areas to which adjustment has to be made: to the external world with all its claims and toils, and the "inner world" which though more archaic, or perhaps because it is so archaic, presents difficult problems of solution.[1] Broadly the eternal problems are those of adjusting between the simultaneously acting impulses of love and hate, i.e. conflict lies within us, therefore we have "tension" within us, whether we like it or not. Furthermore it seems that the individual uses the one to help himself make adjustments in the other.

We must now consider again in more detail our earliest object relationships. When we were frustrated—and it is a myth of the Golden Age to imagine a world without frustration—we responded with rage

---

[1] The ego can be viewed as a frontier phenomenon between these two worlds—the outer world is public or common, the inner one is private, very private, so much so that it is a continual field of discovery, as every poet, artist, and man of feeling knows.

at our frustration and at the world at large (as we then knew it). But our frustrator was our most needed person, and the one who also gave us our comfort and whom we loved. Insofar as this good object was turned "bad" (in our imagination) by our wrath (by being covered with hate) we felt apprehension, insofar as this good object was loved our wrath was a cause of guilt. The origin of guilt is rooted in aggressiveness. We do not feel guilt if we attack an object towards which we entertain no love, but we may even in such attacks produce an unmanageable degree of anxiety because we endow the object with our hate by hating it and fear the redoubled vigour of its revenge.

Thus far we have considered a two-body relationship, of mother and child ("the nursing couple"). But families are made up of at least three people. A further complication comes in with the realisation of the father and his role in relation to the mother and the child. The ambivalence (love and hate towards the same object) especially characteristic of early childhood makes him, too, both a loved and a hated person, whether the child be a boy or girl. It is the proportionate power of the "good" and "bad" images which makes the path of individual development relatively easy or difficult. Privations in feeding, in nursing care, the observation of quarrelling between the parents, the neglect of the one by the other, all tend to strengthen the impression of the "bad" parent figures and hinder the growth of the idea of a harmonious family life. Whatever fosters the impression of "good" parent figures strengthens the belief in the worthwhileness of life and the potential reliability of others.

But the child is not a piece of plastic material merely receiving impressions. The fantasy life to which reference has been made has its own resilience and recuperative power; its content is shaped by the impulses of love and hate. The environment can aid an earlier and more solid acquisition of stability or lead to a retardation of maturation. The effect of environment on this viewing is not so much a "conditioning of reflexes" as a strengthening and enrichment or a weakening and impoverishment of this peculiar intangible thing—the fantasy life. By calling it such, it suggests to some people something nebulous and even negligible; there may indeed be stout-hearted men who would consider all this to be nursery twaddle but would upon occasion salute the flag (their own flag) with a glow of pride and without self-consciousness: that flag is a symbol, and symbols operate in this same fantasy life and upon objects within it.

In its struggle with its own impulses the ego (or executive aspect of the mind) brings processes into operation in order to reduce the confusion that would result if activity directed towards the outer world were disturbed by those clamouring for solution from within. The disturbing impulses and ideas are "repressed", i.e. they are not allowed into consciousness. It is a consequence of repression that people can have the most fantastic ideas about themselves. Naturally only the disturbing impulses and ideas are thus pushed out. But out of sight is not out of mind; what is banished returns in other or symbolic forms and the struggle against these secondary disturbances is renewed afresh. By a process of substitution of one object for another, emotional feelings get transferred onto secondary objects and a new opportunity is provided for dealing with the conflicts (due to ambivalence mainly), but in more attenuated form. It is this process of substitution which both enriches life and provides occasion for confusion. For unless we are not only alive to this possibility but can follow the steps by which it occurs, our own behaviour and that of others seems inexplicable. I want for a moment to return to the relation to the parents: the key to civilisation.

The beginning of social life

Our social life may be said to begin when we deal with two people at once: each has a relation to the other two as well. That problem is satisfactorily solved when the personality of the others is respected, when the relation between the other two members of the triangle is allowed to develop to its fullest extent and each feels that he himself or she herself is not only growing in human understanding but in appreciation of the other's growth. In fundamentals this process is well underway by the fifth year of life, but not, of course, by then as mature as it later becomes. And yet nearly everything I have said so far about the child's mind would lead one to think that such a consummation would be impossible. How is the change brought about? In a word, by the establishment of a function within the mind of the "superego".

When describing the child's early relation to his world it was said that objects were taken in past the barrier between the Me and the Not-Me and constituted an inner world of objects. These taken collectively have their history which is intimately connected with the development of the personality. The most important of these incorporated objects is that of the parent figures. For simplicity we will confine ourselves to the male sex. The boy models himself on his father, not only consciously as we all know, but unconsciously as well. It is this unconscious modelling which is for our present purpose the important aspect.

The "good" father image is clearly a supporting figure; it encourages the boy to a manly development and strengthens his affectionate relation to his mother, and later to women generally, and endows him with a wish in his turn to be a father to his own family. If this were all, our social life would indeed be a paradise. There is the other component. The father (the real father) was actually hated as a rival. To this aspect gets attached the fantasy image of a "bad" father, i.e. on the image of the real father there is projected all of the hate feelings which were roused within the self which could not be dealt with. All the cruelty towards a loved object which arises within the self is ascribed to this figure who becomes the very embodiment of evil. In actual fact the real father is neither so perfect as the fantasied "good" father nor so bad as the fantasied "bad" father; he is a mixture of Good and Bad. The boy's ultimate relation to the real father is determined by his tolerance of his own aggressive or destructive impulses and his capacity to see some virtue even in a rival to his love. Similarly in his relation to his mother, if he can tolerate her "desertion" of him for his father, if he can support some loneliness of spirit without regressing to bouts of impotent rage, if, in other words, he can view her as having a life only part of which he can share, he will be free to look for a partner of his own with whom he can share his life more fully.

Anything which keeps the "good" and "bad" aspects of the parent figures separate in thought-tight, emotion-tight compartments leads to a dangerous splitting in the emotional life later. The proneness of infatuation in the love life and in political life is probably—very probably—derived from an incomplete solution of this task of accepting the "Good-and-Bad" first in ourselves, then in our primary objects, the parents, later in schoolteachers, our companions, and eventually our national leaders.

The superego (which has some of the characteristics of conscience, but is a wider concept) serves the purpose of watching over the instinctual aspects of the mind and by a signal ("a twinge of conscience" in mild instances) gives warning that aggressive action must be curbed. If the superego were rooted in wisdom and benevolence, this institution of the mind would be wholly beneficial. But it, too, is characteristically human: being derived not only, or indeed mainly, from the incorporation into the self of the experience from the outer world, but mainly from within, it has, at least in its early developmental stages, the characteristics of the impulses that were predominant at the time of its inception. Some people's superego therefore is harsh to the point of brutality;

others are blessed with one that is kindly. Of course, if the child's upbringing is gentle and understanding (with firmness if occasion demands it), the superego is more likely to be of that nature too. If the upbringing is erratic, sometimes tyrannical, sometimes indulgent, the superego will not consolidate itself upon models which will assist the child's stability. In severely pathological cases the harshness of the superego is such that the patient is driven to take on himself the punishment of suicide by way of expiation for crimes not of deed but of fantasy.

Dealing with guilt and aggression

It was said that the child's aggression against its loved objects roused feelings of guilt (a feeling that is reinforced by the strictness of the superego). Guilt plays a cardinal part in the development of every human being, but its effects are for the most part unconscious.

One effect of guilt is to increase the impulse to make reparation for the damage done or intended. This "reparative tendency" is one of the most valuable aspects of our cultural life in that by this means we can turn the energy of aggression into constructive channels. The arts and sciences, the maintenance of a cultural level, even the humble duties of the common daily round, are partly prompted and maintained by this "reparative tendency".

To say this is not to deny that there are direct satisfactions in these activities, but it should be recalled that they are reinforced by this means. I would not introduce such a complicated process as the tendency to reparation into a discussion of this kind were it not for the fact that some people deplore the existence of aggression in human nature and try to stamp it out in children as an evil thing. In fact they cannot stamp it out, they can only "drive it underground", i.e. make the child repress it more strongly. Such parents and educators are afraid of expressions of aggression in the young and fear that unless it is "stopped" the child will grow up a delinquent. But the child has from an early age quite strong tendencies to curb his own aggression and to make compensation for the injuries he does in fits of aggression. He may need help in coping with his aggression: parental punishment, if well timed and not too severe, by assuaging the child's feeling of a need for punishment will bring instant relief.[2] The tendency to decent civi-

---

[2] Punishment in itself is not necessarily a harmful thing. Here, as always, it depends on the child's strength and the setting of the action.

lised behaviour does not have to be instilled into a child, but a good home environment brings out self-control and self-reliance earlier and better than a home where parents use their children as a means of getting rid of their own tensions.

A child also needs to discover its own strength, to experience and enjoy all of its instinctual impulses, and aggression is one of them. If its blustering and anger are always taken as a sign of sin, it will become too anxious and inhibited and so will not be able to use its creativeness to the full.

Guilt has a further useful function: a certain quantity of it in the mind seems to act as a sensitizer to current public opinion—too much of it may make the person a craven follower of the opinion of the public or of any powerful demagogue. In this as in all aspects of mental life it is not the presence of a quality that is so important as its strength and the way it interacts with the other aspects of the same personality. When we speak of "too much" of a quality such as guilt, what is meant is that the person is so dominated by it that the rest of the personality is impoverished. Thus for instance any one with too much guilt in his mind (which is not the same, of course, as being aware of the pangs of conscience all the time) will take various measures, without realising as a rule his motives for so doing, to reduce the tension in his mind.

(a) He may at all times feel that he has failed someone, will say "sorry" on any and every occasion, and clutter up his conversation with apologies. This, though tedious, is not incompatible with a high level of cultural production.

(b) He may put himself in the way of danger without taking precautions so that he gets into accidents, and after an accident thus caused he feels wonderfully calm—the injury has assuaged his guilt temporarily and he is therefore for a time relieved of some tension.

(c) He may hand over the control of his life to another who by ruling his life relieves him of responsibility and so he feels that what is done is not a charge on his conscience—many of the "dedications of life" to a cause (religious or political) spring from this motive. The character of the "Ruler" thus chosen depends on the character of the super-ego.

(d) A further stage in the foregoing is when the "Ruler" is chosen because he extorts such a degree of abject submission that it is virtually a form of lifelong punishment. Probably dictators can recruit their servile followers readily when this aspect of the guilt reaction is strong in the population.

(e) A still further stage in the same process in which the need for expiation is especially strong probably leads the dictator's followers to welcome even death on his behalf as a desirable thing.

These are reactions to guilt and are used to allay tension. Although they may not be desired for themselves, they are preferred to the state of mind (the pain of guilt) that the person would experience without them. This incomplete list of reactions to guilt will serve to show two things: first that they have a range spreading from the quite common and quite mild to the severest conditions which are fortunately rare, and secondly, that in some of these reactions the outer world is used "unwittingly" to alter an "inner" tension. Thus those who abject themselves before dictators do not know the reason why they must do so, any more than those that must run dangers and get hurt realise the deeper motives for their actions: in the former case, however, they may experience an excited pleasure in their submissiveness.

Masochism (the condition in which there is pleasure from the experience of pain) is not confined to the enjoyment of physical pain. The most common manifestation of masochism is satisfaction in enduring humiliation. Even this is at times tinged with erotic feeling. In the cases that are most relevant to our present purpose, the tinge of erotic feeling is usually suppressed (i.e. the person himself is not aware of it), but it finds expression in his emotional infatuation for his oppressor, who so far from being thought a brute is regarded as a Saviour. The hostile component of his ambivalent feelings is denied to consciousness and is turned against the self, so that he becomes still more a slave; the positive or friendly feelings flow out uninhibited in rapture.

The reason that guilt has been so much stressed here is that it is an element in the mental life which is forceful and which is of so painful a nature that the sufferer tends to avoid studying within himself both its origins and consequences.

Institutionalising defences

Man's emotional insecurity is a perpetual menace to his peace of mind. The insecurity is primarily internal, but he searches for external aids to help him to bring about a condition of quasi-stable equilibrium. Many social institutions act as a support to the adjustment he has made within himself. Some of the institutions of religion, for instance, clearly minister to the individual's need for punishment, and the submission to the strict rules of his religious order saves the penitent from a deepening insight into the causes of his guilt; he is made easy by the fact that there is an external agency which takes some of the burden of control from himself. Similar are political parties which demand an unwavering obedience of thought as well as of action.

The fact that social institutions act as defences against the disquiet in the mind of those who lean on them is one of the reasons why they are so highly valued. That is, a social institution can be valued both for the benefit it gives in the way of human association, and also—in some cases the more so—because the terms of the association (the rites, rules, conventions and even the mythology) obscure and thus protect the adherents from a recognition of underlying guilt and anxiety-ridden conflicts from which they would otherwise suffer directly. When an institution is valued for reasons such as this, it becomes sacrosanct, for to examine it is thought, or rather felt, to be equivalent to an exposure of its unconscious value and significance to its adherents.

This leads one to the reflection that there would seem to be only two ways to alter human institutions without causing an emotional crisis among the adherents: one way is to replace one institution by another which has the same effect in concealing their unconscious emotional significance, the other is to let the adherents do the changing themselves as they achieve greater understanding and control over that part of their emotional life concerned with public affairs. An example of the former is the embalming and exhibition of Lenin by the authors of the anti-God campaign, who must have known the Russian superstition that Saints do not decompose, i.e. one object of worship was replaced by another, one Saviour by another. The social scientist has to discern the defensive nature of the institutions he is operating on and avoid disturbing the defences until he or society can provide a better, a more normal, i.e. more flexible, solution of the conflicts and anxieties against which a defence is desired.

Social correlates of the superego

The term "superego" covers a wide range of phenomena. At one end of the scale it can include the incorporation into the self of the parental injunctions and examples upon which the boy (for simplicity we will confine ourselves to him) consciously and unconsciously models himself. At the other end of the scale there are fantastic images, which the child's unconscious harbours, of perfect, all-loving, omnipotent parent-figures and at the same time (in the unconscious, contradictions seem to be tolerated) utterly destructive, hateful and equally omnipotent parent-figures. It is a sign of maturation of the personality when the super-ego images are more blended, i.e. there is more tolerance of "good-and-bad" in the same person. The strong separation of "good" from "bad" is a sign of incomplete resolution of the early conflicting impulses in the mind, and when these conflicts are not resolved within the personality there is a tendency to project these opposed and incompatible elements into the environment, which instead of being an intimate blending of "good-and-bad" becomes a divided world of "perfect" and "devilish". We may consider these derivations separately.

Among the derivations of fantastically "good parent" images we may place the concept of Infallibly Good Persons or Institutions, such as for instance an Infallible Pope (the ultra-pious and the simple-minded think of him as a perfect person) or, to the devout followers of the concept, the Communist Party.

There are also simple-minded people who hold the same fantastic view of British Justice. These notions do not correspond with objective reality but with a subjectively toned fantasy the counterpart of which is sought for and then almost delusionally created in the outer world. This tendency leads to the unstable and often dangerous state of infatuation, which is an ascription to a person or an institution of all good qualities while the less good or bad qualities are denied or repressed by the conscious mind.

The derivatives of fantastically "bad parent" images are even more disturbing to public harmony. All forms of race hatred and xenophobia come from the projection of bad or persecuting figures from within the self into the environment and then beyond the frontier of the nation or race.

These concepts should be carried a stage further. A tyrant may be recognised as a bully and a brute consciously, but may nevertheless be an object of unconscious veneration and love. Thus Hitler to many was a sadistic, phallic God, and because of these attributes ascribed to him in fantasy he became irresistible to those who were unwittingly seeking in the outer world some figure on which to place their fantasies of a sadistic monster. They had this need because there was a lack of resolution or synthesis of these components with their opposite in their own personality. War is a social event which favours a splitting of fantasied persons into "all good" or "all bad"; the "good" are thought of as within their own country, the enemies as all bad. Hence, one of the attractions (albeit unconscious) of war is that it justifies or endorses the lack of synthesis of completion of our own maturation and makes our immaturity seem normal; viewed from this aspect war is one of the social institutions which man has devised for solving—though to be sure only temporarily (like a neurotic symptom)—emotional conflicts which he cannot otherwise handle.

It takes all sorts to make a world

During development there are many accretions to the personality. There are many people to whom we feel strong ties of affection or interest and who linger in our mind though our contact with them is over, people with whom we have identified ourselves and from whom we have got much and, through that "living memory" of them within us, still continue to get something of value. Our inner world of people is as rich and versatile as is our experience of ourselves and others; none are so dull as to have none of this within them.

Some people experience satisfaction if the outer world in some good measure matches the variegated pattern of human nature with its manifold diversity and type which they contain within themselves. Such people can tolerate divergence of opinion in their environment and enjoy the idea that opinions and habits of life are so varied. To such, "it takes all sorts to make a world"; the more varied the outer world the more can their own inner world be enriched by feeling their way into modes of life different from their own. Harmony between the outer and the inner world—and both of diverse attributes—gives rest to their spirit.

There is another kind of response to inner complexity, i.e. to make the environment as uniform as possible. If everyone thinks and behaves after the first, then there are no adjustments to make in social life. Internal harmony is effected not by welcoming diversity but by forcing upon the self as well as upon others an unchanging pattern of behaviour. Once the desire for diversity is silenced there is no more trouble, except with the wayward outsider who does not follow the pattern and who therefore must be corrected.

The former of these two contrasting types has a tolerant superego, the latter a strict one, and the former is far less likely to suffer from persecutory ideas than the latter, and is much less likely to turn into a social menace.

Aggressive individualism and aggressive nationalism

It is often assumed that there is an antithesis between international understanding and aggressive nationalism. In the case of individuals there are people—and they are not rare—in which an aggressive element in their relation to others is a necessary ingredient in their understanding of others. They are the active, assertive type in whom there is a more than usual degree of controlled sadism in their personality. It is a matter for investigation whether in national character there may not sometimes be the same factor, i.e. a nation may take a useful and on the whole constructive participation in international affairs so long as it is able to exercise a certain and controlled degree of assertive, even aggressive, nationalism. A further point for enquiry is whether the failure of the League of Nations may not have been due to the fact that it had not the power to be aggressive, and therefore very many people were quite unable in their imagination to bring it into the world of Great Powers. That is to say, the capacity to be aggressive gives substance to the image of the institution. Without weapons of assertion it could not excite sufficient interest in the unconscious fantasy to make it an object of concern to all. This is not the same as saying that the power needed must be on an overwhelming scale—on a scale, for instance, that made it capable of rousing fear—for it to give substantially to that image. Small nations are not feared, but their military zeal gives them nationhood and they are respected.

So strong may this need be for the evidence of aggressiveness that the thought of a world unarmed might be quite alarming; force is not only equated with destructiveness, even in the unconscious mind. Force is also linked with the protection of loved people—an unarmed world, on this viewing, has no wherewithal to curb aggression. The police, who are a force, comfort the worthy citizen not merely because they are a protection from external danger, but because they represent a strong and protecting superego.

Techniques for dealing with discontent on a national level

Some countries have evolved in their political system special techniques for dealing with discontent. The Central Authority is divided into two portions, one fixed and one removable. The fixed portion receives at all times the affection and respect of the people, the removable portion receives the brunt of the people's discontent with the management of affairs. In England the fixed portion is, of course, the Throne; in America it is not the President but the Constitution and the Supreme Court. The removable portion in England is the Cabinet, in America the President and Congress. So long as the removable portion is worth attacking, the fixed portion is safe, and there is continuity in political life.

A second feature of these techniques, which underlies, as I understand it, democratic government, finds its clearest expression in the attitude of His Majesty's Opposition. I take these ideas from a series of leaders in *The Lancet*, but they were first put forward by M. D. Eder soon after the First World War. In the English Parliament His Majesty's Opposition is accorded almost as much respect as His Majesty's Government, for both are loyal to the fixed portion of the Central Authority, both are made up of persons who represent the people, and, when both are of almost equal power, the English have a feeling that their Constitution is safe and that changes will not come at a speed they cannot check.

These two features can be related to the theme "it takes all sorts to make a world" already mentioned, i.e. the notion that the complexity of our inner mental life cannot be adequately represented by a single theme (or political party) but only by an interplay of conflicting forces both of which are subject to an overriding principle—that a Central Authority must have continuity and the removable portions must curb their ambition for absolute power. It may be that this is a solution, perhaps the best so far devised, for dealing with the problem raised in *Totem and Taboo* (Freud, 1912–13) of the rebellion of the sons against the father, adjustments can be freely made but without disturbing that multigenerational pattern (father, sons, and perhaps, also grandparents and grandsons) which seems to be basic to social (and even perhaps personal) growth and enrichment. It is a method of effecting change without rousing anxiety or guilt. Speaking with aphoristic inexactitude, we could extend this theme further by saying that the difference between revolution and reform lies in the fact that the revolutionary evokes guilt but denies it; the reformer tempers his wish for change by an intuitive recognition that when guilt is roused its neutralisation is liable to absorb an undue amount of energy.

There is, however, another technique of human adjustment that is tried from time to time and that merits equal attention. In this there is no two- or multi-party system, no removable portion of the central authority; a one-party system is integrated to the central authority. To express discontent with this party is tantamount to attacking the central authority itself, and that precipitates feelings of anxiety and guilt. It is one of the penalties of a bid for absolute power that so much energy has to be diverted to the suppression of those who want things done another way; a political arrangement in which there is no method of discontent with authority but revolt is bound to increase internal tension.

The importance of this for our present theme is that when a regime regards itself as threatened from within, i.e. when discontent mounts high, by the device of projection the enemy is regarded as beyond the frontier and that in turn increases international tension.

An experiment in technique for dealing with discontent in a closed group and for releasing constructive energy

The psychiatric service in the British Army during the Second World War, under the leadership of Brigadiers J. R. Rees and Sandiford, devised a method by which every psychiatrist felt himself to be a participant in all of the activities of that branch of the Army, and there was therefore hardly a grumble. The country was divided into regions and the psychiatrists working in each region assembled every quarter for a scientific and technical-administrative conference, which was attended by someone from the War Office. At these discussions rank was ignored; any psychiatrist, however junior, could give his views on present and future policy and his memoranda (if submitted) were circulated to his regional colleagues and to the War Office. His views were discussed freely by the War Office representatives, who gave preliminary answers to the points raised.

The success was due to the fact that (a) there was a common enemy and (b) roughly speaking a common skill in contributing to his overthrow; but also (c) discontents were dealt with by face-to-face relationship, and (d) everyone in those conferences was convinced that his constructive ideas would get a hearing: complaints and constructiveness were not led along different channels, both could be expressed to the same authority at the same time. The effect in raising morale was of course considerable, and here is the point germane to our topic: the members of the psychiatric team, who as a team had so few internal disruptive tensions, were free to a quite unusual extent to co-operate in an imaginative way with other branches of the Service.

In framing a research programme to study the influence that makes for international tensions, it is as important to study the channels by which creativeness can flow into a central authority "from below" and the way those channels can be kept open not only for ideas but also for discontent: ideas and discontent are not incompatible.

Two problems for consideration

(a) If the struggle for the ownership of the means of production is as deep-rooted in human nature as some economists tell us, then it would seem probable that its origin is to be found in the family and that the primary impulse is towards possession of the mother, all other means of production being derivatives of that primal source. If this be so, and I am not at all disposed to dispute it, then economic motives in human nature are strongly interwoven with feelings of guilt. A study by analysts in many countries and cultures, East and West, of the impulse to possess the mother invariably discloses guilt reactions. Sometimes the guilt is denied, to the impoverishment of the personality, usually it is not, but it is always there. But these economists who speak much of this impulse to possess the means of production are singularly silent about guilt reactions. Indeed, in my experience in Russia before, during and shortly after the Revolution, one of the surprising features of the Bolsheviks was their silence on the theme of guilt.

If, however, the impulse to possess the means of production is considered to be a purely adult reaction, then we have a new phenomenon to deal with, i.e. a social or economic impulse without roots in childhood. I should regard such a theory on this subject which denied genetic roots in the early developmental years as a myth.

(b) The possession of new weapons inevitably produces, in the case of the individual, an impulse to use them; in the case of a community, it is a matter for investigation whether the invention and monopoly of immensely potent weapons do not put a strain on the administration of their possessor, and whether their effect is not to distort the political structure of the possessing state towards that of an ambitious oligarchy.

Some conclusions

(a) A physician's analogies should be used with caution, but in the absence of a theory of group anatomy and physiology (to make yet another analogy) they may deserve attention.

(b) A physician has to face his patient and listen to his complaints. If he brings his own research puzzles to the doctor–patient relationships he loses touch with the patient. His interview has to be a "two-way" traffic. The same probably applies to the sociologist. Unless a painful problem is felt to be on the way to solution, the people the sociologist interviews will not be able to disclose, because unable fully to appreciate, the origin, extent and consequences of their tensions.

The method of upbringing of children should be studied in relation to:

(i) national character;
(ii) methods of dealing with tension and discontent;
(iii) the type of leader chosen and the relation to him, whether infatuation as towards Hitler or affectionate respect with limited dependence on him as towards Churchill.

(c) A study of the sort of tension we are considering cannot be adequate if it ignores the fact that tension only occurs in actual situations of living people. Those investigating it therefore must stand to gain or lose with those undergoing the tension if they are to produce findings—i.e. techniques of adjustment—that will actually work to effect reduction of tension.

(d) A study should be made of the motives which lead people to affiliate themselves to institutions, e.g. the political parties, the religious orders, the fighting services, the professions, and more temporary and even somewhat unusual associations, such as sports clubs, temperance societies, and the like. Such studies should not stop at conscious answers to questionnaires, nor should they consider as complete a particular investigation which did not show how the joining of the institution solved or attempted to solve the unresolved emotional problems which intrude upon the complicate action in the present.

The same study would also include the reasons for changing institutional affiliations and for ending them.

(e) Bacon said: "It would be an unsound fancy and self-contradictory to expect that things which have never yet been done can be done except by means which have never yet been tried."

The removal of tensions which lead to war is a thing which has never yet been done, but people are slow to try new means to avert it. This is partly because the attitude of man is by no means unanimously against war, partly I surmise (a physician cannot do more) because groups are resistant to an exploration of their psychology particularly in regard to aggression.

For an investigation to hope to succeed in this deep level of human experience there are, in my view, six prerequisite conditions:

TENSIONS THAT CAUSE WARS

(i) The investigation should have no publicity, not that secrecy is desirable, but an enquiry of this sort must be spared crosscurrents.

(ii) No time limit must be set for results.

(iii) The personnel should be familiar with the conflict within themselves regarding their least relished thoughts and impulses, and how they have avoided and eventually made contact with their own unconscious processes.

(iv) They should study both individual tension and intra-group tension on a professional level.

(v) They should be prepared when they have formed conclusions to have them laughed at, attacked, and ignored for a generation, for it is most unlikely that their group findings would not uncover unwelcome truths.

(vi) If, however, their efforts are thus derided and ignored, it does not mean that their results are wholly wrong, but if right that their way of handling the people concerned (in this case anyone interested) has been inadequate. For this investigation is not an academic exercise but a piece of personal experience on a deep level of feeling and significance. Its aim should not be a summary of social dynamics but the beginning of a new phase of human collaboration, where the goal is a more stable social and personal equilibrium. What shape society would then take is yet beyond our ken. It has to emerge from the work of liberation from anxiety and unmanageable guilt.

PART IV

ON THE NATURE OF RELIGIOUS AND MORAL BELIEFS

CHAPTER 15

A study of Quaker beliefs

(1935)

Recent discoveries have thrown light on some aspects of religious belief which had hitherto been obscure. For about a quarter of a century psychoanalysts have been in possession of hypotheses which have enabled us to connect the majority of religious systems with other and better-known mental phenomena of health and illness. But there were certain religious beliefs and practices which were difficult to "place". Chief among these was Quakerism. In the last ten years, however, our knowledge of certain fundamental processes has progressed, largely owing to the researches of Melanie Klein, who has applied Freud's discoveries to the investigation of the minds of young children (Klein, 1932), so that we are now enabled to bring some light to the study of even this obscure problem.

In this paper my concern is far more to extend the application of scientific hypotheses and to increase the number of connections between the phenomena of religion and those of the rest of human life, than to make an ambitious attempt to discover "Transcendental Truth" about Quakerism or anything else.

The Lister Memorial Lecture, 1935, delivered at a Meeting of the Quaker Medical Society.

The character of religious impulses

In the religious impulses of man we are confronted with an urge to satisfy and "complete" his relation to the outer world by means which do not appear to have any direct bearing on the primary impulses to preserve himself or his species. He erects temples to an omnipotent Being of whose existence he has no objective proof, but in whose existence he has the firmest belief. He seeks, under the sway of his religious impulses, or associated ones, to control his environment by magical means—for example, by praying for rain. He tries to produce a right feeling within himself, irrespective of whether this increases or decreases his own chances of survival as in the case of the ascetic, or the well-being of, and his good relation to, his fellow men, in the case of "Holy Wars". Lastly he tries to establish a good, and actually intimate, relation to the Supreme Being who is known to him only in "revelation" and by evidences so vague that if it was a case of tracking an animal by its spoor the quarry would invariably be lost. This is rather a mid-Victorian or Thomas "Huxlean" way of putting the situation, which we shall be able to improve on later.

In his daily life of food-getting and to a less extent in his love-making, man's movements are to a large extent orderly and can be traced to fairly clearly defined impulses or to the results of experience. That is to say, as an adult he seems in many respects to have the characteristics of an animal, as regards predictableness, but in his religious behaviour there appears to be an element of uncertainty, an unpredictability, which suggests that the religious impulse is intimately connected with unstable emotional attitudes to the self and to the environment. The changeableness of his behaviour further suggests that some of his cravings are seldom satisfied and that he does not endure privation easily. If the animals do not get what they want, they endure privation without taking many steps to provide substitute gratifications, but man's capacity to endure privation of instinct is much less and he deflects his aim to other objects. The multifarious expressions of religious activity have been ascribed, and I think rightly, to this capacity of man to deflect his impulses. There is not, I think, sufficient evidence for the commonly held view that the craving for religious experience is one of the primary needs of man; rather, it should be regarded as one of the results of the deflection of the fundamental instincts.

If the adult with regard to the predictability of his behaviour in a given environment resembles the animals fairly closely, we cannot say the same of the child. In infancy the attitude to the environment often changes quickly, from affectionate interest to sudden fear and hostility, showing an unstable mental state. A child will suck its rattle and give signs of enjoying contact with it. At the next instant, he will bang it on the crib, throw it away with a look of disgust, then snatch it and suck it again with evident relish—all within a few seconds. If an adult behaved in this way we should regard him as mentally unbalanced, and there is every reason to regard children's mental equilibrium as unstable; they begin their emotional life in uncertainty and are beset by fantastic fears, bogies and black thoughts. The recent discoveries already mentioned concern the nature of the emotional instability in childhood and the mental processes adopted, albeit unwittingly, to reduce the feeling of insecurity resulting from that instability.

It is relevant to remark here that there appear good grounds for believing that the very strong impulse in man to achieve "completeness" in his relation to his environment, to control it by processes of thought (magic) rather than by action, to effect a right feeling within the self and to establish an intimate relation with a Supreme Being, all arise out of a stage of emotional instability in early childhood which is not completely outgrown. The highest achievements of our culture and the ghastliest of all disorders—those of the mind—are alike traceable to a period of psychic immaturity which persists in the background of the mind throughout life.

Early object relationships

The psychological characteristic of infancy is that the instinctual life is unstable, that is to say, the child is forced to take up attitudes to the people and objects in his environment which he is unable to maintain and he has desires which he is unable to put into action with satisfaction to himself. At one moment he is feeling friendly, at the next moment hostile to the same thing, whether it be his rattle, his own fingers or the mother's breast, and what is more, since the boundary between the self and the outer world, between the me and the not-me, is a hazy one, a change of value involves an alteration in feeling towards the self as well as the world at large. All is good or all is bad—the self included, since there is no "buffer substance" to sustain the self-feeling, to keep up self-confidence, when a black mood begins to come on.

The infant's mood of friendliness or hostility changes for him the character of the object. In technical language the emotion, whether of friendliness or aggression, is attributed to the object, so that in the early days the environment and the self move together so to speak, in oscillation between "nice" or "nasty", "good" or "bad". This attribution to the external object of the emotion that originates in the self (called *production*) is one of the means employed at this infantile period for decreasing mental tension. The other (called *introjection*) is an attempt to become possessed of and to master the object by engulfing it in imagination within the self. When an object is good, there is a wish to suck it into the self; when it is bad, there is a wish to attack it, to bite, cut or tear it to bits and to eat it up. Strange though this mental process may appear to us, we must recollect that the infant's capacity to manipulate an object with his hands is rudimentary compared with his power to chew it. He is a mouth-governed creature.

It is a corollary of the vagueness of the boundary between the me and the not-me that a thing which is thought of as inside the self, can also be regarded as having an element of independence. It is a kind of foreign body within the self. The term "foreign body" must be used with caution, because we think of foreign bodies as objects which have entered the system accidentally or against the wishes of the patient—for example, grit in the eye, or a bullet in the flesh. But in the case we are discussing, the child in its imagination, in order the better to master an object, bites at it, swallows it and then thinks of it as now inside. I have used the word "think" but must hasten to add that it is not a conscious process of introspection or reasoning, but that projection and introjection are unconscious mental processes, though capable of becoming conscious under certain conditions.

It is necessary to lay stress on this complicated problem of the introjection of an external object within the self, because it gives us the key to that remarkable phenomenon basic to Quakerism, namely, the Inner Light. Indeed this process of inclusion of an external thing is at the base of our capacity to respond to and become part of a social culture. Psychoanalysts are, as a result of their observations on small children, coming to the conclusion that maladaptation to a social culture is due to a disorder of the "introjective function". At present this is only a tentative contribution to sociology, but it appears to have enormous possibilities.

The small child has very little capacity for distinguishing gradations between the extremes of very good and very bad. Because of his emotional instability, he cannot easily settle at a stage between the two, nor remain long at either extreme. This is due to lack of fusion of his own tender and aggressive impulses; they operate separately and so lead to violent oscillations in his relation to an object. Now owing to the vagueness of the boundary of the self and the belief that objects, when internalised, retain their characteristics, he is put in a serious difficulty when he is in a rage and, in his imagination, engulfs an object in order to master it. His rage has been communicated to the object by projection, and then it is found to be inside the self as a bad and harmful thing. This greatly increases his need for a good object to put right the harm being done by the bad one. In other words, a state of anger increases the need for a protective agency to undo the harm of one's own aggression. To this need for a protective agency we may ascribe the craving for God. Animals, which are from birth instinctively stable, have no reason to hypothesize such a Being; but to the human infant, in continual need to rectify the results of his own unstable impulses, the concept of a Supreme Being appears a necessity. The biological explanation of the concept of God is, it seems to me, to be found in an (unwitting) endeavour to correct the mental instability which results from our being born psychically immature.

The psychological condition we are describing accounts for the connection to be found in most religions between God and Devil. The tendency of the infant to keep his good object very, very good and to make his bad one very, very bad has already been noted. This finds expression in the Christian Church among believers who exhibit the same degree of faith in the existence of Satan as in the divinity of Christ and console themselves with the idea that "love casteth out sin", in other words that Jesus is stronger than Satan.

If mother and nurse behave to the child in an erratic way, sometimes being short-tempered, sometimes excessively affectionate, the child (always prone to projection) regards the alterations as having emanated from itself and becomes alarmed, not only at the rapid changes produced, but also at its own power.

Within the framework of a stable environment, the baby usually finds it possible to build up an impression of itself as the constructor of a stable world, and this reinforces its trust in itself and in its internalised objects.

A stable emotional environment also helps the child to learn the difference between the me and the not-me, by demonstrating that the behaviour of other people is independent of his moods. Thus the concept of stable external objects arises in his mind.

Since he attributes to others the same processes as go on inside himself, the child regards his mother, when kind, as being full of good objects and the "bad mother" as full of bad objects. The consistent mother is one in whom these contending elements appear to him to have reached stability, and this gives him hope of stability himself. Many people find satisfaction in believing that their God suffered the same mental conflicts that they themselves do. "Jesus was tempted but was without sin." The doctrine that Jesus was a human as well as a Divine Being has been a consolation.

The growth of the concept of stable objects is slow; to begin with, there is a desire for the object to be all of one quality since this facilitates primitive projection and introjection. For instance, we often find in the case of mother–nurse figures that the mother is given all the good qualities and the nurse all the bad ones, a dichotomy which, for all its faults, has the merit temporarily, at least, of facilitating the building up of a picture of a figure that is coherent. Later, when the child, as he invariably does, suffers disappointment in his parent figures through his idealisation of them, i.e. when they do not come up to the fantastically high level that he expects of them, the child splits off a part of his parent-regarding, emotional life and reserves this for his inner or phantasy life and he lets his thoughts dwell on the picture of ideally "helpful" figures who later consolidate into his conception of God. I must, however, emphasise once more that this is not a conscious process of thought; it is a movement of emotional orientation and outlook that occurs outside the range of consciousness. In a word, the concept of God arises because the child needs an idealised object to rescue him from the anxiety which he feels would overwhelm him because of the power of his own destructive impulses and his own bad objects. So long as parents remain idealised they serve this end. When they are seen to have mixed qualities, instead of accepting them for what they are the parent figure is split. The perfect parents are turned into gods, the imperfect ones receive a partial, but on the whole a more stable, allegiance than they had before.

The God concept and mental life

We have traced in outline one of the factors which produce the concept of God in the mental life of the individual, and we may note in passing that the importance of the concept is not diminished by the fact that the existence of a Supreme Being does not readily lend itself to objective verification. It would seem that the function of the God-concept is to diminish mental anxiety, which arises on account of unconscious aggressive impulses threatening the existence of loved objects. In more simple language, the function of God in our minds is to save us from our own destructive tendencies. The need for the concept of God is found wherever there is persistence into later life of the early period of our mental development, the period of emotional instability where those objects (persons) that we most prized were, in our imagination, the victims of our fiercest attacks.

Let us see how these tendencies are dealt with in various types of religions, and what God-concepts have been evolved in different cultures.

Let us consider first the Central Australian Aborigines, the Aranda. The tribe possesses certain magical objects called "churinga". These, if handled in the proper spirit, bestow the power of the "spirit ancestors" upon those that touch them; a laying-on of hands with the direction of the current reversed, so to speak. By the pious manipulation of the sacred objects the believer himself becomes filled with churinga or the spirit of his ancestors. He may indeed reach the state of becoming nothing but churinga, that is he is inspired. It is a fetish-religion, because from the object flows what in Christian idiom would be called "divine-grace". The believer (and who is a doubter among primitive peoples?) finds in the churinga an antidote to his evil passions, his fears and his sense of sin. The introjection of the object, the churinga, is a psychic device for making the interior of the individual safe, and for increasing the believer's confidence in his own powers; "bad" elements are dealt with by means of projection, i.e. they are regarded as external and appear to the believer as demons.

In the religion of the Mongolian tribes on the Siberian border we recognise the concepts and mechanisms with which we are now familiar. The destructive impulses again are projected into the environment on demons, but they are given more human attributes than are those of the Australian Aborigine; they form groups, breed and, above all, fight. The great difference, however, is that the control of the relation between the good and bad spirits and mankind is not direct, but takes place only through the Shaman or priest-medicine man. The laymen do not get power direct from the magical object, as among the Aranda. It is an intercessory religion. The person who has the ecstasies is not the suppliant but the priest; he who trembles and quakes because of the power of the magic within him is the sorcerer who is paid a fee for his services of intermediation.

In a third type of religion the gods are part human, part animal, as in Ancient Egypt and India, showing an emergence into the region of human life from bogey-dom, but the sexual life of the gods is primitive and animal.

A fourth type of religion has consolidated the good and bad figures. There is a Supreme Being, clearly a father figure, who has absorbed all power into himself, as we find in the Jewish, Christian and Mohammedan religions, and the evil or destructive impulses are consolidated into a devil figure or Satan. With this type we find a great deal of bargaining with the Deity for favours; for although there is in all religions a belief in the omnipotence of God, in nearly all there is a counter-belief that the omnipotent God can be controlled by the still more omnipotent magic of the believer's prayers. Quakerism appears to be a singular exception to this, for here the submission to the will of God appears to be complete. There are other ways in which Quakerism is unique. Almost all religions have puberty or initiation ceremonies, which mark the transition to adult sexual life or prepare for it. Our interest in these ceremonies may for the moment be confined to the mere fact of their existence in nearly every religion except Quakerism, which appears to be able to dispense not only with these ceremonies but also with a creed and a totem feast or sacrament of eating its God. Unlike that of the culture in which it arose, Quakerism has no relation to lesser gods or goddesses, in the form of saints. Traditionally, the Quakers have no holy place, do not orient their graves or their places of worship and do not wear mourning for the dead. They ignore titles bestowed by the state, confer none of their own, and do not even distinguish between married or unmarried women in their mode of address. They have no priests and admit women on an equality with men in their ministry and as administrative officers, who are called by the lowly name of clerks. They refused to take oaths, which, before affirmation was allowed as a substitute, led to their exclusion from official positions. The number of important points of difference from other religious bodies is the more astonishing in view of the fact that their doctrine encourages them to join in all public work of a constructive nature. The Quakers may be a peculiar, but they are not an exclusive, people, in the sense that they do not withdraw from the world. I believe it is possible to account for all its peculiar features by one single hypothesis which had already been alluded to, though not in details.

The nature and function of the "Inner Light"

What is the Inner Light? Let us begin by assuming that it is well named. It is *Inner*, that means, I take it, that it is endopsychic. But those who write and speak about it with most experience say that it comes from God. It may, however, be possible to regard the matter in a genetic way, i.e. with reference to the growth of the concept in the mind of the child; in which case we are dealing with a condition where the boundary between the self and an external object is, or rather has been, vague. The object is believed to be internal, and with the cause of the belief we now have to deal.

The object introjected is always an exceedingly valuable thing to the child at the time of the introjection, so much so that it outweighs in importance all other objects. To the Central Australian the churinga represents all that is valuable. It makes the difference between joy and self-confidence, or gloom and emptiness, irrespective of environment. It gives him the capacity to love, and makes him love-worthy. It is a magical love-organ that has the power to transform the world as by its action it transforms the sensations and the sense of well-being in the believer's own body. With the assistance of the churinga he regains in his mind the experience of a time long past when in his phantasy he had assimilated into himself the essence and most potent instrument of life. The reason why the concept retains so much power appears to be due to two causes. In the first place, it is attractive to possess in imagination so good a thing; in the second, it serves as a defence against the opposite concept of bad bogies or demons working destruction within and without. Now if the main function of the Inner Light was to provide a sense of security against demons, Quakerism might have to be classified among the magical cults or religions such as those found in Central Australia. There seem, however, to be grounds for placing Quakerism in an equally surprising though different psychological category, to which after a digression we will return.

It will prove most convenient for the exposition of the hypotheses concerning the function of the Inner Light to make a preliminary, and necessarily cursory, examination of similar though not identical phenomena in other fields. Artists often regard themselves as possessing "a unique gift"; the thought of it as an integral part of themselves is expressed in such phrases as "if I am not a poet I may as well not be alive"—a phrase that implies not only that the poetic gift establishes for them the veritable existence of an inner source of creative power, but also that without it they would feel themselves assailed by a sense of inner futility and annihilation.

The artist and the scientist

A "pure" artist or a "pure" scientist, as Ella Sharpe (1935) has clearly pointed out,[1] is not only one who neglects material gains. He is distinguished also by positive criteria of far greater importance. The "pure" artist or the "pure" scientist is not concerned with the utilitarian value of his labours any more than the child is concerned with the practical application of his play. The product of artist, scientist or child is the result of an inner urge. The "play" is influenced, but not ruled, by factors in the environment. None of the three has a conscience about earning his living. He is content to be supported, so long as he produces his creative work.

If we turn our attention, for the moment, to the artist, we shall recognise the operation of one of the primitive mental mechanisms which we have already discussed. He brings his experience of external events within his personality and there manipulates them. The situation has ceased to be that of an individual *vis-à-vis* an environment, the barrier between the me and the not-me has partially and temporarily vanished. At this stage he cannot do anything but perceive and receive from without; it is an "introjecting" process. The underlying urge in the artist appears to be that of bringing harmony or order into the picture of the world as he sees it. He is not only sensitive to the beauty but is greatly disturbed by the disorder in his picture of what he sees, or rather of what he has experienced in his imagination in the past. The disorder referred to (as the reader will by now be quick to guess) can be traced back to the period of emotional instability in early childhood. There is reason to think that the artist is a person who, for some cause as yet unknown, has experienced at a very early age an unusually severe conflict between loving and destructive impulses, and, being endowed with an unusually high sensibility, feels more acutely than most would do the confusion in his perception of the world.

Is not the element in whose influence the artist subjects his perception the same that the Quakers call the Inner Light? It is the "introjected

---

[1] Most of the points in this paragraph which concern the artist and the scientist are taken from Ella Freeman Sharpe's paper, "Similar and Divergent Unconscious Determinants Underlying the Sublimations of Pure Art and Pure Science" (1935).

good object" with which the artist identifies himself, as does the Quaker, and it is employed to reconstruct the image of the world which the artist, in his unconscious phantasy, imagines has been damaged by his own destructive impulses. His wish is to restore his world to its condition before he wrought havoc in his phantasy, and he does this "magically" by means of artistic production. It is not a facile waving of an all-powerful wand like a conjurer, but the heaviest toil of spirit under the eye of the sternest critic. It must be a perfect production or it will not undo the harm done and restore beauty and order into his world.

We have spoken of the artist as one who introjects in his phantasy elements from the outside world in order to obtain power over them, and after a manipulation of them to form a harmonious unity to produce a work of art. There is a sensuous contact with the objects in the phantasy. Art is closely dependent on fineness of bodily sensibilities.

In the case of the scientist, the interplay is predominantly not that of introjection but of projection; the scientist does not use his body so much as his head in his creative work. The artist feels accurately, the scientist thinks accurately, both have to produce accurate pictures of the world without and within, but the exactness in the one case is in feeling, in the other in abstraction. The "pure" scientist is often inhibited from using his knowledge in "applied science"—that is, for immediately practical ends—but he gets some of his relief from his inner anxieties by knowing that he is doing work that will ultimately benefit mankind.

The Inner Light in relation to creative works

Both artists and scientists seem to employ (but unwittingly) a mental process in which the anxieties consequent on an early and severe disturbance of mental stability, due to the relative strength of the destructive impulse, are rectified by an internal mental factor, which I have called the "introjected good object". Its primary purpose is to reduce anxiety. Its mode of operation differs from one type of case to another, but there it appears to have two functions which are related to one another. The first function is rather like that of a "buffer substance" which helps the ego in its struggle with its own destructive impulses and tides it over a difficult period when the self and the world seem to be hopelessly evil. The second function is to give zest to the ego's constructive activities and, by "making good" the damage that has been done in phantasy, to assuage the pain in the mind caused by the destructive impulses.

Let us take an illustration of the "buffer" effect. The cause of the trouble in the unstable period of childhood is the strength of the destructive impulse in his phantasies. The child bites, cuts up, poisons or peers into the bodies of loved persons, who are, in the surging excitement of the moment, annihilated psychically. The situation can be made clearer if we take a clinical instance from later life after this excited destructiveness has already led to considerable inhibitions. The sawing up of planks, a necessary stage in the construction of a box, may (because of the excitement in the phantasy) be thought of as a destruction of the integrity of the wood, a concept at once thrilling and also the occasion of much anxiety and feelings of guilt. A deeper investigation of the phantasies in such a case shows that there has been a displacement onto the inanimate material (the wood) of the excitement which was originally related to doing these violent actions to people. The displacement of the effect from people to things was made in the first place in order to reduce anxiety and guilt; but the disturbance due to aggressive impulses follows the displacement, and the original worry reappears in the new situation, and action is inhibited, for it becomes as unbearable to saw up planks as to saw up human beings.

The way through this dilemma is provided by the "introjected good object". Fusion of the concept of the finished box with the concept of sawn-up planks diminishes the sense of destructiveness and therefore anxiety is lessened. I have called this the first stage, or the "buffer" effect. The ego is strengthened from within (by the absorption of a good object) against the hate impulses which threaten it. As a result of the reduction of anxiety, the mind is freed from inhibitions and so is enabled to perform elaborate constructive efforts and the path is opened to pleasure in the perfecting of the box. This zest in construction, in "making good" the damage done to the planks by turning them into something better, is what I have called the second function of the internalised good object. The two functions of the "internalised good object" are, first, to effect a better relation to the components within the mind and, then, to produce "good"—that is, pleasing and constructive—effects upon objects in the outer world.

The artist and scientist are fully absorbed in the task of giving maximal opportunity to these effects of the "internalised good object"; it is their life. The process is present in ordinary mortals too, but there is less of the inner urge in their productivity.

The Quaker attitude to art

The characteristic feature of the artist's mental life is the interplay between the impressions he receives from without and the sensuous responses of his own body and its rhythms in his imagination. It appears to be even more necessary for the artist than for the ordinary person to turn his attention outwards from time to time for the passive reception of impressions. Stimulation comes from without; the working over of the impressions is an internal process. With the Quaker it is otherwise. He seems to be more independent of the outer world (though not so independent as the Yogi with whom the Quaker has many interesting points of resemblance but as many points of fundamental difference). The Quaker may be said, in a sense, to live on a store of sensory experience, unfailing as the widow's cruse of oil to which the Inner Light is sometimes likened, taken into the self but never fully absorbed, unchanging as the mother's milk yet never staling to the appetite: a universe of experience within, immutable, eternal. The unchanging character of this inner source of strength depends to a large extent on its being kept away from the taint of other experiences, to which are attributed dangerous sensual qualities. In the Quaker view, a right relation to the source of the experience called the Inner Light requires that there should be restriction of sensual bodily desires and that the Inner Light itself should never be regarded in other than a "pure" or sublimated way. In a sense, the Inner Light is a neuter experience, apparently sexless.

The suppression of sensuality could hardly be carried further in religious belief than is done by the Quakers, and I ascribe their antagonism to art—in the early centuries of Quakerism, at any rate—to a dread lest any rousing of sensuality should jeopardise their relation to the Inner Light.[2]

---

[2] The lengths to which this was carried can scarcely be believed by the younger generation of Quakers; there was no music, no pictures hung on the walls, decorations of all kinds were avoided, the women dressed in "Quaker Grey" and wore a uniform, the men had no collars and at times even no buttons on their coats (I regard the reason given—"wordliness"—as less credible than the symbolic significance of the button itself). Their furniture (of the finest woods and of beautiful grain) must not be polished as this gave a gaudy glint to the room, but oddly enough their table silver, plain and very solid, was kept bright and the panels of their carriages gleamed in street and countryside. They cultivated flowers, and their tables groaned with meats in season.

The Quaker attitude to science

A contrast has been drawn between the artist and the scientist in respect to their relation to sensuous bodily processes: the artist withdraws into his body during the elaborate process of creative work, his field of activity is internal; the scientist goes outward in his creative work to the external world. To express this with aphoristic compactness (and inexactitude) the process *in the artist is corporo-petal, in the scientist corporo-fugal*. But this is not the only difference. For all that the research workers say about their motives being purely theoretical, the scientist is greatly concerned that man should have more control over the phenomena of nature, the artist wishes that mankind should have more delight in it. The impulse to bring more order into the world finds a ready response in Quakers, who seem to be more conscious of the world's confusion (while at the same time borne up by hope, perhaps at times extravagant hope) than most people. The compulsion to pay attention to the order already existing in the outer world characterises the scientist; the compulsion to attempt to bring harmony into what is sometimes euphemistically called "the social order" characterises the Quaker. One of the chief differences lies in the fact that the point of reference in the case of the scientist lies in what does in fact exist, with the Quaker with what he thinks ought to exist. The discrepancy, which may at times exist between these two may explain, in part at any rate, why the Quaker has been more devoted to social reform than to social research.

The nature of a "Concern"

So far as I am aware no definition of a "Concern" exists, and I am not going to be so rash as to attempt one; but it may be possible by examining some of its outstanding characteristics to bring the phenomenon within the framework of theory which we are employing. For convenience, we will divide its features into two groups according as they touch upon the relation of the individual to his God, and upon the relation of the individual to the group. The former may help us to understand the place of "good works" in "the Quaker way of life" and the way in which the Ministry of preaching and "the appearing in supplication" characterise Quaker public worship; the latter may afford us some insight into the bonds which hold the members of the Society of Friends together.

The function of a "Concern" in the individual's relationship to God

A *Concern* is a state of mind (or soul) induced in an individual by a heightening of the action of the Inner Light. The outcome of this state of mind is usually (but not invariably) action, in the form of preaching, prayer, a private talk with a particularly specified person, or a special activity, such as ministering to the sick or afflicted, or something apparently without purpose—going into a field alone and praying aloud, or changing an occupation. It is almost always an addition or alteration to the ordinary routine of life.

Following good medical precedent we may divide the manifestations of the Inner Light in the phenomenon of a Concern into physical and mental.

Physical manifestations of a Concern have diminished in frequency so that they are now rare, but in former times were regarded as normal occurrences. The term "Quaker" gives an indication of their nature. The individual feels within him the power of the Holy Spirit and trembles in all of his limbs. If he is speaking at the time his voice is apt to rise into a high-pitched nasal tremolo, the head is thrown back, the eyes are closed, and occasionally the arms are stretched down with the palms upwards. These phenomena, which vary in proportion and amount in different individuals, are not peculiar to Quakerism. For instance, I have observed them in a Hodja[3] in San Sophia in Constantinople when he was reciting the Koran. "Quaking" also appears in more primitive religious practices—for example, among the Aranda, when "full of churinga", or as Christians would say, "filled with the Holy Spirit". Shaking or quaking is also found, apart from the exercise of religious devotion, among people who suffer from hysteria, and an investigation of these cases reveals a concurrent phantasy with an erotic content, the agitation of the body being an expression of a sexual blended with an aggressive impulse.

The second physical manifestation is not visible; we can only learn it from the reports of those who have experienced it. There is a change of bodily sensation, at first consisting of a faint trembling in the spine and large joints, accompanied at times by an alternation of hot and cold flushes in the back and abdomen, a constriction of the chest, a sense of weight or of oppression. But this gives place to a feeling of peace and

---
[3] A lay preacher or teacher in the Mohammedan Church.

quietness, lightness and unburdensome fullness. Again, apart from religion, we find in patients who undergo these experiences the association with sexual phantasies, so that we may fairly draw the inference that these physical manifestations of a Concern were also related to an aspect of the unconscious part of the mind which derived its energy from the sexual impulse and that the manifestations were not much disguised. I have drawn a distinction between shaking or quaking and the invisible manifestation which might be called Transport. This only serves to illustrate the artificial nature of such classifications, but the two are closely connected, and they are both nearly related to the psychic phenomena described in the term "oceanic feeling".

It is perhaps relevant in this connection to note that with a change in the mode of life of Quakers during the last century shown by an increased pleasure in colour, in clothes, in pictures, music, the theatre, dancing and in sport, the physical manifestations of a Concern have disappeared almost to vanishing point. It is doubtful if anyone born less than a century ago has been, in the literal sense, a Quaker. Nearly forty years ago I saw such a person, who was then about 60, and my grandfather said, in reply to my comment, that the phenomenon was nothing like so vigorous nor so frequent as it was when he was a boy. I remember being somewhat puzzled that a manifestation, said to be due to the most intimate communion with God and therefore to be desired, was passing out of custom among the Quakers or Friends, apparently without regret.

The outstanding *psychical manifestations of a Concern* seem to follow to some extent the same sequence as the physical. Thus there is, as a prodromal symptom, a sense of great oppression, referred to sometimes as "a conviction of sin"; the mind is overpowered by a feeling of littleness and the self is perceived to be feeble. This gives place to a sense of "humiliation before God". In other words, it appears as if a struggle is going on in the mind, first to battle with an inner force or impulse, then at the very brink of defeat to "realise the presence of God", with a sense of helplessness and even of shame. Finally, there is an uplifting of the spirit, an expansion of the soul and, at the same time, a feeling that the boundaries of the self are extended, or at least extensible, to the uttermost ends of space. At this juncture, there is a conviction that there is no limit to the goodness of God nor to the depth of His love.

The term "oceanic feeling" was no doubt coined to express the boundlessness of the experience, but it does not convey the quality—though it may hint at the power of the emotion—which appears to be its content, namely love. If we turn to the investigations which have been made on individuals who have experienced what seems to be an identical emotion, though they have not called it "guidance" or "a Concern", we are struck by the fact that the state of ecstasy is by no means a stable one. The state is dependent on a good relation to an internal object, the Inner Light, and is not due to the establishment of a satisfactory bond to an object in the external world. It is furthermore subject to disturbances from within that are not under the control of consciousness. Deeper investigation shows that the "oceanic feeling" is only maintained by a great effort of control over aggressive impulses directed against the internal object, which is the source of the bliss, but since these impulses of hatred are repressed—that is, kept from consciousness—the person is unaware of them.

Behind the "oceanic feeling" is a state of mental tension. The means taken to reduce the tension differ according to the person's disposition. The artist, for instance, is impelled to produce a work of art by bringing his perceptions of the external world into relation with the experience of his own bodily sensations. With the help of his Inner Light, he is enabled to make a harmony within himself. He then passes on the harmony he has achieved to others, that is his gift to society. The Quaker similarly situated does not use the introjection method, but, rather, the projective. He must do something to the body of society, so to speak. Whereas the sensitive instrument in the case of the artist is his own body, in the case of the Quaker it is the social organisation with which he so closely identifies himself: herein lies one of the differences between the artist and the reformer. The reformer shares with the scientist the impulse to manipulate the external world, but differs from him in important respects. The aim of the scientist's experiments is to test the accuracy of a theory, the aim of the reformer's innovations is to produce a change in the way of other peoples' lives and thought. The accuracy of his own theories seldom enters into the matter. The scientist is, speaking generally, friendly to all other science—that is, he can easily establish an identification with workers in other fields, although less often with his immediate rivals, and he perceives in their work the same motives which guide his own life. This affords him pleasure, and he is satisfied by his place, humble though it may be, in the vast endeavour to conquer the unknown. The reformer, on the other hand, is often jealous of other reformers. He often regards their motives as less worthy than his own; he thinks that they are filching his material and at times even believes that they are doing it damage.

The Quaker's Concern is in some respects related to the impulse to reform, but I have noticed remarkably little of the typical reformer's hostility to other reformers in those who act from a Concern. This may in part be accounted for by the fact that the Quaker regards himself as the *passive* instrument of the Deity to a greater extent than most reformers. There is, however, the further reason that a Concern is usually an injunction to what may be called an *ad hoc* reform; an instance will make this more clear. A Quaker is led by the guidance of the Holy Spirit to preach on a particular occasion, or to go to another part of the world to preach for a few months to a particular group of people. When he has delivered his message he instantly takes his ordinary place in the community; his "call" is not to priesthood but to a particular message. God does not raise up one of his children to be a permanent leader, he treats all alike. This leads us to a consideration of the relation of the phenomenon of a Concern to the bonds which hold the Quakers together.

Quakerism provides a specially interesting field for such an investigation because the bonds of its membership appear to be comparatively simple.

At first it may seem somewhat odd that a concept such as the Inner Light, which is thought of as an unalienable possession of everyone, should in fact draw the Quakers into a compact group. It is, however, probable that the cohesion is due not so much to the Inner Light itself as to a peculiarity of the Quakers towards each other in respect to the supreme rule of the Inner Light in their lives, or their belief that this is the most desirable thing.

The relation between a Concern and the bonds uniting the Quakers into a community

The bonds which hold the Quakers together have not, so far as I am aware, been the object of much study. As this would lead us into a discussion of what is called "group-psychology", I will consider only a few points.

I will ask you to recall the psychological conditions in a Quaker gathering and contrast it with that obtaining in any other sect or religion. There is an air of *expectancy* that is somewhat different in orientation, though not in aim, from that found in other worship. Anyone may have a Concern to preach or pray on any subject whatever. No one knows when the Call may come, or to whom it will come. It would hardly be an exaggeration to say that this lends an element (to be sure in so disciplined a body, only a faintly perceptible element) of excitement to ordinary Quaker worship; but whatever stimulus (and, I think one may add, attraction) that this may in fact exert on the community, it is only an incidental factor in producing unity. But though the pleasure-giving quality of the excitement may in part derive from the element of surprise, it has a more important root in what I would call mutual aid. We notice a somewhat similar thing in the case of groups of artists and scientists, namely an expectancy in everyone that the other members of the group are all doing something creative. This is a pleasant youthful trait and is too often confused with what the dull worldly wise man calls "a mutual admiration Society". There is an element of mutual admiration and a tendency to undue exaltation of the performances of the members or of the group as a whole, but there is another and more valuable process at work as well: the production of an atmosphere of tolerance towards the expression of any idea irrespective of the effect that the idea may have on the individual or on society. I do not want to minimise the dangers of this atmosphere, which, like the hothouse, may stifle hardy growths and let dank weeds flourish.

Before we leave these recurrent comparisons with artists, it may be pertinent to mention that the artist's sense of having a "unique gift" and of being not only a chosen but a superior people would be anomalous in the Quaker; the former says that his power to produce beautiful things is due to his having the special peculiarities of the artist, the latter on the other hand says that he is just the same as everyone else, that God has no favourites among His children. Where spiritual snobbishness does occur among Quakers, it is, I think, like all snobbishness, defensive.

Returning to our Quaker meeting, we find one Friend "labouring under a Concern". I give these words a literal meaning. There is a state of tension or stress in his mind from which he must rid himself. Other Friends identify themselves with him in his travail and give him the support he needs in the struggle of his spirit. The Concern takes on the character of a communal endeavour, first because there is an agreed basis from which to work, namely the most regressive and most primitive position of object relationship, i.e. incorporation within the self and identification; secondly, because the technique of working a way out of the suffering is also mutually agreed to—that is, renunciation of personal wishes and complete, passive surrender to the will of God. It is not necessary, but is felt to be in the highest degree desirable, that the Concern should be declared to the community, for God does not give a Message for the edification of the one but for all. The delivery of a

Message heightens the influence of the Inner Light in all who hear it in the right spirit.

The frequent declaration in the Messages given under Guidance, of a feeling of guilt and of wounds of the spirit caused by refractory elements in the personality, support the view put forward that a precursory condition to a Concern is a state of mental conflict. It would seem that one of the functions of a Quaker community is to assist in the healing of the wounds received by its individual members in that strife, so that one of the bonds which hold Quakers together is a technique for ridding the mind of "the burden of sin" (or better expressed, perhaps, the feeling of guilt).

In the long history of the Society of Friends, the methods employed to this end have varied considerably, from the concept of *Redemption through Grace* to that of *Redemption through Works*, the former being associated with a predominant belief in the efficacy of preaching and prayer, the latter going along with social reform. In the idiom of psychoanalysis, by now I hope familiar, there is a shift from a predominantly introjective to a predominantly projective tendency (the antithesis of artist and scientist). The Redemption through Grace is characteristic of the "buffer effect", that through Works comes nearer to what I have described as the second function of the internalised good object which gives zest to constructive activities.

The bonds of union mentioned so far may be summarised as follows: (1) a state of expectancy shared by all, (2) the identification with the suffering of the Friend labouring under a Concern, (3) "the unity with the Concern" expressed by those who hear the Message, the feeling of unity with the community that this gives the Concerned Friend being communicated back to those who endorse the Concern, (4) the acceptance by the community of the Action (be it Prayer or Reform). And now we may add a fifth point. When the tension is reduced in one, it is reduced in all. The Greeks called their Tragedy cathartic, the same term applies to the Concern.

I should not like to leave the topic of the Concern without mentioning another small point. The artistic conscience is solely concerned to produce a perfect work of art, to worldly needs, such as making a living, the artist is often indifferent. When in a creative mood, he can without sense of guilt be as dependent as is a child for "creature comforts" on those who support him. When not in a creative mood, his social conscience more closely resembles that of the ordinary man. We find the same with the Concerned Friend. He too is, by conscience and

Quaker custom, "released" from the pressure of economic necessity for the duration of his concern. When he "returns his Minute"—that is, reports to his Meeting that his "Concern" has been accomplished—his social obligation to earn his living returns to him. But this exemption from ordinary responsibility is only accorded to those who, like the artist, throw themselves wholly upon the "guidance of the Inner Light". The testing prior to this "release" in the Particular and Monthly meetings is done by a process resembling art criticism—that is, by the incorporation within the self, in the phantasy of the observer, of the object under inspection. In this case, it occurs through the first stirrings and utterance of the Message, by all present, and through an introspective observation of its effect upon the inner or spiritual sensibilities of the Friends, who then give the "Minute".

The relation between the doctrine of the Inner Light and the testimonies against war and against oaths

The doctrine of the Inner Light seems to me different from other religious beliefs on two points: first of all it asserts without reservation that there is a portion of the Divine in every man; that is to say, this spark of the everlasting life is an unalienable and indestructible part of the individual. It is not his by baptism, by special dispensation or by the acquirement of "merit", but his in virtue of his humanity.

The second point is that the Inner Light can fill the whole personality and the whole of life if the individual will give it the opportunity. It is a divine seed that will grow without the watering of tears, it only needs the opening and then it will press its roots into the personality and from there will flourish. The individual is the vehicle of God's power, love and grace. Now, every other Christian body would, I believe, also subscribe to this as the fundamental doctrine of their Faith and then would promptly make numerous additions. The peculiarity of the Quakers is that they not only make no essential additions, but that they believe that additions would weaken their whole position, and, within their framework of reference, I believe they are right.

I have expressed the view that the Inner Light may be regarded as the introjection of a "good object" which removes evil and gives its possessor the capacity to love, with all that that entails, and is a witness also to the fact that he has already received love. The process by which this relationship is established (that of "introjecting" the object) is the most primitive of the mental mechanisms known to us. Other religions employ much more complicated mental processes for the attainment of "completeness" in their relation to their God.[4] It would seem therefore that to explain Quakerism on this basis we have to add another device or mental mechanism, namely regression. That is to say, in order to attain to live a full and active life in the world, the Quaker unwittingly employs once more the simplest and most primitive of all the relationships to the God that we meet in our study of Comparative Religion, and the most primitive mental relationship known to subsist between the child and its object. If this hypothesis be true, it explains at a stroke the majority, if not all, of the peculiarities of Quakerism, the absence of priests, the "equality of the sexes", the absence of titles, even those distinguishing a married woman from a spinster, because, at the level of experience to which the Quaker religion has regressed for the purposes of establishing a relation to God, sex differentiations are not in striking evidence.

In respect to his relationship to God, the Quaker has one more peculiarity that deserves special attention. He does not use the name of God in civil or legal oaths. I believe that the connection of this with the doctrine of the Inner Light may be put briefly in this way. The oath has the power, in primitive belief, to bind not only the man swearing, but the God sworn by. To swear by God's Holy Name is dangerous, because in phantasy that would bring pressure to bear on God and would put Him in the power of the person taking the oath. It is thought to be a blessed thing if God dwells in the bodily temple of a believer, but God must not be made a prisoner. It is essential that the direction of influence is from God to men. It is unholy (or anxiety-provoking) to exert any power in the other direction. Quakers almost alone among religious believers do not bargain with their God.[5]

In his relations with his fellow man, the Quaker is strongly influenced by the doctrine of the Inner Light, especially in his attitude to

---

[4] The Quaker, in my view, can dispense with the Sacrament of the Eucharist not so much because for him every meal is a Lord's Supper (as he says, or used to say), but because the process of incorporating a portion of the Lord has in his phantasy already taken place; that sense of complete union, which the communicant experiences when receiving the Divine Element, is regarded by the Quaker as his permanent privilege and is not dependent on the external circumstances of holy place, holy man, holy time, water, wine, bell, book and candle.

[5] Perhaps it is relevant to this theme to recollect that (at least according to Quaker tradition) they introduced the custom of fixed prices: people are apt to behave to each other as they behave to their God.

killing and to hatred (which in respect to guilt feelings—by reason of identity in unconscious phantasies—are the same as murder). In his spiritual life, the Quaker is safe from the worm of corruption if he does nothing which may destroy the seed of life in another human being, for that is to attack the Inner Light. The Quaker does not object to force to restrain the evil doer, he is not a Tolstoyean Anarchist. The policeman in his view is, or always should be, the criminal's best friend, defending him and society against destructive impulses. The testimony against war is a testimony against aggression, and because it involves the violent death of the host of the Inner Light, it is an outrage against God. Yet, it looks as if the source of that self-confidence, which enables the Quaker to maintain an inner quietness and a gentle tolerance in the face of the greatest external persecution, is threatened from one quarter. The Quaker enjoys in his religion an unprecedented freedom of thought and action, in his life a conspicuous calm, but on one condition—no violence.

The Quaker character

When people use the term "character" they refer to "enduring traits of the personality" (Warren, 1935). It makes the definition more precise if we add "in respect of its object-relationships". That is to say, we think of character in relation to activity, to action directed towards an object (the object may, of course, sometimes be the self). But the essential feature of character, its deep *engraven* nature, lies in its fixity, its rigidity.

The process of character formation is chiefly an internal one. It arises from an internal mental necessity, is not a conscious process and is very little influenced by the conscious efforts of parents, nurses and teachers. Indeed, it is to a very high degree unconscious, and the work of investigating the origins of character formation in an individual meet with a great deal of opposition and defensive argumentation. Clinical experience shows that people have singularly little insight into or knowledge of the factors which formed their character, which is not surprising since character formation is largely defensive. This statement may call for a short explanation: a character trait on closer psychological investigation appears to be due to a special kind of modification of the ego or executive part of the mind. It arises very early in life as a result of an intolerable struggle between instinctual impulses. The way out of the situation of strain which the ego adopts is to capitulate in part to one of the impulses in the conflict, with the result that the ego retains henceforth a special sensitiveness to anything which is related to that struggle. But it is more than sensitiveness, for the ego does not passively shrink back. It actively attempts to quench the heat and power of the impulse that so nearly overpowered it.

In the case of Quakers I think the special feature of their characters as Quakers is due to an early struggle with the destructive component of their instinctual life; in order to neutralise the effects of this there has been a modification of the entire personality. It is not the case of turning away from a painful experience of violence from time to time when the violence is too severe, but of being in a state of permanent orientation to the problem of violence and shaping every action so that it shall be non-violent, and not only every action but every element in belief. The completeness of the renunciation of violence among the Quakers is its striking feature, and in my view accounts for every detail of the intricate pattern of Quaker belief. On this hypothesis I have based my thesis, for I think it lies at the root of the unconscious but strong selective action which has determined both the Quaker's concept of God and his ideal of human relationship.

In this study of Quaker Beliefs I have tried to avoid what I call the "ad hoc" explanations and interpretations of Quakerism, by the employment of a genetic approach, believing that if we study the means by which an individual emerges from the mental chaos of an unstable infancy, we shall be in a better position to relate the features of his life to those of other people than if we assume that he is first and all the time a "Seeker after Truth".[6]

I have put forward the view that besides the Search for Truth, there is a *vis a tergo*—nervous dread, guilt and a feeling of instability—and that without a full consideration of these, our insight into the individual lacks depth.

I believe that a certain amount of obscurity may be found in Quaker thinking because a sufficiently clear distinction is not drawn between the state of mind called "a Discovery of Truth" and a sudden, temporary relief of mental tension. It is not uncommon to find in clinical psychology that a sudden relief of tension is ascribed to causes that have but little relation to the mental change. So I have been put on my guard against accepting, at face value, statements about sudden enlightenment, revelation and Divine Inspiration. In particular, I have noticed that the object which is thought to have reduced the strain is

---

[6] One of the earliest Quaker descriptions of themselves.

given an overvaluation, which is apt to encumber the individual's subsequent mental development. As Quakerism is with some people a powerful means of relieving mental strain, at least for a time, I think it has come in for more appreciation among Quakers than it deserves. It is not an infallible remedy for the ills resulting from an unstable infancy, and it is not made more efficacious by doubling the dose; that is, it may be better in a given case, if Quakerism is not found satisfying to the mind, to turn to some other mode of detensioning than to think that what is needed is more and ever more Guidance from the Inner Light. After all, Quakerism does not resolve the conflicts left over from the past; it only quietens them.

I should have liked to extend the scope of these enquiries, to discuss the individual who has what I have called "the Quaker Character" but has not been able to leave his own Church to "join the Friends"; conversely, there are those of "birthright Membership" and whose Ministry has been Recorded, but who nevertheless find it necessary to communicate in other Churches as well. Then we have those who "join" the Society of Friends. All of these raise problems of the greatest psychological interest, and I am sure that research in this direction would throw light, not only on the character and history of the Society of Friends, but on wider problems of the interplay between individual differences and the stability and inter-relation of groups.

In spite of all that has been written about Quakerism, the exploration of that field, to my way of thinking, has hardly begun.

CHAPTER 16

The need for a belief in God

(1937)

In this paper I am mainly concerned with one important aspect of religion—that is, belief in God. But since this is too wide, it will be narrowed still further to the need or compelling necessity which some people feel to believe in God, and within the smaller field we may consider why others feel no such need. I would like to emphasise at the very beginning that a subject like this should be studied historically. I consider that there is no value in such a statement as "the conclusion of science, or psychoanalysis, on this, or any other subject, is so-and-so . . ."; but rather that "with such and such material available the following theory was advanced to explain it . . ." In a word, the important thing is to follow the movement of scientific thought and to see how it deals with the matter in hand, rather than to adopt a general or philosophical attitude about it, which nearly always turns out in the end to be ill-founded.

The study of religion is not the main concern of psychoanalysis, in the same way that it is the main concern of theology, and this is perhaps an advantage, because the subject is seen in an everyday setting. It is

---

This was the third of a series of lectures on the "Psychology of Religion", given at the Caxton Hall, London SW1, in November and December 1937.

given no more and no less importance than the patient himself contributes to it.

Above all, the religious impulse is seen in the context which is not so readily available by any other means.

The historical evolution of psychoanalytic theories

Now, the manifestations of the religious impulse, the need for belief in God, and for help from God, have been roughly speaking the same during the last few decades, but there has been an evolution in psychoanalytic ideas about the material presented to us. I propose to deal chiefly with that evolution, and for greater clarity I will divide the subject into three periods: the first was up to 1921, with special emphasis on the latter part of that time; the second, from 1921 to 1932; and the third from that date to 1937. I must add that these dates are only approximate, but they will serve as a reminder, a never-too-often-repeated reminder, that every scientific idea is dated and can only be used to full advantage if its place in the evolution of scientific thought is realised.

For long ages man has prayed to and spoken of God as his Father. He is regarded as the producer of His own people, and indeed of the whole world. The first explanation given for this way of regarding God is of course that, before the forces of nature, man is as helpless as a child, and that as a child turns to its Father for help and security, so man, repeating an early attitude of mind, turns to God as if he was an infant and God was a protecting parent.

With this view no psychoanalyst would quarrel, but it obviously does not explain enough of the facts. In the first place most primitive people, and indeed some not so primitive, have many gods, widely differing in characteristics, some wholly virulent, some kindly. So our first step is to say that the figure of God does not resemble the Father as the child *actually* saw him but as the child imagined him to be—and with that step we pass from the non-analytic to the psychoanalytic basis of study. I wish to repeat this point because it is sometimes thought—for example, recently by a previous Dean of St. Paul's—that "the idea of God is in many cases closely connected with the *memory* of the father". It is not the memory of a real person but the image or images which the child evolves, the world which he creates when his impulses are passionately strong and his power of control is weak. It is these *images*, which continue to live on actively in the unconscious, that influence his conception of God, and of everything else. If we include the child's phantasies about its father, we have the basis for a far closer resemblance to the image of his God. The omnipotence attributed to the father is displaced onto the God, who can do everything he wants to, whereas the child cannot. It seems that there is a strong tendency to cling to the notion that thoughts are in fact omnipotent, that we can get what we want if we wish hard enough. Experience shows us that this is false, but our need for the comfort that *somewhere*, in *some* field of experience, our wishes will not be denied us, is so strong that we cling to the illusion that omnipotence is still possible, that we *shall* get what we want. If we cannot have this power for ourselves, we put it into commission, so to speak, omnipotence is given into God's safe-keeping. Looked at in this way, the need for belief in God resolves itself into a need to keep alive the illusion that our wishes will be granted, with the proviso that we now obey God as in the past we obeyed our parents, when we found that we did actually get so many of our wishes fulfilled.

There can be no doubt that this illusion of wish-fulfilment has played a great part in the development of religion and has led, and still leads, many to lean on their faith. But two reflections at once arise in our minds. The first is that this way of thought belongs to the more primitive or less spiritual religions, and the second is that it may strike us as odd that with so many satisfactions actually obtained from the parents, there should be in childhood such a strong desire for more and yet ever more satisfaction, mounting to the craving for control of God-like power, the state of having every wish fulfilled, which is a definition of omnipotence.

The re-discovery of the totem

All this may be regarded as a preliminary to a brief discussion of what I have called the first of the three periods. We are not primarily concerned with the psychoanalytic theory of the development of the God-concept, but we may note in passing its ontogenesis: how the emotional attitude towards the father is split in infancy into two parts, that attaching to the father-proper and that displaced onto an outside object. If this object is an animal and the culture is primitive, the displaced portion exalts the animal to a quasi-God position and is revered as the totem, who is sacrificed and eaten, adored and destroyed. We might note in passing that this arrangement is not without its advantages in that the emotional relations to the actual father are eased, if the ambivalence can be worked off on the totem–animal–god. It is difficult for anyone with a tendency to use biological concepts not to see a survival value in

THE NEED FOR A BELIEF IN GOD 297

totemism. The relation to the family is preserved, in spite of the strong emotional forces of sex and aggression, which if left unchecked would wreck the family and therefore jeopardise the chances of survival of the children.

Apart from this biological aspect, the splitting of the emotional life into two parts serves a further cultural function. While the emotion attaching to the parents can be reduced in amount, or at any rate kept fairly stable, that part which is displaced onto images or phantasies is capable of a great deal of elaboration. It is thus possible to build up a culture within the castles in the air, in daydream, and later to adapt our everyday life to it, or bring it into relation with our mundane existence in the form of art, religion, science and politics.

The split in the emotional life is never complete; there is always some ambivalence (often a great deal) towards the parents, and towards the idealised images which lend their strength to the God-concept. There is a tendency to constancy in affection as well.

The purpose of the first manipulation of emotional attachments was to preserve a good relation to a definite object (the father or parental figure), but the emotion belonging to the idealised objects undergoes a further treatment. The cleavage in this case is in respect to the kind of emotion. All the benevolent feelings are concentrated on the God-concept, the hostile are concentrated on the Devil-concept. The purpose of this separation of God and Devil is to reduce the ambivalent feelings towards them both. The God can be loved without fear and the devil hated without remorse. These God and Devil images are not to be regarded as dumping grounds for surplus emotional products. They have in the mind a life of their own and a character showing traces of their own in the phantasies about the parents. They do not behave as parents, they represent the small child's phantasy of parental behaviour, which is a very different thing.

We cannot leave what I have called the first phase of the theory without a reference to the development of the theory of the ego-ideal, which also brings us to the second phase of the theory. The ego-ideal is a part of the ego, it is not an external thing. It is a modification of a part of the self, and at first Freud regarded it as being derived from internal forces, namely from the child's own self-love, but soon he added the idea that it is also derived from parental injunctions. That is to say, the child takes into himself the admonitions of his parents; they become a part of himself, critical of his misdeeds and serving out punishments for evil actions, and *intentions*. Thus the *conscience* was conceived of as being derived from an interplay of an *external* (environmental, parental) factor and an *internal* (instinctive) factor. It requires but one more step in this argument to get fresh light on the origin of the God-concept: it is the projection into the outside world (into heaven) of this ego-ideal. Some of the work of conscience is done within the ego, some is now given the power of an external force—the admonishing voice comes from without.

The evolution of an ideal

Further light was thrown on this problem from a study of melancholia, in which, as is well known, the patient suffers from excessive scruples of conscience. Here as in other cases the disease processes magnify a normal process, so that it becomes more clearly visible. From a study of the processes in melancholia (and also in mourning), it seemed clear that what happens is that a once loved but now inaccessible person, removed from the scene by death or a sudden rupture of love relationships, is incorporated within the ego. Thus in melancholia and in mourning, the image of the dead person is set up within the self, and another way of modifying the self is disclosed. There were the modifications due to rational experience, in which the ego discovered the limitations of its powers. Then there was the modification due to parental injunctions, and now comes a third way, In order to keep alive in the imagination a person once loved and now departed, the ego incorporates the image of that person in the self—in other words, it is built into the self. Thus the ego manages to keep contact with something that has vanished; but it gets modified in the process. If this process of incorporating a vanished object only resulted in mourning and melancholia, it would have no particular interest to anyone but psychiatrists, but it appears to be a normal process, though usually of course not carried to the extremes just mentioned. If an idealised object is lost as an ideal, then it may set up within the self in the way described. Now, the child develops an idealised picture of the parents, but they do not ever live up to that ideal. The fall of the parents from Godhead is a precondition for the massive disturbance of the ego, which instituted the human conscience. The projection of that conscience outward is the precondition for the development of a concept as powerful in action, as intimate in its operation, as is that of God.

This theory has more in it than appears from the rough outline I have just given. Remember, it was not devised to explain the origin and nature of the God-concept; its main purpose was to explain the conditions found in the narcissistic neuroses, in melancholia, and in certain of the phenomena of falling in love. The theory of the origin of the God-concept is a by-product only. But it explains something that has not received, in my view, so satisfactory an explanation by other means, namely the intimate relation between the God-concept and the social conscience. For the projection of the conscience into the outer world takes two directions. One is directed to heaven, so to speak, and furnishes energy to the God-concept; another part is directed to the community and returns as social conscience and social feeling. The theory spans a number of phenomena and brings them into a new relationship. To one man the most terrible thing in the world is to lose his belief in God; to another the most terrible thing is to lose contact with the moral values of the community in which he lives. Most people are between these extremes and have some of the characteristics of both. To lose belief in God in this sense is to lose belief in an ideal—that is, to be plunged into a condition where a loved object has vanished.

"But", you may say, "is religion only a sort of cure for grief?" Is God only a sort of holy tombstone erected in the phantasy of the child for a fantastic parent-image he imagines he has lost? I should welcome such an expostulation, for it would show an intuitive realisation that something has been omitted throughout from this glib exposition. At the beginning of this paper I referred to that period of development of the mind when wishes, thoughts and intention were equated with deeds. I have, however, said nothing of the early emotional conflicts of childhood, nothing of the pain and consequent guilt experienced by us all, when we hated those who stood in the path of our love and loved them as well—the hate of the boy for his father, the girl for her mother; a driving bitter hate that wills their humiliation or their death. This is the lot of every one of us to experience. Somehow or other we have to live through this stormy time, when we are too dependent to pack up and go, too dependent physically and too in need of the love of our parents. Yet, notwithstanding all this hate, there is a great tenderness in the boy's relation to his father and in the girl's feelings for her mother, and there is a longing in the heart of every child to see its parents happy together. But there is a blasting, devastating hate and jealousy as well. There is, however, a way out of this awful predicament. The admonitions of the parents against jealousy, hate and all evil-doing are taken into the self, the forces of self-love are now put at the service of this idealised self, and the curbing of the hate and destructive impulses becomes one of the most highly prized functions of the ego. The image of the ego-ideal is not merely that of an aggrandised self, but the guardian of morality and the beginning of the reign of law. The guardian of morality, though feared, is loved and admired. Belief in his existence is, in the unconscious mind, the same as giving support to his existence. Doubt is felt to be lethal to the process of idealisation, and only by the exaltation of the power of a stern father can the devastating influence of hate be checked.

Perhaps another objection will arise at this point, and I may be asked whether this picture of a poor, weak ego, this cork on the ocean waves of passion, has not been a bit overdrawn. Just as, before, the objection led us to see that the factor of guilt had been omitted, so now we are reminded that the first-mentioned method by which the ego gets modified by experience has been overlooked. Yes, it is true that this ego, this executive part of the self, does in fact grow up. I have drawn a picture of it as needing help of a magical kind in dealing with its fears of its own instincts, an ego in distress from fears and guilt, an ego uncertain of itself, horrified at its own passions, and feeling helpless before them.

But if this weak and harassed ego can in fact grow up, don't let us go to the other extreme and say that because the ego can grow up, the adult has, therefore, left these childish fears behind. The ego cannot grow up when these fears are too strong.

Now about fifteen years ago I wanted to put the psychoanalytic theories on the problems of religion that I have described to a test, and I chose for a beginning a sect without ritual, creed, priesthood, sacred days, sacred places, or sacraments, and yet a sect that every thinking Buddhist, Mohammedan and Christian would say was truly religious and one furthermore that has rather a reputation in the world at large in this respect. The scope of psychoanalytic theory at that time did not seem to me to be adequate to explain the case I wanted to study, namely Quakerism [see chapter 15]. I thought, and I still think, that psychoanalytic theory at that period had not covered an aspect of religion, which in Quakerism is conspicuous (partly because there is not much else to look at), namely what the early Quakers called the "inwardness" of religion. Ritual is not religion, nor are the observance of holy places or the submission to and the support derived from a creed an essential feature of the religious life. The test of a theory is its capacity to explain the less obvious as well as the more obvious features to be examined. Further light on this matter came from a new field of study. As often happens, one field of investigation is studied, instruments of research are devised, then they are seen to apply to a new topic. This leads to a modification of theory, which is then reapplied to yet another field and re-modified, and so on, again and again. Thus light was thrown on religious trances and ecstasies by a study of hysteria, on ritual by a study of obsessional neurosis, on the formation of an ideal by studying a form of insanity, and on conscience by an examination of melancholia. Then at the point where all these fields meet—in the study of the child—we get light on them all.

The search for goodness

We have called the first referred to in this paper, "The *Re*-discovery of the Totem" and the second, "The Evolution of an Ideal", so that to the third period we may give the title, "The Search for Goodness". The third period, according to the classification we are using, centres on the researches by Melanie Klein on the emotional life of small children. But it also throws light on the mental life of adults as well, and with that we shall be concerned. In our clinical work, we meet with a striking phenomenon, which occurs with such regularity that it deserves to be considered as a general feature of mankind. We find that our patients cherish, in secret, a phantasy of a special kind: it is for a good person or thing. It is really difficult to get them to talk about this object. In most cases, they hardly realise the importance it plays in their lives. In not a few, the object is wholly concealed from consciousness. A man or boy who says that he hates his father, that he always has hated him, and that their relation has always been a bad one, will nevertheless bring forward material which shows that there is in the back of his mind— in the unconscious—an image of a father-figure who is loving and kind and towards whom the patient has deep respect and affection. The same may, of course, be found in respect to a mother-image as well. If this was the case only in "shut-in", morose people, one could dismiss it as just another instance of shyness, but the same is found in those who flaunt their open minds before their friends, those who have, or rather say they have, no secrets. If the circumstances of the disclosure of this cherished figure are examined, it is found that the person can hardly bear that this good object shall run the risks of contact with such dangers as lurk about. The analyst of a sudden is felt to be unreliable, he will jeer, is over-critical, does not understand the true nature of affection, is cold, crafty and so on. It does not take much perception to see that we are faced here with a very complicated situation. This cherished good thing is associated in the patient's mind with a lot of hostile thoughts, and these, in proximity to what is regarded as good, are unbearable. So the bad thoughts, the coldness, craftiness, over-critical attitude, jeering, are projected onto the analyst, and the patient is in the position of the protector of the good thing. Sometimes it is the other way about: the patient feels him/herself to be all these bad things and the analyst to be a good object wanting to reveal a piece of good news, to become a good or protecting figure. But this situation is also felt to be dangerous to the good thing, because of the patient's badness.

In a brief description I cannot convey one point of great significance, namely that this is felt to be a matter of overwhelming importance to the patient. Note that it is not like the conscious embarrassment accompanying the confession of some guilty deed. It has not lain on the mind like a weight. It is usually a slow discovery, a realisation that something is gradually emerging into consciousness, and for no observable reason it is accompanied by these dreadful forebodings.

I cannot go now into the details of the chains of evidence that lead from this observation, back to the early object-relationships in childhood, but I want to single out a feature common to all of these situations that can be given a generic name: "the relation to a good object". Now what is a "good object" in this sense, and what is "goodness"? *A good object is one which gives content.* This is not really an easy oversimplification; it describes a primitive relation of the ego to an object in the outer world. If that object brings content, peace of mind, a stifling of hunger, relief from pain, it is felt to be good, and it is loved. More of that goodness is desired, and yet more. The very goodness of it stirs up greed, and, if the situation arises, as indeed it must, jealousy and hate follow in the train of that desire for more of the good thing.

Hate is a terrible thing. In a padded cell physical violence can be let loose without harm, but in the mind there are no padded cells; hate pursues its object and leaves a trail of devastation. Worst of all, the object hated is also loved. The situation becomes intolerable for it means that access to the good object is barred by this hate, or by the dread of the emergence of this hate. A device for overcoming the difficulty is adopted. The badness is projected outwards onto an object in the environment, and when that object is hated the relation to the good object is eased. The matter does not stop here: the object hated is not an indifferent one. It is hated because of its relation to the good object, and that forms a tie to it. In the typical oedipal situation, for instance, the boy cannot in his jealousy endure the father, but he also has feelings of affection for him. The mother is also hated for her affection for the father; and in this welter of hate, which we all endured at our most impressionable period of growth, we feel an estrangement and isolation which is the pattern of all subsequent feelings of loneliness. A remedy (as early as projection) lies to hand in *introjection*—the incorporation into the self of objects which the ego needs. And it is by the process of introjection that the ego acquires objects within itself that have, to a certain extent, an independent existence and yet are contained within the ego-system.

At this point I want to call your attention to the development of the psychoanalytic theories about the ego. Earlier we discussed the relation of the ego to the ego-ideal, which was, in part, of external origin. The ego-ideal was that by which the ego measured itself in terms of right and wrong. The introjected elements in the ego, like the ego-ideal, are also derived in part from the outer world, but insofar as they are not external and concrete things but concepts (and our concepts are coloured by our own mood), the introjected elements in the ego are derived from our own emotional life as well as from perceptions from without. We can call them by a special name: "internalised objects". Now these "internalised objects" can be good or bad, but whichever they are, they continue to exert an influence on the ego. Consider the nature of the "good internalised objects". They are precipitates from "good" experiences of the ego, having some of the quality of those experiences. The form can vary. It is to the small infant food, good and warm milk. (I am leaving it to the reader each time to translate this into psychological terms, i.e. the presentation in the mind of the good quality of the milk ... etc.) It can be a genital experience, it can be an experience of the perception not of a part of the body, but of the whole personality of the father or mother. But, whatever it is, so long as it is included in the ego in the way described, it belongs to this class of "good internalised objects". Similarly with the bad objects. These are the harrowing, persecuting objects within the personality, the precipitates of old hates that live on in the self, embittering good relationships, jeopardising trust in love and friendship, and making, on the smallest provocation, the world within and without seem evil.

Now in the more primitive levels of the mind everything is concrete. A bad impulse is conceived—no, that isn't a plastic enough term—is felt to be a solid object, a thing. So the ego, that part of us which is nearest to the flesh and blood of animal creation, is felt to have these good and bad internal objects within it (that is, as the unconscious pictures it), and they can be displaced outwards or drawn back into the self, as if they were solids. This, in part, explains the notion, mentioned earlier, of the conscience being projected outwards and lending its power to the God-concept. These internalised objects are living and can be killed in our phantasy, of course. Perhaps I have said enough for you to see that there is a relation between these internalised objects and the ego-ideal later called the superego. There is a continuous development of this mental function from a primitive, almost physical, substratum to the most highly developed conceptions of the mind, finding expression in ideals, social feeling and the conscience. By now, I hope I have been able to give an adequate picture of the ego's position. It is faced with the outer world that it cannot easily control, and also with this inner world, these internalised objects, which are much more under its dominion, though not completely so. And let me repeat, these internalised objects stand for external loved and hated objects. Ego activity is thus oriented in two directions, outwards and inwards, and an action related to an external object may have—does, in our phantasy, have—an effect on the constellation of these internal objects. A kindness to a person in the outer world is, in one part of the mind, a good deed done to an internal object, who is in need of it. Loathe an external object, and some object within gets the loathing too. Outer and inner life cannot be separated. How often we wish they could be separated! How we wish that our actions should cause no inner perturbations, no guilt. But what a lot we should lose if outer and inner were shut off from one another. How pale and shallow our present experiences would be if they did not rouse the inner life to the depths and cause an awakening of the old conflicts and the profound peace which followed the solution of them. The hedonists call for a life of pleasing experience, the artists know better; pain is mixed with pleasure, and if we are to deal truly with our experience, we must be ready to endure the echoes of old battles before we can evolve out of ourselves a new harmony. Perhaps the artists are revered by mankind, and their work is loved, because it gives us, at one and the same time, a picture not only of the lovely things we see in the world around us, but also an insight into that strained and struggling life within, deep in our unconscious, where everything is so intense and where our treasure is hid. This treasure, hidden in the depths of the self, brings me back to the old Quaker saying about the inwardness of religion.

Belief in God as belief in a power to protect what is good

Reverting to the concept of the good and bad internalised objects, we find a number of ways in which the ego adjusts their relationship to one another. First, there is the projection of the good objects into the outer world. The representation of this is not as simple as these words might imply: the good object is given form or quality suited to the environment of the projection. Thus the projection of the good object into an

THE NEED FOR A BELIEF IN GOD   305

environment where hate is absent gives us a picture of heaven. There the good object is safe. The belief in such a place expresses, as realised in the imagination, a need for an environment, *which the ego itself does not provide*, where that most valuable possession—the good object—may exist securely. We see the same process at work in lower levels of spiritual growth, in the projection into images of wood and stone of the treasured part of the self. The idol which is adored must be kept from harm. And I would remind you that there is no mutual exclusiveness in these two processes—that is, the same person can divide the location of his good objects, part in heaven, part in the image. This is what we all do throughout our lives. We do not keep all of our eggs in one basket, as the homely phrase goes. Most religious people have an element of image worship in them, and apart from religion we commonly endow special places with this quality of giving us peace and meriting our love. I must not digress, but you can see the connection here with science and exploring. The good object must be found, cost the search what it may.

But this projection is not a very stable process. In order that an environment may be created that contains no hate, for instance, another one must be created that contains nothing else. Heaven has its counterpart in hell. And hell is a ghastly place, made tolerable only by turning it into a pleasure ground for sadistic phantasies. When hell breaks its bounds, as our forefathers well knew, who grew up, as it were, in the shadow of its walls, a breach in those ramparts makes the very throne of God unsafe. This experiment of our forefathers in separating good and bad, like all such attempts, was no solid foundation for a developing spiritual life. So much energy must go into keeping the elements separate that there is too little left for a vigorous search for goodness in the world of human beings. Those who make this effort at separation are, of course, doing so for the better preservation of what is good. No one would stop them in this action of love, or rather in this search for love, because for them it is the best means to this end, but it is not the only way. The projection into heaven and hell are not the only means of displacing the objects into the outer world. There are human relationships which, one would think, would be specially fitted for the displacement. But we must recollect that it was because of the pain and the strain of our own hatred, which imperilled human relationships, that the trouble began. The idealisations and the projections we have been talking about arise, and are used, because they help us to deal with that strain. We should never lose sight of the fact that, however crude and cruel a system of religious thought may be (and if we survey the history of religion there are some dark places), these systems, even the worst, were attempts to keep the good objects from annihilation by man's own inner hate. Their function was, in the main, to protect the good.

The denial of goodness

I want now to discuss the method of trying to deal with this dilemma by the denial of goodness and of spiritual values. This tendency, now so widespread, to deny goodness and any values that do not appear before our eyes as wealth, power or fame, to return from internal to external things, is, I think, due to the same root causes. The inner life is denied value, because people despair of keeping in touch with the good that is there. It is easier to follow the visible good of riches, power and fame, and a person can more easily win approval from his fellows by these means. There may be environmental factors which favour the overvaluation of external goodness to the disadvantage of internal goodness. Science is responsible for much of the increased power over the environment, and this perhaps is the reason why so many people who are sensitive to the things of the spirit, ruthlessly and, as I think, blindly attack science. We are now in a transition period without a new scale of values and without the old modes of keeping in contact with goodness. It needs a capacity for a focused, perhaps rather abnormal, kind of love for external things before a man can create a new environment for his inner treasures. Lucky are the artists in this, for without this gift mankind settles into a cynicism and a despair. Love loses its power, even pleasure goes, and listlessly men drift towards a negative Nirvana, not to a place where all is peace because the strife within the mind is settled, but to a place of no strife, because nothing is worth struggle.

The search for a belief in goodness

I want to summarise what I have said with a consideration of this search for goodness. It seems that man is impelled to search for something more than the means of subsistence and the immediate needs of sex. He desires to find objects which bring him peace of mind, which do not change in their character of giving him the satisfaction that he needs, and which give him a feeling of permanence and security in a changing, unstable world. We find this quality of change and insecurity, present to a high degree, in the emotional life of childhood. At that time, the same objects are both loved and hated, and the child feels insecure in his capacity to love, doubting the love of others, and afraid of the contents of his mind. What he cherishes within himself is not safe from his own evil thoughts, what he loves in the outside world never fulfils his every need. He is driven to take measures to avert despair. By an unwitting process, the good objects are displaced from the dangerous self to places of better security, and objects thought to be good are incorporated into the matrix of the self to bring consolation and security against his own instability. But doubt follows hard on the heels of love, and hate follows desire; nothing now in his outer or in his inner world is sure. A temporary respite is obtained by splitting experiences into good and bad categories, by heaping up trust in the good, and by avoidance and denial of hate, greed and destructiveness. But the need to carry on the process of division is accentuated by the fear that the two will mix again and the good will be lost for ever.

However, the splitting into good and bad categories may effect a temporary reduction in mental strain, and better relations between good and bad objects, and inner and outer objects, can then be established. For, one of the paramount tendencies in the mind—probably a derivative of the impulse of love—is to effect a synthesis in two functions that are in antagonism. By distributing interest, by having regard to a wider range of objects thought of as good, the ego is spared some of its terrors; for any tendency to focus all goodness on one object evokes the tendency to concentrate all the hostile impulses on the same object. One special case of this general process is found in the God-concept. When the mind attempts to picture all goodness in one Being, and to make all that is of worth derive from one source, inevitably that Being becomes the recipient of unconscious hate. An inner struggle then begins, and one phase of that struggle is a wrestling with doubt. Belief in the goodness of God is redoubled in order to counter this doubt until the primary need of the individual for a more certain belief that God is good, and is not being hated, is again fulfilled. An old struggle, dating from the time when thoughts were regarded as having omnipotent power, has taken possession of the individual.

Those whose business it is to minister to the religious needs of the community know this syndrome well. It is a counterpart, in religious experience, of the terrific sexual overestimation of a loved object, that must not be thought ill of, which we find commonly in adolescence.

There is a tendency in religion to press for belief and trust in God as an ideal, irrespective of the particular needs of the individual, just as there is a tendency among a far less, indeed a quite unorganised, body of opinion to press the claims of idyllic love to the exclusion of all other kinds of relationship.

The majority of mankind do not respond wholeheartedly to either appeal. The reason for this appears to lie in the following considerations. Though there is, as I have tried to describe, a dread of hate that is turned against loved and valued objects, and that dread may amount to panic, it is the common experience that aggression does not invariably destroy, and indeed, if well in harness, it may actually do good. It seems further to be a condition for trust in the goodness of others that we should also recognise, in its true light, their badness and, furthermore, that we should not fear to see our hatred of them, though we owe so much to their love, which usually we return. We are full of good and bad impulses, those precipitates of our own passions and of the impact of environment on our growing minds, which we experience as those internalised good and bad objects, of which mention has been made. If we can recognise and accept the true character of these impulses—that is to say, if we can recognise without grudge, the harm that has been done to us, and without paralysing guilt, the harm that we have wanted to do; if we can accept the love that is offered to us, without evoking greed, and give love without demanding immediate return—then we are on the way to establishing an equilibrium between the past and the present, and between inner and outer values. As a result of that equilibrium, we become able to put our trust in, and to give value and love, to everyday things. It may be that we shall be swept into positions of passionate desire. The result does not matter, because if this equilibrium is achieved, we shall have a sure foothold in this solid and good world of ours, the world of everyday people and everyday things, from which we spring.

CHAPTER 17

Man without God?

(1950)

A belief in one God or in many gods is almost universal in mankind, but there are individuals—and worthy ones—who live full, kindly and creative lives without, apparently, any such belief. So a belief in God, though widespread, is not a necessity in Man's life, as are oxygen and food. Without these last, no one can live for long; without a belief in God, however, some people can develop harmoniously—indeed, it is sometimes difficult to tell from their behaviour, even under stress, whether those people believe in God or not.

How the idea of God arises

I think it unwise to make general statements on a subject of this kind because general statements so often express the aspirations of the speaker rather than a reflection of what we see in the world around us. Instead, I want to put some questions, as much to myself as to you: when does the idea of God come into the individual's mental life? Is

---

This paper, which was first published in *The Listener* (14 December 1950, Vol. 44, No. 1137), was based on a talk broadcast as the fifth of eight contributions by different speakers on the theme "Man without God?"

there in the course of a man's life a change or series of changes in the pattern or quality of this idea? What function does the God-idea serve in the development of the personality? Can the idea of an omnipotent God ever act as an inhibiting factor in the growth of the personality or of the intelligence? Is it possible that disbelief may be an endeavour to free the mind from an unnecessary constraint? What factors alter an individual's apparent need for God, and is there a direct or an inverse relation between the need for God and other of man's needs? And lastly, under what conditions does a person become, or appear to become, independent of a belief in God?

In my view simple points like these should always be considered by those who are interested in Man's relation to God before they tackle more complicated problems. To many of these questions answers can be found without a profound knowledge of psychology, still less of theology, and independently of the findings of the psychoanalysts. I will not bore you by trying to answer these questions in a way that you can do equally well for yourself without psychoanalytic theories to help you, but, since the work of Sigmund Freud chiefly, and of Sandor Ferenczi and Melanie Klein, have helped me to put these questions and to get some answers, I will approach this problem with their psychoanalytic work in mind, though what has been made of that work is, of course, my responsibility.

The idea of God comes gradually, and is built up partly by the child's own phantasies and partly by what its parents tell it. Children have magical beliefs—magical beliefs about the power of their own thoughts and wishes. It is not always easy for us as adults to remember these thoughts and feelings, but it is almost certain we all had these magical thoughts once. Then a change occurs: we cease to some extent to hold these beliefs about ourselves, but we ascribe these powers to our parents and later to God. Some people create for themselves, so to say, a climate of powerful thoughts, strong and dogmatic ideologies, theologies, all sorts of "ologies" (including scientific arrogance), and whether they believe in God or not they certainly behave as if they believed in the magical power of thought—omnipotence is not far from what most people think of when they think of God.

In our present-day Western monotheistic culture, God is to most people almost synonymous with love. The idea of a loving God is derived from the relation to the parents, but it is not at all a simple evolution: it is a representation in the child's mind of what it pictured its parents to be—usually a very different thing. In the turbulent moods of childhood, things at times feel to be all good or all bad—all white or all black, no grey. And so at first parent-images are coloured white or black and from them come both gods and devils. By the way, why don't we hear so much about the devil in these days? Satan for centuries held the imagination of preachers and their adult audiences; now apparently he does not exist. I wonder, perhaps, was Satan a creation of the imagination, a sort of mass delusion? But there are many children still who find no difficulty in believing in some kind of arch-devil. As children grow older the idea seems to fade out, perhaps because it is not supported by the cultural outlook of the adults of their generation. Anyway, it is not difficult to see where the idea came from.

But let us return to the idea of God. It begins in the child's mind as an act of synthesis, of creation; the images of many good things and people are fused into a unified fissure of the good all-loving God. It is a valuable supporting idea in what may be only a transitional period. But why is there this need for support? What spiritual dangers does the child—or anyone—risk from being alone? The dangers of this kind do not come from without but from within.

Very early—all too early for our placid development—we are seized with hate, hate even for those we love, and this hate embitters us even to ourselves. (I think this may have something to do with what ordinary people would call Original Sin.) Our need for love—indeed our greed for love—springs from the anguish that because of our selfishness and hate we are not worthy of love; we need to be reassured that we are love-worthy and so, being in childhood inexperienced and immature, we build up a concept of a Being so powerful and loving as to endure unwaveringly the devastation of our sin and hate.

Can Man live without God? Must he forever look for support and comfort in God's everlasting arms? Why, the very images employed by those who speak of God's infinite mercy point to a stage of development of character and strength which in other respects we all outgrow. It would seem that the idea of God as a support originates in and relates to a difficult period of our personality development, when we were ridden by our instincts, when we had not mastered our desires and when our lives were often clouded by anxiety, depression and guilt. But we all know one of the ways we overcame some of the troubles of childhood. There developed in our minds ideals of good behaviour, ideals modelled originally on the image we held of our parents, and we carried within us this representative of those we loved as a pattern and guide, who reproved us when we transgressed, and encouraged us when we obeyed our ideals or our conscience. Sometimes, but not always, the conscience is projected onto God. Many people, and among them men of good will and staunch character, come to dispense with these attributes of omnipotence and infallibility even in their consciences; they acquire a warm and living tolerance for the failings of others without yielding to or being dismayed by their own frailty.

The idea of God as a check to our unconscious impulses

Now I want to raise another question. Surely by the time there is a developed conscience, we should know our strength and weakness in the face of our desire, even of our selfish and destructive impulses. It is just at this point that psychoanalytic experience comes in usefully: the mighty agency of heaven and of the gods is not cherished in the mind primarily to cope with the temptations besetting our mature selves; it is used to keep in check the ever-lively impulses which live on in our unconscious minds, dating from our childhood. Those unconscious impulses, when kept from mind, cannot be resolved, and while they remain unconscious the worry they cause can never be finally allayed. Like bogies whose size depends on the degree of our fear, whose power grows with our hate, the sins of childhood's thoughts haunt men's minds and many people think a supra-human power is needed and only a supra-human power can check those haunting thoughts and evil impulses—without the aid of omnipotent power there is no peace. However, we must remember that most people do not feel a continuous need for God; usually they only feel it in face of an event which stirs up childhood's phantasies beyond the pitch of their tolerance. Then, too, there are those who avoid the pain of conflict by denying the evil within themselves. Such people may have successful outward-turned lives, but they lack something of depth and tenderness.

I could briefly summarise one aspect of the God-idea by saying: the idea of God is a mental process—one of the ways of preserving within the mind the living presence of persons and things which in childhood, and later, we experienced as "good". By "good" I mean, in this context, anything which helps us to feel the power and presence of love in others and in ourselves and which sustains our courage. The employment in the mental economy of the omnipotent element is not a necessary part of the supporting function which we associate with the Good or need associate with God. Not all men feel a need for God. Some by reason of their strength and the harmony of their development know how to endure the tragedies of existence alone, and to retain that sensitiveness to suffering and to joy in themselves and others, which makes our human lot so infinitely rich and varied. When I speak thus about these men without God, I am thinking of those who have faced their inner struggles bravely and tenderly, being brave in themselves and tender towards others. Mankind is enriched by their presence and their number is not few.

CHAPTER 18

The development of the moral function

(1951)

One of the social functions of the educator is to provide a transitional community[1] between the culture of the infant and the culture of the adult. The culture of the adult is a learned reaction which nevertheless cannot be taught. Despite this fact, however, the role of the educator is important, though not essential, in effecting a smooth transition from the one culture to the other.

That transition is most effective when the development of the moral function of the individual has a tempo that is within that individual's capacity (Susan Isaacs, 1930), and has a direction which is in general conformity with the custom of the time; thus the educator has no absolute standards, no final goals (save in his own incommunicable imagination), but must employ the methods of society (which, however, he can vary within limits) in order to further one of the functions of society in respect to the child, i.e. to absorb it.

In an adult world, children are a minority group without adequate power of representation in that world (M. Crichton-Gordon, personal

---

This paper first appeared as chapter four in *The Yearbook of Education, 1951* (London: Evans Bros., in association with the Institute of Education of the University of London, 1951).

[1] See p. 334 for notes on the "Transitional Community".

communication 1950); one of the functions of the educator is to be such a representative of this minority, and in this role to protect the developing child during the important phase of transition; the educator is thus an interpreter of the adult world to the child, and the culture of the child to the adult world.

Unlike the lower-animal kingdom, the human species is not governed by rigid patterns of behaviour common to all members of the species. During the development of the human individual there is great scope for the acquisition of behaviour of a widely varied kind (far more varied than occurs in any other animal); one of the means by which this flexibility and adaptability are achieved is through the medium of the moral function.

The type of behaviour possible in the human species, though very wide in variety, is limited in range in any individual. The limitations of range are of two kinds, a conscious will or choice and an unconscious force operating within the mind or personality, which in some directions restricts, in others develops, the scope of action; of the two sorts of limitation the latter is by far the more important. Thus mankind has not a conscious control of his destiny, neither has the individual. The latter often thinks he has, but this is an illusion fostered, indeed sometimes cherished, to give him temporary peace of mind when faced with crisis.

Man shares with other animals the capacity to pass on to the next generation a genetic (gene-governed) structural and functional pattern of growth and behaviour. Man also passes on—but not by the physical medium of germ-plasm—a cultural pattern of behaviour which is most transmissible during the years when the individual is most plastic, that is, during development. At this time the teacher may exert a limited but lifelong influence on the individual.

The culture pattern transmitted from one generation to another is mainly a product of the influence of the moral function upon the developing individual. Much in a culture that seems on first observation to be unconnected with these ideas or ideals is on closer examination found to be intimately related to them.

The pattern of a culture is a unity; it cannot *be constructed* by an individual, however tyrannical and powerful or clever and persuasive, out of the "raw material" of humanity, it can only be modified. That is, man has not complete mastery even over "cultural inheritance"; when he has more knowledge of the origin of the moral function and its influence on human personality he will be in a better position to control his destiny. Mendel's and Bateman's discoveries have made the plant and animal breeder less dependent on empirical methods when evolving new shapes of plant or animal, but the laws governing the transmission of cultural inheritance are even more difficult to understand. Psychologists are making a beginning in this direction, notably those who take cognisance of the unconscious as well as the conscious processes in the mind.

The pattern of a culture is a unity. Even a great deal of knowledge about its parts does not necessarily tell us much about the whole. As in the case of a culture, so in the case of an individual, the greatest circumspection must be employed in making generalisations from studies of particular "unit elements"; nowhere is this more true than in the case of the origin and development of the moral function.

Yet another difficulty in making an objective study of the moral function lies in the fact that the observer is usually either a part of the culture to which the person studied belongs, or else he is a stranger to it and liable to the distortions of ignorance as well as of prejudice. The major difficulty lies in the resistance roused in the observer's mind to any disturbance of his own equilibrium; it is very rare that there are not "internal defences" against the implications, to the self and to others, of what is seen when the minds of others are looked at objectively. This notion of "internal defences" is important for an understanding of the moral function. Most of the confusion and sterility of discussions on the moral function is due to lack of attention to this process of defence.

In the foregoing paragraphs the word "culture" has been frequently and perhaps too widely used. It includes in this connection—though this use is admittedly irregular—the "culture" of the infant's and small child's mind. The gulf between the mental processes of childhood and those of adulthood is greater than between those of the European adult and the remotest of darkest Africa's inhabitants; to admit the possibility of prejudice in the latter example is not only common, it is now culturally demanded; to admit and really accept it in the former example is alarming—it means that we have a tremendous task in even beginning to understand our own children and our young pupils. We erect cultural edifices upon sites of our choosing without being able to explore the foundations of those sites, and in those edifices not only then, but in later years, when we in turn become dependent again, we too will have to live.

One of the tasks of the educator is to interpret the culture of the child to the adult and the culture of the adult to the child: it is an awkward fact that important mental and emotional elements in childhood are repressed and remain unconscious, which is apt to make "reading the child's mind" almost like guesswork.

At this point, if indeed not earlier, the writer should perhaps have made reference to the modesty of his equipment and the tentative nature of his conclusions; but now I say simply that I am grateful for this opportunity to address another profession than my own, and just a little doubtful whether my readers will be as interested in my approach to this matter as I am in theirs: for in becoming a doctor and a psychoanalyst I had to be educated, whereas to be a teacher it is not necessary (though it may be an advantage) to be psychoanalysed.

First approach to the problem

In the preceding section a hint was given of the approach to the moral function, which will be followed in this paper: it will be viewed as a combination of a biological and a social function. Its roots lie in our animal nature and at the same time it is in part shaped by the experience of childhood and, to a less extent, adult life. No animal, however much it is brought up as a human being, would develop a moral function at all comparable with that of a human being; and no human being brought up, if it were possible, apart from human society would, it is believed, develop a moral function such as ours. There is thus something peculiar in the animal nature of the human infant which makes it susceptible to the influence of human society, and maybe there is something in adults which makes them wish to influence their offspring more thoroughly and earnestly than grown-up animals train their young. This human peculiarity appears to turn on two things; the infant is more immature in executive function than in emotional needs; the capacity "to put two and two together" and to organise his behaviour so that it shall satisfy his requirements is less developed than the recognition of what he wants and does not want. Though there is a clear perception of *things* desired, there is a poor control over the means for attaining the objects or goals desired. Infancy is thus a period of intense frustration and, just as no man of developed sensibilities would willingly and for long exchange his human attributes and immerse himself in the community of animals (Freud, 1930a), so no one, however hard his lot, would be likely to exchange his adult world for the emotional turbulence and frustrations of infancy. Between us and the beasts there is a gulf of incomprehensibility; between us and infancy there is the veil of amnesia—we do not desire to know, really to know and feel, with the impact of the unscreened perception, what life was then like. True, there are moments, most precious for confidence and courageous progress through difficulty, when in the earliest days there was utter satisfaction in living (Scott, 1948). But it is the times of frustration, baffled by unknown forces, which contribute to the mental pains which we adults screen from our memory and fondly imagine never existed, or at most were only the moving shadows of a passing cloud.

Our infancy, the foundation of our mental lives, is no solid rock of sturdy animal nature, but a condition of constant adjustment to rapid ups and downs, earthquakes: the infant's greatest need is for a stabiliser, and one component in this stabiliser is the moral function. When disordered—all functions are liable to disorder—what should be a stabiliser may itself become an agent for more disorder within the personality; even the stabiliser is not always reliable.

The mind may be pictured as a regulating apparatus whose function is to keep tension as low and constant as possible. The moral function is a protective function. The thing protected in the first place is the self; later, and by a curious mutation of instinct, it protects the community.

The span of life and the observers

"We start as specks of jelly," as a writer once said in *The Lancet*, "and we end as life-size corpses." Between these terminal events a person goes through many changes. Who observes those changes? Does anyone observe all of them?—No. Does anyone observe more than a few of those changes? Even that simple question cannot be easily answered: no one observes the important first nine months of life; after birth a few people may observe the first few years; after that, observation is divided between parents and teachers, pastors and doctors, later between parents and employers, and so on; even in marriage the most devoted partner sees only a part of the other's day; only in old age is observation of behaviour reduced again to a few persons, perhaps in the end to a partner in marriage or a nurse.

It is well to state the embarrassing conclusion as clearly as possible: direct observation by an individual of the behaviour of another individual over long and significant periods of change is rare. Where the period of possible observation is intimate, as in the case of parents, it does not cover the whole span of life, and where it is long, covering most of the span, as with doctors and clergy who live throughout their lives with the same patients and parishioners, it is not intimate. Teachers see much that is highly important, but only for a part of the day and only for a few years. Even where special techniques of research are employed for examining the mind, the data provided by the investigations do not cover the whole field—clearly we must make do at present with partial answers.

Two modes of approach to the problem

There are two ways of approaching the problem of the growth of the moral function. The older way is to assume that the moral function is implanted in man from an external source, i.e. God, and that throughout life man gropes with greater or less success towards the realisation of the ideal which exists, already formed, in the mind of the Creator. The attainment of that ideal is a task that must from the nature of things be for ever unfulfilled, the act of striving being evidence, for those who experience it, of the presence and power of God within themselves. This way of approach has been employed for several thousand years; it labours, however, under a disadvantage in that there is a basic postulate of a perfection of behaviour to which all men ideally should attain. When this is made the basis of observation and still more of upbringing, there is a tendency for the observer and the guide to consider themselves competent (by reason of age or for whatever other reason) to perceive and interpret the Divine will; this sometimes works to the disadvantage of the child who, besides being rather confused by the different interpretations of his teachers, is not led to accept standards of behaviour which relate directly to his own development.

Another approach to the problem is based on a different postulate, i.e. that the growth of the moral function within the personality is a personal achievement in each individual in adapting himself, his animal self and his desires, to the culture of the society in which he grows up, and that investigation should be turned to the processes by which one phase of development leads under the dual influence of instinctual and environmental forces to the next stage of the moral function. On this viewing the moral function may be regarded as the highest development of biological evolution and not as a derivative of anything lying outside the animal kingdom in its widest aspect.

This paper will be concerned with this second postulate.

What biological function does a moral function play?

A creature that lives quite alone has no need for morality; such a function would play no part in its life, and if such isolation had existed from birth or from a very early age it is difficult to see how it would be acquired. Morality is a social function which serves the purpose of attaining and maintaining a harmonious relation with a society which is regarded as "good". The moral function is of slow growth and is liable to disturbances of development, which may be noted by any observer or may be seen only by one who has not been subject to the same disturbing influences himself. Thus a person with "a fierce conscience" is not observed to be unusual by those who through upbringing have acquired the same sort of fierce consciences, but he may be regarded as a very odd sort of person, if not definitely abnormal, when he goes abroad or moves into a company of people with different standards.

The origins of the moral function are primitive

If we are going to look into the origins of the moral function, we must begin with processes which at first sight seem hardly recognisable as such, and, as the earlier we go back in an individual's history the more nearly do we come to a physiological, almost animal, level, we must be prepared for humble origins of what later becomes one of man's greatest achievements.

When we consider the primitive nature of the small child's mental processes and at the same time consider the nature of the demands made on him to regulate his behaviour—in particular the fact that the control of his sphincters is to many children one of the first criteria by which they can please their parents and earn the titles of "good" or "bad"—it is not surprising that some psychologists have sought the first stages of morality in "sphincter morality" (Ferenczi, 1925). This is no more a belittlement of later developments than to say that man's origin can be traced through the lower primates, even to still lower animals, and it is of course only a partial explanation. But there is no gainsaying that in our society the training of the body's habits makes a deep impression on the child and colours his attitude, on the one hand to his body and its functions, and on the other to the relation of friendly co-operation with or hostility to those on whose good regard he so greatly depends. One baby was clean and dry, requiring no diapers even at night, before the age of nine months; forty years later he said, "It has taken me all this time to get over that terrible start, and I am only just learning to relax". With his bowels and bladder he was "good", but for the rest he was beneath all resentful and irritable though longing to be—and eventually becoming—charming and easy-going with others where there was no real occasion for protective self-assertion.

Another child, brought up in an "all-electric house", while still a crawler used to go to the power plugs, extend one hand nearly touching the forbidden switch, and then smack it with her other hand, shaking her head and saying a primitive "no". "Good" and "bad" behaviour, even among children in the crawling stage, is thus not only a matter of sphincters, but appears to be always associated with movements, i.e. with action, of some kind.

It is desirable to have a frame of reference, perhaps an over-simple one, by which to designate the parts or aspects of the personality engaged in these inner and outer moral controversies. The hand of the crawler extended towards the electric switch had, for the child herself, during that particular game a different "meaning" from the other hand which smacked. The former was connected with its activities that were influenced by impulses of curiosity, of mastery and of exploration; the smacking hand was most probably during that game an embodiment within the self, a representative, of prohibiting parents.

A simple frame of reference and nomenclature

Without a simple nomenclature, we shall be tied to illustrations or anecdotes. Freud's (1923b) frame of reference[2] is the simplest which at the same time is at all adequate. If the executive part of the mind or personality is called the *ego*, the part which checks the ego's behaviour can be called, without giving it an exalted valuation, the *superego*. That leaves us with the part which manifests itself in urges to action of all primitive kinds, and first Groddeck (1923) and then Freud (1923b) called this part the It or impersonal part of the self, or (to keep it Latin) the Id.

It was due to impulses of *id* origin that the child extended her hand towards the switch; the superego part caused the other hand to smack; mediating between these two was the ego.

At one time it was thought that the superego was a part of the ego modified by parental injunctions, whose "Thou shalt not . . ." became a part of the child's thinking and self-controlling processes—later (Freud, 1923b) the incorporation of the parents' attitude was seen to have another or supporting side. It is as if a part of the ego accepted the parental attitude as though it were its own so that they no longer had

---

[2] See p. 334 for notes on "The Ego and the Id".

need to say "Do not do that or we won't love and cherish you (or we will be angry with you), or do this and we shall be pleased with you"—such functions become part of the child's own ego behaviour or rather its superego behaviour.

Though the superego is to some extent moulded on injunctions and encouragements, it would be a mistake to imagine that at any time in the child's development it is a simple matter to modify or mould the superego, or the child's ideals, or its moral function—far otherwise. The child's ego, fortunately, is not a plastic lump, like wax, ready to receive whatever imprint the environment shoves upon it. The development of the superego is an active process within the mind; the superego meets a biological need (adaptive), and so the total personality is involved in it; but it is an unconscious process, and for this reason, until researches into the operation of unconscious mental processes had disclosed their way of working, the development of even this important function was utterly obscure.

The beginning of social life

Social life begins when a person finds it necessary to adjust to two or more persons at once; the human family usually provides this prerequisite condition. But the child is ill prepared for the problem of a three-person relationship; he is emotionally unstable, is dependent on his parents, and has as a background of his own experience a babyhood by no means free from trouble. The boy, for instance, finds himself in conflict with his father particularly in his striving to obtain and retain the central and sole place in his mother's affections. An implacable hostility to a person so powerful and so near would fill his life with fear and anxiety. But there is in everyone a certain tendency to bisexuality, and the father is liked and admired as well as being regarded as a rival to be got rid of. The quandary is overcome by a process (apparently peculiar to human beings) in which the attributes of the parent of the same sex are taken into the self: the boy identifies himself with his father and accepts parental admonitions as if they were issued by a part of himself. A part of his own ego becomes modified by his experience of the environment which is most precious to him, i.e. his parents; thus there is an "inclusion" of the social environment within himself which goes on behaving in a lively way both as part of him and as part of the environment.

The liveliness or the livingness of the portion of the environment included within the self (the superego) is an important part of its function. It is not as if the parent's "You are not to do that" set up a kind of reflex blockage of the impulse to do that particular thing; we do not as adults take into ourselves the sayings of others as if they were telegrams containing just words and instructions, and still less do we do so as children. Our lives are not spent in the execution of formulations like those newly constructed electronic calculating machines into which are fed specific instructions to act in such and such a way—press the button and the machine does the rest. Our lives are lived all the time with people; if through identification with our father we are restraining ourselves from a desired activity it is as if he was present *within us* holding back our hand.

"But," you may say, "this is all phantasy!" Yes, that is exactly what it is and why it is so important. Our mental life begins, certainly our social life begins—and continues—in the movement and interaction of people in their various relations to one another, now loving, now quarrelling, now remote, now close, but all the time in vital relationships. A child can commit to memory a command or an encouragement, but that does not modify the personality, it does not "get inside", it does not exercise a "superego" function nor alter the moral ideas.

We all know that children people every cranny of their world with creations of their imagination, but these phantasied objects are not entirely new constructions having no relation whatever with what they have experienced before. The phantasied objects, their own little people, or giants, for that matter, have attributes some of which are taken from one person, some from another, but blended and recombined to form just such a figure as is needed in the drama of their imagination at the moment. As it is in their imagination—so it is with their inner world, it too is peopled with all sorts of creations, sublime and terrifying, all of them immortal.[3]

---

[3] When a reluctant feeder is having porridge spooned into her mouth with the words "This is for Daddy", then with the next spoonful "This is for Mummy" ... and so on through the whole Table of Kindred and Affinity till the dish is finished, I ask myself this simple question, "Who is being, fed, and where?" (a) The child is being fed, (b) Mummy and Daddy and the rest seemingly are being fed, (c) since the child does not turn the spoon to these and others but takes the porridge into herself, these others must get it when it gets inside herself. While I hold fast to the boundaries of anatomy, I can get nowhere near an understanding of the mind and social concepts of a small child, but if I assume that when a child accepts such "play" then there must be some "meaning" in it—these people are inside somewhere or other. I would not have given such simple nursery experiences had I not

This inner world is no *camera obscura* which reflects faithfully the outer world in miniature. It is too much coloured by the child's own emotions, and the phantasies shaped by those emotions, for any such photographic analogy to be employed. The inner world is a theatre of operations in which the child (we adults do it too) is for ever playing over and over again the emotional problems which preoccupy him—and most important of these is the relation of the parents to one another, their love-making, their quarrels, their having children, killing children and cooking and eating them, and reviving them again, and so on. The dramas are most varied; now tender, now brutal, according as the child feels at the moment. The parent-figures who play a prominent part in these dramas are not like the real parents; they are what the child at the moment phantasies them to be, but though only made in imagination they are for the moment and in the life and action of the phantasy real.

The term "inner world" has been used in the singular; it seems, however, that there is a hierarchy or stratification of these phantasy theatres of operation, the earliest and most primitive being "deepest" or least accessible to consciousness, the more recent being more superficial and as a rule more easily made conscious. The phantasy activity in every level has the same purpose, i.e. to reach a solution to an unresolved emotional problem, but there is a "super-objective", as Konstatin Stanislavsky (1936) calls it in *An Actor Prepares*, namely to produce a solution that will solve the problems at every level simultaneously.

All this is getting complicated, and I can hear some readers say, "Heaven above, does every little brat have all that going on within him—spare us from psychology!" Be patient with me, I am soon coming to clearer matters.

We are now considering the beginnings of social life: all this is by way of saying that there are patterns in the inner world which are the most personal and cherished possessions of the child, which affect his outlook on the social patterns which he sees in the world of men and women and children around him.

---

found in the course of psychoanalytic work that these "games" are meaningful, that is to say, they are related to the experiences of the child—and the experiences in his imagination, which are of course in their frame of reference real. "A thing is real", said Kurt Lewin, "if it has effects"; these childhood's imaginings have effects, therefore they are real, though maybe only real for the child himself.

I sometimes wish that the philosophers who talk learnedly about "mind and body" problems would let themselves be bothered with small children's play: from such mouths we learn how little we know.

Let us now go back to the theme of the beginning of this section, the difficult position of the boy, for instance, faced with the two parents he is fond of, but of whom one is a rival. It was said that he identified himself with his father and took him as a model. This, however, is in fact a continuous process. There is a hierarchy of models thus acquired—the more primitive ones are harsher in outline, more all-black or all-white, than the later ones; the earlier ones are hardly human at all, if by human one means that they are a blending of good and bad, of strength and weakness—but once incorporated in the inner society they have their place there no matter how crude and seemingly unassimilable they may be. The word "models" has been used: it is incorrect if by models we mean what the conventions of the adult world would call "ideals"; there can, after all, be models of all kinds, and the "inclusions" within our personality are of all kinds, at first, anyway.

But the child soon looks away from home for models. One of the great advantages of going to school (dare I say the greatest advantage?) is that the child is afforded an opportunity to assimilate other models than those of his parents.

There is a propulsion away from home, no matter how pleasant the home may be; home is a place of conflict and jealousy as well as a refuge and a secure place of comfort. The child needs a wider world where his new acquaintances, among adults as well as children, will be those with whom he is less emotionally involved. But the need for such new acquaintances springs in part—not entirely, his growing curiosity and desire for experiment in social relations supplies the other part—from a satiation with the interaction of the same, ever the same, emotionally supercharged outer world with his inner world, for the interaction of the two worlds is going on all the time.

The beginning of moral feelings

We feel guilt when, and only when, we do or intend an injury to a loved object (person or thing or abstraction such as Truth): if we had no aggressive impulses we would never feel guilt; if we had no love within us—love and a desire to cherish—we would never feel guilt. But we have love and hate within us from the earliest age and for the same person; therefore, from the earliest age we are liable to feelings of guilt. If it is preferred that the term "guilt" be kept for the highly developed response which we know in consciousness as "pricks of conscience", then we could coin a term for the primitive sort and speak of "proto-guilt". The point is not important.

On this view, guilt can begin very early; indeed, since the infant loves the breast and often is angry with it, guilt can begin—"proto-guilt", if you wish—in the first year of life. There is some ground for thinking that it does.

What does guilt "say" to the ego? In more prosaic language, what effect does a pang of guilt have upon the executive function of the mind? First, it calls a halt to the guilt-provoking action, and then, when the love impulses gain momentum, it induces a restitutive response, a making good the bad action done. Under the influence of the restitutive impulse the object is cherished sometimes more fondly than before the guilt-provoking act was done; indeed, the restitutive impulse is a reinforcement of the love impulse in our personal and social relations; in this we are different from the animals, who pine but do not mourn, who caress but do not find themselves in those enduring bonds which we call love.

What has been said about guilt thus far is valid for a two-person relationship, for example the "nursing-couple" (Middlemore, 1941) of mother and child; it acquires a greater richness and power when the three-person relationship of two-parents-and-child are the interacting group. In this case the boy can model himself upon the father so that both the inhibiting element and the restitutive element have guides, so to speak, in which they can run. But it is not easy! The previous section said nothing if it did not make plain that there is interaction between the outer and the inner worlds, or the outer and the inner society, as I prefer to think of it, and that the inner society is a complex of stratified reactions interplaying with one another. There is not one "superego", in other words, but a hierarchy of superegos or inclusions of external persons (modified by the mood at the moment of inclusion); at least, this is so in the early years, and those are the ones we are considering at the moment.

This is not a stage at which one should stop—it is too depressing with this entwined mass of unresolved emotional entanglements. Nevertheless, I propose to jump to a condition of maturity in the moral function and then work back to the present difficult point, discussing on the way the disorders of the moral function—what increases and what diminishes the likelihood of such disorders.

The optimum development of the moral function

What are the components of the moral function, and what service does it perform in the normal healthy adult? The part of the mind responsible for the moral function is the superego. It is *vigilant*, it watches the intention to action in respect to loved objects (persons and things and valued abstract ideas). Its vigilance is directed to the protection of good objects from any damage or hurt which they may receive as a result of the action prompted by the instinctual part of the self (the *id*).

Under the guidance of the superego the ego looks inwards to the instinctual part of the self, and also, without such guidance, it looks outwards to the external world. In a mature, healthy adult, the ego (Executive), recognising that the instinctual element is as much a part of the self as any other part of it, is ready to assess the degree of its (the ego's) responsibility for its acts and to compare this both with the standards required by society and with its own feelings for the fitness of the act or intention in the circumstances under consideration.

The healthy, mature adult ego is neither intimidated by the selfishness and aggressiveness it discerns within the self (the *id* part), nor is it complaisant to its demands for satisfaction. Even under pressure from the superego, the ego does not find secret outlet for aggression by turning the aggression against itself in an orgy of self-punishment, nor does it allow an orgy of misdeeds to be followed by a severe process of "un-guilting" by penitences and the like.[4] The act and the consequences are considered as a unity before the action takes place; finally, the decision as to the rightness or the wrongness of the action (considered in respect to the effect on good objects) has to be taken independently, quite independently, of the opinion of the community on the matter, the final decision being taken after that too has been considered.

A person who behaved in this way has some claim to wisdom in the matter of morals, and at least in respect to loved objects he could be gentle. He would not be harsh, either, with himself, for such a person would regard his own self as among the good objects to be protected. His own self? What self? What of all those "inclusions", that "internal society", that seemed so bewildering in a previous section: are all of them to be protected too? Even the harsh uncouth parts? This "optimum" just described combines tolerance with feeling, endurance and love. Such a combination is not beyond human compass, though there are many forces—often institutionalised forces—which would persuade us that morality is not showing virtue if it does not demand mortification of the flesh and penances of the spirit.

---

[4] The old-regime Russians were prone to this behaviour; cf. Gorer and Rickman, *The People of Great Russia* (1949).

That terrible Greek proverb, "Count no man happy till he is dead", speaks both of the misery which may befall the contented man and of the triumph over calamity which may bring joy in the last days of a life of struggle. So, surely, it is with this matter of the attainment of a mature and wholesome—a life-giving and supporting—moral function: who can say that in the blunderings and struggles of the most wayward there is not at least a tendency to attain tolerance within and without and thus find peace?

Hindrances to the development of the moral function

The poor devil who has to endure the often clamant demands of the instincts on the one hand, the restraints of conscience or superego on the other, and all the time earn a living and keep a fairly clear slate in the outer world is, of course, the ego, or Executive. Whatever adds to his burden prolongs his task of making a final adjustment of these various claims.

One of the most difficult people he has to deal with in the outer world is the person who is in authority over him and whom he is trying to respect, but who is anxious to take short cuts to morality. There is a proper tempo in the assimilation of problems of morality which is peculiar to every individual, and nothing is harder—just as nothing in the long run is more rewarding—than a perception of that tempo. Short cuts to morality are neither moral nor are they short.

Morality cannot be implanted in a person, it can grow only at its own time and in his own way. Certain types of behaviour can, of course, be forced on a child or on an adult, but that is not morality. Morality is not behaviour in conformity to a standard of conduct, but the expression of good relationship already existing in the mind and finding expression in everyday action and in crisis.

Morality involves a sensitive perception of the codes of ethics in the community, but the person must not lose himself in an identification with that community; one of the values of morality is its highly individual quality; perhaps, indeed, that is one of its chief biological (survival) values.

If a child is taught to connect "good" and "bad" with actions and not with his feeling about people, he will tend to split action from feeling, and the end of that is a rigid type of personality who becomes more and more, instead of less and less, one who goes blindly "with the crowd". Those who are concerned with moral education know well that the final result of their endeavours may not be apparent for years after their contact with the children is finished, and that if they look for immediate results visible and satisfying to themselves they may be setting store by superficially polished manners instead of a basic integrity of character. It was not for nothing that so many of the foregoing pages were filled with descriptions, inadequate as I know them to be, of the "serial deposits of experience", or the "inclusions of external personalities" within the self, or superegos, nor that I described at such length their interaction; a new experience has to work its way through and into the stratifications in the "internal society". To say this is not to belittle good manners, but only that they must come from within if they are to endure stress, and when pressed upon a person from without there is apt to be distortion of the internal processes of social relationships.

Though in our society at the present time a high value is attached to love, and indications of aggression and hate are considered to be of themselves antisocial, it is well to ponder on the cost of (and the possibility of sudden reactions from) such a dichotomy. If a small child says to another, "Oh, I hate you!" this is by many considered a dreadful thing. To be sure, for the moment the social situation is somewhat disquieted, and there is an air of expectancy, possibly of some apprehension, but before we pass a moral judgement on a child who speaks thus there are a number of considerations which may pass under our notice. The double love-and-hate feelings are very common in our earliest years, and it is, after all, quite an achievement for us to be able to experience these oscillations without disturbing our relationships with people. This child may be in the process of mastering its hate feelings by giving conscious expression to them. Furthermore, we grown-ups heard the child say it to another: were we, who stood so near, not also in the social setting of that malediction—weren't we meant to hear, was it not said to test our tolerance or to force us to aid the speaker to stop his flow of wrath from going farther? I cannot answer these questions (partly because the above is a hypothetical case), but I can say that merely to stop the expression of such emotions because on general principles they are thought unseemly is not, in my view, an aid to the development of a sensitive and tolerant moral function. This is not the same as saying that any child can say and do whatever he likes when he likes; the child needs our help, help to adjust to his inner needs as well as to society's.

In an earlier section it was said that there was a continual pressure to complete in the present the unresolved emotional situations of the past, i.e. the ego has to face two ways, the outer world and its demands in the present, and the inner feelings (instinct-demands) plus the past as yet unsatisfied dissatisfactions. Those who have to bring up and educate children have ever before them young creatures doing or wanting to do the very things they themselves desired to do and could not do with any real content.

"Those kids stir up my complexes!" as a young teacher once said with enviable insight: she at any rate would not be caught unawares. Referring back to those sections dealing with the interaction of an external and an internal society, the latter by no means entirely harmonious, does not a teacher facing a difficult class feel the discord outside herself awakening responses within herself from the somewhat discordant inner, internalised past experiences? Has not she in such a case a double task to perform: to quell an inner as well as an outer hubbub? What she brings to the one task she will bring to the other. If we are agreed that discipline must be maintained, there are still two possible ways of looking at it: one way is that noise and confusion are in themselves wrong; the other way is to regard them as inconvenient and perhaps ungracious. The way taken will depend on the moral attitude of the disciplinarian.

Returning to the superego again, the teacher is endowed by the child with ego-ideal qualities which were originally felt towards the parents. To view any infringement of the code of behaviour as a thing which cannot possibly be looked upon with a sense of humour tends to activate in the child's mind the phantasy of blind and harsh parental disciplining and the phantasy of harsh relations generally in the home. Insofar as the child is saddled with much unresolved guilt the experience of stern reproofs will be a temporary assuagement of his guilt feelings; but if the aim of the teacher is to aid the child's ego to adjust to the claims of impulse, of inner conscience and of outer society, then rigid schemes of behaviour will be avoided as tending to benumb the recognition and the enjoyment of the inner experiences even though they may need curbing, for when we look with unabashed gaze into ourselves we find enjoyment (albeit with a blush) at many of the thoughts and impulses we prefer not to display or perform.

Now, what part of the teacher's behaviour or personality gets absorbed into her pupils' personalities? Is it her *injunctions* to keep quiet, or is it her *way* of handling the unruliness? Put in other terms, is it her conscious behaviour or her unconscious behaviour which really influences them most? In my view the latter (the unconscious) behaviour is the most influential, and I think it is a recognition of this which makes some parents and teachers nervous before their charges; they do not feel that they have sufficient control over themselves to be able to handle the parent–child (teacher–child) relationship.

When referring to the early development of the superego, we had occasion to consider the role of the sphincters in the child's growing self-control and in his social relationships. These bodily functions and sensations, as well as those derived from the genitals, are a source of delight and satisfaction to the child. These excitations enhance and give "body" to phantasies—those most precious of all human characteristics—and afford a link between the animal, the "proto-mental" (Bion, 1948), part of ourselves and the nexus of personal relationships in which we live. These phantasies, as we would expect, contain mixtures of loving and destructive components, and in the course of his life each child, adolescent and adult has to work out for himself the untangling of these two opposing tendencies in his phantasy life and to canalise both of them constructively. It is a task of the greatest delicacy, and, perhaps fortunately, most of it goes on subliminally, i.e. outside the range of consciousness.

But those who have responsibility for the upbringing and education of children inevitably have to face the fact of the child's sensuality. Since the child himself needs help in resolving his conflicts over his sensual feelings, he often so shapes his behaviour (rarely by direct requests for help, more often by actions which excite attention and even reprimand) that the adult is compelled to face the issue too. What would be the aim in such a case?

If morality is an invigilating function in the mind to preserve good objects from injury caused by the self, and if what has been said above is true—that love and hate impulses are often closely interwoven—and if the child is troubled, and if the ego, which has the job of testing reality, is to be supported in its hard but practical tasks—then, though it is difficult, the path is fairly plain. An alliance has to be made with the ego, not with the superego (which looks only within) nor with the *id* (which considers only immediate release of tension), and in making that alliance the facts must be considered: the child is troubled because he feels a wrong has been done, so his worry is intelligible and, because he would not worry if he did not love, it seems to the onlooker—and perhaps some day to himself—that the situation is not hopeless, as the child at the moment feels; these double feelings everyone knows to be painful, but they are soluble in the end. Alliances made with the conscience against sensuality, or sensuality against conscience, or on the child's side against the parents, or the other way about, only add to the burdens of the part of the child's personality which finally has to decide on its course of action—his ego.

It hinders the child's ego in its difficult assay and difficult decision if the adult—who is virtually called into consultation (to butt in without being asked is an almost inexcusable trespass)—brings forward his own problems for solution simultaneously, i.e. by making this an occasion for the working through of his own problem of dealing with sensuality, conscience, love and hate and by taking sides for or against the parents in that—for the child—still unclosed issue of the parent-child relationship. In a word, each generation has to solve its own problems, and if bridging of generations is to be done in moments of conflict, the point of contact should be the ego.

How difficult this subject is! For despite what I have just said it is perfectly evident that the vehicle of culture transmissions is via the superego! But I was also not entirely wrong: in moments of conflict let the bridge be the ego (any clinician would say the same), but when looking at the general stream of culture transmission we must consider the superego.

The moral function as a vehicle of cultural transmission

Born dependent, impulse-ridden, fickle, egoistic, body-bound, we grow up—if the Fates do but grant us grace—into independent, controlled (but spontaneous), constant, reasonably unselfish, spiritually far-seeing and yet body-enjoying adults.

One of the means by which this remarkable transformation takes place is through the process of superego formation. We take into ourselves the personalities of those we lean on and admire; by so doing not only do we get help to curb our wayward impulses, but through the simultaneous action of sublimated love and hate impulses we receive an impetus to acquire from our model skills in social adaptations (and even skills in craftsmanship), and through an identification with our model we gain the support of a kindly mentor when we falter and of a comforter in our despair. We use the experience and the love we have for parents and their surrogates to help us in our dependent years, till we have mastered our desires or at least ceased to fear them—then only do we grow up.

The tie with the older generation must some day end, useful and fruitful though it was. How does it end? Is there a shift of the function from one part of the mind to another? From the superego to the ego? Does the ego gain in insight and knowledge of its instinctual part (its id), so that the person can decide for himself what is right and wrong without reference to what father taught, what the school code was, what society thinks? All this I believe to be so, but there is a precondition to the attainment of this goal: the pain of conflict must be faced, the fact of frustration and despondency at our own waywardness and hurtfulness is to be reckoned with as part of our very nature. If we idealise ourselves or our motives or seek to smother our antagonism by over-idealising others, if we work out, in our emotional life in relation to others, problems of our own which only we can face within ourselves—then we shall be for ever dependent on the aid of father's admonitions and of codes of conduct that we must blindly obey.

But as we grow up facing our own troubles as best we may, these "inclusions", so often referred to, become absorbed as parts of our own ego, and thus we grow in stature to be the equals of those who were once our teachers and our guides.

There seem to be two kinds of cultural transmission: in the cases where the superego element is unabsorbed and in the cases where it is assimilated. The former is more noisy, more reforming, more intrusive; the latter quieter and perhaps more wise. The former seeks, but unwittingly, to pass on to the next generation *its defences* against the disturbance deriving from our animal nature; the latter has to be sought out, and if its aid is required it does not flinch from the painful experience of facing again the tragedies of our human lot for another's sake. Between these two kinds of helper Youth thinks he can make a choice, but, for better or worse, the decision is made according to unconscious forces in the mind, and over these he has no control.

Perhaps it is as well at the present time that this should be so. The activity of the moral function is one of Man's most precious cultural achievements, and until we know much more about it a dogmatic attitude is more likely to be injurious than helpful. The greatest enemy of the developing moral function is the person who is certain that he knows the answers for others as well as for himself. Morality does not, in essence, consist in *doing* particular things and not doing others, but in the person *feeling* the impulses of the love and hate, first in himself and then in others, and choosing so far as is possible the more constructive, the less disruptive, pathway in social relationships.

The growth of the moral function is best outlined as the change from dogmatism to exploration and choice; from sudden, all-or-none, explosive responses in situations involving moral choice to graduated, controlled responses; from reflex or reactive action to consideration; from automatism to love.

Notes on the "Transitional Community"

One of the most important ideas in sociology in the last decade is found in the concept of Transitional Communities (Wilson et al., 1947) and what is probably subtly related to it, the "Transitional Object" referred to by D. W. Winnicott (1955).

The Transitional Community idea arose during the war when the problems arose of settling repatriated prisoners of war. A. T. M. Wilson, W. R. Bion, T. F. Main, Ferguson Roger, E. L. Trist, and others realised that to construct a community (Civilian Resettlement Units) for the purpose of making a smooth transition for a specified body of persons from one community to another involved far more than making a "transit camp"—it called for a study of the dynamics of both terminal communities and the special needs of a community where transition and not permanence was to be its essential characteristic (Curle & Trist, 1947). The importance of this to education is immediately apparent, not merely as a check to such *clichés* as "In my school we prepare for citizenship", but as stimulus to prior examination of just what forces operate in the community of the nursery and family on the one hand and on the other in the post-school communities which the pupil will enter finally. Integrative studies of this kind are at the moment in their infancy, but they may well revolutionise our views on education. It might be thought that such a subject was irrelevant to the topic of this paper, but the question of morale is central to the effective working of transitional communities, and these depend on the growth and development of the moral function.

Notes on "The Ego and the Id"

This frame of reference was of slow growth. In 1911 Freud began to view a part of the ego as an ego-ideal; this was further developed in a paper on narcissism in 1914 (1914c); in 1916–17, when dealing with melancholia, the relation of the ego to parental authority and loss of loved objects was included in the concept (1917e); in 1921 the relation of the ego-ideal—now called superego—to group psychology was considered (1921c); and the threefold frame of reference, ego–superego–id, was published in 1923 (1923b). Each extension of the general concept was made in response to developments of clinical observation which showed that former theories were not adequate to explain the phenomena observed. The process of extension and change continues; for this reason, every use of a technical concept should be given its date.

The work of Melanie Klein (1932, 1949) has placed the *beginning* of the superego function still earlier than did Freud—indeed, to the first year of life; this should remind us that the moral function in its early stages is very primitive and does not manifest itself to the casual, or for that matter to the worried, onlooker in the same way as it does later in development. This paper has been greatly influenced by the work of Melanie Klein, but the responsibility for the views contained in it is mine alone; I would not like to saddle Freud, or her, with these opinions. The most important writings for educationalists on the relations of these three institutions of the mind to school life are to be found in the writings of Susan Isaacs (1930, 1933, 1948).

APPENDIX 1

Memorandum on Criteria which may be employed by the Training Committee regarding the suitability of Candidates at various stages in their Training

To the Training Committee at Lt Col Bowlby's request
From John Rickman, 10th Jan 1945

1. The following Memorandum is based on the assumption that the Institute is clearly distinguishing its function as a therapeutic establishment from its function and social duty to train as many of the best Candidates as it can find who will become future teachers & trainers of analysts and others in related subjects, and that the Training Committee is oriented to this latter purpose, i.e. to teach teachers in the present phase.

2. The second assumption is that the Training Committee will not employ the same criteria for Candidates who are going to use their psychoanalytic knowledge in non-therapeutic fields as for those who are. In the past it was said that Candidates who began with the idea of doing therapy in fact ended up by doing it, and therefore it was not expedient to have two kinds of criteria. If a higher level of Candidate is obtained it is less likely that this dilemma will arise; in any case it will not arise without warning, but the Training Committee should have a policy ready to meet the case. In the following notes it is assumed that the full therapeutic training is meant unless otherwise specified.

3. *Criteria for acceptance of a Candidate after a months' "trial"*:

    (a) *Sympathy, or a feeling for personal relationships,* that is above the average. A quick-flashing insight into parts of problems is a "counter-pointer"; slowness to see the detail is not a bar if the Candidate can keep in contact with the *person as a whole* whom he is dealing with while he gropes to a better understanding.

(b) *Stability of Character, shown by*

(i) his capacity for combining resistance to pressure with adaptation to others in the pursuit of a developing social relationship and in the pursuit of personal happiness

(ii) he should have *done* something, not merely be a person of promise (it is true that this point should be settled before the three months probationary period begins, but if the criteria are really going to be oriented to training of teachers of ps-an ideas it is important to keep the therapeutic impulse of analysts under observation if not control)

(iii) these two criteria exclude the grosser forms of neurosis and psychosis and do include, and indeed underline, a capacity for constructiveness.

(c) With a demonstrated stability in guiding his course in life and a feeling for personal relationships as well; it is also assumed that the Candidate is interested in making the *psychological approach* the medium for attaining goals (i) in his work as a field for exploration and exploitation, (ii) as a means of living and as a vehicle for competitive impulses.

(d) His *tolerance*—his capacity to see the good in other people's views is of more importance than mere enthusiasm for his own; this tolerance must however be combined with a capacity to resist pressure.

(e) His *intelligence*. Since ps-an is passing into a phase of expansion it is very important that the candidates should be chosen with a view to their capacity to influence other people's views.

(NB: re "d" above—there are unusually intolerant people who are at the same time unusually creative—the creativeness has to be outstanding to outbalance the intolerance.)

GENERAL NOTE: No mention has been made of specifically psychoanalytic points such as a feeling for the unconscious. I think it unlikely that anyone who has passed high, so to speak, in the foregoing points would be without it.

With regard to the non-therapists, all of the above criteria apply.

APPENDIX 1   339

4. *Criteria for Starting Seminars and Lectures:*

(i) When the Candidate shows that he wants to meet teachers and colleagues to get something from them into himself for use and not to use the occasion of the lecture-room for quick intellectual victories on a new battleground, and when he shows a capacity to co-operate—in rivalry, it may be—with his equals.

(ii) The foregoing depends on his stability of character, on positive or constructive feelings for personal relationships and on the psychological approach.

(iii) A mature candidate could begin in say six months or less if he had no previous knowledge of the subject, but if a Candidate had no previous knowledge of the subject that fact and its cause needs inquiring into; one with foreknowledge could begin after a few weeks, i.e. soon after the probationary period.

5. *Criteria for taking patients under control:*

(i) If he has a responsible attitude to others and has clinical experience already he should have patients within a few months of beginning post-probationary analysis, provided that

(a) his past history has shown that he has been able to keep a clinical objectivity during periods of emotional stress

(b) he has not "clinical anxiety", i.e. fear of patients or his attitude towards them

(b) the Training Committee is going to take a matter-of-fact attitude (as is done in teaching hospitals) about students' relation to patients, i.e. it is assumed that it is an ordinary event and that mistakes will be made. The analogue to "clinical anxiety" is "teacher's anxiety".

The foregoing paragraph relates of course to some of our new Candidates who have had years of clinical-psychological experience and have taken on their hands life-&-death responsibility for other people, i.e. who are clinically mature but not yet trained in a new technique—a common situation in a progressive teaching centre where new therapeutic methods need to be learned from ward & recreation ground observation.

"Clinically-psychologically-lay" Candidates are those who have not had the aforementioned responsible experience. "Clinical-psychological-laity" has nothing to do with medicine as such; e.g. a Probation Officer might have had just the experience of responsibility for another's welfare that the psychiatrist has. Very rarely has an educationalist had enough of this kind of experience to remove him from the "c-ps-lay" class; very few parents could qualify even on the basis of having had a difficult family because an essential of this quality is that the responsibility is carried *professionally*, not as a direct expression of parental love.

Where the Candidate is "clinically lay" the analyst has to assess his capacity to maintain a professional relationship during trying moments.

A professional relationship between doctor and patient (analyst and analysand) may be defined as one in which the doctor meets the problems which the patient and the disease set him by a further exploitation of the professional methods and skill he has acquired from his teachers and colleagues; i.e. the tension set up in the doctor by the exacerbations of the patient's illness finds relief by activities which while keeping the interests of the patient in view employ and only employ the methods of his profession and its basic sciences. This in turn depends on his belief in (identification with) the professional techniques he is acquiring from his teachers and colleagues, which again depends on the stability of his positive transferences.

Should non-therapist Candidates have patients as part of Training?

Personal analysis (called sometimes, but inadvisedly, "didactic analysis") should be the beginning not the end or goal of the candidate's analytic experience; fully to understand the field of forces operating in an analysis, these forces must be seen from the position of the analyst too; further, since ps-an is an instrumental science* a student should learn to handle the instrument lest he develop an over-theoretical attitude to the subject—these considerations point to non-therapists having patients under control. But the non-therapists need not be turned into clinicians not taught advanced psychotherapy, not for the matter of that advanced psychopathology; it should suffice if they have two patients provided that they are carefully selected cases.

6. *Criteria for the Final Qualification*

(i) Clinical resoluteness or decisiveness is one of the main final criteria; i.e. to know when to stop or change a therapeutic measure.

(ii) The ps-an instrument needs delicate handling; an over-passive attitude is as clinically wasteful as an over-active one is clinically distorting—a balance needs to be struck. But since this will be rarely achieved by the time the question comes up for decision, the development of the candidate must be the guide. If he was over-passive at the beginning and is becoming more active, or even overdoing it a bit, he is fairly safe—and so with over-activity.

(iii) The Candidate's capacity to talk to non-analytic colleagues about *their* clinical therapeutic problems in a way that is helpful to both parties is a good criterion that the analytic training is reaching maturation. (This point is specially important if the teaching of teachers is one of the main selection guides; but it also applies in ordinary cases of therapeutic education.)

(iv) Is the Candidate by now a *professional* & a trooper, a chap who will slog along at a job using only tools that he knows will be of use and ready to consult a colleague in a businesslike way before he does anything unusual?

(v) Is he from-the-heart co-operative with other professionals? (This point is important if we are going to teach teachers.)

7. *A general note on Criteria*

In the foregoing it has been assumed that the Training Committee can establish criteria out of their heads, so to speak, and thus judge the timing of the Candidate's advancement.

Another aspect needs consideration: Candidates and Trainers alike compose the "Field of Training" in which both operate. Reciprocal inhibition may delay maturation, i.e. the Training Committee or its organs (training analysis or lecturers) may maintain a discouraging attitude to the Candidate who responds by passive resistance which may manifest itself, for instance, by not reading up the subject.

Only if the Criteria are viewed in the "Field of Training" as a whole will flexible and realistic judgements be formed.

8. *A general note on these Criteria*

It will not have escaped the notice of readers of the foregoing pages that I have made little use of psychoanalytic terms, and it may even be thought at first sight but little use of psychoanalytic concepts, by which to judge the Candidate. I sat on the Training Committee for a decade or more, and, looking back on the experience, the feature I now realise that I did not miss (but perhaps should have done) was the professional line, which I have so much stressed here. I heard many other (and changing) criteria on psychoanalytic lines, but the general and simpler criteria were, if my memory serves me, perhaps somewhat neglected.

The Change in orientation of the Training Committee to a wider outlook makes these general or professional standards more than ever worthy of consideration.**

NOTES ON THE TWO ASTERISKED TERMS. (These two notes were of course not sent with the memorandum to Lt Col Bowlby, because my use of them is familiar to the members of the Committee.)

* *Psychoanalysis as an Instrumental Science*. This is the key to my philosophical or scientific approach to psychoanalysis, viz. that the Transference Situation is *the* instrument of research of psychoanalysts, that the modifications of the instrument alter the character of the data which it affords, that a personal analysis has the purpose of reducing the number of unrecognised modifications in the instrument of research or therapy, and so on. It need hardly be said that "brass Instruments" were not meant.

** *Change in Orientation in the Training Committee* refers to a Social purpose; it has nothing to do with scientific ideas. We have a Scholarship Fund; the change in orientation referred to is to divide the scholarships between those likely to be good research workers and those likely to make a good functional penetration of psychoanalysis into other related branches of activity, e.g. Child Guidance, Education, Anthropology, Sociology and the like.

J.R.

APPENDIX 2

A note on the concept of "dynamic structure" and field theory

1. The notion of an organism being impelled by an "instinct" to seek object relationships has long been familiar. The notion received an addition from Freud—that the organism (in man) had erotogenic zones which oriented it in particular ways to its object and further that the zones contributed, besides an orientation of body, an attitude of mind and tendencies to behave in ways characteristic for each zone, i.e. instinct impulse *through the channel of* non certain zones of the body determined behaviour.

2. The next important theoretical addition (viewed solely from the angle of the present paper) was that the organism was not a solid thing whose envelope was sensitive to external stimuli and internal instincts but that it could *contain* bits of the outer world and continue to behave to them as if they were simultaneously both me and not-me (Freud's ego-ideal in "On Narcissism", 1914c, plus "Mourning and Melancholia", 1917e, and *The Ego and the Id*, 1923b; also Abraham's "A Short Study of the Development of the Libido", 1924).

Notes for a talk given by John Rickman to the British Psychoanalytical Society on 21 February 1945. Sylvia Payne was in the Chair and the following were present: A. Stephen, K. Stephen, Herford, Winnicott, Usher, Heimann, Money-Kyrle, Pratt, Taylor, Milner, Sheehan-Dare, Ries, Bonnard, Bowlby, Klein, Gillespie, Riggall, Rickman. *Guest*: Lt. Col. Sutherland, *Candidate Guests:* Wride, Warburg, Poznanska (Segal), Rosenfeld. Dr Payne opened the Discussion and the following took part in it: A. Stephen, K. Stephen, Winnicott, Usher, Heimann, Money-Kyrle, Bonnard, Bowlby, Klein, Gillespie, Sutherland. Dr Rickman replied.

3. The connection between the superego (SE) and the child's earliest identifications (Klein, 1932) and the concept of internal objects as having an important relation to one another and that relation having an important bearing on the behaviour and mood, the orientation and development of the organism (Klein), and most recently Scott's "Body-Schema theory"—all these events should be brought into relation with the notion of "dynamic structure" and field theory.

4. The latter two theories are supplementary to psychoanalytic theories, and the "models" or constructs at first look odd and unfamiliar.

5. The "total-ego" (TE) as a "dynamic structure". The TE means something as wide as Scott's "Body Schema". I do not use his Body Schema because I do not want to encroach on his as yet unpublished thesis. It will be assumed for the purpose of this paper that the TE has "dimensions" in space and time and that a description lying on one "plane" or dimension has no "reality" (i.e. has no effects) if taken in isolation.

6. The SE co-ordinate is the region of the TE which is concerned with identification and introjection of objects. Fenichel (1946, p. 37) wrote: "A primitive attempt at mastering intense stimuli consists in the primitive ego's imitating that which is perceived. Apparently perceiving and changing ones own body according to what is perceived were originally one and the same thing ... it is a kind of identification, the awareness of which brings perception ... another primitive reaction to the first objects appears simple and more comprehensible: the infant wants to put them into its mouth ... the first reality is what one can swallow." Jones (1912) wrote: "Introjection may be regarded as only a special form of identification." Freud (1927c, p. 35): "At the very beginning, in the primitive oral phase of the individual's existence, object cathexis and identification are hardly to be distinguished from each other." Again (1917e): "Object choice develops from a preliminary stage of identification ... the way in which the Ego first adopts an object." Again: "The Ego is weak, it borrows energy from the Id and one of its 'tricks' is the method of identification." Klein (1932, p. 28n): "The child's earliest identifications should already be called super-egos." (Idem, p. 322): "The attainment of a state of harmony ... is founded on the existence of a good relationship between her ego and its identifications"—this by way of preliminary.

7. For the moment, let attention be confined to the *SE series*, i.e. to the sequence of identifications which are spread out in the "time dimen-

sion". It is a characteristic of the TE that identifications or introjections or SEs are never "lost"; they persist with varying "strength" throughout life.

8. These SEs are cathected with +ve or –ve charges, i.e. the objects tend to be drawn together in bonds of love and creativeness or related to one another in hate or repulsion and destructiveness. These SE-bodies form one of the "armatures" of the TE.

9. The armature consists of a *serial arrangement of SEs* all of which are activated simultaneously by the "forces of the TE" (the id) and they influence each other's activity, i.e. the earliest SEs influence the "capacity" of the later ones. (The analogy of the dynamo must be used with caution since the physical machine is not capable of much functionable change without re-winding—again, by analogy, ps-an treatment provides opportunity for re-winding.)

10. Another "model" can be used, viz. the protein molecule which has an orderly array of parts structurally arranged in respect to each other. This model also has the disadvantage of being static, whereas the interrelation of the parts should be governed by the relation of the parts in the whole (cf. Gestalt concepts and the "fluid crystal" of the chromosomes).

11. The relation between the early introjected parent images influences the relation existing between later parent images on the one hand and the "shape" of the developing ego on the other. Ego and SE are interconnected functional systems.

12. Apropos the "forces of the TE", i.e. those which "activate" the "armature of the SEs"—these can be grouped under the two classes +ve and –ve. The different structures and functions of the body ego (the part of the TE that is not SE) provide a means for discharge or dispersal of those +ve and –ve charges or cathexes *vis-à-vis* the outer world; the differentiated structure and functions of the SE-armature provide a means for discharge of these +ve and –ve cathexes which relate to those past experiences which proved insoluble in the past and which were "stored" in the TE system as SE formations. (This notion accords with Freud's theory of frustration in the aetiology of the SE and underlies Ferenczi's Thalassic theory). In the SE-armature the past lives in the present, but it has no power in itself, it has effectiveness only in the "field of forces" +ve and –ve provided by that aspect of the body-ego

called the id. Further, the TE needs the SE armature as much as it needs any part of the body-ego, for without the SE (which is a stabilizer of the TE) the TE would be deadlocked by its past frustrations still existing in the present.

13. Apropos "structure" and "function"—it is a question where the emphasis lies.

> Structure is merely a persistent function while function is merely a series of changing structures. [Lundberg, 1939, p. 49]

> In using the concept of "function", the temporal continuity of pattern occupies the centre of attention to the immediate exclusion of considerations that relate to spatial changes among the parts of the pattern. ... In "function" the emphasis is upon a sequence of continuum in time of the essential pattern. In "structure" the emphasis is upon discontinuity among the parts. [Chapin, 1935, pp. 60–61]

The "psychological field" is a mathematical spatial construct to which all psychological behaviour may be ordered. All psychological events (perception, emotion, behaviour) may be said to occur in the psychological field, just as electrical events occur in the electromagnetic field or events of free fall occur in the gravitational field.

To the psychologist behaviour is analysable as an example of goal-integrated activity. The psychological field is a construct to which all psychological activity (i.e. behaviour) may be ordered. It is spatial in the sense in which space has been defined above, and likewise mathematical. The idea of the psychological field may perhaps be clarified by comparing it with mathematical and physical fields. Mathematical fields are spatial regions which may be either scalar or vector fields. A scalar field is a region where every point may have an associated set of magnitudes. A vector field is a region where every point is characterised by both direction and magnitude. The points in the psychological fields are associated with both direction and magnitude, but these may for the present only be non-metrically defined.

The force (language of constructs) to which the behaviour (language of date) of both is to be ordered represents a directed magnitude. The value of this vector depends on its position in the field. It is well known that when the goal is nearly attained the magnitude of the vector is greater. The direction of vectors in the psychological field may be defined for certain problems through the distinctive path between points within the field. Consequently the chief methodological difference between the psychological field and the physical field is that direction and magnitude of the point values within the psychological field are not as yet to be given with the same precise definition.

One may use the construct of the psychological field for several types of psychological problem. "Sensory fields" are constructs applicable to problems of perception. Various regions in the visual field, for instance, have definite values in the perceptual process, and perception depends on the structure of the visual field. "Individual action fields" are constructs which allow adequate ordering of the observed facts concerning goal behaviour. The "social field" is a construct to which problems of sociology may be ordered.

"Field structure". By it we mean the variation in the precision with which the position of points may be given in the field. We call fields "unstructured" where it is impossible to give the position of (i.e. distinguish) points. A field is said to be "structured" when one can distinguish larger regions but not infinitely small regions within it.

We must begin with a few definitions of topological concepts. Any segment of space represents a region, and all spatial configurations (or figures) are regions.

A "line-region" connecting two points is called a path. Psychological activity of all sorts will be ordered to a path and maybe aid to represent a "locomotion" in the psychological field. Regions are further characterised as bounded and unbounded, limited and unlimited, and onefold, twofold, to n-fold connected.

Regions in the psychological field are marked off by boundaries. The psychological significance of boundary is that in crossing a boundary the individual's reactions are changed. Individual point-regions within a bounded region are said to have membership-character within that region. Consequently by membership-character we mean the pattern of reaction tendencies common to all the members of a group. The dynamics of the field determine the variation in membership-character among the individuals.

All individuals within a bounded social region are affected in their behaviour through the fact that they have membership-character within this region. The boundary may be said to be quasi-physical, quasi-social, or quasi-conceptual.

Quasi-physical are boundaries like prison walls and club buildings. The quasi-social boundaries are those where social institutions and mores mark off the regions. The quasi-conceptual are those where intellectual factors function as boundaries. Psychologically a boundary represents a barrier to locomotion. This barrier is not necessarily impenetrable, but in crossing it the individual becomes ordered to a new social region and his "psychology" is changed. It is convenient to distinguish between two types of psychological barrier, both of which represent topologically bounded social regions.

Fluidity: By the degree of fluidity of a medium is meant the ease of locomotion in the medium. Ease of locomotion depends not only on the fluidity of the medium, but also on the distribution of barriers in the medium and on internal psychological factors. It has meaning, however, to speak of the varying fluidity of psychological fields in themselves.

Permeability: By the degree of permeability of a barrier is meant the ease with which locomotions are executed through the barrier. Here one distinguishes between group- and inner-barriers.

Vectors: The forces activating all locomotions in the psychological field are to be ordered to the concept of vector. These vectors represent forces causing psychological locomotion and are directed magnitudes. Their analogies in physical fields are the lines of field force within these fields.

APPENDIX 3

Quotations researched by Lucy Rickman Baruch

On 5 September 1944 John received a letter from the War Office, AMD11:

> My dear John, I have been so concerned about your illness, and am thirsting for the latest news of you. I do hope that things have really settled down and that you are going still to be able to give us lots more of this brilliantly good work that you have handed out so liberally to the Army. On the other hand, you must take sensible care of yourself and try not to take on things until you are fit to do so. . . . With very best wishes to you, Your sincerely, J. R. Rees, Brigadier. [CRR/F19/32]

What I [P.K.] had failed to find, as I worked with our Archives, was any description of John's "brilliantly good work" that he "had handed out so liberally to the Army".

Recently, Lucy Rickman Baruch has found letters to her from both her mother and her father, when she was at College in America, during the war. She copied extracts for me from some of these letters, which include John's comments about his work and how it was appreciated. These extracts make sense of what J.R. Rees was referring to in his letter quoted above and also they show Rickman's surprise at the interest and impact of the work that he was doing, on his medical and military authorities.

On 4 September 1939, John Rickman joined the Emergency Medical Service at Haymeads Hospital, Bishop Stortford

> On 7 January 1940 John wrote: "Researches keep me busy . . . results are a matter of interest to High Quarters . . . Panic paper in the Lancet did me a favour . . . there will be tales to tell when this war is over."

On February 20 1940 Rickman wrote: "Lectured to 400 ARP Wardens of Marylebone at Langham Hotel: "Quite like old times . . . rousing the meeting. . . some questions frightened me . . . lack of common sense."

On 23 August 1940, John Rickman moved to Wharncliffe Hospital, Emergency Medical Service, Sheffield, where he was in charge of a Special Centre for Neurosis

On 28 November 1940 Rickman wrote: "It is odd as I have said before that a longish Quaker line should throw up one who is introducing innovations into Army training".

On 6 December 1940 John wrote: "The Northern Command people were here yesterday and their praise for this place is unabated, which is an encouragement."

On 17 January 1941 John wrote: "I am going to begin writing this up soon. Our records top the thousand mark, which is bit of a change as regards statistics from No. 11, Kent Terrace!" [John's home]

On 9 February 1941 he wrote: "I have spent three 12 hour days and far into the night explaining "The Wharncliffe Methods" as they are called; then pulling my weight with the rest in keeping the clinical work going. So I am off on holiday, 6 days in London at libraries."

In a letter to Lucy dated 18 February 1941 Lydia Rickman wrote: "He is in most excellent form. I have never seen him in better, full of enthusiasm about his job & the innovations & experiments he is trying, and quite flabbergasted by the sensation his methods are causing both in medical and military circles. He finds it rather a burden having to demonstrate them to visitors so constantly, for that means working all hours to catch up the time he has had to devote to the visitors. He really has got a job that gives scope for his ingenuity & imagination, and I wonder if he will ever be content to go back to private practice. If he ever does, his present new contacts ought to serve him well as a source of patients."

On 23 March 1941 John Rickman wrote: "I heard from the Source that our results are better than anywhere else; so it gives me an excuse to throw my weight about. It's an interesting business and I never thought I should be in it in the way I am."

On 21 March 1942 he wrote: "First day in the Army." [Aldershot]

[*Pearl King*]

REFERENCES

Abraham, K. (1924). A short study of the development of the libido. In: *Selected Papers of Karl Abraham*. London: Hogarth Press, 1927.
Ahrenfeldt, R. H. (1958). *Psychiatry in the British Army in the Second World War*. London: Routledge and Kegan Paul.
Bion, W. R. (1948). *Experiences in Groups*. London: Heinemann.
Breuer, J., & Freud, S. (1893–95). *Studies on Hysteria. S.E. 2*.
Brooke, R. (1912). The Old Vicarage, Grantchester. *Collected Poems*. London: Penguin, 1916.
Brown, D. F. (1936). *Psychology and the Social Order*. New York & London: McGraw-Hill.
Cantril, H. (Ed.) (1950). *Tensions that Cause War*. Urbana, IL: University of Illinois Press.
Chapin, F. S. (1935). *Contemporary American Institutions*. New York: Harper & Row.
Clark, D. H. (1996). *The Story of a Mental Hospital: Fulbourn, 1858–1983*. London: Process Press.
Curle, A., & Trist, E. (1947). Transitional communities and social re-correction. *Human Relations*, 1: 244–288.
Dicks, H. (1970). *Fifty Years of the Tavistock Clinic*. London: Routledge & Kegan Paul.
Eitingon, M. (1925). International Training Board. *International Journal of Psycho-Analysis*, 6.
Fenichel, O. (1946). *The Psychoanalytic Theory of Neurosis*. London: Routledge & Kegan Paul, 19892.
Ferenczi, S. (1919). The phenomena of hysterical materialisation. In: *Further Contributions to the Theory and Technique of Psychoanalysis*. London: Hogarth Press, 1926.

Ferenczi, S. (1925). Psychoanalysis of sexual habits. In: *Further Contributions to the Theory and Technique of Psychoanalysis*. London: Hogarth Press, 1926.

Freud, A. (1979). Personal memories of Ernest Jones. *International Journal of Psycho-Analysis*, 60: 285–286.

Freud, S. (1895f). A reply to criticisms of my paper on anxiety neurosis. *S.E. 3*.

Freud, S. (1896c). The aetiology of hysteria. *S.E. 3*.

Freud, S (1900a). *The Interpretation of Dreams*. *S.E. 4/5*.

Freud, S. (1901a). *On Dreams*. *S.E. 5*.

Freud, S. (1904a). Freud's psycho-analytic procedure. *S.E. 7*.

Freud, S. (1905d). *Three Essays on the Theory of Sexuality*. *S.E. 7*.

Freud, S. (1911b). Formulations on the two principles of mental functioning. *S.E. 12*.

Freud, S. (1912–13). *Totem and Taboo*. *S.E. 13*.

Freud, S. (1912b). The dynamics of transference. *S.E. 12*.

Freud, S. (1914c). On narcissism: an introduction. *S.E. 14*.

Freud, S. (1917e). Mourning and melancholia. *S.E. 14*.

Freud, S. (1920g). *Beyond the Pleasure Principle*. *S.E. 18*.

Freud, S. (1921c). *Group Psychology and the Analysis of the Ego*. *S.E. 18*.

Freud, S. (1923b). *The Ego and the Id*. *S.E. 19*.

Freud, S. (1925d). *An Autobiographical Study*. *S.E. 20*.

Freud, S. (1926d). *Inhibitions, Symptoms and Anxiety*. *S.E. 20*.

Freud. S. (1927c). *The Future of an Illusion*. *S.E. 21*.

Freud, S. (1930a). *Civilization and its Discontents*. *S.E. 21*.

Gillespie, W. R. D. (1952). *Annual Report of the British Psycho-Analytical Society*. London: BPAS.

Glover, E. (1940). *An Investigation into the Technique of Psychoanalysis*. London: Bailliere Tindall and Cox.

Glover, E., & Ginsburg. M. (1934). The psychology of peace and war. *British Journal of Medical Psychology*, 14: 288–293.

Gorer, G., & Rickman, J. (1949). *The People of Great Russia*. London: Cresset Press.

Groddeck (1923). *The Book of the It*. London: Vision Press, 1961.

Harrison, T. (2000). *Bion, Rickman, Foulkes and the Northfield Experiments: Advancing on a Different Front*. London: Jessica Kingsley.

Isaacs, S. (1930). *Intellectual Growth in Young Children*. London: Kegan Paul.

Isaacs, S. (1933). *Social Development in Young Children*. London: Kegan Paul.

Isaacs, S. (1948). *Childhood and After*. London: Kegan Paul.

Jones, E. (1912). The section of suggestion in psychotherapy. In: *Papers on Psychoanalysis* (3rd edition). London: Bailliere Tindall & Cox, 1923.

Kardiner, A. (1977). *My Analysis with Freud: Reminiscences*. New York: Norton.

King, P. H. M. (1988). Activities of British psychoanalysts during the Second World War. In: E. Timms & N. Segal (Eds.), *Freud in Exile*. New Haven & London: Yale University Press.
King, P. H. M. (2002). Review of *Bion, Rickman and Foulkes and the Northfield Experiment: Advancing on a Different Front* by T. Harrison. *Psychoanalytic Psychotherapy*, 16 (1): 90–97.
King, P. H. M., & Steiner, R. (Eds.) (1991). *The Freud-Klein Controversies 1941–45*. London: The Institute of Psycho-Analysis and Routledge & Kegan Paul.
Klein, M. (1932). *The Psychoanalysis of Children*. London: Hogarth Press, 1975.
Klein, M. (1940). Mourning and its relation to manic depressive states. In: *Contributions to Psychoanalysis, 1921–1945*. London: Hogarth Press, 1975.
Klein, M. (1945). The Oedipus complex in the light of early anxiety. In: *Contributions to Psychoanalysis, 1921–1945*. London: Hogarth Press, 1975.
Klein, M. (1949). A psycho-analytic study of the manic-depressive states. In: *Contributions to Psychoanalysis, 1921–1945*. London: Hogarth Press, 1975.
Klein, M., & Riviere, J. (1937). *Love, Hate and Reparation. Psycho-Analytical Epitomes, No. 2*. London: Hogarth Press and the Institute of Psycho-Analysis.
Lewin, K. (1947). *Resolving Social Conflicts: Field Theory in Social Sciences*. Washington: American Psychological Association, 1997.
Lundberg, G. A. (1939). *Foundations of Sociology*. New York: MacMillan
Main, T. (1946). Forward psychiatry in the army. *Proceedings of the Royal Society of Medicine*, 38: 140–142.
Menninger, K. (1946). Foreword. *Bulletin of the Menninger Clinic*, 10: 65.
Middlemore, M. P. (1941). *The Nursing Couple*. London: Hamish Hamilton.
Money-Kyrle, R. (1939). *Superstition and Society. Psycho-Analytical Epitomes, No. 3*. London: Hogarth Press and the Institute of Psycho-Analysis.
Money-Kyrle, R. (1944). Towards a common aim: a psychoanalytical contribution to ethics. *British Journal of Medical Psychology*, 20: 105–117.
Payne, S. (1957). Foreword. In: J. Rickman, *Selected Contributions to Psychoanalysis*, ed. W. C. M. Scott. London: Hogarth Press and the Institute of Psychoanalysis.
Rees, J. R. (1945). *The Shaping of Psychiatry by War*. London: Chapman and Hall.
Rickman, J. (1926–27). A survey: the development of the psychoanalytical theory of the psychoses 1894–1926. In: *Selected Contributions to Psychoanalysis*, ed. W. C. M. Scott. London: Hogarth Press and the Institute of Psychoanalysis, 1957.
Rickman, J. (1928). *Index Psychoanalyticus: 1893–1926*. London: Hogarth Press.
Rickman, J. (1934). Discussion. *British Journal of Medical Psychology*, 14: 288–293.

Rickman, J. (Ed.) (1936). *On the Bringing Up of Children*. London: Kegan Paul.
Rickman, J. (Ed.) (1937). *A General Selection from the Works of Sigmund Freud. Psycho-Analytical Epitomes, No. 1*. London: Hogarth Press and the Institute of Psycho-Analysis.
Rickman, J. (1938). Pamphlet. Reprinted from *The Medical Press and Circular*, 7 September 1938. Also in *British Medical Societies: Their Early History and Development* (chapter 9). London.
Rickman, J. (Ed.) (1939). *Civilization, War and Death: Selections from Three Works by Sigmund Freud. Psycho-Analytical Epitomes, No. 4*. London: Hogarth Press and the Institute of Psycho-Analysis.
Rickman, J. (1949). An Editor retires. *British Journal of Medical Psychology*, 22: 1.
Rickman, J. (1950). On the criteria for the termination of an analysis. *International Journal of Psycho-Analysis*, 31: 200.
Rickman, J. (1951a). Methodology and research in psychopathology. *British Journal of Medical Psychology*, 2: 1–7.
Rickman, J. (1951b). Reflections on the function and organization of a psychoanalytical society. *International Journal of Psycho-Analysis*, 32: 218–237.
Rickman, J. (1957). *Selected Contributions to Psychoanalysis*, ed. W. C. M. Scott. London: Hogarth Press and the Institute of Psychoanalysis.
Scott, W. C. M. (1948). *Proceedings of the International Conference on Medical Psychotherapy*, 3: 49–50.
Sharpe, E. F. (1935). Similar and divergent unconscious determinants underlying the sublimations of pure art and pure science. *International Journal of Psycho-Analysis*, 11: 12.
Stanislavsky, C. (1936). *An Actor Prepares*, ed. E. R. Hapgood. New York: Taylor & Francis, 1989.
Trist, E. L. (1985). Working with Bion in the 1940s: the group decade. In: M. Pines (Ed.), *Bion and Group Psychotherapy*. London: Routledge & Kegan Paul.
Warren, H. C. (1935). *Dictionary of Psychology*. London: Allen & Unwin.
Wilson, A. T. M., et al. (1947). Transitional communities and social reconstruction. In: E. Trist & H. Murray (Eds.), *The Social Engagement of Social Science, Volume 1* (pp. 88–111). London: Free Association Books, 1990.
Winnicott, D.W. (1955). Transitional objects and transitional phenomena: a study of the first not-me possession. *International Journal of Psycho-Analysis*, 34: 89–97.

INDEX

Adam, R., 33, 38
aggression:
   causes of war, 248–249
   and cooperation, 167–169, 171
   and group-ideal, 171
   and guilt, 250–251, 254–256
   humiliation, 256
   individualism and nationalism, 259–260
   mother–infant relationship, 250–251
   party politics, 179–180
   response to by homogeneous group, case study, 161–164, 171–172
   and security, 27
aggressive impulses, 27, 162, 164–165, 167–168, 171, 176, 186, 249
air raids, panic, 184–196
Alder, V., 91, 92
Allport, G. W., 62
Altounyan, E., 8
American Psychoanalytical Association (APA), 63
anthropology:
   interviewing technique, 148–156
   and psychoanalysis, 113–114, 241
anxiety:
   in air raids, 184–196
   and creativity, 279–280
   definition, 184–185
   fear, 129
   and magical beliefs, 194–195
   and mastery of sources of danger, 193–194
   paralysis in, 177
   reduction of through group membership, 192–193
   and science, 206
   strain arising from danger, 190–192
   see also fear
appeasement, and wars, 247
art:
   and artist, 278–279
   Quaker attitude to, 281
authority:
   and protection, 189
   submission to, 195–196

Bacon, F., 264
Balint, M., 5, 39
Barbour, R. F., 37
Bartemeier, L., 54, 58
Baruch, L. R., 6
Bibring, E., 29
biological function, and moral function, 319–320

Bion, W. R., 33, 38, 39, 49, 114, 155, 237, 243, 334
   Northfield Military Hospital, 40–43, 54
   and Rickman:
      Intra-Group Tensions in Therapy, 42–43, 220–234
      letter to, 49–50
   Wharncliffe experiment, 35–36
Body Schema, 344
boundaries, 347–348
Bowlby, J., 30, 34, 38, 39, 55, 57, 61
Breuer, J., 73
Bridger, H., 38, 57
British Journal of Medical Psychology, 13, 17, 23
   Rickman's retirement, 65–66
British Psychoanalytical Society, 14–15, 19, 29
Brown, J. F., 33
Bryan, D., 13, 15, 19
Bryant, G. R., 35
Burlington, D., 29

Cantril, H., 62
Carroll, D., 25
case studies:
   aggression, response to by homogeneous group, 161–163, 164, 171–172
   analysis as examination of nascent dreams, 90–92, 93
   guilt, and first-aid psychotherapy, 121–128
cathexis, and ego-ideals, 79–80
Chadwick, M., 20
Chapin, F. S., 346
child(ren):
   and aggression, 254–255
   identification, 175–176
   mental life of as unfinished, 173–174
   phantasy in play, 173
   process of projection, 176–177
   social life, development from childhood, 322–325
   see also infancy

classification, scientific method, 101
cooperation, and aggression, 167–169, 171
"Coffee Pot" discussions, 44
Collingwood, D., 8
communities:
   transitional, 334
   uniformity and diversity in, 159–183
compassion, 135, 138
concern, and Quakerism, 282–289
conscience, 175
   and ego-ideal, 297–298
   see also moral function; superego
countertransference, 101
creativity:
   artist and scientist, 278–279
   Inner Light (Quakerism), 279–280
   and reparation, 280
   see also art
Crichton-Gordon, M., 314
criticism, hostility discharge, 107
culture, and moral function, 314–317, 332–333

dangers:
   internal and external, 190–194
   submission to authority, 195–196
   see also anxiety; fear
data, scientific method, 99–102
Debenham, G., 36
defence(s):
   against object loss, 124–125
   and social institutions, 256–257
dependence, hate, love, and religion, 299–300
depression, 167
Dicks, H. V., 56, 57
discontent:
   dealing with, in closed group, 262
   political systems, 260–262
diversity:
   exploration of through imagination, 173–175
   free trade as danger to, 170
   heterogeneous group(s), 173, 180–183

and uniformity of group-ideal, 177–180
and imagination, 173–175
and inner complexity, 259
and uniformity in communities, 159–183
dream(s), 12
  analysis as examination of nascent dreams, 90–93
  manifest and latent contents, 75
  patient's story like manifest dream, 129
  psychoanalysis and experimental psychology compared, 8990
dynamic structure, 343–348

Eder, M. D., 24, 261
education, professional, 198, 218–219
ego:
  and belief in God, 300
  as boundary phenomenon, 242, 250
  and development,
    early, 175
    as growth of internal society, 141–142
  -ideal:
    and conscience, 297–298
    and impulses, 211
    and narcissism, 79–80
    professional, 212–215, 217, 219
    self-control, 189
    see also superego
  and internalised objects, 303–304
  and object relations, 82
  Shamanism, mastering excitement, 203–204
  superego and id, 80–81, 321–322, 326–328, 334–335, 345
  total-ego (TE), 344
Egypt, Rickman's work in, 64–65
Eitingon, M., 15
Emergency Medical Services (EMS), 31–32
  Hospital, Haymeads, 34
  Psychiatrists' Conferences, 36–37
envy, and group bonds, 189

family(ies):
  idealised, and idealised group, 165–167
  and ownership of means of production, 263
  parents, and beginning of social life, 252–254
  see also child(ren); father(s); infancy
fascism, impact of rise of, 26–29
father(s):
  as good and bad object, 252–253
  relationship with mother and child, 251
fear:
  air raids, panic, 184–196
  and anxiety, 129
  definition, 184–185
  see also anxiety
Fenichel, O., 344
Ferenczi, S., 19–20, 23, 110, 243
field:
  structure, 347
  theory, dynamic structure, 343–348
first aid, 119–131
fixation, 177–178
Flatland (Square/Abbott), 9
fluidity, 348
four-person psychology, 111
Fox, T. F., 2, 10, 27
free association, and transference, 73–74, 76, 77
free trade, as danger to diversity, 170
Freud, A., 26, 28, 55, 61, 63
  tribute to Jones, 29
Freud, S., 13, 241, 243
  definition of fear and anxiety, 184–185
  ego, superego, id, 321, 334
  ego-ideal, 297
  group psychology, 112
  object cathexis and identification, 344
  threatened by annexation of Austria, 28
function, and structure, 346

General Selection from the Works of Sigmund Freud (Rickman), 25
Germany, Nazis in power, 26
Gillespie, R. D., 29–30
Gillespie, W., 3–5, 31, 63
Ginsberg, M., 23
Glover, E., 14, 16, 23, 24, 31, 54, 55
   World War II, 29–30
Glover, J., 14–16
God:
   belief in, and ego, 300
   concept, 274–276
   and function of concern in Quakerism, 283–286
   see also Quakerism; religion
goodness, search for, 301–304, 306–308
Greenacre, P., 63
Groddeck, G., 321
group(s):
   aggression and cooperation, 167–169, 171
   bonds:
      and envy, 189
      and self-control, 188–189
      -cohesive and group-destructive, 141
   factors leading to uniformity in political field, 169–172
   heterogeneous, 173
      and diversity, 180–183
      and uniformity of group-ideal, 177–180
   -ideal:
      and aggression, 171
      uniformity as, 160–165
      uniformity of, 177–180
      uniformity of, and political repression, 169–172
   idealised, and idealised family, 165–167
   internal and external dangers, 189–192
   organised, panic in, 186–187
   psychology, 112
   tensions, research in, 155
therapy:
   intra-group tensions, 220–234
   Northfield experiment, 42–43
   unorganised, panic in, 187–188
guilt:
   and aggression, 250–251, 254–256
   beginning of moral feelings, 325–326
   religion, 203

Haddon, A. C., 12, 154
Hargreaves, R., 34–36, 38, 54
   group therapy, 42–43
Harrison, T., 6
Hart, B., 36, 37, 43
hate:
   dependence and religion, 299–300
   and group membership, 192
   and love, 81, 308, 311, 329
   and search for goodness, 302
Haymeads Memorandum, 34
Heimann, P., 26, 63
hell, 305
heterogeneous groups, *see* diversity
Hinshelwood, R. D., 6
Hitler, A., 246, 258
Hitschmann, E., 14
Hoffer, H., 29
Hoffer, W., 29, 54, 55
Hogarth Press, 15, 17
Hopkins, P., 21, 25
hostility discharge, and criticism, 107
humiliation, and aggression, 256
hypnosis, origins of psychoanalysis, 73–74
hypotheses, scientific method, 102–103

id, ego, superego, 80–81, 321–322, 326–328, 334–335, 345
ideal, formation of and religion, 298–301
idealisation:
   and fixation, 178

of group, and idealised family, 165–167, 171
and impulses, 176
and instabilities of homogeneous groups, 179
and repression, 171
and war, 178
see also ego-ideal; identification
identification:
  and aggressive phantasies arising from danger, 191
  and destructiveness, 179
  in early development, 175–176
  and introjection, 344
  and object cathexis, 344
  see also idealisation
imagination, exploration of diversity, 173–175
impulses:
  aggressive, 27, 162, 164, 165, 167–168, 171, 176, 186, 249
  destructive and constructive, 167, 177, 209–210
  and ego, 82, 175
  God as check to, 312–313
  and guilt, 83–84
  hostile and friendly, 139
  and idealisation, 176
  and internal dangers, 190, 191
  love and hate, 138, 168, 171, 178, 182, 186, 196, 251
  and need for scapegoats, 172
  professional, 209–211
  and religion, 205
  repressed aggressive, 249
  role of psychoanalysis, 73, 74, 89, 92–93
  and Shamanism, 201
  transference, 76
  un-adult nature of, 77
  unfulfilled, 174
  unprofessional, 212–218
  see also phantasy
Index Psychoanalyticus 1893–1926, 17
individualism, and nationalism, 259–260

infancy:
  frustration, 317–318
  insecurity, origins of, 250–251
  moral function, origins of, 320–321
  object relations, 271–274
  sexuality, 77–79
  stability, 273–274
  see also child(ren); family(ies)
infants, choosing new objects, 177
Inner Light (Quakerism):
  creative works, relation to, 279–280
  nature and function, 277–278
  and object relations, 272, 277
  war and oaths, testimonies against, 289–291
insecurity, origins of, 249–252
instinct, 343
Institute of Psychoanalysis, establishment of, 14–15
internal objects, 344
  see also object relations
internal society, ego-development, 141–142
internalised objects, 82
  and ego, 303–304
International Journal of Psychoanalysis, 14
International Psychoanalytical Association (IPA), first congress after World War II, 63
International Psychoanalytical Library, 15, 17
interpretation, 92–94
Interpretation of Dreams, The (Freud), 12
interview:
  influence:
    of past emotional experiences, 152–153
    influence of social field, WOSB, 140–147
  psychiatric, WOSB, 132–139
  technique, 148–156
Intra-Group Tensions in Therapy (Bion and Rickman), 42–43, 220–234

360   INDEX

introjection, 272, 302–303
  and identification, 344
Isaacs, S., 24, 25, 34, 55, 335

Jaques, E., 57
Jones, E., 13–16, 20, 21, 22, 24, 30, 31, 55, 58, 63
  and Germany's annexation of Austria, 28
  and immigration of Viennese analysts, 28–29
  on introjection, 344
  Kleinian ideas, attitude to, 53
  Rickman, criticism of, 28–29
  support for analysts threatened by fascism, 26

Kardiner, A., 14
Kerr, M., 57
Kerri, R. S. R., 39
Khan, M., 5–6
Klein, M., 19, 25, 34, 54, 269, 301
  on identification, 344
  on superego, 175, 335
Kleinian ideas, reaction to in USA, 51
Knight, R. P., 50, 51–52, 54
knowledge, and magic, 208
Kris, E., 29
Kris, M., 29
Kubie, L., 54

Lancet, The, Rickman's editorials for, 27, 31, 56
Langdon-Davies, J., 28
Lantos, B., 29
Lawrence, T. E., 8
League of Nations, insufficient aggression, 260
Lewin, K., 33, 36, 53, 60, 112, 141
Lewis, A., 36, 37
Lewis, L. C., 10–11
Limentani, A., 6
line-region, 347
London Clinic of Psychoanalysis, 15–16

love:
  and hate, 81, 308, 311, 329
  as hoped-for cure to loss of object, 125
  phantasy of independence of fate, 168–169
Low, B., 15, 23, 24, 54
Lundberg, G. A., 156, 346

McDougall, W., 12, 154
magic:
  knowledge and professionalism, 208
  magical beliefs, craving for security, 194–195
Main, T. F., 60, 334
Maine, H., 208
masochism, humiliation, and aggression, 256
means of production, and family, 263
Menninger, K., 54
Menninger, W. C., 54
Merchant of Venice, 87–88
Mitchell, T. W., 18
Mitsch (Friedlander), Kate, 26
Money-Kyrle, R.:
  development of, 326–328
  normality, 246–248
moral function, 314–335
  beginning of, 325–326
  and biological function, 319–320
  cultural transmission, 332–333
  culture, 314–317
  hindrances to development of, 328–332
  primitive origins, 320–321
  see also superego
moral negativism, tensions as cause of wars, 248
Moreno, J. L., 53
multi-person psychology, 111–112
Myers, C. S., 12, 154

nameless horror, panic in organised groups, 187

narcissism, and ego-ideal, 79–80
nationalism, and individualism, 259–260
nature, attitude to in Shamanism and religion, 204
negative attitudes, 138
Newman, W., 45, 46, 48
normality, 246–248
Northfield Military Hospital, experiment, 40–43, 54
"Number and the Human Sciences" (Rickman), 18
nursery conflicts, projection in groups, 182

oaths, and Quakerism, 289–291
obituary, Rickman's, 66
object(s):
  cathexis, and identification, 344
  definition, 141
  good and bad, 140–141
  internal, 344
    good, and creativity, 280
  internalised, 82
    and ego, 303–304
  loss, defence against, 124–125
  relations, 81–84
    crisis due to loss of satisfaction in, 129
    ego, 82
    importance to psychoanalysis, 95
    in infancy, 271–274
    search for goodness, 301–304
objectivity:
  capacity for, 215
  scientific method, 106
  of scientist, 205–207
observation, scientific method, 99–102
Oedipus complex, 78
  three-person psychology, 111
omnipotence, phantasy of God as father, 295–296
On the Bringing up of Children (Rickman), 25

one-person psychology, 110
oral tradition, 2

pacifism, tensions as cause of wars, 247–248
panic, in air raids, 184–196
paralysis, anxiety, 177
paranoid tendencies, and wars, 246–247
parents, and beginning of social life, 252–254
Patterson, A. S., 47
Payne, S., 3, 5, 23, 24, 25, 30, 55, 58, 60, 63
Pear, T. H., 57
Penrose, L., 8
permeability, 348
personality, external, and internal society, 142
phantasy:
  and beginning of social life, 323–324
  constructive and destructive, professional impulses, 209–211
  God as father, 295–296
  love, phantasy of independence of fate, 168–169
  and play, 173
  seduction, 78
  Shamanism and religion, 203
  strains arising from danger, 190–191
  and unprofessional impulse, 212
  see also impulses
play, and phantasy, 173
political repression, uniformity in group-ideal, 169–170
Posnanska, Hanka (Hanna Segal), 26
prediction, scientific method, 113
professionalism, 197–219
  education, 198, 218–219
  psychological basis for, 209
  status and contract, 208
  and unprofessional impulse, 212–218

projection:
    and belief in God, 298, 299
    in early development, 176–177
    hatred, and search for goodness, 302
    heaven and hell, 304–306
    heterogeneous groups, 181–182
    idealised family, 165
    idealised group, 168
    international tension, 262
    nursery conflicts, 182
    paranoid tendencies, 246
    protecting good objects, 179
    and Quakerism, 272, 273, 274, 275
    racism and xenophobia, 258
    and science, 279
    Shamanism, 200
protection, and Authority, 189
psychiatric interview, WOSB, 132–139
psycho-social relationships, 115
psychoanalysis:
    and anthropology, 113–114
    as blow to man's narcissism, 112
    definition, 71
    and experimental psychology compared, 85–97
    origins, 73–75
    theory, development of, 73–84
"Psychoanalytical Epitomes" (book series), 25
psychology, experimental, vs. psychoanalysis, 85–97
psychotherapy:
    first aid, 119–131
    and research, 153
Public Lectures Programme, 23–25

quackery, 212–218
Quakerism:
    art, attitude towards, 281
    artist and scientist, 278–279
    beliefs of, 269–293
    character, 291–293
    Concern, a, 282–289
    and God:
        concept of, 274–276
        and function of Concern, 283–286
    Inner Light:
        nature and function of, 277–278
        and object relations, 272, 277
        relation to creative works, 279–280
        testimonies against war and oaths, 289–291
    and object relations, 271–274
    quaking, 283
    and religious impulses, 270–271
    science, attitude towards, 282
    see also religion

Ramzy, I., 64
Rank, O., 14
reassurance, danger of, 130
Rees, J. R., 32–33, 37, 48, 50, 262
"Reflections of the Function and Organisation of a Psychoanalytical Society" (Rickman), 25
regions, 347
religion:
    and God:
        belief in, need for, 294–308
        as check to unconscious impulses, 312–313
        concept of, 274–276
        as father, phantasy, 295–296
        wrath of, fear of, 207–208
    and goodness, 301–304, 306–308
    heaven and hell, 304–306
    ideal, formation of, 298–301
    and Satan, 311
    and Shamanism, 202–205
        Shaman, Priest, and Scientist, 207
    totem, 296–298
    see also Quakerism
reparation:
    and creativity, 280
    dealing with aggression, 254
    impulses, 209–210
repression:
    and idealisation, 171

of aggressive impulses, 249
and substitution, 252
research:
and psychotherapy, 153
research techniques, 153–156
Richardson, L. F., 57
Rickman, L., 5, 11, 13, 14, 47
Rivers, W. R. H., 12, 114, 154
Riviere, J., 16
Roger, T. F., 33, 38, 334
Roheim, G., 13, 18, 27, 29, 67
prediction, 114
Romano, J., 54
Rosenfeld, E., 26
Rosenfeld, H., 26
Russia, Rickman's experiences in, 9–11, 26

Sandiford, H. A., 45, 50, 262
scapegoats, 167, 168, 171, 172
Schmideberg, M., 19
Schmideberg, W., 19
science:
hypotheses, 102–103
observation, 99–102
Quaker attitude to, 282
scientific method, 98–108
scientist, 205–207, 278–279
verification, 103–105
Scott, C., 5, 30, 31, 37, 344
security:
and aggression, 27
craving for and magical beliefs, 194–195
lack of, origins of, 249–252
seduction, phantasies of, 78
Segal, H. (H. Posnanska), 26
Selected Contributions to Psychoanalysis (Rickman), 17, 25
self-control:
group bonds, 188–189
panic in organised groups, 186
sensory fields, 347
sexuality, infancy, 77–79
Shamanism:
ego-ideal, 211
and religion, 202–205

Shaman, 198–202
vs. Priest and Scientist, 207
Shaping of Psychiatry by War, The (Rees), 32–33
Sharpe, E., 278
silence:
holding, 46
psychiatric, 136–137
Slater, E., 36
social factors, importance of recognised in World War II, 33
social field, 347
social life:
development from childhood, 322–325
parents and beginning of, 252–254
social relationship, analyst–analysand, 93–94
social setting, psychiatric interviews at WOSB, 139
society, internal, and ego-development, 141–142
sociology, 244–245
sociotherapy, 238
splitting, 176, 253
role of totem, 297
and search for goodness, 301–304, 307
and superego, 257–258
stability, infancy, 273–274
Stanislavsky, K., 324
Stephen, A., 3, 9, 23, 24, 55
Stephen, K., 23, 25
Story of a Mental Hospital: Fulbourn 1858–1983 (Clark), 12
structure, and function, 346
subjectivity, and scientific method, 100–101, 103, 105, 106
sublimation, 168
substitution, and repression, 252
superego, 175
beginning of moral feelings, 325–326
beginning of social life, 322–325
curbing cruel impulses, 212
dynamic structure, 344–345

superego (*continued*):
    early development of, 330–331
    id and ego, 80–81, 321–322, 326–328, 334–335, 345
    and impulses, 210–211
    social correlates of, 257–259
    and social life, 253–254
    see also ego-ideal; guilt; moral function
"Survey: The Development of the Psychoanalytical Theory of the Psychoses 1894–1926" (Rickman), 17
Sutherland, J. D., 38, 47, 54, 57, 65
Syria, Rickman's work in, 64–65
Szalai, A., 62

TE (total-ego), 344
tension:
    psychodynamic factors behind wars, 241–265
    reducing, Quakerism, 285
Tensions that Cause Wars (Cantril), 62
Thompson, G., 47
Thorne, A., 38
Thorner, H., 26
three-person psychology, 111
totem, 296–298
training, after World War II, 58–61
transference:
    definition, 72
    and free association, 73–74, 76, 77
    impulses, 76
    interpretations in first aid psychotherapy, 131
    and third party, 75–77, 81
    two-person psychology, 110–111
transitional community, 334
Trist, E. L., 36, 38, 57, 115, 334

unconscious:
    God as check to unconscious impulses, 312–313
    scientific method, 101
    see also impulses; phantasy
UNESCO, Tensions Project, 62–63

uniformity:
    and diversity in communities, 159–183
    as group-ideal, 160–165
    of group-ideal, demand for, in heterogeneous groups, 177–180
    need for in group-ideal, 169–172
United States, contact with psychoanalysts from, 50–54
Usher, R., 63

vectors, 348
verification, scientific method, 103–105

Walters, A. W., 57
war:
    aggression, 248–249
    and appeasement, 247
    and idealisation, 178
    moral negativism, 248
    pacifism, tensions as cause of, 247–248
    paranoid tendencies, tensions as cause of, 246–247
    psychodynamic factors, 241–265
    and Quakerism, 289–291
    as therapy, 235–240
    see also World War II
War Office Selection Board (WOSB):
    influence of social field, 140–141
    psychiatric interview, 132–139
    Rickman's work in, 4, 43–50
Wharncliffe experiment, 34–36
Whitehorn, J., 54
Wilbur, G. B., 18
Wilson, A. T. M., 46, 56, 57, 334
Winnicott, D. W., 30, 111, 334
Wittkower, E., 38, 223
work, constructive and destructive impulses, 167–168
World War II:
    at WOSB, 43–50
    Emergency Medical Services (EMS), 31–32, 36–37

EMS Psychiatrists' Conferences, 36–37
Haymeads EMS Hospital, 34
impact of events leading up to, 26–29
Northfield Military Hospital, 40–43
officer selection, 38–40
proposal to teach at Menninger Clinic, 50–53
recognition of social factors, 33
Rickman active in British Society, 54–55
Rickman on, 31
Wharncliffe experiment, 34–36
see also war
WOSB, *see* War Office Selection Board:

Yates, S., 23, 24, 34